SPARKS

A Reader to Energize Writing

Second Edition

Donna Barnard
Orange Coast College

Kendall Hunt
publishing company
4050 Westmark Drive • P O Box 1840 • Dubuque IA 52004-1840

Cover image copyright © ilbok, 2009. Used under license from Shutterstock, Inc.

Kendall Hunt
publishing company

www.kendallhunt.com
Send all inquiries to:
4050 Westmark Drive
Dubuque, IA 52004-1840

Copyright © 2009 by Donna Barnard

ISBN: 978-0-7575-6220-4

Kendall/Hunt Publishing Company has the exclusive rights to reproduce this work, to prepare derivative works from this work, to publicly distribute this work, to publicly perform this work and to publicly display this work.

All rights reserved. No part of this publication may be reproduced, stored in a retrieval system, or transmitted, in any form or by any means, electronic, mechanical, photocopying, recording, or otherwise, without the prior written permission of the copyright owner.

Printed in the United States of America
10 9 8 7 6 5 4 3

Dedicated to
Barbara Underwood
in admiration of her courage

Brief Contents

Detailed Contents   vii
Essays by Rhetorical Mode   xi
Essays by Subject and Theme   xiii
Style Guide   xv
Assignment Guide   xvii
Acknowledgments   xix
Preface   xxi
User's Guide   xxiii
Survival Kit   xxv

SECTION ONE   Telling Tales: Essays from Memory   1

SECTION TWO   Figuring It Out: Essays that Explain and Explore   51

SECTION THREE   Heating It Up: Essays that Argue   189

SECTION FOUR   Laughing Out Loud: Essays that Satirize and Amuse   269

SECTION FIVE   Writing Strategies   313

SECTION SIX   Research   337

Glossary   349

Index   355

Contents

Essays by Rhetorical Mode   xi
Essays by Subject and Theme   xiii
Style Guide   xv
Assignment Guide   xvii
Acknowledgements   xix
Preface   xxi
   Why This Book?   xxi
User's Guide   xxiii
   How to Use This Book   xxiii
Survival Kit   xxv
   I'm in College. Now What?   xxv
   Tips for Success   xxv
   Reading Tips   xxvi
   "Learning to Read and Write" by Fredrick Douglass   xxix
   Advice for Working in Groups   xxxiv
   Peer Evaluations: Responding to Your Classmates' Work   xxxv

SECTION ONE — Telling Tales: Essays from Memory   1

Introduction   1
Essays   3
   "A Voice for the Lonely" by Stephen Corey   3
   "Modern Times" by Lawrence Weschler   10
   "Burl's" by Bernard Cooper   17
   "The Courage of Turtles" by Edward Hoagland   31
   "Children in the Woods" by Barry Lopez   44

SECTION TWO — Figuring it Out: Essays that Explain and Explore   51

Introduction   51
Essays   53
   "On the Uncertainty of the Future" by Yoshida Kenko   53
   "Museum Piece" by David Huddle   57
   "Nourishing Awareness in Each Step" by Thich Nhat Hanh   62
   "Toys" by Roland Barflies   68
   "Mute Dancers: How to Watch a Hummingbird" by Diane Ackerman   74
   "Roll Over Bach, Too!" By Jack Kroll   83
   "Prince: The Fargodome" by Chuck Klosterman   91
   "A Box Filled with Magic" by Martin Scorsese   100
   "Monster Mash" by Jack Kroll   108

"City Out of Breath" by Ken Chen   114
"Hair" by Diane Ackerman   122
"Indian with a Camera" by Leslie Marmon Silko   130
"Joyas Voladoras" by Brian Doyle   138
"American Children" by John Updike   144
"Musical Awakenings" by Clayton S. Collins   150
"Disposable Rocket" by John Updike   159
"Graven Images" by Saul Bellow   167
"Black Widow" by Gordon Grice   176

SECTION THREE **Heating It Up: Essays That Argue   189**
Introduction   189
Essays   191
"The Little Mermaid" by Pauline Kael   191
"Drugs" by Gore Vidal   196
"Naps" by Barbara Holland   202
From "The Culture of Celebrity" by Joseph Epstein   210
"Fiddling While Africa Starves" by P. J. O'Rourke   220
"About Men" by Gretel Ehrlich   228
"Folktale Liberation" by Alison Lurie   236
From "The Content of Our Character" by Shelby Steele   251
"Letter to His Master" by Frederick Douglass   260

SECTION FOUR **Laughing Out Loud: Essays that Satirize and Amuse   269**
Introduction   269
Essays   271
"Cat Bathing as Martial Art" by Bud Herron   271
"Name That Tone" by Louis Menand   277
"From How to Drive Fast" by P. J. O'Rourke   284
"Mortality" by Bailey White   291
"Turbulence" by David Sedaris   297
"Advice to Youth" by Mark Twain   306

SECTION FIVE **Writing Strategies   313**
Writing Basic College Essays   313
Getting Started   313
Organizing and Writing   314
Revising and Editing   316
Titles, Introductions, Conclusions   317
Traditional Brainstorming   320
Strategies for Writing From Memory   321
Purpose   321
Zooming In   321
Transitions   322

Evoking Senses 322
Point of View 322
Writing Strategies for Explaining and Exploring Ideas 323
Comparison and Contrast 323
Cause and Effect 324
Explaining a Process 325
Writing Strategies for Defining Terms 326
Purpose 326
Language Resources 327
Examples 328
Debunking Misconceptions 328
Writing Strategies for Arguing 328
Stating Your Point 329
Supporting Your Point 329
Refuting the Opposition 329
Organization 330
Writing Strategies for Classification 330
Purpose 331
Ruling Principle 332
Support 332
Labels 332
Organization 333
Summarizing 333
Tips for Writing Summaries 334
Paraphrasing 334
Plagiarism and General Advice for Using Sources 335

SECTION SIX

Research 337

Basic Sources 337
The Internet 338
Evaluating Internet Sites 339
Favorite Search Engines 339
Basic Documentation 340
Format 340
Parenthetical References 341
Works Cited 342
Works Cited Sample 346
Sample First Page 348

Glossary 349

Index 355

Essays by Rhetorical Mode

NARRATION

"A Voice for the Lonely" by Stephen Corey
"City Out of Breath" by Ken Chen
"Mortality" by Bailey White
"A Box Filled with Magic" by Martin Scorsese
"Turbulence" by David Sedaris
"Prince: The Fargodome" by Chuck Klosterman
"Burl's" by Bernard Cooper
"Learning to Read and Write" by Frederick Douglas
"Disposable Rocket" by John Updike
"The Courage of Turtles" by Edward Hoagland

DESCRIPTION AND METAPHOR

"Museum Piece" by David Huddle
"Joyas Voladoras" by Brian Doyle
"Mute Dancers: How to Watch a Hummingbird" by Diane Ackerman
"Hair" by Diane Ackerman
"Burl's" by Bernard Cooper
"Disposable Rocket" by John Updike
"The Courage of Turtles" by Edward Hoagland

ILLUSTRATION/EXEMPLIFICATION

"The Little Mermaid" by Pauline Kael
"Naps" by Barbara Holland
"Joyas Voladoras" by Brian Doyle
"Hair" by Diane Ackerman
"Mute Dancers: How to Watch a Hummingbird" by Diane Ackerman
"A Box Filled with Magic" by Martin Scorsese
"Roll Over Bach, Too!" by Jack Kroll
"Monster Mash" by Jack Kroll
"Musical Awakenings" by Clayton Collins
"Folktale Liberation" by Alison Lurie
"Black Widow" by Gordon Grice
"Fiddling While Africa Starves" by P. J. O'Rourke
From "The Content of Our Character" by Shelby Steele
"Disposable Rocket" by John Updike
"The Courage of Turtles" by Edward Hoagland

DEFINITION

"On the Uncertainty of the Future" by Yoshida Kenko
"Hair" by Diane Ackerman
"Joyas Voladoras" by Brian Doyle
From "The Content of Our Character" by Shelby Steele
From "The Culture of Celebrity" by Joseph Epstein

PROCESS

"Cat Bathing as Martial Art" by Bud Herron
"Mute Dancers: How to Watch a Hummingbird" by Diane Ackerman
"Disposable Rocket" by John Updike
"Black Widow" by Gordon Grice

COMPARISON/CONTRAST

"The Little Mermaid" by Pauline Kael
"City Out of Breath" by Ken Chen
"Mortality" by Bailey White
"Disposable Rocket" by John Updike

CAUSE AND EFFECT

"Drugs" by Gore Vidal
"Toys" by Roland Barthes
"A Box Filled with Magic" by Martin Scorsese
"Letter to His Master" by Fredrick Douglass
"Nourishing Awareness in Each Moment" by Thich Nhat Hanh
"The Courage of Turtles" by Edward Hoagland
"Folktale Liberation" by Alison Lurie

ARGUMENTATION

"The Little Mermaid" by Pauline Kael
"Drugs" by Gore Vidal
"Naps" by Barbara Holland
From "How to Drive Fast" by P. J. O'Rourke
"Nourishing Awareness in Each Moment" by Thich Nhat Hanh
"About Men" by Gretel Ehrlich

"Fiddling While Africa Starves" by P. J. O'Rourke
"Folktale Liberation" by Alison Lurie
From "The Content of Our Character" by Shelby Steele
"Letter to His Master" by Frederick Douglass

ANALYSIS

"Museum Piece" by David Huddle
"Toys" by Roland Barthes
"On the Uncertainty of the Future" by Yoshida Kenko
"Nourishing Awareness in Each Moment" by Thich Nhat Hanh
"Name That Tone" by Louis Menand
"Prince: The Fargodome" by Chuck Klosterman
From "The Culture of Celebrity" by Joseph Epstein
"American Children" by John Updike
"The Indian with a Camera" by Leslie Marmon Silko
"About Men" by Gretel Ehrlich
"Disposable Rocket" by John Updike
"Graven Images" by Saul Bellow
"The Courage of Turtles" by Edward Hoagland
"Folktale Liberation" by Alison Lurie

Essays by Subject and Theme

IDENTITY/GROWING UP

"A Voice for the Lonely" by Stephen Corey
"City out of Breath" by Ken Chen
From "How to Drive Fast" by P. J. O'Rourke
"Mortality" by Bailey White
"Hair" by Diane Ackerman
"Advice to Youth" by Mark Twain
"A Box Filled with Magic" by Martin Scorsese
"Name That Tone" by Louis Menand
"Indian with a Camera" by Leslie Marmon Silko
"Burl's" by Bernard Cooper
"Learning to Read and Write" by Frederick Douglass
"Disposable Rocket" by John Updike
From "The Content of Our Character" by Shelby Steele

NATURE

"Mute Dancers: How to Watch a Hummingbird" by Diane Ackerman
"Joyas Voladoras" by Brian Doyle
"Black Widow" by Gordon Grice
"Children in the Woods" by Barry Lopez
"The Courage of Turtles" by Edward Hoagland

MUSIC, FILM, AND ART

"The Little Mermaid" by Pauline Kael
"Museum Piece" by David Huddle
"A Voice for the Lonely" by Stephen Corey
"Roll Over Bach, Too" by Jack Kroll
"Prince: The Fargodome" by Chuck Klosterman
"Monster Mash" by Jack Kroll
"A Box Filled with Magic" by Martin Scorsese
"Musical Awakenings" by Clayton S. Collins
"American Children" by John Updike
"Folktale Liberation" by Alison Lurie

SOCIAL, CULTURAL, AND HISTORICAL

"Drugs" by Gore Vidal
"Naps" by Barbara Holland
"City Out of Breath" by Ken Chen
"Modern Times" by Lawrence Weschler
"Toys" by Roland Barthes
"Name That Tone" by Louis Menand
"Fiddling While Africa Starves" by P. J. O'Rourke
"Folktale Liberation" by Alison Lurie
"Burl's" by Bernard Cooper
From "The Culture of Celebrity" by Joseph Epstein
"The Indian with a Camera" by Leslie Marmon Silko
"Learning to Read and Write" by Frederick Douglass
"Letter to His Master" by Frederick Douglass
"About Men" by Gretel Ehrlich
From "The Content of Our Character" by Shelby Steele

Style Guide

See specific readings for exercises on these style techniques. For brief explanations—including common errors such as fragments, comma splices, and run-on sentences—see the glossary.

ALLITERATION: "Naps," "Mute Dancers: How to Watch a Hummingbird," "Prince."

APPOSITIVES: "Modern Times."

CONCLUSIONS: "Joyas Voladoras."

COLONS: "American Children," "City Out of Breath," "Drugs," "Content of Our Character."

DASHES: "Modern Times," "Museum Piece," "Graven Images," "How to Drive Fast," "Black Widow," "Indian with a Camera."

DESCRIPTION AND SENSORY WRITING: "A Voice for the Lonely," "Burl's."

DETAILS AND WORD CHOICE: "Joyas Voladoras," "American Children," "The Little Mermaid," "Mortality."

DIALOGUE: "Turbulence."

EXAMPLES: "A Box Filled with Magic," "The Little Mermaid."

INTRODUCTIONS: "Riddles," "Mute Dancers: How to Watch a Hummingbird," (Teaming Up #1), "Roll Over Bach, Too!"

LISTING: "The Indian with a Camera," "American Children," "Disposable Rocket," "The Content of Our Character."

QUESTIONS: "Nourishing Awareness in Each Moment," "Roll over Bach, Too."

PERIODIC AND LOOSE SENTENCES:
    PERIODIC—"Children in the Woods," "Mute Dancers: How to Watch a Hummingbird."
    LOOSE—"Letter to His Master," "How to Drive Fast," "Advice to Youth," "Folktale Liberation."

SEMI-COLONS: "City Out of Breath," "Hair."

TITLES: "Monster Mash," "Name That Tone."

TONE: "Toys."

TRANSITIONS: "About Men."

WORD PLAY (SIMILE, METAPHOR, PERSONIFICATION, HYPHENATED WORDS): "The Courage of Turtles," "Joyas Voladoras" (Teaming Up #2), "Musical Awakenings," "The Culture of Celebrity," "Fiddling While Africa Starves."

Assignment Guide

Refer to specific readings for writing assignments using one or more of these rhetorical modes.

ANALYZING AND EXPLAINING: "A Voice for the Lonely," "Modern Times," "Burl's," "The Courage of Turtles," "Museum Piece," "Toys," "Mute Dancers: How to Watch a Hummingbird," "Roll Over Bach, Too," "A Box Filled With Magic," "Monster Mash," "The Indian with a Camera," "Musical Awakenings," "Disposable Rocket," "Black Widow," "The Culture of Celebrity," "Fiddling While Africa Starves," "About Men," "Cat Bathing as Martial Art," "How to Drive Fast," "Turbulence," "Folktale Liberation."

ARGUMENTATION: "Children in the Woods," "A Box Filled With Magic," "City Out of Breath," "Black Widow," "The Little Mermaid," "Drugs," "Naps," "Fiddling While Africa Starves," "The Content of Our Character," "Letter to His Master," "Name That Tone."

CAUSE/EFFECT: "Nourishing Awareness in Each Moment," "Hair," "How to Drive Fast," "Advice to Youth."

COMPARISON/CONTRAST: "On the Uncertainty of the Future," "Museum Piece," "Nourishing Awareness in Each Moment," "Toys," "Roll Over Bach, Too!" "Prince," "Monster Mash," "City Out of Breath," "Hair," "The Indian with a Camera," "Joyas Voladoras," "American Children," "Disposable Rocket," "The Little Mermaid," "Naps," "Letter to His Master," "Cat Bathing as Martial Art," "Name That Tone."

CLASSIFICATION: "Mortality," "Turbulence."

DEFINITION: "The Culture of Celebrity," "About Men," "The Content of Our Character."

DESCRIPTION: "Museum Piece," "Toys," "Prince," "Monster Mash," "City Out of Breath," "Hair," "American Children," "Graven Images," "Fiddling While Africa Starves," "About Men," "How to Drive Fast," "Mortality," "Turbulence."

NARRATION: "A Voice for the Lonely," "Burl's," "The Courage of Turtles," "Children in the Woods," "On the Uncertainty of the Future," "American Children," "On the Content of Our Character," "Turbulence," "Advice to Youth," "Folktale Liberation."

PROCESS ANALYSIS: "Mute Dancers: How to Watch a Hummingbird," "Graven Images," "Cat Bathing as Martial Art," "Advice to Youth."

RESEARCH: "A Voice for the Lonely," "Modern Times," "Burl's," "The Courage of Turtles," "Toys," "Mute Dancers: How to Watch a Hummingbird," "Hair," "Musical Awakenings," "Graven Images," "Black Widow," "Drugs," "Naps," "Fiddling While Africa Starves," "The Content of Our Character," "Advice to Youth."

Acknowledgments

In memory of Ed Dornan, I'll always be grateful for his help getting me started in writing, teaching, and publishing. This book wouldn't have happened without him.

And I can't forget Steve Rigolosi—a belated thanks for your guidance, quick responses, and hard work on the first edition of *Sparks*.

A special thanks to those extraordinary professors Alice Brekke and Eileen Lothamer—colleagues, friends, mentors—for setting me on my life's path, helping me achieve my goals, and encouraging me throughout this endeavor. You changed my life.

Muchas gracias to Gary and Glynis Hoffman and their book *Adios, Strunk and White* for helping me find my writer's voice and transforming my writing. A gal couldn't have better office mates or friends. Thank you for always being there.

And what would I have done without fellow writer, friend, track buddy, and idea man Gene Garofolo? Thanks for those brainstorming sessions during painful workouts but pleasant coffee sessions.

A nod to Jen and the crew at The Neighborhood Cup in Aliso Viejo for keeping me supplied with tea and homemade scones while I took up space in their coffee shop writing this second edition.

A big thanks to Janice Samuels, Ryan L. Schrodt, and Renae Horstman at Kendall Hunt for the hard work on the second edition. You helped make the process smooth.

Finally, my thanks to reviewer colleagues for their many insightful suggestions on the first edition. Your advice was invaluable. You'll find many of your suggestions incorporated into this second edition:

> Teresa Gibbons, Grand Valley State University, Michigan
> Beth Hash, Bluefield State College, West Virginia
> Greg Kemble, Yuba College, California
> Rick Ladonsi, Grand Valley State University, Michigan
> Richard Levesque, Fullerton College, California
> Dr. Gary Sligh, Lake-Sumter Community College, Florida
> Dr. Melanie Wagner, Lake-Sumter Community College, Florida

Preface

WHY THIS BOOK?

Today's students are, in general, technology savvy and media-saturated. They deserve a reader that speaks their language, sparks their interest, challenges their assumptions, incites their passions. Online research in academic databases, photographs for writing prompts, cartoons for analysis, film connections, and a smorgasbord of essays should all be a part of a 21st-century reader if teachers want to help motivate developmental writing students—in an increasingly visual culture—to want to read and write.

I've kept the diverse classroom—the different backgrounds and age groups—in mind, and while I can't promise students will like every essay, I think they'll find something that will interest and challenge them, perhaps shock them. Donald Murray in "What Is a Practical Education?" wrote that a good college "must be an uncomfortable place, a threatening place, a challenging place." He believes students should be offered ideas and theories that shake them up, make them think, maybe even frighten them; the more students are shocked and challenged in college, according to Murray, the more prepared they'll be for life. I chose the essays with Murray's philosophy in mind, arranging essays from easiest to most complex within each section, offering students readings they can feel comfortable with and ones that will test their abilities.

In addition to essays and the exercises that go with them, the book offers sections on surviving college, writing strategies for different essay styles, and basic tools for researching and documenting sources. The "User's Guide" gives tips on negotiating the text as well as alternative tables of contents; in the "Survival Kit" section, students will discover tips for succeeding in college, advice for becoming better readers, diplomacy for working in groups, and ways to respond to their classmates' work.

Essay topics range from music and film to toys and automobiles, hummingbirds and turtles to war and technology. Section One, "Telling Tales: Essays From Memory" includes a diversity of writers writing in the personal voice, sharing stories about their lives and experiences: topics include, war and technology, nature, sexual identity, and culture; in "Figuring It Out: Essays That Explain and Explore," the writers attempt to make sense of the world by explaining and analyzing art, music, film, sports, the media, history, and social issues; "Heating It Up: Essays That

Argue" contains opinion essays on technology, fairy tales, social issues, and racism. Not everyone reacts to humor in the same way—what's funny to one person may leave another wondering what the laughter is all about—but the "Laughing Out Loud: Essays That Satirize and Amuse" section attempts to provide a diversity of humorous styles from P. J. O'Rouke's outrageous satire on teens drinking and driving to the more subtle humor of Bailey White's "Mortality."

After the essay sections, there are strategies for writing essays and an introduction to research and documentation using the Modern Language Association (MLA) style.

I've tried to keep the book as jargon-free as possible, using terminology only when necessary. Instead of confusing students with the different names for clauses and phrases, I've labeled most of them dependent or independent word groups. When I do mention a term, it will be in bold; students can turn to the glossary for an explanation.

The styling exercises that accompany the essays are designed to make students think about how good writers accomplish good writing. Some students think good writers are born that way, but writing—as teachers know—like any skill, can be learned with diligence, patience, and desire. Focusing on style—especially sentence structures—not only spices writing, but teaches correctness: modeling advanced sentences reinforces punctuation and grammar.

The assignments and style techniques are tried and true. I thank my students for sometimes double-acting as guinea pigs. While some of the techniques may seem advanced or difficult (some may seem too simple, depending on your students' level), I assure you that with some practice my students mastered at least some—if not all—of them.

From the more advanced student to the struggling writer, the book attempts to interest and challenge your students, make them better thinkers and writers, and help them find their voices.

User's Guide

HOW TO USE THIS BOOK

Because most essays are hybrids, blending various modes and themes, I've not organized the book in the strictly traditional rhetorical or thematical arrangement, though I've added alternative tables of contents to help you find your way around the book if you're more comfortable with those systems. A narrative can present an argument and almost always contains description; an exemplification essay might also define; a classification essay may explain and so forth, so I've divided the book into four sections: In Telling Tales: Essays from Memory, you'll find a diversity of voices telling their stories, relating their experiences, making their points through memories. Figuring It Out: Essays That Explain and Explore contains essays that attempt to make sense of the world, of history, nature, art, and the human mind. Heating It Up: Essays That Argue, while containing some traditional arguments, also presents viewpoints in a variety of forms, and the Laughing Out Loud section offers narration, satirical arguments, process analysis, and other styles. Within each section, I've attempted to arrange the essays, questions, and assignments from simpler to more complex, an arrangement I owe to my students; they've illustrated to me through their writing, questions, and class discussion which assignments and readings present more challenges.

Because I cover style as it relates to the essays, you might find a technique covered in different spots in the book, which might seem repetitive, but techniques need practice for mastery, and it's possible to read many of the essays and not run across a particular technique even though it's offered several times in the book. The **periodic** and **loose** sentences might accompany several essays because the sentences themselves take on many forms. Colons and semicolons can be used in a variety of ways. I've focused on these styles because students often come to college without some of the tools that spark writing—or haven't practiced them since early high school. Modeling good writers improves writing.

If you're working from a rhetorical mode perspective, the assignment arrangement, too, may be unfamiliar because you might find narrative assignments, for example, in every section. The Assignment Guide at the beginning of the book will tell you where to find writing ideas compatible with narration, description, argumentation, cause/effect, and so forth.

Two other features of this book attempt to help you understand the essays. The Dustbin of History and Culture (meant ironically) preceding each essay explains references to history, culture, literature, or other areas that might be unfamiliar (the "dustbin of history" is a phrase Greil Marcus borrowed from Leon Trotsky for his book of the same title; Greil argues that history *does not* belong only to the past, relegated to the dustbin). Though some of the references may seem obvious to you, they may not to others, and the allusions are there because my students have asked me, "What's that mean?" While a feather quill might seem obvious to most, I've had several students ask me about it, students unfamiliar with cultures or historical periods where feather quills might be common, and some students might be embarrassed to ask about a reference that the rest of the class takes for granted. At other times, I list cultural references that might be familiar but detail and context of time and place might be elusive.

The second feature, the Exploring Language section, defines words and gives ideas for usage. Practice using the words, as they'll do you little good otherwise. The more words you add to your vocabulary arsenal, the more complex your reading, thinking, and writing skills become.

I've tried to make it easy for you to navigate the book, but let me know if there's something I didn't think of that might make it easier for you. I welcome your comments.

Survival Kit

I'M IN COLLEGE. NOW WHAT?

Congratulations! You're in college. A good decision. Now what? If college overwhelms you at first, or if you find you're struggling, you're not alone. Many students have a tough time adjusting to college. Others glide. Even the best students fumble at times, so I offer these tips to give you a hand up.

TIPS FOR SUCCESS

First, find out what resources your college has to help you. Is there a tutoring center? A writing lab? Learning disabled center? Financial aid? Make use of these resources. One of my students didn't know that she could get free health care on campus in our health center, so she suffered with a health problem, missed classes and work, and fell needlessly behind at school. If your reading skills need some polish, find out if your school offers reading courses. Do you have trouble spelling? See if there's a spelling course or computer lab with a spelling tutor. The same goes for weaknesses in grammar, math, or any area. Seek and ye shall find.

Consider your workload. Talk to your counselor about your schedule and whether it's too much. If you're working full time and taking five or six classes, you may be overdoing it, though ultimately only you can answer that question. But if you're struggling in classes, it may be time to reconsider.

Get organized. Some schools have classes in surviving college, often offered through counseling. Be sure to have a good notebook with a section for each class, and take notes. Unless you have a photographic mind, you can't possibly remember everything important the teacher says. Write it down, especially if it's on the board or overhead projector. If a teacher repeats an idea, write it down. If you must be absent, get someone in class to take notes for you. Offer to return the favor. While this may seem obvious, I often see students neglect note taking and then wonder why their grades suffer.

Homework can be overwhelming. Set aside time each day to study. Budget your time: study, work, play. Yes, play is important. We all need time away from work to do the things we enjoy. The word *recreation* means to re-create, so budget time to recreate yourself. The general rule for studying is to budget two hours of study time for each hour spent in class, so a three-hour class requires six hours a week of studying. As for work, only you can decide what you need to do, but try to schedule your life wisely.

Don't be afraid to ask questions. Raise your hand. If your teacher has an office and office hours, make use of them. Be sure you understand the homework assignments. If you don't, get clarification. If you miss class, find out what you missed. Assume you missed something.

Read the syllabus and know the teacher's rules. Know how many absences each teacher allows, and keep track when you miss. Don't assume a teacher will take late homework if you've been sick. If you must miss class, get your homework to school somehow, by friend, relative, courier.

Buy the books. If you can't, find out if the library has them or if the teacher has placed them on reserve. Don't sit in silence, not understanding lectures and failing tests because you don't have the books. Find out what help is available. You might be eligible for financial aid.

Many students don't realize the abundance of resources available on campus, often for free. Surviving college means balancing your time, staying organized, and seeking help when you need it. Ask. Your college wants to help.

READING TIPS

In a visual culture where most of our stories come in the form of movies or television and our news from the Internet and television, where films make it easy for us to avoid reading difficult classic literature like Shakespeare and Homer why, then, should we bother to read, other than learning basic communications skills so we can surf the net and fill out job applications?

Reading does more than provide information. It hones intelligence, forces interaction with the text, teaches vocabulary through context, sharpens critical thinking skills, improves verbal and written communication, and illustrates punctuation and difficult sentence structure. You think in language. The more you read, the more language you learn, and the more sophisticated your thinking and analysis become. What you get from reading versus viewing is incalculable.

To be a successful college student, you need to read actively. When you sit down to read, do so with a highlighter, notepad, and dictionary. Looking up words in a dictionary can be tedious—but if you want to learn, to improve reading, to be able to think more complexly, then a dictionary is a must. If you stop to look up every unfamiliar word, you'll get bogged down, so mark the words and reach for the dictionary later. Don't just find the words and jot down their meanings; figure out the context and match the proper definitions. Practice using the words in daily conversations and writings. If you look up the meaning but never use the word, you probably won't remember it.

Highlight passages you think meaningful or don't understand or passages the teacher points out. Try to figure out the writer's main idea and key supporting points. If you have difficulty interpreting a passage—and you've looked up unfamiliar words—write questions that you'd like answered about the passage in the margin next to it; if you don't write down questions as they occur to you, chances are you'll forget by the time class discussion rolls around.

Here are some points to consider when you're **annotating** the text:

1. Ask a question about a concept you don't understand, and then attempt to answer it.
2. Compliment the writer on style: strong word choices, description, specific detail, **metaphor and simile**, **personification**, use of punctuation, sentence structure (for example, **loose** and **periodic** sentences), a hook in the introduction, a snazzy title. You can also complain about any of these techniques.
3. Point out the main idea or thesis of the essay and the supporting evidence.
4. Comment on the strength of the argument or point. Agree or disagree.
5. Look for smooth transitions between paragraphs or ideas within paragraphs.
6. Pinpoint the tone or mood of the essay: academic/analytical, casual, melancholy, contemplative, humorous, cynical, joyful, poignant, and so on.
7. Mention the essay's organization. Is it chronological (order of events), point-by-point, or some other method?

If you're like me, sometimes you read a passage only to find you have no idea what you just read. It's normal for your mind to drift, but make every effort to get back on task. Read the passage again, highlighter and pencil ready. If you're highlighting and making notes, looking up words and thinking about definitions, you'll be an active reader, more likely to absorb material.

Textbooks usually suggest that you read an assignment or essay at least three times: once through quickly to survey, a second time to question the content, and a third time to review. Although I also suggest you try to read three times, I know crowded schedules don't always permit this type of diligence, but you should at least highlight, question, and look up words. Try to read a difficult piece at least twice. Don't give up in frustration if the reading is particularly hard. It's tough at times—I sloughed through some pretty leathery Anglo-Saxon literature as a graduate student—but sticking it out is the only way.

If you're not convinced as to the benefits of reading, think about what it would be like to be denied the privilege. Frederick Douglass, an American slave, tells his story in the following essay, "Learning to Read and Write," from his famous work, *Narrative of the Life of Frederick Douglass*.

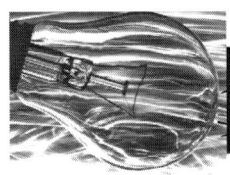

LEARNING TO READ AND WRITE

Frederick Douglass

1\. I lived in Master Hugh's family about seven years. During this time, I succeeded in learning to read and write. In accomplishing this, I was compelled to resort to various stratagems. I had no regular teacher. My mistress, who had kindly commenced to instruct me, had, in compliance with the advice and direction of her husband, not only ceased to instruct, but had set her face against my being instructed by any one else. It is due, however, to my mistress to say of her, that she did not adopt this course of treatment immediately. She at first lacked the depravity indispensable to shutting me up in mental darkness. It was at least necessary for her to have some training in the exercise of irresponsible power, to make her equal to the task of treating me as though I were a brute.

2\. My mistress was, as I have said, a kind and tender-hearted woman; and in the simplicity of her soul she commenced, when I first went to live with her, to treat me as she supposed one human being ought to treat another. In entering upon the duties of a slaveholder, she did not seem to perceive that I sustained to her the relation of a mere chattel, and that for her to treat me as a human being was not only wrong, but dangerously so. Slavery proved as injurious to her as it did to me. When I went there, she was a pious, warm, and tender-hearted woman. There was no sorrow or suffering for which she had not a tear. She had bread for the hungry, clothes for the naked, and comfort for every mourner that came within her reach. Slavery soon proved its ability to divest her of these heavenly qualities. Under its influence, the tender heart became stone, and the lamblike disposition gave way to one of tiger-like fierceness. The first step in her downward course was in her ceasing to instruct me. She now commenced to practise her husband's precepts. She finally became even more violent in her opposition than her husband himself. She was not satisfied with simply doing as well as he had commanded; she seemed anxious to do better. Nothing seemed to make her more angry than to see me with a newspaper. She seemed to think that here lay the danger. I have had her rush at me with a face made all up of fury, and snatch from me a newspaper, in a manner that fully revealed her apprehension. She was an apt woman; and a little experience soon demonstrated, to her satisfaction, that education and slavery were incompatible with each other.

3   From this time I was most narrowly watched. If I was in a separate room any considerable length of time, I was sure to be suspected of having a book, and was at once called to give an account of myself. All this, however, was too late. The first step had been taken. Mistress, in teaching me the alphabet, had given me the *inch,* and no precaution could prevent me from taking the *ell.*

4   The plan which I adopted, and the one by which I was most successful, was that of making friends of all the little white boys whom I met in the street. As many of these as I could, I converted into teachers. With their kindly aid, obtained at different times and in different places, I finally succeeded in learning to read. When I was sent on errands, I always took my book with me, and by going one part of my errand quickly, I found time to get a lesson before my return. I used also to carry bread with me, enough of which was always in the house, and to which I was always welcome; for I was much better off in this regard than many of the poor white children in our neighborhood. This bread I used to bestow upon the hungry little urchins, who, in return, would give me that more valuable bread of knowledge. I am strongly tempted to give the names of two or three of those little boys, as a testimonial of the gratitude and affection I bear them; but prudence forbids;—not that it would injure me, but it might embarrass them; for it is almost an unpardonable offence to teach slaves to read in this Christian country. It is enough to say of the dear little fellows, that they lived on Philpot Street, very near Durgin and Bailey's shipyard. I used to talk this matter of slavery over with them. I would sometimes say to them, I wished I could be as free as they would be when they got to be men. "You will be free as soon as you are twenty-one, *but I am a slave for life!* Have not I as good a right to be free as you have?" These words used to trouble them; they would express for me the liveliest sympathy, and console me with the hope that something would occur by which I might be free.

5   I was now about twelve years old, and the thought of being *a slave for life* began to bear heavily upon my heart. Just about this time, I got hold of a book entitled "The Columbian Orator." Every opportunity I got, I used to read this book. Among much of other interesting matter, I found in it a dialogue between a master and his slave. The slave was represented as having run away from his master three times. The dialogue represented the conversation which took place

between them, when the slave was retaken the third time. In this dialogue, the whole argument in behalf of slavery was brought forward by the master, all of which was disposed of by the slave. The slave was made to say some very smart as well as impressive things in reply to his master—things which had the desired though unexpected effect; for the conversation resulted in the voluntary emancipation of the slave on the part of the master.

6   In the same book, I met with one of Sheridan's mighty speeches on and in behalf of Catholic emancipation. These were choice documents to me. I read them over and over again with unabated interest. They gave tongue to interesting thoughts of my own soul, which had frequently flashed through my mind, and died away for want of utterance. The moral which I gained from the dialogue was the power of truth over the conscience of even a slaveholder. What I got from Sheridan was a bold denunciation of slavery, and a powerful vindication of human rights. The reading of these documents enabled me to utter my thoughts, and to meet the arguments brought forward to sustain slavery; but while they relieved me of one difficulty, they brought on another even more painful than the one of which I was relieved. The more I read, the more I was led to abhor and detest my enslavers. I could regard them in no other light than a band of successful robbers, who had left their homes, and gone to Africa, and stolen us from our homes, and in a strange land reduced us to slavery. I loathed them as being the meanest as well as the most wicked of men. As I read and contemplated the subject, behold! that very discontentment which Master Hugh had predicted would follow my learning to read had already come, to torment and sting my soul to unutterable anguish. As I writhed under it, I would at times feel that learning to read had been a curse rather than a blessing. It had given me a view of my wretched condition, without the remedy. It opened my eyes to the horrible pit, but to no ladder upon which to get out. In moments of agony, I envied my fellow-slaves for their stupidity. I have often wished myself a beast. I preferred the condition of the meanest reptile to my own. Any thing, no matter what, to get rid of thinking! It was this everlasting thinking of my condition that tormented me. There was no getting rid of it. It was pressed upon me by every object within sight or hearing, animate or inanimate. The silver trump of freedom had roused my soul to eternal wakefulness. Freedom now appeared, to disappear no more forever. It was heard in every sound, and seen in every thing. It was ever present to torment me with a sense of my wretched condition. I saw nothing without seeing

it, I heard nothing without hearing it, and felt nothing without feeling it. It looked from every star, it smiled in every calm, breathed in every wind, and moved in every storm.

I often found myself regretting my own existence, and wishing myself dead; and but for the hope of being free, I have no doubt but that I should have killed myself, or done something for which I should have been killed. While in this state of mind, I was eager to hear any one speak of slavery. I was a ready listener. Every little while, I could hear something about the abolitionists. It was some time before I found what the word meant. It was always used in such connections as to make it an interesting word to me. If a slave ran away and succeeded in getting clear, or if a slave killed his master, set fire to a barn, or did any thing very wrong in the mind of a slaveholder, it was spoken of as the fruit of *abolition*. Hearing the word in this connection very often, I set about learning what it meant. The dictionary afforded me little or no help. I found it was "the act of abolishing"; but then I did not know what was to be abolished. Here I was perplexed. I did not dare to ask any one about its meaning, for I was satisfied that it was something they wanted me to know very little about. After a patient waiting, I got one of our city papers, containing an account of the number of petitions from the north, praying for the abolition of slavery in the District of Columbia, and of the slave trade between the States. From this time I understood the words *abolition* and *abolitionist,* and always drew near when that word was spoken, expecting to hear something of importance to myself and fellow-slaves. The light broke in upon me by degrees. I went one day down on the wharf of Mr. Waters; and seeing two Irishmen unloading a scow of stone, I went, unasked, and helped them. When we had finished, one of them came to me and asked me if I were a slave. I told him I was. He asked, "Are ye a slave for life?" I told him that I was. The good Irishman seemed to be deeply affected by the statement. He said to the other that it was a pity so fine a little fellow as myself should be a slave for life. He said it was a shame to hold me. They both advised me to run away to the north; that I should find friends there, and that I should be free. I pretended not to be interested in what they said, and treated them as if I did not understand them; for I feared they might be treacherous. White men have been known to encourage slaves to escape, and then, to get the reward, catch them and return them to their masters. I was afraid that these seemingly good men might use me so; but I nevertheless remembered their advice, and from that time I resolved to run away. I looked forward to a time at which it would be safe for me to escape. I was too young to think of doing so immediately; besides, I wished to learn how to write, as I might have occasion to write my own pass. I consoled myself with the hope that I should one day find a good chance. Meanwhile, I would learn to write.

8   The idea as to how I might learn to write was suggested to me by being in Durgin and Bailey's ship-yard, and frequently seeing the ship carpenters, after hewing, and getting a piece of timber ready for use, write on the timber the name of that part of the ship for which it was intended. When a piece of timber was intended for the larboard side, it would be marked thus—"L." When a piece was for the starboard side, it would be marked thus—"S." A piece for the larboard side forward, would be marked thus—"L.F." When a piece was for starboard side forward, it would be marked thus—"S.F." For larboard aft, it would be marked thus—"L.A." For starboard aft, it would be marked thus—"S. A." I soon learned the names of these letters, and for what they were intended when placed upon a piece of timber in the ship-yard. I immediately commenced copying them, and in a short time was able to make the four letters named. After that, when I met with any boy who I knew could write, I would tell him I could write as well as he. The next word would be, "I don't believe you. Let me see you try it." I would then make the letters which I had been so fortunate as to learn, and ask him to beat that. In this way I got a good many lessons in writing, which it is quite possible I should never have gotten in any other way. During this time, my copy-book was the board fence, brick wall, and pavement; my pen and ink was a lump of chalk. With these, I learned mainly how to write. I then commenced and continued copying the Italics in Webster's Spelling Book, until I could make them all without looking on the book. By this time, my little Master Thomas had gone to school, and learned how to write, and had written over a number of copy-books. These had been brought home, and shown to some of our near neighbors, and then laid aside. My mistress used to go to class meeting at the Wilk Street meeting-house every Monday afternoon, and leave me to take care of the house. When left thus, I used to spend the time in writing in the spaces left in Master Thomas's copy-book, copying what he had written. I continued to do this until I could write a hand very similar to that of Master Thomas. Thus, after a long, tedious effort for years, I finally succeeded in learning how to write.

ADVICE FOR WORKING IN GROUPS

Your instructor has just asked you to break into groups to work together on a project—perhaps one of the Teaming Up exercises in this book—or for peer evaluations or discussion. You may dislike this idea, feeling that you always get stuck with the bulk of the work, or perhaps you just prefer to work alone; or you might relish the idea, enjoying the group interaction and break from routine. Whether you love or loathe it, you may be asked to participate, so here are a few guidelines to help your group get along, split up the work fairly, stay focused on the task, and get the most out of the session.

1. Introduce yourselves and perhaps exchange phone numbers in case you have questions later.
2. Draw up some rules of civility. How will you handle discussion to ensure that each member gets a chance to speak? What will you do about an unruly or rude student? What will you do if a member of the group doesn't show up with a crucial part of the project? What happens if a team member slacks off, bringing shoddy work or none at all?
3. Consider assigning each member a daily task: discussion director, note taker, reader (someone to read passages or directions to the group), typist, spokesperson. You can alternate the jobs each time you split into groups or keep the same tasks.
4. Split up the work fairly. If the project involves research, be sure that each person is responsible for a portion. If you're writing a group essay, assign each person a paragraph to work on at home.
5. Stay focused. If you notice your group deteriorating into discussion of the latest football score or concert attended, try to steer the members back to work. It's natural to get sidetracked, but if it happens too frequently, you're in danger of not completing the work, irritating the teacher, and embarrassing yourselves in front of the rest of the class.
6. Keep noise to a minimum.
7. If you give it a good try and feel you just can't work with your group, it's okay to ask the teacher if you can switch teams, but do it diplomatically. Tell your group that you plan to ask for a transfer, citing philosophical differences. Or say something polite like "I've really enjoyed working with you but would like to try another group, get to know some new people." Don't leave the group with ill feelings.

In general, be courteous to your group and the rest of the class. Follow that golden rule to treat others as you would like to be treated.

PEER EVALUATIONS: RESPONDING TO YOUR CLASSMATES' WORK

Reading and responding honestly to your peer's writing can be difficult. Afraid to offend, you offer only positive remarks, ignoring the flaws, sending the poor soul home with the mistaken impression he or she has written a masterpiece. Or perhaps you're the critical type, finding fault with everything, not offering a kind word, demoralizing your classmate into giving up. Neither response is ideal, but perhaps a balance between the two will help the student discover the positive aspects of his or her work as well as what might need revision. Following are some questions that might help you evaluate another's work kindly but constructively. You'll need a separate sheet of paper, a pen, and a highlighter.

Note: Do not edit another student's work by correcting grammar, punctuation, and spelling. That's the student's job. It's all right to point out that an essay contains several **comma splices** or other errors, but leave the detective work to your peer.

1. Start out positive. What do you like best about the paper? Be specific. Instead of "I really like how you describe things," write "The line in your essay *A thick layer of snow covers the road, and the leafless trees impose a sinister feel; our steps on the crunchy snow break the silence* is so vivid I feel like I'm there. Well done!"
2. Does the essay have a title that grabs your interest? If not, make suggestions or refer the student to the index of this book to look up strategies for creating snappy titles.
3. Does the introduction hook the reader? If not, again refer the student to the index to look up strategies for writing introductions.
4. Does the essay have a thesis or make a point? What is the point? If you are not sure, ask the writer. Does the thesis address the prompt?
5. Does the writer use vivid detail so that you see, hear, smell, feel, taste the experience? If not, tell the writer where you think more detail or description is needed.
6. Is the writing specific, using strong verbs and nouns? ("Joe ambled along the rocky shore" is stronger than "The boy walked along the beach.") Point out sentences that could be more specific.

7. Does the writer provide enough examples to support his or her point? Are the examples appropriate, or would others be stronger?
8. Is the paper well organized? Does the writer make clear paragraph breaks with **transitions**? Is each paragraph organized around a central idea, or do details wander away from the topic? Does each paragraph support the main idea of the essay?
9. Are there any mechanical errors that detract from the paper, like frequent misspellings, punctuation problems, fragments, run-on sentences, shifts in tense or person, or other errors?
10. How is the writing style? Are the sentence patterns varied (short, medium, long sentences)? Can some sentences be combined? Does the writer use **figurative language**? Does the writer rely on too many "to be" verbs (is, are, was, were, be, being, been, am)? Use your highlighter to highlight each "to be" verb. More than three or four per page signals weak verb use. Is the writing clear? Are there spots where you're not sure of the meaning?

Telling Tales: Essays from Memory

INTRODUCTION

A song or a whiff of perfume is a time machine, instantly transporting you back to another moment and place. Feelings, smells, colors come into sharp focus, and you're reliving the moment: your first kiss, disappointment, heartbreak, betrayal. Memories—whether dreamlike and poignant or nightmarish and disturbing—influence you, your decisions and reactions. A memory of mom and dad fighting through a divorce might make you skittish about marriage; an unkind teacher telling you you're no good at math can cause you to avoid college majors that require crunching numbers; a gentle comment from an adult about your talent in art can set you on your life's path. Powerful stuff.

Memories motivate some of the finest writing. Most of the essays in this section come from the writers' thoughts and feelings and stories of a particular time and place, memories so vivid that the writers want to share their experiences with you, move you, shake you, cause you to reflect. In his essay "Modern Times," Lawrence Weschler wants you to think about the marvels and menaces of war fought with modern technology. Barry Lopez reflects on nature and our responsibility toward children in "Children in the Woods." In a series of fable-like stories, Edward Hoagland, in "The Courage of Turtles," relates his boyhood interest in turtles and conveys empathy for their plight at the hands of humans. In a forthright account, Bernard Cooper, in "Burl's," tells us of his struggle growing up homosexual. From turtles to sexual identity, Desert Storm to Roy Orbison, these writers offer themselves to you. Read. Reflect. Enjoy.

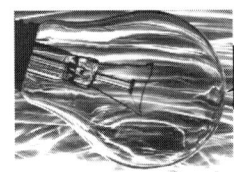

A VOICE FOR THE LONELY

Stephen Corey

Stephen Corey is an editor and author of poetry and essays. In this piece, he reminisces about the death of singer Roy Orbison of "Pretty Woman" fame, speculating on friendship, the impact of music, and "forces of circumstance and the fate of inches."

1   The right silence can be a savior, especially in these days of motorcycles, leaf blowers, and malls that thrum with a thousand voices and dozens of sundry machines. Five or six days a week, I get up pretty early—generally around 4 A.M.—and one of the things I like most about those last hours of darkness is their stillness. The house is quiet, the streets are quiet, and (except on weekends, when some of the serious drunks are hanging on) the all-night restaurants are quiet. Reading and writing and thinking come more easily when you know you won't be interrupted, and over the past 20 years I've never found a better mental bodyguard than the hours before dawn.

2   I got my first serious training as an early riser when I acquired a newspaper delivery route in seventh grade: three miles of widely scattered houses on the edge of Jamestown, New York, and beyond—just me, the moon, darkness, and the various faces of silence. I recall stopping my brisk walk sometimes, especially in winter when every step squeaked and crunched on the snow that nearly always covered the ground, and marveling at how there were no sounds except those of my own making. But just as often, that quiet made me nervous, even though my hometown was awfully safe in those days. I learned to offset the urge to look over my shoulder by carrying a pocket-sized transistor radio.

3   The music helped me to cope with more than just the empty morning streets—I was, as I said, in seventh (and then eighth, and finally ninth) grade during those lone marches. In short, I was just learning something of what much of that music was about: love—lost, found, hoped for, and despaired of.

4   Most habits die hard, and old ones can seem immortal. Last week, I was up as usual at 4 A.M., and I headed out in the car toward the nearest newspaper box. As always during these quick runs, I flipped

"A Voice for the Lonely," copyright © 1989 by Stephen Corey. Reprinted by permission of the author.

on the radio for some wake-up rhythms to jolt my system for the solitary work time soon to come back at the house.

5   Instead of music, I caught the voice of the all-night deejay just as she was saying, "We have tragic news in over the wire: singer Roy Orbison is dead . . ." She gave a quick flurry of details (heart attack, Hendersonville, North Carolina, hospital), repeated the central fact—"Roy Orbison, dead at 52"—and then (my heart applauds her still for this) said not a word but cut straight into "Only the Lonely."

6   There I was, cruising down the abandoned city street with the radio now up as loud as I could stand it, mouthing the rising and falling words, rocking side to side as I held the wheel, and riding Orbison's wailing, nearly-cracking voice back 24 years to the passenger seat of Jon Cresanti's Volkswagen beetle.

7   We're told these days that the hottest and fastest wire into memory is our sense of smell, but music must run a close second. Some songs carry us into a certain mood, some to a general region of our past lives, and some to a very particular moment and situation in time. Jon and I were brought together by chance and loneliness for a couple of months during our sophomore year in high school. The alphabetical seating in our homeroom put us next to each other in the back row, and Jon was a talker. We hadn't known each other before: we came from different parts of town, had different friends, and moved through different sequences of classes. But for a while we found a bond: my girlfriend had recently dropped me after more than a year of going steady, and Jon had eyes for a girl who had none for him.

8   I had time—all the time I was no longer spending with my girl. John had a car and was old enough to drive it, having failed a grade and thereby become a crucial year older than the typical sophomore. I signed on board, and we cruised day after day, weekend after weekend, killing time and eating at the wondrous new "fast food restaurant" that had just opened. We sat in his car eating 15-cent hamburgers and 12-cent french fries near the real golden arches, the kind that curved up and over the entire little structure (no inside seating, no bathrooms)—and, naturally, listening to the radio. The Four Seasons were with us, as were The Beach Boys, Nat King Cole, The Supremes.

9   But in those two desperate months of shotgunning for Jon, there was only one song that really mattered, one song we waited for, hoped for, and even called the radio station and asked for: Roy Orbison's "Pretty Woman."

10 That opening handful of heavy guitar notes (a lovesick teenager's equivalent of Beethoven's Fifth) carried us into a world of possibility,

a world where a moment's fancy could generate love, where losers could be winners just by wishing for success. The pretty woman walks on by, and another failure has occurred—but suddenly, the downward sweep of the wheel is reversed as the woman turns to walk back; and there is nothing in the world but fulfillment of one's dreams.

11   Pop songs are full of such stuff, of course, and have been for as long as the phonograph record and the radio have been with us; we get all kinds of talk about the importance of television in modern life, but I think we need more examination of the ways we have been encompassed by music. I'm not talking about ranting "discussions" of the immorality of certain strains of pop music, but some real studies of the much wider and deeper implications of growing up in a world awash with radio waves.

12   Needless to say, I wasn't concerned about such matters there in the McDonald's parking lot. I wouldn't even have thought about what it was in Orbison's singing that made him so important to me. I took the words of the song's story for their relevance to my own emotional state, and I floated with those words inside a musical accompaniment that both soothed and roused my fifteen-year-old body.

13   When I heard of Orbison's death, I found myself wanting to figure out just what it was in that strange voice that might have been so compelling for me and others across the years. I think it might be in the way the voice itself often seems about to fail: in Orbison's strange and constant modulations, from gravelly bass-like sounds to strong tenor-like passages to piercing falsetto cries, there is the feeling for the listener that the singer is always about to lose control, about to break down under the weight of what he is trying to sing. Never mind that this is not true, that Orbison's style was one carefully achieved; what we are talking about here is emotional effect, the true stuff of pop and country music.

14   If Roy could make it, we could make it. And if Roy could stand failing, so could we.

15   This feeling of camaraderie with the faraway record star increased for me, I think, the first time I saw him. He was so ordinary-looking— no, he was so *homely,* so very contrary to what one expects romantic musical heroes to look like. He was *us.*

16   The right singer, the right sadness, the right silence. The way I heard the story of the death of Orbison's wife in 1966 (and the way I'll keep believing it) was that the two of them were out motorcycling when an errant car or truck hit them from an angle. She was riding just a few feet to the side of and behind him, so the other vehicle

clipped the back of his cycle but caught hers full force. I've never gotten over this chilling illustration of the forces of circumstance and the fate of inches, so much so that over the years I have regularly found the story called to mind for retelling in classrooms or at parties.

17   I graduated from high school the year of the accident, and Orbison disappeared from the national music scene. (It wasn't until recently that I heard how the death of two sons by fire in 1967 compounded Orbison's private tragedies.) Oddly, there is a way in which the disappearance or the death of a singer these days doesn't really matter to his or her listeners, since that person is still present in exactly the same way as before. All the songs take on a slightly new cast, but the singer still lives in a way that one's own deceased relatives and friends cannot.

18   When my girl wanted me back, I dropped Jon's friendship and never tried to regain it—a not-very-commendable way to be. But we were glued for a while by those banging Orbison notes and those erratic vocals, and maybe that was enough, or at least all that one could hope for.

19   Music can block out silence, on dark scary roads and in moments of loneliness. But there's also a sense or two in which a song can create silence: when we're "lost in a song" the rest of the world around us makes, for all practical purposes, no sound. And in an even more strange way, a song we love goes silent as we "listen" to it, leaving us in that rather primitive place where all the sounds are interior ones— sounds which can't be distinguished from feelings, from pulsings and shiverings, from that gut need to make life stronger than death for at least a few moments.

20   When "Only the Lonely" faded, that wonderful deejay still knew enough not to say a word. She threw us straight forward, 4:15 A.M., into "Pretty Woman."

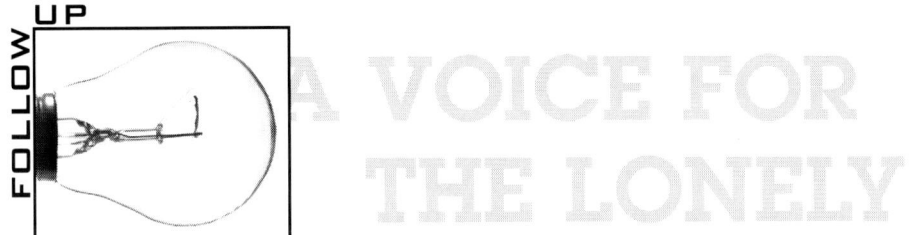

Exploring Language

camaraderie: a feeling of getting along, friendship, or kinship.
erratic: irregular or unpredictable.
modulations: changes in tone or pitch.
sundry: various or miscellaneous.
thrum: strum, as in playing a stringed musical instrument.

USAGE Notice how Corey uses *thrum* in his opening paragraph to describe noises not related to music. Consider other words connected to music that might be used in unusual ways.

Thinking and Talking Points

1. Corey writes, "We're told these days that the hottest and fastest wire into memory is our sense of smell, but music must run a close second." How so? Is there a particular song that helps you travel to another place and time?
2. Reread paragraph #17. What does Corey mean by the songs take on a slightly new cast"?
3. Reread paragraph #19. What does Corey mean by "there's also a sense or two in which a song can create silence"? Can you give a personal example?
4. What is the purpose of Corey's essay? Is it just a tribute to Roy Orbison, or does he have another purpose?
5. Corey writes, "I've never gotten over this chilling illustration of the forces of circumstance and the fate of inches." What does he mean? What's your definition of fate?

Styling

Corey uses sensory words to describe the silence he experienced on his paper route:

> I recall stopping my brisk walk sometimes, especially in winter when every step *squeaked* and *crunched* on the snow that nearly

always covered the ground, and marveling at how there were no sounds except those of my own making.

PRACTICE Fill in the blanks with words that convey sound. Before filling in the blanks, make a list of possibilities, picking out the strongest choices.

Every beat of the drum _____ and _____ my ears.

As it spun out of control, the car _____ and _____, finally crashing into the living room of the house across the street.

Bells _____ and _____ from the cathedral tower.

YOU TRY IT Write five sentences that use the sense of sound.

Teaming Up

1. **A Good Warm-up for Writing Idea #3.** Bring in an article on a favorite singer, alive or dead. Before you come to class, write a summary of the article. In your group, do a **freewrite** on why you like this particular singer or group. Read your freewrites aloud in your group. Who has the most convincing freewrite? You can use your summary and freewrite for Writing Idea #3.

2. **A Good Warm-up for Writing Idea #2.** At home, freewrite on the idea of fate. To what degree do you think fate controls our lives? Why? What's your experience with fate? Read your freewrites in your group, comparing responses, debating the issue.

Writing Ideas

1. Write an essay about a friend who was once very close to you. Explain what made the friendship special and why the friendship broke off. If music played a role in the memories, describe it, modeling Corey when he writes about his memories of John, making use of the sense of sound (see the Styling exercise above).

2. Corey writes about the death of Roy Orbison's wife, stating, "I've never gotten over this chilling illustration of the forces of circumstance and the fate of inches." Write an essay about a time when you first realized

you were—to some degree—at the mercy of fate. Use at least one of the senses in your essay: sight, sound, smell, touch, taste.

3. Use your school or local library's online periodicals database and find an article on a singer you admire. Use the information to write a tribute, as Corey does, to this singer. Write about the music's impact on you, either emotionally or as a memory link. If the singer has died, write about where you were when you heard the news and your reaction. Use the sense of sound in your essay (see the Styling exercise above).

Essay and Film Connections

In "Musical Awakenings," Clayton Collins writes about music's ability to heal, and Jack Kroll, in "Roll Over Bach, Too," writes an essay about the Beatles and their tremendous impact on music and culture. "Prince" by Chuck Klosterman expresses the author's admiration of Prince as a genius. Collins mentions several films in his essay.

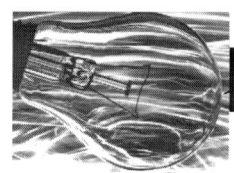

MODERN TIMES

Lawrence Weschler

> Lawrence Weschler, on the first day after Desert Storm, is both fascinated and repelled by a war fought with technology. He recounts the coldness of the news media, which celebrates the clean aerial strikes, but ignores the carnage left behind. Think about his connection of the war with the victims of the San Francisco earthquake.

DUSTBIN OF HISTORY AND CULTURE

DESERT STORM: The Persian Gulf War between the United States and Iraq in 1991.

1   The morning after the launching of Desert Storm, a group of us at my office were talking about this awesome new thing that has entered the world, these awesome new things: this unprecedented kind of warfare with its truly precision, pinpoint aerial bombing; this unprecedented kind of war where, thanks to the various satellite technologies, you get to hear the results of that bombing instantaneously, as it's happening. Modern, we said, high-tech, uncanny, eerie, futuristic. And yet, of course, at another level, there's nothing new here. On the ground, the carnage of war, the gore, the frantically desperate attempts at rescue, the bitterly expiring hopes—they're all the same as they've ever been.

2   One of my friends there at the office that day commented on the way he'd been haunted all morning by the memory of an article he'd read last year—he couldn't remember where—about the San Francisco earthquake. About this young couple who'd been buried alive together in a small room in their collapsed apartment, their bones crushed in debris up to their waists, the two of them huddled together in this narrow air pocket. And of how the rescuers finally got to them—but at that very moment the wreckage caught fire; they were able to free up the husband, but he was forced to leave his wife behind and she perished in the flames.

3   We were all silent for a moment—CNN in the background was cross-cutting between the latest Pentagon briefing and live coverage of a speech by the Turkish prime minister in Ankara.

"Modern Times" from *Everything that Rises: A Book of Convergences* by Lawrence Weschler (McSweeney's, 2007). Reprinted by permission of the author.

4   "Wait a second," my friend said. "I remember: it was in the *Whole Earth Review.* In fact, I bet we can even access it over Nexus." Our office is tied into one of those computerized data bases which offers continuously updated access to the complete back-contents of hundreds of newspapers and periodicals. My friend set himself down before the system's console, revved up the machine, punched in a few key words—*earthquake* and *fire* and *rescue* and *couple*—and instantaneously that very article appeared on the screen. He punched a few more buttons and the console's neighboring printer revved up and began spewing out a copy. The whole process didn't take more than a few moments.

5   The account, by Stewart Brand, was every bit as compelling as our colleague had remembered it. It turned out that Brand himself had happened to be visiting the neighborhood at the moment the earthquake struck and that he'd played an impromptu part in the volunteer rescue attempts: he'd been one of those on the outside, scrambling through the wreckage. "Of course, it wasn't as direct and purposeful as this brief account makes it seem," he records. "A real rescue is dreamy and hesitant, full of false starts and conflicting ideas, at times frantic and focused, at times diffuse. It is a self-organizing process, neither quick nor tidy. . . ." Much later, weeks after the disaster, he'd gone back and interviewed several of the principals from that evening's incident, including Bill Ray, the husband, who was still recovering at a hospital. In his article, Brand interwove their stories, and his account climaxed as the firemen were being driven back by the flames:

> "I told Janet," [this is Ray talking] "I told her 'I'm going to get free, and we're both going to get free.' I assumed that I was binding her and that if I could get loose, then she could get loose. You just start pulling with everything you've got. You reach up and you pull on the lathe and the plaster, and it's breaking off in your hand. . . . Janet was screaming because it was a lot of pain and her arms were trapped, and a picture frame of glass was cutting her.
>   "Then I got free, but she still wasn't. I tried to pull her out. Smoke was coming in. You could hear the flames cracking and popping. She couldn't pull herself loose, and I couldn't get to her."
>   What they said to each other then, Bill Ray prefers to keep private. "Then I left," [Ray recalls] "I crawled out that hole. . . ."

6   And so forth. That terrible lacuna—the private moment, what they possibly could have said to each other—has haunted me, too, ever since I read it. And, of course, I've been imagining the hundreds

of variations of that scene being played out half a globe away; the fact that accidental strikes on civilian targets are purportedly being kept to a minimum doesn't comfort me in the least. I envision seventeen-year-old boys scrambling desperately to rescue their buddies, having to abandon the attempt in the face of further bombardments, and the image is in no way softened by the allegedly mitigating circumstance that the boys in question may be wearing uniforms.

7   But, strangely, the image that really haunts me, and the one I just can't shake, is that of my colleague in the eerie glow of his Nexus console, calmly punching that set of keys, activating the machine—the machine silently humming away, surveying the veritable continents of information before it, instantaneously targeting its quarry, yanking it out of the endless field and delivering it up to us whole. The surgical precision of the whole process. For a moment that morning, my colleague seemed to me like one of those amazing young officers strapped to his battle station aboard the AWACs control planes circling high above Saudi Arabia—coolly surveying his console, punching in the coordinates, splaying out the information, directing the entire battle.

8   CNN, Nexus, AWACs—they're all of a piece. And the carnage on the ground is something entirely else, almost infinitely removed.

Exploring Language

carnage: the leftovers from slaughter, usually referring to dead people, especially after a battle.
diffuse: to scatter or spread.
eerie: ghostly or spooky.
impromptu: spontaneous or unrehearsed.
lacuna: break or interruption; cavity.
mitigating circumstances: special situations that allow for tolerance when leniency might not otherwise be permitted.
quarry: the victim or prey that one is hunting or focusing on.
splaying: spreading out.
uncanny: strange, weird, extraordinary.
unprecedented: never seen before; new, unrivaled.

USAGE Examine the author's use of *mitigating* and *eerie*. Why do you think he made these particular choices? Here's a vocabulary challenge: use *uncanny, eerie,* and *quarry* in the same sentence.

Thinking and Talking Points

1. Why do you think the piece is called "Modern Times"? Give examples from the essay.
2. Explain the connection between the war and the earthquake. Why is Weschler's friend "haunted all morning" by the memory of an earthquake incident? What's significant about the friends' silence after hearing the earthquake story in paragraph #2 and the CNN coverage in the background?
3. What is Weschler's point? Do you think he's saying that war is not justified? Or is he just lamenting the need for war? Find evidence in the article to support your response.
4. Why is Weschler haunted by the image of his colleague at the console of the computer?
5. How do you think this highly technological war differs from previous wars like Vietnam and War World II? What does Weschler indicate he

thinks? What's the emotional or psychological difference for the soldiers? Can you relate his ideas on war and technology to the Iraq war?

Styling

Weschler uses variations of **loose** and **periodic** sentence styles and dashes for writing spice (for more on using dashes, see the Styling section with David Huddle's "Museum Piece"). But let's take a look at a sentence with dashes that set off an **interrupting clause** called an **appositive**. Appositives rename, describe, or give more information about **nouns** (subjects) and help eliminate clunky clauses using *who* and *which*. Here's Weschler's sentence:

> My friend set himself down before the system's console, revved up the machine, punched in a few key words—*earthquake* and *fire* and *rescue* and *couple*—and instantaneously that very article appeared on the screen.

The group of words set off by dashes is an appositive because it renames *key words*. Notice that Weschler's sentence would be complete without the appositive:

> My friend set himself down before the system's console, revved up the machine, punched in a few key words, and instantaneously that very article appeared on the screen.

You have a choice of setting off interrupters with commas, dashes, or parentheses. When interrupting a sentence with a list, as Weschler does, it's a good idea to use dashes, especially when the list contains commas. Dashes will help avoid misreading. If Weschler had used commas instead of the dashes and conjunctions, and if the key words had not been italicized, the sentence would be confusing:

> My friend set himself down before the system's console, revved up the machine, punched in a few key words, earthquake, fire, rescue, couple, and instantaneously that very article appeared on the screen.

Weschler also uses appositives with commas to rename nouns:

> Much later, weeks after the disaster, he'd gone back and interviewed several of the principals from that evening's incident, including Bill Ray, the husband, who was still recovering at a hospital.

The husband renames the noun *Bill Ray*.

Identity the appositives in the following sentences; notice which ones require dashes for clarity.

Her acupuncturist, Jerry, moved to Thailand.

The orchids—dendrobiums, oncidiums, cymbidiums, and cattleyas—bloomed a riot of colors.

My dog, a lazy Golden Retriever, is loveable but useless.

PRACTICE Fill in the blanks below with words or phrases that describe, rename, or give extra information about the nouns.

My college, _____, changes to a sixteen-week semester next spring.

Her car, _____, sat crumpled in the corner of the police impound yard.

The band, _____, drew a large crowd at the county fair.

The vegetable garden—_____—grew despite neglect.

YOU TRY IT Create five sentences of your own with appositives, using dashes and a list in at least two of them. Use this technique in one of the Writing Ideas below.

Teaming Up

1. Have each group member bring in some information about the reasons behind the Persian Gulf War (or another war), half of the group finding arguments justifying the war, half against it. Discuss these reasons and whether or not you think the war was justified.

2. **A Good Warm-up for Writing Idea #2.** In your group, make a list of technological advances that have had an impact on people's lives. Discuss the positive and negative aspects of these technologies. Compare your results with those of the other groups in your class.

Writing Ideas

1. Using a list from "Teaming Up" activity #2, choose one technological advance to explore. Write an essay that discusses the advantages and disadvantages of the technology, proposing a solution to minimize the disadvantages.

2. Research the public's reaction to the Persian Gulf War; then research the reaction to the Vietnam War or Iraq. Write an essay describing these reactions and the reasons behind them. What has changed culturally or socially to cause a change in attitude?
3. Research diary entries from soldiers—perhaps their postings on online communities—about the war or other aspects of being in the military. Then write your own diary entries from the perspective of a soldier. You can create a day-in-the-life story using description and narration, or present it as blog writing.

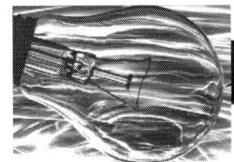

BURL'S

Bernard Cooper

Bernard Cooper is a writing teacher whose work has been published in Harper's Magazine, The Paris Review, and Best American Essays. "Burl's" appeared in the Los Angeles Times Magazine and Best American Essays. In this essay, a young Bernard Cooper discovers that things aren't always as they appear: life is more complex and ambiguous than he thought. He ponders this idea using a series of incidents that contribute to or lead up to this realization, as well as an epiphany about his own sexual identity and "the hazy border between the sexes."

1   I loved the restaurant's name, a compact curve of a word. Its sign, five big letters rimmed in neon, hovered above the roof. I almost never saw the sign with its neon lit; my parents took me there for early summer dinners, and even by the time we left—father cleaning his teeth with a toothpick, mother carrying steak bones in a doggie bag—the sky was still bright. Heat rippled off the cars parked along Hollywood Boulevard, the asphalt gummy from hours of sun.

2   With its sleek architecture, chrome appliances, and arctic temperature, Burl's offered a refuge from the street. We usually sat at one of the booths in front of the plate-glass windows. During our dinner, people came to a halt before the news-vending machine on the corner and burrowed in their pockets and purses for change.

3   The waitresses at Burl's wore brown uniforms edged in checked gingham. From their breast pockets frothed white lace handkerchiefs. In between reconnaissance missions to the table, they busied themselves behind the counter and shouted "Tuna to travel" or "Scorch that patty" to a harried short-order cook who manned the grill. Miniature pitchers of cream and individual pats of butter were

See "Writing Idea" #1.

© vgstudio, 2009. Used under license from Shutterstock, Inc.

"Burl's" from *Truth Serum* by Bernard Cooper. Copyright © 1996 by Bernard Cooper. Reprinted by permission of International Creative Management, Inc.

extracted from an industrial refrigerator. Coca-Cola shot from a glinting spigot. Waitresses dodged and bumped one another, frantic as atoms.

4   My parents usually lingered after the meal, nursing cups of coffee while I played with the beads of condensation on my glass of ice water, tasted Tabasco sauce, or twisted pieces of my paper napkin into mangled animals. One evening, annoyed with my restlessness, my father gave me a dime and asked me to buy him a *Herald Examiner* from the vending machine in front of the restaurant.

5   Shouldering open the heavy glass door, I was seared by a sudden gust of heat. Traffic roared past me and stirred the air. Walking toward the newspaper machine, I held the dime so tightly it seemed to melt in my palm. Duty made me feel large and important. I inserted the dime and opened the box, yanking a *Herald* from the spring contraption that held it as tight as a mousetrap. When I turned around, paper in hand, I saw two women walking toward me.

6   Their high heels clicked on the sun-baked pavement. They were tall, broad-shouldered women who moved with a mixture of haste and defiance. They'd teased their hair into nearly identical black beehives. Dangling earrings flashed in the sun, brilliant as prisms. Each of them wore the kind of clinging, strapless outfit my mother referred to as a cocktail dress. The silky fabric—one dress was purple, the other pink—accentuated their breasts and hips and rippled with insolent highlights. The dresses exposed their bare arms, the slope of their shoulders, and the smooth, powdered plane of flesh where their cleavage began.

7   I owned at the time a book called *Things for Boys and Girls to Do*. There were pages to color, intricate mazes, and connect-the-dots. But another type of puzzle came to mind as I watched those women walking toward me: What's Wrong With This Picture? Say the drawing of a dining room looked normal at first glance; on closer inspection, a chair was missing its leg and the man who sat atop it wore half a pair of glasses.

8   The women had Adam's apples.

9   The closer they came, the shallower my breathing was. I blocked the sidewalk, an incredulous child stalled in their path. When they saw me staring, they shifted their purses and linked their arms. There was something sisterly and conspiratorial about their sudden closeness. Though their mouths didn't move, I thought they might have been communicating without moving their lips, so telepathic did they seem as they joined arms and pressed together, synchronizing their

heavy steps. The pages of the *Herald* fluttered in the wind. I felt them against my arm, light as batted lashes.

10   The woman in pink shot me a haughty glance and yet she seemed pleased that I'd taken notice, hungry to be admired by a man, or even an awestruck eight-year-old boy. She tried to stifle a grin, her red lipstick more voluptuous than the lips it painted. Rouge deepened her cheekbones. Eye shadow dusted her lids, a clumsy abundance of blue. Her face was like a page in *Things for Boys and Girls to Do,* colored by a kid who went outside the lines.

11   At close range, I saw that her wig was slightly askew. I was certain it was a wig because my mother owned several; three Styrofoam heads lined a shelf in my mother's closet; upon them were perched a Page-Boy, an Empress, and a Baby-Doll, all in shades of auburn. The woman in the pink dress wore her wig like a crown of glory.

12   But it was the woman in the purple dress who passed nearest me, and I saw that her jaw was heavily powdered, a half-successful attempt to disguise the telltale shadow of a beard. Just as I noticed this, her heel caught on a crack in the pavement and she reeled on her stilettos. It was then that I witnessed a rift in her composure, a window through which I could glimpse the shades of maleness that her dress and wig and makeup obscured. She shifted her shoulders and threw out her hands like a surfer riding a curl. The instant she regained her balance, she smoothed her dress, patted her hair, and sauntered onward.

13   Any woman might be a man. The fact of it clanged through the chambers of my brain. In broad day, in the midst of traffic, with my parents drinking coffee a few feet away, I felt as if everything I understood, everything I had taken for granted up to that moment—the curve of the earth, the heat of the sun, the reliability of my own eyes—had been squeezed out of me. Who were those men? Did they help each other get inside those dresses? How many other people and things were not what they seemed? From the back, the impostors looked like women once again, slinky and curvaceous, purple and pink. I watched them disappear into the distance, their disguises so convincing that other people on the street seemed to take no notice, and for a moment I wondered if I had imagined the whole encounter, a visitation by two unlikely muses.

14   Frozen in the middle of the sidewalk, I caught my reflection in the window of Burl's, a silhouette floating between his parents. They faced one another across a table. Once the solid embodiments of woman and man, pedestrians and traffic appeared to pass through them.

15 There were some mornings, seconds before my eyes opened and my senses gathered into consciousness, that the child I was seemed to hover above the bed, and I couldn't tell what form my waking would take—the body of a boy or the body of a girl. Finally stirring, I'd blink against the early light and greet each incarnation as a male with mild surprise. My sex, in other words, didn't seem to be an absolute fact so much as a pleasant, recurring accident.

16 By the age of eight, I'd experienced this groggy phenomenon several times. Those ethereal moments above my bed made waking up in the tangled blankets, a boy steeped in body heat, all the more astonishing. That this might be an unusual experience never occurred to me; it was one among a flood of sensations I could neither name nor ignore.

17 And so, shocked as I was when those transvestites passed me in front of Burl's, they confirmed something about which I already had an inkling: the hazy border between the sexes. My father, after all, raised his pinky when he drank from a teacup, and my mother looked as faded and plain as my father until she fixed her hair and painted her face.

18 Like most children, I once thought it possible to divide the world into male and female columns. Blue/Pink. Rooster/Hens. Trousers/Skirts. Such divisions were easy, not to mention comforting, for they simplified matter into compatible pairs. But there also existed a vast range of things that didn't fit neatly into either camp: clocks, milk, telephones, grass. There were nights I fell into a fitful sleep while trying to sex the world correctly.

19 Nothing typified the realms of male and female as clearly as my parents' walk-in closets. Home alone for any length of time, I always found my way inside them. I could stare at my parents' clothes for hours, grateful for the stillness and silence, haunting the very heart of their privacy.

20 The overhead light in my father's closet was a bare bulb. Whenever I groped for the chain in the dark, it wagged back and forth and resisted my grasp. Once the light clicked on, I saw dozens of ties hanging like stalactites. A monogrammed silk bathrobe sagged from a hook, a gift my father had received on a long-ago birthday and, thinking it fussy, rarely wore. Shirts were cramped together along the length of an aluminum pole, their starched sleeves sticking out as if in a halfhearted gesture of greeting. The medicinal odor of mothballs permeated the boxer shorts that were folded and stacked in a built-in drawer. Immaculate underwear was proof of a tenderness my

mother couldn't otherwise express; she may not have touched my father often, but she laundered his boxers with infinite care. Even back then, I suspected that a sense of duty was the final erotic link between them.

21 Sitting in a neat row on the closet floor were my father's boots and slippers and dress shoes. I'd try on his wingtips and clomp around, slipping out of them with every step. My wary, unnatural stride made me all the more desperate to effect some authority. I'd whisper orders to imagined lackeys and take my invisible wife in my arms. But no matter how much I wanted them to fit, those shoes were as cold and hard as marble.

22 My mother's shoes were just as uncomfortable, but a lot more fun. From a brightly colored array of pumps and slingbacks, I'd pick a pair with the glee and deliberation of someone choosing a chocolate. Whatever embarrassment I felt was overwhelmed by the exhilaration of being taller in a pair of high heels. Things will look like this someday, I said to myself, gazing out from my new and improved vantage point as if from a crow's nest. Calves elongated, arms akimbo, I gauged each step so that I didn't fall over and moved with what might have passed for grace had someone seen me, a possibility I scrupulously avoided by locking the door.

23 Back and forth I went. The longer I wore a pair of heels, the better my balance. In the periphery of my vision, the shelf of wigs looked like a throng of kindly bystanders. Light streamed down from a high window, causing crystal bottles to glitter, the air ripe with perfume. A makeup mirror above the dressing table invited my self-absorption. Sound was muffled. Time slowed. It seemed as if nothing bad could happen as long as I stayed within those walls.

24 Though I'd never been discovered in my mother's closet, my parents knew that I was drawn toward girlish things—dolls and jump rope and jewelry—as well as to the games and preoccupations that were expected of a boy. I'm not sure now if it was my effeminacy itself that bothered them as much as my ability to slide back and forth, without the slightest warning, between male and female mannerisms. After I'd finished building the model of an F-17 bomber, say, I'd sit back to examine my handiwork, pursing my lips in concentration and crossing my legs at the knee.

25 One day my mother caught me standing in the middle of my bedroom doing an imitation of Mary Injijikian, a dark, overeager Armenian girl with whom I believed myself to be in love, not only because she was pretty but because I wanted to be like her. Collector of effortless

A's, Mary seemed to know all the answers in class. Before the teacher had even finished asking a question, Mary would let out a little grunt and practically levitate out of her seat, as if her hand were filled with helium. "Could we please hear from someone else today besides Miss Injijikian," the teacher would say. *Miss Injijikian.* Those were the words I was repeating over and over to myself when my mother caught me. To utter them was rhythmic, delicious, and under their spell I raised my hand and wiggled like Mary. I heard a cough and spun around. My mother froze in the doorway. She clutched the folded sheets to her stomach and turned without saying a word. My sudden flush of shame confused me. Weren't boys supposed to swoon over girls? Hadn't I seen babbling, heartsick men in a dozen movies?

26   Shortly after the Injijikian incident, my parents decided to send me to gymnastics class at the Los Angeles Athletic Club, a brick relic of a building on Olive Street. One of the oldest establishments of its kind in Los Angeles, the club prohibited women from the premises. My parents didn't have to say it aloud: they hoped a fraternal atmosphere would toughen me up and tilt me toward the male side of my nature.

27   My father drove me downtown so I could sign up for the class, meet the instructor, and get a tour of the place. On the way there, he reminisced about sports. Since he'd grown up in a rough Philadelphia neighborhood, sports consisted of kick-the-can or rolling a hoop down the street with a stick. The more he talked about his physical prowess, the more convinced I became that my daydreams and shyness were a disappointment to him.

28   The hushed lobby of the athletic club was paneled in dark wood. A few solitary figures were hidden in wing chairs. My father and I introduced ourselves to a man at the front desk who seemed unimpressed by our presence. His aloofness unnerved me, which wasn't hard considering that no matter how my parents put it, I knew their sending me here was a form of disapproval, a way of banishing the part of me they didn't care to know.

29   A call went out over the intercom for someone to show us around. While we waited, I noticed that the sand in the standing ashtrays had been raked into perfect furrows. The glossy leaves of the potted plants looked as if they'd been polished by hand. The place seemed more like a well-tended hotel than an athletic club. Finally, a stoop-shouldered old man hobbled toward us, his head shrouded in a cloud of white hair. He wore a T-shirt that said "Instructor"; his arms were so wrinkled and anemic, I thought I might have misread it. While we followed him to the elevator, I readjusted my expectations, which had

involved fantasies of a hulking drill sergeant barking orders at a flock of scrawny boys.

30   The instructor, mumbling to himself and never turning around to see if we were behind him, showed us where the gymnastics class took place. I'm certain the building was big, but the size of the room must be exaggerated by a trick of memory, because when I envision it, I picture a vast and windowless warehouse. Mats covered the wooden floor. Here and there, in remote and lonely pools of light, stood a pommel horse, a balance beam, and parallel bars. Tiers of bleachers rose into darkness. Unlike the cloistered air of a closet, the room seemed incomplete without a crowd.

31   Next we visited the dressing room, empty except for a naked middle-aged man. He sat on a narrow bench and clipped his formidable toenails. Moles clotted his back. He glistened like a fish.

32   We continued to follow the instructor down an aisle lined with numbered lockers. At the far end, steam billowed from the doorway that led to the showers. Fresh towels stacked on a nearby table made me think of my mother; I knew she liked to have me at home with her—I was often her only companion—and I resented her complicity in the plan to send me here.

33   The tour ended when the instructor gave me a sign-up sheet. Only a few names preceded mine. They were signatures, or so I imagined, of other soft and wayward sons.

34   When the day of the first gymnastics class arrived, my mother gave me money and a gym bag and sent me to the corner of Hollywood and Western to wait for a bus. The sun was bright, the traffic heavy. While I sat there, an argument raged inside my head, the familiar, battering debate between the wish to be like other boys and the wish to be like myself. Why shouldn't I simply get up and go back home, where I'd be left alone to read and think? On the other hand, wouldn't life be easier if I liked athletics, or learned to like them?

35   No sooner did I steel my resolve to get on the bus than I thought of something better: I could spend the morning wandering through Woolworth's, then tell my parents I'd gone to the class. But would my lie stand up to scrutiny? As I practiced describing phantom gymnastics, I became aware of a car circling the block. It was a large car in whose shaded interior I could barely make out the driver, but I thought it might be the man who owned the local pet store. I'd often gone there on the pretext of looking at the cocker spaniel puppies huddled together in their pen, but I really went to gawk at the owner, whose tan chest, in the V of his shirt, was the place I most wanted to

rest my head. Every time the man moved, counting stock or writing a receipt, his shirt parted, my mouth went dry, and I smelled the musk of sawdust and dogs.

36   I found myself hoping that the driver was the man who ran the pet store. I was thrilled by the unlikely possibility that the sight of me, slumped on a bus bench in my T-shirt and shorts, had caused such a man to circle the block. Up to that point in my life, lovemaking hovered somewhere in the future, an impulse a boy might aspire to but didn't indulge. And there I was, sitting on a bus bench in the middle of the city, dreaming I could seduce an adult. I showered the owner of the pet store with kisses and, as aquariums bubbled, birds sang, and mice raced in a wire wheel, slipped my hand beneath his shirt. The roar of traffic brought me to my senses. I breathed deeply and blinked against the sun. I crossed my legs at the knee in order to hide an erection. My fantasy left me both drained and changed. The continent of sex had drifted closer.

37   The car made another round. This time the driver leaned across the passenger seat and peered at me through the window. He was a complete stranger, whose gaze filled me with fear. It wasn't the surprise of not recognizing him that frightened me, it was what I did recognize—the unmistakable shame in his expression, and the weary temptation that drove him in circles. Before the car behind him honked, he mouthed "hello" and cocked his head. What now, he seemed to be asking. A bold, unbearable question.

38   I bolted to my feet, slung the gym bag over my shoulder, and hurried toward home. Now and then I turned around to make sure he wasn't trailing me, both relieved and disappointed when I didn't see his car. Even after I became convinced that he wasn't at my back— my sudden flight had scared him off—I kept turning around to see what was making me so nervous, as if I might spot the source of my discomfort somewhere on the street. I walked faster and faster, trying to outrace myself. Eventually, the bus I was supposed to have taken roared past. Turning the corner, I watched it bob eastward.

39   Closing the kitchen door behind me, I vowed never to leave home again. I was resolute in this decision without fully understanding why, or what it was I hoped to avoid; I was only aware of the need to hide and a vague notion, fading fast, that my trouble had something to do with sex. Already the mechanism of self-deception was at work. By the time my mother rushed into the kitchen to see why I'd returned so early, the thrill I'd felt while waiting for the bus had given way to indignation.

40   I poured out the story of the man circling the block and protested, with perhaps too great a passion, my own innocence. "I was just sitting there," I said again and again. I was so determined to deflect suspicion away from myself, and to justify my missing the class, that I portrayed the man as a grizzled pervert who drunkenly veered from lane to lane as he followed me halfway home.

41   My mother cinched her housecoat. She seemed moved and shocked by what I told her, if a bit incredulous, which prompted me to be more dramatic. "It wouldn't be safe," I insisted, "for me to wait at the bus stop again."

42   No matter how overwrought my story, I knew my mother wouldn't question it, wouldn't bring the subject up again; sex of any kind, especially sex between a man and a boy, was simply not discussed in our house. The gymnastics class, my parents agreed, was something I could do another time.

43   And so I spent the remainder of that summer at home with my mother, stirring cake batter, holding the dustpan, helping her fold the sheets. For a while I was proud of myself for engineering a reprieve from the athletic club. But as the days wore on, I began to see that my mother had wanted me with her all along, and forcing that to happen wasn't such a feat. Soon a sense of compromise set in; by expressing disgust for the man in the car, I'd expressed disgust for an aspect of myself. Now I had all the time in the world to sit around and contemplate my desire for men. The days grew long and stifling and hot, an endless sentence of self-examination.

44   Only trips to the pet store offered any respite. Every time I went there, I was too electrified with longing to think about longing in the abstract. The bell tinkled above the door, animals stirred within their cages, and the handsome owner glanced up from his work.

45   I handed my father the *Herald*. He opened the paper and disappeared behind it. My mother stirred her coffee and sighed. She gazed at the sweltering passersby and probably thought herself lucky. I slid into the vinyl booth and took my place beside my parents.

46   For a moment, I considered asking them about what had happened on the street, but they would have reacted with censure and alarm, and I sensed there was more to the story than they'd ever be willing to tell me. Men in dresses were only the tip of the iceberg. Who knew what other wonders existed—a boy, for example, who wanted to kiss a man—exceptions the world did its best to keep hidden.

47 It would be years before I heard the word "transvestite," so I struggled to find a word for what I'd seen. "He-she" came to mind, as lilting as "Injijikian." "Burl's" would have been perfect, like "boys" and "girls" spliced together, but I can't claim to have thought of this back then.

48 I must have looked stricken as I tried to figure it all out, because my mother put down her coffee cup and asked if I was O.K. She stopped just short of feeling my forehead. I assured her I was fine, but something within me had shifted, had given way to a heady doubt. When the waitress came and slapped down our check—"Thank You," it read, "Dine out more often"—I wondered if her lofty hairdo or the breasts on which her nametag quaked were real. Wax carnations bloomed at every table. Phony wood paneled the walls. Plastic food sat in a display case: fried eggs, a hamburger sandwich, a sundae topped with a garish cherry.

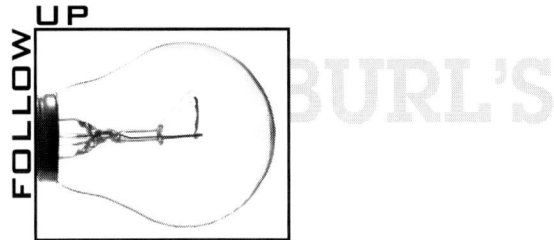

Exploring Language

akimbo: hands on the hips and elbows turned outward.
cloistered: secluded or sheltered from the world.
conspiratorial: suggestive of having a conspiracy, which means having a secret or plot.
elongated: stretched out or lengthened.
ethereal: delicate or rare; otherworldly.
frothed: bubbled or foamed.
garish: tasteless and/or flashy; excessively ornate.
haughty: arrogant or scornful.
incredulous: astounded, shaken, shocked, surprised.
insolent: bold, rude, discourteous.
periphery: on the edge or border.
reconnaissance: an information-gathering mission. The military often sends reconnaissance missions made up of a few people (sometimes only one) into enemy territory to gather information about the other side.
scrupulously: carefully, exactly, meticulously; honestly.
synchronizing: happening at the same time.
telepathic: being able to communicate through the mind rather than words or gestures.
voluptuous: suggesting fullness of form and beauty; sensual.

USAGE Create **personification** using the words *insolent* and *haughty* to describe an object. For example, Cooper writes, "The silky fabric—one dress was purple, the other pink—accentuated their breasts and hips and rippled with insolent highlights." The word *insolent* is a human quality, but he uses it to describe the highlights in their dresses. Make a list of as many objects as you can, and then try *insolent* and *haughty* in front of each one. Choose your best combination and write a sentence.

Thinking and Talking Points

1. Examine Cooper's word choices, particularly how he uses strong **verbs** like *hovered* and *rippled*. What other style techniques does

Cooper use in his essay? Find *similes* and *metaphors* and explain what they add to the essay.

2. At what point in the essay did you first suspect Cooper is leading up to a realization about his own sexual identity? What clues can you find early in the essay?

3. Discuss Cooper's parents and their reaction to their son's not-so-masculine qualities. How do they cope with the situation? Is their reaction typical of many parents? Do you think they ever accept young Bernard's sexual orientation? What clues in the essay lead you to this conclusion?

4. Cooper writes, "Like most children, I once thought it possible to divide the world into male and female columns." What blurs this line for young Bernard? To what extent do you divide the world along gender lines? What other situations can you think of where things aren't always what they appear?

5. Analyze the structure of this essay. Why does Cooper begin and end with the restaurant? In what way are the series of events he describes related? Why does he put them in the order he does? What conclusion do they lead to about the world?

Styling

Slowing down time like a slow motion camera, Cooper takes a slice of time—a few seconds—and describes it in minute detail, stretching a few seconds onto a canvas, creating a vivid portrait of the two women who walk by him on the sidewalk outside of Burl's. He could have written, "Two women dressed as men walked by me on the sidewalk." We wouldn't be nearly as intrigued nor surprised. He teases the reader, leading up to realization that these two women are men, recreating the experience he had as a young boy, puzzling over it, finally astounding himself and the reader with the line—set off by itself—"The women had Adam's apples." His slow motion technique creates a sense of reality, pulling the reader into the piece, making us see the event through young Bernard's eyes.

PRACTICE Reread the section where Cooper describes seeing the two women on the sidewalk. Examine how he slows down time, zooming in on the details. Make a lists of word choices and phrases he uses to accomplish this goal. Underline or list strong verb choices and **figurative language**.

Now, think of a meaningful event in your life, perhaps one that led you to some realization about the world. Choose something that happened in a short period of time so you can zoom in close on the details. If you can't recreate a scene, sit in a public place and people-watch until you see an interesting person or event to describe. Make a list of details. Pay close attention. If you're writing about a person, you might list things like this: frayed collar, cracked toenails, lipstick-smeared mouth. Think about fabrics, accessories, expressions. If you get stuck, reread Cooper's piece for ideas.

YOU TRY IT Using your list of details, write a paragraph or two describing a person or event. If it's a person, he or she should be in motion. Use slow-motion-camera writing to zoom the reader in on the action. Use at least one *simile* or *metaphor*, strong *verbs,* and lots of details. Make use of the senses: touch, taste, smell, sound, sight.

Teaming Up

1. In your group, make a list of big things (a whale, for example). Think of at least ten items. Next, replace the word *continent* in Cooper's sentence, "The continent of sex had moved closer." Try out each word on the list. Do any of them work as well as Cooper's choice as a metaphor? Discuss Cooper's use of *continent* to describe sex. Why does it work so well? What word choices on your list flopped? Why?

2. **A Good Warm-up for Writing Idea #2.** Before class, brainstorm and do a **freewrite** about a time you had a child-to-adult epiphany, a time when you realized that appearances can be deceiving. In class, study the photo and discuss what the reality might be behind the picture. Now share your freewrites. Do any of them match up with the pictures studied?

Writing Ideas

1. **Photo Connection:** Study the photo on page 17. Write a story about the picture, using the reality-is-more-complicated-than-it-seems idea.
2. Write an essay about an awareness you had as a child that things aren't always what they seem. Think of several events that led to, contributed to, or confirmed this epiphany, and use them to lead the reader to your realization.

3. Visit an online database that subscribes to periodicals, such as Infotrac, available at your public or college or university library. Do some research on the controversy surrounding the genetic link to sexual orientation. Look at both sides of the issue. Write an essay explaining the controversy.

Film and Essay Connections

"Oranges and Sweet Sister Boy" by Judy Ruiz—not in this text, but in *Best American Essays* college edition—makes a good companion essay to "Burl's." "Graven Images" by Saul Bellow discusses the media's power to control our image by the photographs they print, and the image we have of ourselves vs. the reality of the image on paper. The film *The Crying Game* explores the appearances-vs.-reality theme. If you haven't seen it, I won't spoil the surprise.

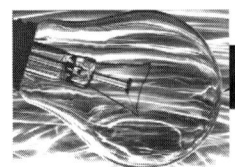

THE COURAGE OF TURTLES

Edward Hoagland

Edward Hoagland is best known for his nature and travel essays, with several collections to his credit, among them Walking the Dead Diamond River, The Final Fate of Alligators, *and* The Courage of Turtles. *In this essay from the book of the same title, Hoagland expresses his admiration of these creatures through anthropomorphizing and a series of stories resembling fables.*

DUSTBIN OF HISTORY AND CULTURE

BERET: French, a cap with no visor, usually made of wool.
BON MOTS: French, literally meaning "good word"; clever remark or witticism.
IDÉE FIXE: French meaning fixed idea; obsession.
MARGAY CAT: A small, spotted, forest-dwelling cat of Central and South America, closely resembling the ocelot.

1   Turtles are a kind of bird with the governor turned low. With the same attitude of removal, they cock a glance at what is going on, as if they need only to fly away. Until recently they were also a case of virtue rewarded, at least in the town where I grew up, because, being humble creatures, there were plenty of them. Even when we still had a few bobcats in the woods the local snapping turtles, growing up to forty pounds, were the largest carnivores. You would see them through the amber water, as big as greeny wash basins at the bottom of the pond, until they faded into the inscrutable mud as if they hadn't existed at all.

2   When I was ten I went to Dr. Green's Pond, a two-acre pond across

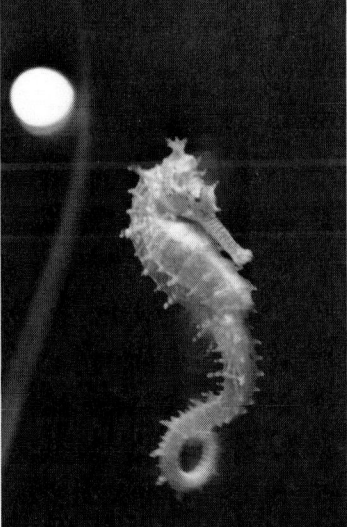

See "Teaming Up" #3.

© Teri Hammaren, 2009. Used under license from Shutterstock, Inc.

"The Courage of Turtles" from *The Courage of Turtles* by Edward Hoagland. Published by Lyons & Burford. Copyright © 1968, 1970, 1993 by Edward Hoagland. Reprinted by permission of Lescher & Lescher, Ltd. All rights reserved.

the road. When I was twelve I walked a mile or so to Taggart's Pond, which was lusher, had big water snakes and a waterfall; and shortly after that I was bicycling way up to the adventuresome vastness of Mud Pond, a lake-sized body of water in the reservoir system of a Connecticut city, possessed of cat-backed little islands and empty shacks and a forest of pines and hardwoods along the shore. Otters, foxes, and mink left their prints on the bank; there were pike and perch. As I got older, the estates and forgotten back lots in town were parceled out and sold for nice prices, yet, though the woods had shrunk, it seemed that fewer people walked in the woods. The new residents didn't know how to find them. Eventually, exploring, they did find them, and it required some ingenuity and doubling around on my part to go for eight miles without meeting someone. I was grown by now, I lived in New York, and that's what I wanted to do on the occasional weekends when I came out.

3   Since Mud Pond contained drinking water I had felt confident nothing untoward would happen there. For a long while the developers stayed away, until the drought of the mid-1960s. This event, squeezing the edges in, convinced the local water company that the pond really wasn't a necessity as a catch basin, however; so they bulldozed a hole in the earthen dam, bulldozed the banks to fill in the bottom, and landscaped. the flow of water that remained to wind like an English brook and provide a domestic view for the houses which were planned. Most of the painted turtles of Mud Pond, who had been inaccessible as they sunned on their rocks, wound up in boxes in boys' closets within a matter of days. Their footsteps in the dry leaves gave them away as they wandered forlornly. The snappers and the little musk turtles, neither of whom leave the water except once a year to lay their eggs, dug into the drying mud for another siege of hot weather, which they were accustomed to doing whenever the pond got low. But this time it was low for good; the mud baked over them and slowly entombed them. As for the ducks, I couldn't stroll in the woods and not feel guilty, because they were crouched beside every stagnant pothole, or were slinking between the bushes with their heads tucked into their shoulders so that I wouldn't see them. If they decided I had, they beat their way up through the screen of trees, striking their wings dangerously, and wheeled about with that headlong, magnificent velocity to locate another poor puddle.

4   I used to catch possums and black snakes as well as turtles, and I kept dogs and goats. Some summers I worked in a menagerie with the big personalities of the animal kingdom, like elephants and

rhinoceroses. I was twenty before these enthusiasms began to wane, and it was then that I picked turtles as the particular animal I wanted to keep in touch with. I was allergic to fur, for one thing, and turtles need minimal care and not much in the way of quarters. They're personable beasts. They see the same colors we do and they seem to see just as well, as one discovers in trying to sneak up on them. In the laboratory they unravel the twists of a maze with the hot-blooded rapidity of a mammal. Though they can't run as fast as a rat, they improve on their errors just as quickly, pausing at each crossroads to look left and right. And they rock rhythmically in place, as we often do, although they are hatched from eggs, not the womb. (A common explanation psychologists give for our pleasure in rocking quietly is that it recapitulates our mother's heartbeat *in utero*.)

5   Snakes, by contrast, are dryly silent and priapic. They are smooth movers, legalistic, unblinking, and they afford the humor which the humorless do. But they make challenging captives; sometimes they don't eat for months on a point of order—if the light isn't right, for instance. Alligators are sticklers too. They're like war-horses, or German shepherds, and with their bar-shaped, vertical pupils adding emphasis, they have the *idée fixe* of eating, eating, even when they choose to refuse all food and stubbornly die. They delight in tossing a salamander up towards the sky and grabbing him in their long mouths as he comes down. They're so eager that they get the jitters, and they're too much of a proposition for a casual aquarium like mine. Frogs are depressingly defenseless: that moist, extensive back, with the bones almost sticking through. Hold a frog and you're holding its skeleton. Frogs' tasty legs are the staff of life to many animals— herons, raccoons, ribbon snakes—though they themselves are hard to feed. It's not an enviable role to be the staff of life, and after frogs you descend down the evolutionary ladder a big step to fish.

6   Turtles cough, burp, whistle, grunt and hiss, and produce social judgments. They put their heads together amicably enough, but then one drives the other back with the suddenness of two dogs who have been conversing in tones too low for an onlooker to hear. They pee in fear when they're first caught, but exercise both pluck and optimism in trying to escape, walking for hundreds of yards within the confines of their pen, carrying the weight of that cumbersome box on legs which are cruelly positioned for walking. They don't feel that the contest is unfair; they keep plugging, rolling like sailorly souls—a bobbing, infirm gait, a brave, sea-legged momentum—stopping occasionally to

study the lay of the land. For me, anyway, they manage to contain the rest of the animal world. They can stretch out their necks like a giraffe, or loom under-water like an apocryphal hippo. They browse on lettuce thrown on the water like a cow moose which is partly submerged. They have a penguin's alertness, combined with a build like a brontosaurus when they rise up on tiptoe. Then they hunch and ponderously lunge like a grizzly going forward.

7   Baby turtles in a turtle bowl are a puzzle in geometrics. They're as decorative as pansy petals, but they are also self-directed building blocks, propping themselves on one another in different arrangements, before up-ending the tower. The timid individuals turn fearless, or vice versa. If one gets a bit arrogant he will push the others off the rock and afterwards climb down into the water and cling to the back of one of those he has bullied, tickling him with his hind feet until he bucks like a bronco. On the other hand, when this same milder-mannered fellow isn't exerting himself, he will stare right into the face of the sun for hours. What could be more lionlike? And he's at home in or out of the water and does lots of metaphysical tilting. He sinks and rises, with an infinity of levels to choose from; or, elongating himself, he climbs out on the land again to perambulate, sits boxed in his box, and finally slides back in the water, submerging into dreams.

8   I have five of these babies in a kidney-shaped bowl. The hatchling, who is a painted turtle, is not as large as the top joint of my thumb. He eats chicken gladly. Other foods he will attempt to eat but not with sufficient perseverance to succeed because he's so little. The yellow-bellied terrapin is probably a yearling, and he eats salad voraciously, but no meat, fish, or fowl. The Cumberland terrapin won't touch salad or chicken but eats fish and all of the meats except for bacon. The little snapper, with a black crenelated shell, feasts on any kind of meat, but rejects greens and fish. The fifth of the turtles is African. I acquired him only recently and don't know him well. A mottled brown, he unnerves the greener turtles, dragging their food off to his lairs. He doesn't seem to want to be green—he bites the algae off his shell, hanging meanwhile at daring, steep, head-first angles.

The snapper was a Ferdinand until I provided him with deeper water.

9   Now he snaps at my pencil with his downturned and fearsome mouth, his swollen face like a napalm victim's. The Cumberland has an elliptical red mark on the side of his green-and-yellow head. He is benign by nature and ought to be as elegant as his scientific name (*Pseudemys scripta elegans*), except he has contracted a disease of the

air bladder which has permanently inflated it; he floats high in the water at an undignified slant and can't go under. There may have been internal bleeding, too, because his carapace is stained along its ridge. Unfortunately, like flowers, baby turtles often die. Their mouths fill up with a white fungus and their lungs with pneumonia. Their organs clog up from the rust in the water, or diet troubles, and, like a dying man's, their eyes and heads become too prominent. Toward the end, the edge of the shell becomes flabby as felt and folds around them like a shroud.

10   While they live they're like puppies. Although they're vivacious, they would be a bore to be with all the time, so I also have an adult wood turtle about six inches long. Her top shell is the equal of any seashell for sculpturing, even a Cellini shell; it's like an old, dusty, richly engraved medallion dug out of a hillside. Her legs are salmon-orange bordered with black and protected by canted, heroic scales. Her plastron—the bottom shell—is splotched like a margay cat's coat, with black ocelli on a yellow back-ground. It is convex to make room for the female organs inside, whereas a male's would be concave to help him fit tightly on top of her. Altogether, she exhibits every camouflage color on her limbs and shells. She has a turtleneck neck, a tail like an elephant's, wise old pachydermous hind legs, and the face of a turkey—except that when I carry her she gazes at the passing ground with a hawk's eyes and mouth. Her feet fit to the fingers of my hand, one to each one, and she rides looking down. She can walk on the floor in perfect silence, but usually she lets her plastron knock portentously, like a footstep, so that she resembles some grand, concise, slow-moving id. But if an earthworm is presented, she jerks swiftly ahead, poises above it, and strikes like a mongoose, consuming it with wild vigor. Yet she will climb on my lap to eat bread or boiled eggs.

11   If put into a creek, she swims like a cutter, nosing forward to intercept a strange turtle and smell him. She drifts with the current to go downstream, maneuvering behind a rock when she wants to take stock, or sinking to the nether levels, while bubbles float up. Getting out, choosing her path, she will proceed a distance and dig into a pile of humus, thrusting herself to the coolest layer at the bottom. The hole closes over her until it's as small as a mouse's hole. She's not as aquatic as a musk turtle, not quite as terrestrial as the box turtles in the same woods, but because of her versatility she's marvelous, she's everywhere. And though she breathes the way we breathe, with scarcely perceptible movements of her chest, sometimes instead she pumps her throat ruminatively, like a pipe smoker sucking and puffing. She waits and

blinks, pumping her throat, turning her head, then sets off like a loping tiger in slow motion, hurdling the jungly lumber, the pea vine and twigs. She estimates angles so well that when she rides over the rocks, sliding down a drop-off with her rugged front legs extended, she has the grace of a rodeo mare.

12   But she's well off to be with me rather than at Mud Pond. The other turtles have fled—those that aren't baked into the bottom. Creeping up the brooks to sad, constricted marshes, burdened as they are with that box on their backs, they're walking into a setup where all their enemies move thirty times faster than they. It's like the nightmare most of us have whimpered through, where we are weighted down disastrously while trying to flee; fleeing our home ground, we try to run.

13   I've seen turtles in still worse straits. On Broadway, in New York, there is a penny arcade which used to sell baby terrapins that were scrawled with bon mots in enamel paint, such as KISS ME BABY. The manager turned out to be a wholesaler as well, and once I asked him whether he had any larger turtles to sell. He took me upstairs to a loft room devoted to the turtle business. There were desks for the paper work and a series of racks that held shallow tin bins atop one another, each with several hundred babies crawling around in it. He was a smudgy-complexioned, bespectacled, serious fellow and he did have a few adult terrapins, but I was going to school and wasn't actually planning to buy; I'd only wanted to see them. They were aquatic turtles, but here they went without water, presumably for weeks, lurching about in those dry bins like handicapped citizens, living on gumption. An easel where the artist worked stood in the middle of the floor. She had a palette and a clip attachment for fastening the babies in place. She wore a smock and a beret, and was homely, short, and eccentric-looking, with funny black hair, like some of the ladies who show their paintings in Washington Square in May. She had a cold, she was smoking, and her hand wasn't very steady, although she worked quickly enough. The smile that she produced for me would have looked giddy if she had been happier, or drunk. Of course the turtles' doom was sealed when she painted them, because their bodies inside would continue to grow but their shells would not. Gradually, invisibly, they would be crushed. Around us their bellies—two thousand belly shells—rubbed on the bins with a mournful, momentous hiss.

14   Somehow there were so many of them I didn't rescue one. Years later, however, I was walking on First Avenue when I noticed a basket of living turtles in front of a fish store. They were as dry as a heap

of old bones in the sun; nevertheless, they were creeping over one another gimpily, doing their best to escape. I looked and was touched to discover that they appeared to be wood turtles, my favorites, so I bought one. In my apartment I looked closer and realized that in fact this was a diamondback terrapin, which was bad news. Diamondbacks are tidewater turtles from brackish estuaries, and I had no seawater to keep him in. He spent his days thumping interminably against the baseboards, pushing for an opening through the wall. He drank thirstily but would not eat and had none of the hearty, accepting qualities of wood turtles. He was morose, paler in color, sleeker and more Oriental in the carved ridges and rings that formed his shell. Though I felt sorry for him, finally I found his unrelenting presence exasperating. I carried him, struggling in a paper bag, across town to the Morton Street Pier on the Hudson River. It was August but gray and windy. He was very surprised when I tossed him in; for the first time in our association, I think, he was afraid. He looked afraid as he bobbed about on top of the water, looking up at me from ten feet below. Though we were both accustomed to his resistance and rigidity, seeing him still pitiful, I recognized that I must have done the wrong thing. At least the river was salty, but it was also bottomless; the waves were too rough for him, and the tide was coming in, bumping him against the pilings underneath the pier. Too late, I realized that he wouldn't be able to swim to a peaceful inlet in New Jersey, even if he could figure out which way to swim. But since, short of diving in after him, there was nothing I could do, I walked away.

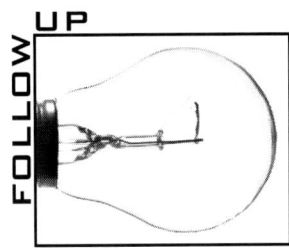

FOLLOW UP: THE COURAGE OF TURTLES

Exploring Language

amicably: friendly, peaceable.
apocryphal: doubtful, false; can also imply mythical.
benign: gentle, gracious; of mild character.
brackish: salty or not appealing to the taste; repulsive.
canted: slanted or tilted.
carapace: protective shell or shell-like covering.
convex: a surface that curves outward; concave curves inward.
crenelated: dented or notched.
elongating: lengthening or extending.
estuaries: where rivers—fresh water—meet the sea.
forlorn: in despair or depressed.
giddy: light-hearted or silly.
gimpy: with a limp; handicapped.
governor: in this context, an attachment to a machine or engine to regulate or control speed, like on a car.
id: psychological term referring to the part of the unconscious that embodies the instinctual need and desires, like pleasure.
humus: decomposed animal or vegetable material in soil.
ingenuity: inventive or skillful.
inscrutable: in this context—inscrutable mud—not able to see through it; unfathomable.
interminably: seemingly unending.
lush: luxuriant, abundant vegetation.
metaphysical: abstract thought; sometimes refers to the supernatural.
menagerie: a collection of varied and usually unusual animals, though can refer to people or things.
morose: gloomy, sullen.
napalm: a jellylike, inflammable substance used in bombs.
nether: lower or under; below the surface.
ocelli: a simple eye or an eye-like spot as on a peacock's feathers.
parceled: a quantity or unit of something bundled or packaged up for sale.
portentous: ominous or threatening; momentous.

priapic: phallic, or penis-like.
perambulate: walk or stroll about.
rapidity: quickness.
recapitulate: to repeat in a summarized form.
ruminatively: to meditate or ponder.
stickler: perfectionist; an unyielding person.
untoward: improper; unfavorable or unfortunate.
vivacious: lively, spirited.
voracious: consuming large quantities, as in "voracious appetite" or "voracious reader."

USAGE Use three of the words from the list to describe an animal in one of the Writing Ideas or in Teaming Up #3.

Thinking and Talking Points

1. Hoagland uses anthropomorphizing (assigning human characteristics or personality traits to animals) of turtles throughout the essay. An example would be the quality of courage, a trait generally associated with humans. How do the turtles display courage? Locate other human characteristics like courage and then discuss why you think he relies so heavily on this technique.
2. Examine where Hoagland compares turtles to other animals. What is his purpose with these comparisons?
3. In addition to anthropomorphizing, Hoagland uses other style devices: simile, metaphor, vivid description, sentence variety—long, medium, and short sentences—and punctuation marks such as dashes and semi-colons. Choose at least one of each style and discuss how the style enhances the essay.
4. Several stories—often compared to fables—concerning turtles connect to make a point in this essay. What do you think is the overall purpose? Identify the moral of each story and the order in which he arranges them. Discuss why he chooses to end the essay with the story of the Diamondback turtle.
5. What does the essay imply about human interference with animal habitat? Is there an environmental commentary embedded here?

Styling

Adding comparisons in the form of **simile** and **metaphor** to your essay helps your reader envision size, shape, swiftness, slowness, facial features—almost anything. It goes beyond mere description, elevating your writing to sharpness and clarity. Edward Hoagland, instead of using boring measurements for size, describes snapping turtles "as big as greeny wash basins" and a hatchling as "not as large as the top joint of my thumb." For other details, he describes baby turtles "as decorative as pansy petals," for movement "rolling like sailorly souls" and "hunch and ponderously lunge like a grizzly going forward." Students sometimes complain that they're not creative enough to write **figurative language**, but you can learn to write strong comparisons by using simple techniques and remembering a golden rule—if you've heard it before, don't use it. It has become a **cliché**. Strive for originality.

Here is how to get started. If you want to describe, for example, how fast an animal moves, think of all the things that move swiftly and make a list: shooting stars, a magician's sleight of hand, bottle rockets, a jet fighter. The list could go on and on, but when choosing which comparison to use, think about the tone, the feeling you want your reader to experience about the animal. A shooting star might imply fading-into-the-background; a magician's sleight of hand may lend mystery; a jet fighter a fierce or battle-like tone; a bottle rocket, a sudden burst of speed. Then pick the best one and write a sentence about it. One student wrote about dolphins riding in the wake of the boat, "Suddenly, they were off like bottle rockets."

Practice

Think of an animal or person to write about. Make a list of features you'd like to describe. Following the instructions above, brainstorm a list for each feature. Then create a fill-in-the-blank comparison, something like the following:

As fast as (or as slow as) _____

A nose like _____

As big as (or as small as) _____

A body like (choose a shape to compare, for example a football)

_____

Don't limit yourself to these examples. Try to come up with some of your own.

YOU TRY IT   Create sentences for each of your best comparisons. You might also try dropping *like* or *as* for a more direct metaphor.

Teaming Up

1. **Anthropomorphizing: A Good Warm-up for Writing Idea #1:** In small groups (or as a class with the teacher writing suggestions on the board), brainstorm a list of human character—or personality—traits like humility, patience, greed. Write down at least twenty. Next, individually write a type of animal at the top of a sheet of paper. Take three minutes to write down any human character traits (you can use them from the list or create your own) that might be associated with that animal. At the end of three minutes, pass the paper to the right. Each person must then continue the list they have received. For the second round, work for two minutes. Repeat this process a third time, working for one minute. Give the list back to its original owner. Now each person has a brainstorming list to use for Writing Idea #1.

2. **A Good Warm-up for Writing Ideas #2 and #3:** Each student brings one of *Aesop's Fables* to class. In small groups, read each fable and choose one to present to the class. Identify and discuss the elements of fables listed in Writing Idea #3 and summarize and outline the chosen fable. Decide who will present which element to the class (each student should be responsible for at least one of the elements). For the presentation, each team member explains to the class how one element functions in the story. You might choose one student to summarize the story.

3. **Photo Connection:** In small groups, study the photo of the animal. Individually, write a paragraph describing the animal, using at least one **simile**. For example, in "The Courage of Turtles" Hoagland compares turtles with similes like "as big as greeny wash basins" and "as decorative as pansy petals." Take turns reading each other's paragraphs, picking out your favorite descriptions and similes. Co-write a paragraph, combining the best efforts of each student. Read the co-written paragraph to the class.

Writing Ideas

1. Research a wild animal you admire and write an essay that uses **anthropomorphizing** to humanize the creature. The essay can be humorous, mourn the plight of the animal, argue whether or not the animal should be kept as a pet (no giraffes, rhinos, or other animals that would not make reasonable pet choices; consider ferrets, snakes, racoons, wild birds, or other small creatures), or admire the animal's

ability to survive, either in the wild or in an environment encroached on by development.
2. Write an essay that uses a series of stories (from your own experience) with morals. Before writing, find a copy of *Aesop's Fables* (some available online) and read a few stories to help you understand the format. All stories should connect to illustrate an overall point. Be sure to use proper **transition**.
3. Write your own **fable** (a story where animals represent humans to teach lessons or morals concerning humans; "The Ant and the Grasshopper" in *Aesop's Fables* is a good example). Involve at least two animals using the elements of fables: characters and setting, action/dialogue, conflict, events that result from the conflict, and a moral. Read several fables—some available online—to warm-up.

Essay and Film Connections

Several animal essays in *Sparks* include "Mute Dancers: How to Watch a Hummingbird" by Diane Ackerman, "Black Widow" by Gordon Grice, "Joyas Voladoras" by Brian Doyle, and "Cat Bathing as Martial Art" (anonymous). For films, consider *Grizzly Man, Winged Migration,* and, of course, *March of the Penguins.*

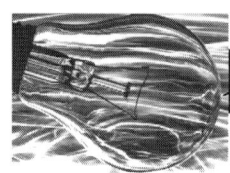
CHILDREN IN THE WOODS

Barry Lopez

Barry Lopez is a novelist, essayist, and winner of many awards including a Guggenheim Fellowship. A naturalist, Lopez writes about our responsibility to enlighten children to the delights of nature rather than lecture to them, "rather to encourage by example a sharpness of the senses."

1   When I was a child growing up in the San Fernando Valley in California, a trip into Los Angeles was special. The sensation of movement from a rural area into an urban one was sharp. On one of these charged occasions, walking down a sidewalk with my mother, I stopped suddenly, caught by a pattern of sunlight trapped in a spiraling imperfection in a windowpane. A stranger, an elderly woman in a cloth coat and a dark hat, spoke out spontaneously, saying how remarkable it is that children notice these things.

2   I have never forgotten the texture of this incident. Whenever I recall it I am moved not so much by any sense of my young self but by a sense of responsibility toward children, knowing how acutely I was affected in that moment by that woman's words. The effect, for all I know, has lasted a lifetime.

3   Now, years later, I live in a rain forest in western Oregon, on the banks of a mountain river in relatively undisturbed country, surrounded by 150-foot-tall Douglas firs, delicate deerhead orchids, and clearings where wild berries grow. White-footed mice and mule deer, mink and coyote move through here. My wife and I do not have children, but children we know, or children whose parents we are close to, are often here. They always want to go into the woods. And I wonder what to tell them.

4   In the beginning, years ago, I think I said too much. I spoke with an encyclopedic knowledge of the names of plants or the names of birds passing through in season. Gradually I came to say less. After a while the only words I spoke, beyond answering a question or calling attention quickly to the slight difference between a sprig of red cedar and a sprig of incense cedar, were to elucidate single objects.

"Children in the Woods" from *Crossing Open Ground* by Barry Lopez. Copyright by Barry Holstun Lopez. Reprinted by permission of SLL/Sterling Lord Literistic, Inc.

5 I remember once finding a fragment of a raccoon's jaw in an alder thicket. I sat down alongside the two children with me and encouraged them to find out who this was—with only the three teeth still intact in a piece of the animal's maxilla to guide them. The teeth told by their shape and placement what this animal ate. By a kind of visual extrapolation its size became clear. There were other clues, immediately present, which told, with what I could add of climate and terrain, how this animal lived, how its broken jaw came to be lying here. Raccoon, they surmised. And tiny tooth marks along the bone's broken edge told of a mouse's hunger for calcium.

6 We set the jaw back and went on.

7 If I had known more about raccoons, finer points of osteology, we might have guessed more: say, whether it was male or female. But what we deduced was all we needed. Hours later, the maxilla, lost behind us in the detritus of the forest floor, continued to effervesce. It was tied faintly to all else we spoke of that afternoon.

8 In speaking with children who might one day take a permanent interest in natural history—as writers, as scientists, as film-makers, as anthropologists—I have sensed that an extrapolation from a single fragment of the whole is the most invigorating experience I can share with them. I think children know that nearly anyone can learn the names of things; the impression made on them at this level is fleeting. What takes a lifetime to learn, they comprehend, is the existence and substance of myriad relationships: it is these relationships, not the things themselves, that ultimately hold the human imagination.

9 The brightest children, it has often struck me, are fascinated by metaphor—with what is shown in the set of relationships bearing on the raccoon, for example, to lie quite beyond the raccoon. In the end, you are trying to make clear to them that everything found at the edge of one's senses—the high note of the winter wren, the thick perfume of propolis that drifts downwind from spring willows, the brightness of wood chips scattered by beaver—that all this fits together. The indestructibility of these associations conveys a sense of permanence that nurtures the heart, that cripples one of the most insidious of human anxieties, the one that says, you do not belong here, you are unnecessary.

10 Whenever I walk with a child, I think how much I have seen disappear in my own life. What will there be for this person when he is my age? If he senses something ineffable in the landscape, will I know enough to encourage it?—to somehow show him that, yes, when people talk about violent death, spiritual exhilaration, compassion, futility,

final causes, they are drawing on forty thousand years of human meditation on *this*—as we embrace Douglas firs, or stand by a river across whose undulating back we skip stones, or dig out a camas bulb, biting down into a taste so much wilder than last night's potatoes.

11   The most moving look I ever saw from a child in the woods was on a mud bar by the footprints of a heron. We were on our knees, making handprints beside the footprints. You could feel the creek vibrating in the silt and sand. The sun beat down heavily on our hair. Our shoes were soaking wet. The look said: I did not know until now that I needed someone much older to confirm this, the feeling I have of life here. I can now grow older, knowing it need never be lost.

12   The quickest door to open in the woods for a child is the one that leads to the smallest room, by knowing the name each thing is called. The door that leads to the cathedral is marked by a hesitancy to speak at all, rather to encourage by example a sharpness of the senses. If one speaks it should only be to say, as well as one can, how wonderfully all this fits together, to indicate what a long, fierce peace can derive from this knowledge.

CHILDREN IN THE WOODS

Exploring Language

alder: a type of tree.
camas: a lily bulb that's edible.
deduce: to conclude or suppose.
detritus: loose material or debris caused by deterioration.
effervesce: to delight or excite; can also mean to bubble or hiss, but Lopez means that the raccoon's jaw continued to excite them the rest of the afternoon, setting the tone for the day.
elucidate: to clarify (make clear) or explain.
extrapolation: reasoning; prediction from what is known. By visual extrapolation, Lopez means that by looking at the jaw fragment they were able to figure out the animal's size.
ineffable: this word has several **connotations**, but here Lopez means transcendent; rising above the material to the spiritual.
insidious: treacherous or deceitful; harmful.
maxilla: jaw
myriad: a large or vast number; countless.
osteology: branch of anatomy that deals with bones.
propolis: a gooey, resin-like substance bees collect from the buds of trees.
surmised: guessed.
undulating: moving in waves or swells.

USAGE Use *insidious* and *undulating* to describe an animal.

Thinking and Talking Points

1. In paragraph #2, Lopez writes, "Whenever I recall it I am moved not so much by any sense of my young self but by a sense of responsibility toward children, knowing how acutely I was affected in that moment by that woman's words." How was he affected? In what way does he mean "a sense of responsibility toward children"? Do you agree that adults have this responsibility toward children?

2. In paragraph #11, Lopez writes about a moving look he saw on a child's face while in the woods: "The look said: I did not know until now that I needed someone much older to confirm this, the feeling I have of life here. I can now grow older, knowing it need never be lost." What is it that may be lost when we grow older?
3. Lopez writes that he stopped speaking so much with the children during their walks in the woods, and instead wishes "to encourage by example a sharpness of the senses." Find examples in the essay where he teaches the senses by example rather than speech. Do you agree with him about using examples rather than words?
4. In the last paragraph, he uses the metaphor of a door to a small room versus the door to a cathedral to illustrate opening the woods to a child. Explain the **metaphor**. He also states, "The brightest children, it has often struck me, are fascinated by metaphor." Do you agree? Why or why not?
5. Lopez writes, in paragraph #9, "The indestructibility of these associations conveys a sense of permanence that nurtures the heart, that cripples one of the most insidious of human anxieties, the one that says, you do not belong here, you are unnecessary." What associations? What does he mean that these associations "cripple one of the most insidious of human anxieties"?

Styling

Lopez uses a variety of sentence structures and style techniques—strong verbs and nouns, specific language, dashes, metaphor—but here's a short, eloquent sentence style for you to try, which Lopez uses in paragraph #3:

> White-footed mice and mule deer, mink and coyote move through here.

Notice how Lopez breaks down his list of animals into two groups:

> White-footed mice and mule deer
> Mink and coyote

He uses multiple subjects in his sentence, grouping them two by two: *mice and deer* followed by a comma and then *mink and coyote*. Lopez also adds some specifics, *white-footed* to describe mice and *mule* to illustrate the type of deer. This structure is easy to follow and gives pizzazz to your **sentence variety**. A similar style exercise accompanies "Mute Dancers: How to Watch a Hummingbird" by Diane Ackerman.

PRACTICE Fill in the blanks below with subjects that go together. Notice where the comma separates the two sets of items. Be specific.

_____ and _____ , _____ and _____ swam lazily in the ocean.

_____ and _____ , _____ and _____ grew in my neighbor's garden.

_____ and _____ , _____ and _____ struggled to finish the marathon.

YOU TRY IT Now write five sentences of your own based on the above model. Use this structure in your next writing assignment.

Teaming Up

1. Lopez writes, "Whenever I walk with a child, I think how much I have seen disappear in my own life. What will there be for this person when he is my age?" Have each member in your group bring in an article on some aspect of the environmental debate: endangered animals, deforestation, ozone layer. Be sure to bring in articles on both sides of the issue. For example, should fishermen be allowed to catch tuna with nets? Environmentalists claim nets also catch dolphins, killing the creatures, while commercial fishermen claim few dolphins are killed and they need the nets to fish more efficiently. Read the articles in your group and decide which ones have the strongest arguments. Now you have research to use in an essay.
2. Each member write a quick paragraph about their childhood experiences with nature and how they interact with nature now. Read each paragraph and discuss the experiences. Has much changed since childhood? Have some of you lost the sense of wonder at nature? Discuss differing viewpoints.

Writing Ideas

1. Lopez remembers a comment a woman made to him on a trip to Los Angeles that influenced his life. Write an essay about a time an adult—or another child—said something that influences you now, as an adult. Use the sentence structure from the Styling section in your essay.

2. Lopez begins his essay remembering a special trip to Los Angeles. Write an essay that describes a time you took a special trip or visited a special place. It doesn't have to be a long journey; I might write about a safari to the vacant field behind my house at age ten, with canteen, sack lunch, and imagination as companions, describing the weasels and wild flowers, rubbish and decayed vegetation. Use the sentence structure from the Styling section in your essay.
3. Research an endangered or almost extinct animal. Write an essay arguing whether or not more money should be spent to save the animal from extinction. Be sure to write about causes (why the animal has become endangered) and effects (what might be the result of losing the animal, either environmentally or otherwise). Use the sentence structure in the Styling section.

Essay and Film Connections

For essays on nature, see "Black Widow" by Gordon Grice, "The Courage of Turtles" by Edward Hougland, and "Joyas Voladoras" by Brian Doyle. For essays with childhood themes see "Burl's" by Bernard Cooper and "A Voice for the Lonely" by Stephen Corey.

A film you might enjoy that deals with an orphaned boy trying to make it on his own and the unlikely woman who reluctantly befriends him is *Central Station,* a foreign film with subtitles.

SECTION TWO

Figuring It Out: Essays That Explain and Explore

INTRODUCTION

Visit an art museum and gaze at a Jan Vermeer painting through David Huddle's eyes. Find out why Roland Barthes thinks French toys reflect French culture. Learn about the secret lives of hummingbirds with Diane Ackerman. Discover music's healing power with Clayton Collins. Explore Hong Kong with Ken Chen. In this section, writer's attempt to explain some aspect of the world, from hair to hearts, cameras to culture.

These essays—like most—are hybrids, often blending rhetorical modes, so they don't always fit into a classic argument, narrative, definition, or other organization (see Section Five). Some contemplate, like Brian Doyle in "Joyas Voladoras," a seemingly on-the-surface meditation of animal facts, but his conclusion hints at heartbreak; others complain, as does Roland

Barthes in his analysis of French toys. Others reminisce: Martin Scorsese in "A Box Filled With Magic"; or amuse: John Updike in "Disposable Rocket," a lamenting look at the male body, its betrayal as it ages; reveal our darker motivations: "Monster Mash" by Jack Kroll. All analyze.

Trying to light some aspect of a complex world invites critical thinking, research, rumination. Analysis is an important skill, in college and in the rest of your life. Whether you're exploring the reasons why some people watch horror films or the workings of the heart, zooming in and examining a topic in depth fires the neurons in your brain and helps you look at the many facets of a subject.

As you read, study how these writers organize their essays, but also pay attention to the thinking process evident in the writing. How do they arrive at their conclusions? What evidence do they use for support? *How* you say something is as important as *what* you say, so examine style—figurative language (metaphor, simile, personification), **sentence variety**, punctuation, **transition**. Seeing how others craft their essays helps you learn how to be a better writer and thinker.

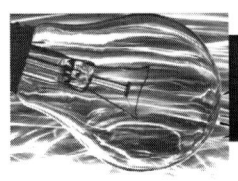

ON THE UNCERTAINTY OF THE FUTURE

Yoshida Kenko

In this short essay, Japanese poet, essayist, and Buddhist priest Yoshida Kenko (approximately 1283–1350) ruminates on how uncertainty, to some extent, controls our lives. Kenko, a prominent literary figure in his day, is still an important part of Japanese education.

1   You may intend to do something today, only for pressing business to come up unexpectedly and take up all of your attention the rest of the day. Or a person you have been expecting is prevented from coming, or someone you hadn't expected comes calling. The thing you have counted on goes amiss, and the thing you had no hopes for is the only one to succeed. A matter which promised to be a nuisance passes off smoothly, and a matter which should have been easy proves a great hardship. Our daily experiences bear no resemblance to what we had anticipated. This is true throughout the year, and equally true for our entire lives. But if we decide that everything is bound to go contrary to our anticipations, we discover that naturally there are also some things which do not contradict expectations. This makes it all the harder to be definite about anything. The one thing you can be certain of is the truth that all is uncertainty.

FOLLOW UP ON THE UNCERTAINTY OF THE FUTURE

Thinking and Talking Points

1. Summarize Kenko's purpose in this short meditation. What support does he use?
2. To what extent does the author think uncertainty plays a role in our lives?
3. How relevant is this essay to modern life? Give examples to support your view.
4. What point does the essay make about contrary expectations (expecting things will go wrong)?
5. What tone does Kenko take when addressing his readers? Study his **point of view** for help discerning his tone.

Teaming Up

1. Each member of the group make a list of expectations—things that you are reasonably certain will go smoothly. The list can be composed of anything from technology expectations (cell phones, computers, Tivo) to more meaningful expectations (medical test results, a job interview, a marriage proposal). Hand your list to the person on your right. Each person, on a scale of one to ten (ten being absolutely certain, one being will never happen) rate each item on the list. Discuss the results. Are the results in favor of optimism or pessimism?
2. **A Good Warm-up for Writing Idea #1:** Individually, write a paragraph about a time you had an expectation that turned out the opposite, something you thought would happen but didn't (you can brainstorm ideas first with the group). After writing your paragraph, read them aloud and decide who has the best one to read to the class.

Writing Ideas

1. Write an essay about a time you had an expectation that turned out to be a disappointment (or a time you had a negative expectation that turned out positive). Describe the anticipation leading up to the expectation, the event itself, and your feelings afterward.

2. Compare the writing style and philosophy of Yoshida Kenko's essay to Thich Nhat Hanh's piece "Nourishing Awareness in Each Moment." Is there a similarity in the thought of these two Buddhists from very different time periods?
3. Write your own meditation on something from your daily life: an emotion (anger, joy, depression, grief, humility), a philosophy or belief (destiny, solitude, death), an institution (marriage, education, medicine), nature (many essays in the book provide examples of reflections on nature, and pair well with Thich Nhat Hanh's essay, "Nourishing Awareness in Each Moment").

Essay Connections

Thich Nhat Hanh's "Nourishing Awareness in Each Moment" (a rumination on television and mood by a modern Vietnamese monk) pairs up well with Kenko's essay. Joseph Epstein's "The Culture of Celebrity" comments on our obsession with famous people, connecting well with Hanh's piece. Many reflective nature essays appear in this book, teaming up with Hanh's ideas of solitude and meditation rather than noisy television that can affect mood.

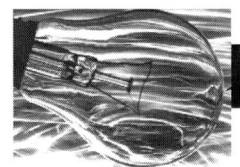

MUSEUM PIECE

David Huddle

David Huddle is a university professor and writer of fiction and nonfiction. He's written a collection of essays titled "The Writing Habit" as well as a novella, three collections of poetry, and four collections of short stories. In this short piece, he describes three paintings by Jan Vermeer, focusing on "A Lady Writing," proclaiming, "All those art history courses, all these visits to the museum, attending lectures, reading catalogs: nothing teaches you just to look the way you're doing it now!"

DUSTBIN OF HISTORY AND CULTURE

JAN VERMEER: Dutch painter who lived from 1632–1675.
FEATHER QUILL: A feather with a hollow reed used as a pen.

1   Jan Vermeer's *The Girl with the Red Hat* always appealed to you because of that hat. Incredible scarlet aura spinning around her head like pure energy. Mouth open. Delicate coating of light that makes you think she's just licked her lips. Got to appreciate the composition. Lively and precise at the same time. The face of the girl isn't much. You like the look of her hat. You know it excites her to be wearing that hat. But there's nothing about the actual person. What she has to say wouldn't be much. Features are crude. Common girl all dressed up.

2   Another Vermeer here you've gotten to know. *Maiden with a Flute*. Little sister of *The Girl with the Red Hat*. Not nearly

See "Thinking and Talking Points" #1.

A Lady Writing by Jan Vermeer. 1962.10.1. (1664)/PA: Vermeer, Johannes, A Lady Writing, Gift of Harry Waldron Havemeyer and Horace Havemeyer, Jr., in memory of their father, Horace Havemeyer, Image courtesy of the Board of Trustees, National Gallery of Art, Washington, c. 1665, oil on canvas, .450 × .399 (17¾ × 15¾); framed: .683 × .622 × .070 (26⅞ × 24½ × 2¾)

"Museum Piece" by David Huddle. Originally appeared in *In Short: A Collection of Brief Creative Nonfiction*, W. W. Norton and Company, 1996. Reprinted by permission of the author.

as flamboyant, but it's another composition that makes you smile. They're both paintings that have some wit.

3   This one day, instead of passing with a quick pause-and-look, the way you always have before—maybe because the room is empty, and you have plenty of time—you take one step closer to the third of those Vermeers: *A Lady Writing.* One step closer to a picture you've seen dozens of times before.

4   The lady of the picture isn't really writing. She's stopped writing. Her pen—it's a small feather quill—is still in place on the paper. Her other hand is holding the page down. She's just looked up. You've interrupted her. Her face has this expression that is warm and so complex. But that expression is not for you—it's left over from the moment before she saw you. She looks that way because of whatever it was she was writing. It has to be a letter: this lady is writing to her good friend—or maybe to her sister—about something that really pleases her. You wonder what it could be. You can almost sense the pleasure flying away from her as she stops her writing.

5   She isn't beautiful. The way her hair is fixed, it looks like she's put it up in curlers. But you get her whole life out of this picture. All those art history courses, all these visits to the museum, attending lectures, reading catalogs: nothing teaches you just to look the way you're doing it now! Thousands of days of this lady's living click into this single instant. Across three hundred years of time, she looks you straight in the eyes. *Look,* she says. *Go ahead and look. My life feels to me the same as yours feels to you—so full I could burst with it. Please let me get back to my letter. You go on with whatever you're doing out there in the twentieth century.*

MUSEUM PIECE
FOLLOW UP

Thinking and Talking Points

1. **Photo Connection:** Study the painting of *A Lady Writing,* and then reread Huddle's description. What is your reaction? Is it similar to Huddle's or do you have a different response?
2. As a student, you've probably been told to avoid "you" when writing essays. Why do you think Huddle uses "you" to address the reader? In what situations might it be acceptable to address the reader so casually?
3. Huddle breaks another general writing rule: don't use sentence **fragments**. Sometimes, though, fragments can work to the writer's advantage. Examine the fragments. Why do you think Huddle uses them?
4. In the last paragraph, what point does Huddle make about enjoying versus studying paintings? Rewrite his point in your own words. What other subjects might apply to his point?

CAUTION While writers often use **fragments** for a particular effect, I caution beginning writers against using them until they have mastered **complete sentences**. You don't want to be guilty of a writing error.

Styling

This short essay pops with style, making it difficult to focus on just one technique. In addition to breaking writing rules in favor of style, Huddle also uses **simile**: "Incredible scarlet aura spinning around her head like pure energy." His detailed descriptions and lively word choices draw you into the essay. But let's look more closely at how he uses dashes (—), a writing tool that students aren't often taught. Dashes can be used in place of commas around groups of words called **interrupters** because they interrupt the main sentence to add information or detail:

> Her pen—it's a small feather quill—is still in place on the paper.

Huddle could write, "Her pen is still in place on the paper." The clause "it's a small feather quill" interrupts the main sentence with extra information. Those dashes shout at the reader, *Hey, look at me!* The writer could use commas or parentheses instead of dashes, but he chose the stronger dashes to draw attention to the feather quill. Study the other dashes in the essay. Notice that dashes can also be used to set off a phrase, clause, or another sentence at the end of a sentence.

SAMPLE SENTENCE WITH DASHES   The Okapi—like a creature out of a fairy tale—is an animal that looks half giraffe, half zebra.

PRACTICE   Fill in the blank between the dashes with a descriptive or informational phrase.

> The child—_____—shoved cake greedily into her mouth.

YOU TRY IT   Create three sentences of your own using dashes. It might help to write a simple sentence first, inserting the interrupting words and dashes later.

   Tip: parentheses whisper, commas talk, dashes shout.

Teaming Up

1. Bring to class a picture of a painting or other artwork that appeals to you. One place to look is the Metropolitan Museum Web site—you can visit almost any museum online and print pictures. Before coming to class, **freewrite** about the picture. What does the picture make you think about? What feeling do you get from looking at it? What details stand out the most? Group up in teams of three to five members. Don't discuss your freewrite yet. Each person pass his or her picture to the right. Study the picture you've been handed. Now freewrite about it. Pass pictures to the right and freewrite two more times so that each person has written about three pictures plus his or her own. Pull out the freewrite you did at home. Group all of the freewrites with the picture they are about. Read the freewrites and discuss your reactions. What details or reactions seem to be the same in the majority of freewrites? Did feelings differ significantly on the same picture? Which picture got the most varied reactions? Save all of your freewrites—you might be able to use some of the details in one of the Writing Ideas.
2. Go to the library and find art criticism on some of Jan Vermeer's paintings. You'll find books on art criticism in the reference section as well as the regular book stacks. Sister Wendy's criticisms of art are a good place to start—her writing is not muddled with overblown language. If you have trouble finding an article, ask the librarian. In your group,

read the criticisms and compare them to Huddle's essay. Which piece did you enjoy the most? Which one gives the most insight into the painting? Study the style in each article. Do the writers of these articles use strong style, as Huddle did?

CAUTION   Avoid the Web when looking for criticism. The Web is full of dubious articles. You can search for hours without finding anything. You're better off visiting the library at your college or in your community.

Wrting Ideas

1. Find a painting or photograph of an historical event: *Third of May* by Francisco Goya; *Washington Crossing the Delaware* by Emanuel Gottlieb Leutze; *Death of Socrates* by Jacques-Louis David. You can also use photographs—try visiting an online photography exhibit or a book like the *History of Rock and Roll;* possibilities are endless. Next, study the picture and imagine yourself there: sights, sounds, smells, feelings, tastes. Choose a point of view: who will you be, an observer of the scene or one of the characters in the picture? Be sure to look up the historical facts. Facts must be accurate, but you can invent the sensory details. Now, write an essay narrating the event. Stick to the picture as much as possible. Practice using dashes.
2. Browse through some art books and choose an artist who interests you. Choose three paintings by the same artist. Following Huddle's model, write an essay discussing the three paintings. Notice that Huddle saves the painting that he reacts to the most strongly to discuss last, spending two full paragraphs on it. Use **simile** and strong description. Try at least one sentence style you've learned in this book.
3. Find a painting—a portrait—of a person who seems to be speaking to you. You can use the Web site or visit the library. After studying the portrait you chose, write an essay using details to describe the painting and what you imagine the person is thinking. Write in the present tense and address the reader as "you."

Film and Essay Connections

John Updike's essay "American Children," like Huddle's essay, analyzes art in an easy-to-understand manner. The film *Artemisia* (1997), a historical drama set in 17th-century Italy, is based on the true story of the first woman to achieve success as an artist. The film gives a good look at the time period—though Italian rather than Dutch—of Jan Vermeer. It's a bit immodest, rated R.

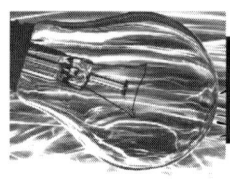

NOURISHING AWARENESS IN EACH MOMENT

Thich Nhat Hanh

Spiritual leader and Zen monk Thich Nhat Hanh has many achievements: he founded a Buddhist university in Vietnam and a social services school for youth, taught at the Sorbonne and Columbia University, chaired the Buddhist delegation in the Paris Peace Talks, was nominated by Martin Luther King Jr. for the Nobel Peace Price, has helped refugees all over the world, founded a meditation in south of France (where he lives as an exile from his native country), and written many books on Buddhist thought and meditation, including The Art of Power, Anger, The Miracle of Mindfulness, and Peace is Every Step, where "Nourishing Awareness in Each Moment" appears. In this essay, he wonders why people will watch bad television programs rather than cherish solitude, believing that when we watch bad television, "we become the TV program."

1   One cold, winter evening I returned home from a walk in the hills, and I found that all the doors and windows in my hermitage had blown open. When I had left earlier, I hadn't secured them, and a cold wind had blown through the house, opened the windows, and scattered the papers from my desk all over the room. Immediately, I closed the doors and windows, lit a lamp, picked up the papers, and arranged them neatly on my desk. Then I started a fire in the fireplace, and soon the crackling logs brought warmth back to the room.

2   Sometimes in a crowd we feel tired, cold, and lonely. We may wish to withdraw to be by ourselves and become warm again, as I did when I closed the windows and sat by the fire, protected from the damp, cold wind. Our senses are our windows to the world, and sometimes the wind blows through them and disturbs everything within us. Some of us leave our windows open all the time, allowing the sights and sounds of the world to invade us, penetrate us, and expose our sad, troubled selves. We feel so cold, lonely, and afraid. Do you ever find yourself watching an awful TV program, unable to turn it off? The raucous noises, explosions of gunfire, are upsetting. Yet you don't get up and turn it off. Why do you torture yourself in this way?

"Nourishing Awareness in Each Moment" from *Peace is Every Step* by Thich Nhat Hahn, copyright © 1991 by Thich Nhat Hahn. Used by permission of Bantam Books, a division of Random House, Inc.

Don't you want to close your windows? Are you frightened of solitude—the emptiness and the loneliness you may find when you face yourself alone?

3   Watching a bad TV program, we *become* the TV program. We are what we feel and perceive. If we are angry, we are the anger. If we are in love, we are love. If we look at a snow-covered mountain peak, we are the mountain. We can be anything we want, so why do we open our windows to bad TV programs made by sensationalist producers in search of easy money, programs that make our hearts pound, our fists tighten, and leave us exhausted? Who allows such TV programs to be made and seen by even the very young? We do! We are too undemanding, too ready to watch whatever is on the screen, too lonely, lazy, or bored to create our own lives. We turn on the TV and leave it on, allowing someone else to guide us, shape us, and destroy us. Losing ourselves in this way is leaving our fate in the hands of others who may not be acting responsibly. We must be aware of which programs do harm to our nervous systems, minds, and hearts, and which programs benefit us.

4   Of course, I am not talking only about television. All around us, how many lures are set by our fellows and ourselves? In a single day, how many times do we become lost and scattered because of them? We must be very careful to protect our fate and our peace. I am not suggesting that we just shut all our windows, for there are many miracles in the world we call "outside." We can open our windows to these miracles and look at any one of them with awareness. This way, even while sitting beside a clear, flowing stream, listening to beautiful music, or watching an excellent movie, we need not lose ourselves entirely in the stream, the music, or the film. We can continue to be aware of ourselves and our breathing. With the sun of awareness shining in us, we can avoid most dangers. The stream will be purer, the music more harmonious, and the soul of the filmmaker completely visible.

5   As beginning meditators, we may want to leave the city and go off to the countryside to help close those windows that trouble our spirit. There we can become one with the quiet forest, and rediscover and restore ourselves, without being swept away by the chaos of the "outside world." The fresh and silent woods help us remain in awareness, and when our awareness is well-rooted and we can maintain it without faltering, we may wish to return to the city and remain there, less troubled. But sometimes we cannot leave the city, and we have

to find the refreshing and peaceful elements that can heal us right in the midst of our busy lives. We may wish to visit a good friend who can comfort us, or go for a walk in a park and enjoy the trees and the cool breeze. Whether we are in the city, the countryside, or the wilderness, we need to sustain ourselves by choosing our surroundings carefully and nourishing our awareness in each moment.

NOURISHING AWARENESS IN EACH MOMENT

Exploring Language

hermitage: a place where one can live in solitude; a retreat.
raucous: rough-sounding, harsh.

USAGE Use *raucous* in a sentence to describe one of the following: laughter, sporting event, specific television program, particular music or song, or something mechanical (for example, a machine, tool, or musical instrument).

Thinking and Talking Points

1. Hanh writes, "Sometimes in a crowd we feel tired, cold, and lonely." How do you think he means that it's possible to be lonely in a crowd? What evidence does he give for this statement?
2. Another statement Hanh writes, "Our senses are our windows to the world, and sometimes the wind blows through them and disturbs everything within us," is a **metaphor**. Explain the comparison. What other metaphors does he use?
3. What connection does he make between our fear of solitude and bad television programs? Do you agree that bad television programs affect our mood? How might it negatively "guide us, shape us, and destroy us"? Are some people afraid of being alone and need noise to distract them? What do you think they fear?
4. Bad television, according to Hanh, is not the only thing that affects our mood. What other "lures" do you think pull us away from "ourselves"? What examples does he mention?
5. What solution does Hanh propose to the problem he presents? Do you agree or disagree with his ideas? Provide evidence to support your view.

Styling

This essay uses several thought-provoking questions that speak directly to the reader. Though often students are taught not to use questions, this style—when done well—can create moments of hesitation, causing the reader to think and attempt to answer.

> In paragraph two, Hanh writes, "Do you ever find yourself watching an awful TV program, unable to turn it off?" and, "Why do your torture yourself this way? Don't you want to close your windows? Are you frightened of solitude—the emptiness and loneliness you may find when you face yourself alone?"

Hanh asks questions that he believes most people will—if they're honest with themselves—have to answer yes. Notice that the first question asks something that most of us have found ourselves doing, so we nod, almost smiling in agreement. But the second question catches us off guard: we've probably not thought of it as torturing ourselves. The question stops us momentarily, making us wonder why we watch such bad programs. It's a gentle reprimand. The third question, "Don't you want to close your windows?" applies to an earlier metaphor of the senses being windows to the world; in other words, he's asking, "Don't you want to stop the torture?" The final question gets to the heart of his point: we're afraid of solitude, of being alone with ourselves, so we'll use any device to distract us from ourselves. These statements wear a costume, disguised as questions.

PRACTICE   Make a list of other negative behaviors people participate in to ward off loneliness or to procrastinate.

YOU TRY IT   Take one behavior from your list and create a series of thought-provoking questions that are really statements in disguise. Follow the above example, building your questions to a conclusion about the behavior.

Teaming Up

1. **A Good Warm-up for Writing Idea #1:** The Styling makes a good Teaming Up activity. Make a group brainstorming list; select one item and have each member of the team write as many questions as possible in five minutes. Next, read all of the questions and decide which ones to use to create the Styling paragraph. Build your questions to a conclusion about the behavior.

2. **A Good Warm-up for Writing Idea #2:** As a group, brainstorm a list of television programs you have watched that you consider bad

by Hanh's standards. Next to each one, write why you think each program has a negative impact. Co-write a paragraph about these programs, describing the programs and their effects, and attempt to explain why you watch them.

Writing Ideas

1. Write an essay that explores another distraction people use as an avoidance technique. Examine the causes (what, how, and why people are avoiding) and effects (what long-term harm this behavior does to the individual or to others). Some examples might be the boss who never delegates (or delegates too much), a sibling who avoids family confrontations, or the spouse or partner who always agrees or backs down to avoid conflict.
2. Write an essay about the effect of bad television programs on our minds and moods. Explore and explain why people watch such programs and how they're harmful (or write a defense of such programs).
3. Compare the style and Buddhist thought in Hanh's essay to Yoshida Kenko's "On the Uncertainty of the Future." Though of vastly different centuries, what do these two essays have in common?

Essay Connections

Yoshida's Kenko's "On the Uncertainty of the Future" is an obvious choice. Another commentary on modern life is Joseph Epstein's "The Culture of Celebrity." Louis Menand's "Name That Tone" comments on a new cell phone ring tone that only people under twenty can hear.

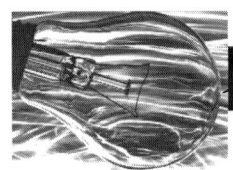

TOYS

Roland Barthes

> In his book Mythologies, influential French essayist and literary critic (1915–1980) Roland Barthes examines hidden assumptions in popular culture. In the essay "Toys," he studies how French toys reflect modern French life, becoming "microcosms of the adult world." He argues that most toys stifle creativity and that "the adult Frenchman sees the child as another self." He also discusses the materials from which the toys are made, and how most toys are made of "graceless material" like plastic or complex chemical compositions rather than wood or other natural materials.

DUSTBIN OF HISTORY AND CULTURE

JIVARO HEAD: reference to a South American tribe who preserved the heads of their enemies (a practice known as headhunting) by removing the skull and packing it with hot sand, which shrank the head but kept the facial features intact.

NAPPIES: a British term meaning diapers.

1   French toys: one could not find a better illustrations of the fact that the adult Frenchman sees the child as another self. All the toys one commonly sees are essentially a microcosm of the adult world: they are all reduced copies of human objects, as if in the eyes of the public the child was, all told, nothing but a smaller man, a homunculus to whom must be supplied objects of his own size.

See "Teaming Up" #1.

2   Invented forms are very rare: a few sets of blocks, which appeal to the spirit of do-it-yourself, are the only ones which offer dynamic forms. As for the others, French toys *always mean something*, and this something is always entirely socialized, constituted by the myths or the techniques of modern adult life: the Army, Broadcasting, the Post Office,

© charles taylor, 2009. Used under license from Shutterstock, Inc.

"Toys" from *Mythologies* by Roland Barthes, translated by Annette Lavers. Translation copyright © 1972 by Jonathan Cape Ltd. Reprinted by permission of Hill and Wang, a division of Farrar, Straus and Giroux, LLC. and The Random House Group Ltd.

Medicine (miniature instrument-cases, operating theatres for dolls), School, Hair-Styling (driers for permanent-waving), the Air Force (Parachutists), Transport (trains, Citroëns, Vedettes, Vespas, petrol-stations), Science (Martian toys).

3   The fact that French toys *literally* prefigure the world of adult functions obviously cannot but prepare the child to accept them all, by constituting for him, even before he can think about it, the alibi of a Nature which has at all times created soldiers, postmen and Vespas. Toys here reveal the list of all the things the adult does not find unusual: war, bureaucracy, ugliness, Martians, etc. It is not so much, in fact, the imitation which is the sign of an abdication, as its literalness: French toys are like a Jivaro head, in which one recognizes, shrunken to the size of an apple, the wrinkles and hair of an adult. There exist, for instance, dolls which urinate; they have an oesophagus, one gives them a bottle, they wet their nappies; soon, no doubt, milk will turn to water in their stomachs. This is meant to prepare the little girl for the causality of house-keeping, to 'condition' her to her future role as mother. However, faced with this world of faithful and complicated objects, the child can only identify himself as owner, as user, never as creator; he does not invent the world, he uses it: there are, prepared for him, actions without adventure, without wonder, without joy. He is turned into a little stay-at-home householder who does not even have to invent the mainsprings of adult causality; they are supplied to him ready-made: he has only to help himself, he is never allowed to discover anything from start to finish. The merest set of blocks, provided it is not too refined, implies a very different learning of the world: then, the child does not in any way create meaningful objects, it matters little to him whether they have an adult name; the actions he performs are not those of a user but those of a demiurge. He creates forms which walk, which roll, he creates life, not property: objects now act by themselves, they are no longer an inert and complicated material in the palm of his hand. But such toys are rather rare: French toys are usually based on imitation, they are meant to produce children who are users, not creators.

4   The bourgeois status of toys can be recognized not only in their forms, which are all functional, but also in their substances. Current toys are made of a graceless material, the product of chemistry, not of nature. Many are now moulded from complicated mixtures, the plastic material of which they are made has an appearance at once gross and hygienic, it destroys all the pleasure, the sweetness, the humanity of touch. A sign which fills one with consternation is the

gradual disappearance of wood, in spite of its being an ideal material because of its firmness and its softness, and the natural warmth of its touch. Wood removes, from all the forms which it supports, the wounding quality of angles which are too sharp, the chemical coldness of metal. When the child handles it and knocks it, it neither vibrates nor grates, it has a sound at once muffled and sharp. It is a familiar and poetic substance, which does not sever the child from close contact with the tree, the table, the floor. Wood does not wound or break down; it does not shatter, it wears out, it can last a long time, live with the child, alter little by little the relations between the object and the hand. If it dies, it is in dwindling, not in swelling out like those mechanical toys which disappear behind the hernia of a broken spring. Wood makes essential objects, objects for all time. Yet there hardly remain any of these wooden toys from the Vosges, these fretwork farms with their animals, which were only possible, it is true, in the days of the craftsman. Henceforth, toys are chemical in substance and colour: their very material introduces one to a coenaesthesis of use, not pleasure. These toys die in fact very quickly, and once dead, they have no posthumous life for the child.

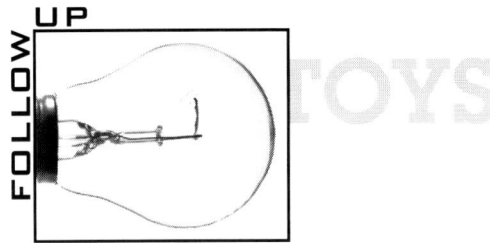

Exploring Language

abdication: relinquishing power or responsibility.
bourgeois: the middle class.
coenesthesis: psychology term that refers to the idea that the senses—our exploration of the natural world and materials—help determine our overall bodily awareness and vitality.
consternation: sudden bewilderment, alarm, or fear.
demiurge: creator.
fretwork: design created by interlacing pieces or patterns made by perforation (cutting or punching holes).
homunculus: a fully formed, miniature human being.
inert: no power of motion; sluggish or inactive.
microcosm: a miniature world.
prefigure: represent or suggest.
Vosges: a range of mountains in NE France.

Thinking and Talking Points

1. What, in Barthes view, do French toys say about French culture?
2. Barthes claims, "All the toys one commonly sees are essentially a microcosm of the adult world." Do you think his examples of French toys are any different from American toys in being imitations of adult objects? List specific examples.
3. Do these types of toys—imitations of adult objects—stifle creativity? What types of toys encourage creativity? Defend your position with specific examples from your own experience.
4. Is Barthes comment on gender bias in toys—that dolls that wet, etc., prepare the little girl for a life of motherhood and housework—valid today? Are toys still divided along gender lines? Give specific examples to support your stand.
5. Examine the last paragraph. What point is Barthes making about the materials used to create modern toys? Do you agree with him? Why or why not?

Styling

In his last paragraph, Barthes creates two tones by contrasting plastic and metal toys to wood toys, bringing the wood to life with words like pleasure, sweetness, softness, natural warmth, poetic; he sentences plastic and metal toys to death with graceless, gross, hygienic, destroys, chemical coldness. He carefully chooses each word, using qualities usually associated with humans, and our senses naturally warm to the wood while rejecting the plastic and metal.

PRACTICE For each object or place listed think of a tone or mood you associate with that object, and then think of at least six qualities to help convey that tone: cemetery, cafeteria, airport, basketball, cell phone.

YOU TRY IT Pick your favorite list from above and write a paragraph describing the object or place. Next, write a paragraph that conveys the *opposite* tone of the one you created.

Teaming Up

1. **Photo Connection:** Examine the toy in the photo, and have each member of the group write a description of the toy that conveys a tone. Read each other's descriptions, and then combine your best efforts to co-write a paragraph to read to the rest of the class.

2. **Good Warm-up for Writing Idea #2:** Each member of the group bring in research on toys from a particular decade; decide ahead of time who will research each decade. If possible, bring in a picture of a toy from that era. Compare the toys through the decades. What has changed? How do the toys reflect the decade? What can you learn about that decade from examining the toys? How do they differ from today's toys? Are there any similarities? Compare your results to other groups in the class.

3. **Good Warm-up for Writing Idea #3:** Each member of the group bring in research on toys from another culture. If possible, bring in a picture of at least one toy from that culture. Compare the toys from each culture. How do the toys reflect the culture? What can you learn about the culture from examining the toys? How do they differ from American toys? Are there any similarities?

Writing Ideas

1. Write an essay about a favorite childhood toy or other object, why it was a favorite, and what it says about you. Describe the toy or other object in some detail, what emotional importance it had in your life (made you feel secure, served as a confidant, etc.), and what happened to the toy. Do you still have it? Did it get sold at a garage sale? Passed onto a sibling? Or did it just quietly fade away?
2. Choose a particular toy and examine how it has changed throughout the decades, perhaps from the forties to present day. Some examples might be baby dolls, military toys, lunch boxes, action figures, coloring books. Comment on how the changes in each decade reflect that era and the tone of the times. Has that type of toy improved or declined in quality or some other way?
3. Research toys from another culture and write an essay that examines what the toys say about that culture. What did you learn about the culture by examining the toys?

Essay Connections

Other essays that examine culture include "About Men" by Gretel Ehrlich, Ken Chen's "City Out of Breath," and "The Culture of Celebrity" by Joseph Epstein. The book, *Mythologies,* from which "Toys" was taken, examines other cultural phenomena.

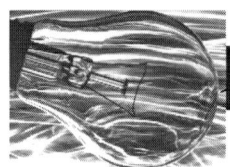

MUTE DANCERS
How to Watch a Hummingbird

Diane Ackerman

Diane Ackerman's fascination with nature and the senses combine in this essay. Using mythology and fact, she heightens the reader's awareness of the wonder of hummingbirds. She's the author of "A Natural History of the Senses," a national bestseller made into a PBS special.

DUSTBIN OF HISTORY AND CULTURE

LI'L ABNER: A comic strip by cartoonist Al Capp introduced in 1934 and continuing until 1977. The strip satirically commented on public figures and current events through hillbilly characters in a place called Dogpatch.

NORTHERN LIGHTS: A spectacular atmospheric light show also known as the aurora borealis or polar lights. Lights of various hues shift and dance.

1   A lot of hummingbirds die in their sleep. Like a small fury of iridescence, a hummingbird spends the day at high speed, darting and swiveling among thousands of nectar-rich blossoms. Hummingbirds have huge hearts and need colossal amounts of energy to fuel their flights, so they live in a perpetual mania to find food. They tend to prefer red, trumpet-shaped flowers, in which nectar thickly oozes, and eat every 15 minutes or so. A hummingbird drinks with a W-shaped tongue, licking nectar up as a cat might (but faster). Like a tiny drum roll, its heart beats at 500 times a minute. Frighten a hummingbird and its heart can race to over 1,200 times a minute. Feasting and flying, courting and dueling, hummingbirds consume life at

See "Teaming Up" #1.

Preying Mantis. © Eric Lawton, 2009.
Used under license from Shutterstock, Inc.

"Mute Dancers: How to Watch a Hummingbird" by Diane Ackerman, originally published in *The New York Times Magazine*, May 29, 1994. Copyright © 1994 by Diane Ackerman. Reprinted by permission of William Morris Agency, LLC on behalf of the Author.

a fever pitch. No warm-blooded animal on earth uses more energy, for its size. But that puts them at great peril. By day's end, wrung-out and exhausted, a hummingbird rests near collapse.

2   In the dark night of the hummingbird, it can sink into a zombielike state of torpor; its breathing grows shallow and its wild heart slows to only 36 beats a minute. When dawn breaks on the fuchsia and columbine, hummingbirds must jump-start their hearts and fire up their flight muscles to raise their body temperature for another all-or-nothing day. That demands a colossal effort, which some can't manage. So a lot of hummingbirds die in their sleep.

See "Teaming Up" #1.

Grasshopper. © Evgeniy Ayupov, 2009. Used under license from Shutterstock, Inc.

3   But most do bestir themselves. This is why, in American Indian myths and legends, hummingbirds are often depicted as resurrection birds, which seem to die and be reborn on another day or in another season. The Aztec god of war was named Huitzilopochtli, a compound word meaning "shining one with weapon like cactus thorn," and "sorcerer that spits fire." Aztec warriors fought, knowing that if they fell in battle they would be reincarnated as glittery, thuglike hummingbirds. The male birds were lionized for their ferocity in battle. And their feathers flashed in the sun like jewel-encrusted shields. Aztec rulers donned ceremonial robes of hummingbird feathers. As they walked, colors danced across their shoulders and bathed them in a supernatural light show.

4   While most birds are busy singing a small operetta of who and what and where, hummingbirds are virtually mute. Such small voices don't carry far, so they don't bother much with song. But if they can't serenade a mate, or yell war cries at a rival, how can they perform the essential dramas of their lives? They dance. Using body language, they spell out their intentions and moods, just as bees, fireflies or hula dancers do. That means elaborate aerial ballets in which males twirl, joust, sideswipe and somersault. Brazen and fierce, they will take on large adversaries—even cats, dogs or humans.

5   My neighbor Persis once told me how she'd been needled by hummingbirds. When Persis lived in San Francisco, hummingbirds often attacked her outside her apartment building. From their perspective she was on *their* property, not the other way round, and

they flew circles around her to vex her away. My encounters with hummingbirds have been altogether more benign. Whenever I've walked through South American rain forests, with my hair braided and secured by a water-proof red ribbon, hummingbirds have assumed my ribbon to be a succulent flower and have probed my hair repeatedly, searching for nectar. Their touch was as delicate as a sweat bee's. But it was their purring by my ear that made me twitch. In time, they would leave unfed, but for a while I felt like a character in a Li'l Abner cartoon who could be named something like "Hummer." In Portuguese, the word for hummingbird (*Beija flor*) means "flower kisser." It was the American colonists who first imagined the birds humming as they went about their chores.

6   Last summer, the historical novelist Jeanne Mackin winced to see her cat, Beltane, drag in voles, birds and even baby rabbits. Few things can compete with the blood lust of a tabby cat. But one day Beltane dragged in something rare and shimmery—a struggling hummingbird. The feathers were ruffled and there was a bit of blood on the breast, but the bird still looked perky and alive. So Jeanne fashioned a nest for it out of a small wire basket lined in gauze, and fed it sugar water from an eye dropper. To her amazement, as she watched, "it miscarried a little pearl." Hummingbird eggs are the size of coffee beans, and females usually carry two. So Jeanne knew one might still be safe inside. After a quiet night, the hummingbird seemed stronger, and when she set the basket outside at dawn, the tiny assault victim flew away.

7   It was a ruby-throated hummingbird that she nursed, the only one native to the East Coast. In the winter they migrate thousands of miles over mountains and open water to Mexico and South America. She may well have been visited by a species known to the Aztecs. Altogether, there are 16 species of hummingbirds in North America, and many dozens in South America, especially near the equator, where they can feed on a buffet of blossoms. The tiniest—the Cuban bee hummingbird—is the smallest warm-blooded animal in the world. About two and one-eighth inches long from beak to tail, it is smaller than the toe of an eagle, and its eggs are like seeds.

8   Hummingbirds are a New World phenomenon. So, too, is vanilla, and their stories are linked. When the early explorers returned home with the riches of the West, they found it impossible, to their deep frustration, to grow vanilla beans. It took ages before they discovered why—that hummingbirds were a key pollinator of vanilla orchids—and devised beaklike splinters of bamboo to do the work of birds.

9   Now that summer has come at last, lucky days may be spent watching the antics of hummingbirds. The best way to behold them is to stand with the light behind you, so that the bird faces the sun. Most of the trembling colors aren't true pigments, but the result of light staggering through clear cells that act as prisms. Hummingbirds are iridescent for the same reason soap bubbles are. Each feather contains tiny air bubbles separated by dark spaces. Light bounces off the air bubbles at different angles, and that makes blazing colors seem to swarm and leap. All is vanity in the end. The male's shimmer draws a female to mate. But that doesn't matter much to gardeners, watching hummingbirds patrol the impatiens as if the northern lights had suddenly fallen to earth.

Exploring Language

benign: gentle, kind.
bestir: get moving. Impress your friends with this one by saying, "Bestir yourself," instead of "Hey, get off the couch, let's go."
colossal: huge, enormous. A good word to replace humongous, which has been banished to the realm of slang.
iridescence: glistening, shimmering, rainbow colors that change with movement. Use *iridescence, glisten,* or *shimmer* in one of the Writing Ideas below.
mania: enthusiasm taken to the extreme; can also refer to a mental illness.
torpor: sluggishness; couch-potato mode.

USAGE   See *bestir colossal, iridescence.*

Thinking and Talking Points

1. Though the essay is subtitled "How to Watch a Hummingbird," Ackerman gives very little advice on how to watch these creatures. How, then, does the essay teach you to watch hummingbirds?
2. Ackerman uses lively **verbs** in her essay to create action, words like *jump-start* and *fire up* (paragraph #2) and *needled* (paragraph #5). Find other action words in the essay and discuss their effectiveness. Try changing these words to more common ones, *needled* to *bothered,* for example. Does the essay lose anything by these changes?
3. Ackerman uses **simile** and **metaphor** to give spark to her essay: "And their feathers flashed in the sun like jewel-encrusted shields" (paragraph #3). Go on a hunt for other similes and metaphors and make a list. Discuss why metaphor might be an important style tool in academic essays—a research paper, for example—rather than just poetry and other fiction. For more on **figurative language**, see the Styling section with "Musical Awakenings."
4. Ackerman writes that hummingbirds communicate through dance, "they spell out their intentions and moods just as bees, fireflies or

hula dancers do." What other creatures communicate silently? In what ways do humans communicate nonverbally?
5. What is Ackerman's purpose for writing this essay? Is it merely to inform, or can you find another reason? State her purpose in your own words.

Styling

Some of the style techniques in this essay are examined in the Thinking and Talking Points, so let's look closely at a sentence style you can model. Ackerman writes:

> Feasting and flying, courting and dueling, hummingbirds consume life at a fever pitch.

Ackerman introduces her complete sentence—*hummingbirds consume life at a fever pitch*—with two sets of words that describe *how* the hummingbirds consume life. She links two words ending in *ing* with *and*: *feasting* and *flying*. Then she uses a comma followed by two more words ending in *ing*: *courting* and *dueling*. Notice the comma before the beginning of the complete sentence (beginning with *hummingbirds*). Also notice that the words linked with *and* go together in some way: feasting and flying both begin with *f*. Courting and dueling, while seemingly opposite activities, often connect in the animal world as males duke it out for the attention of a female.

   Note: This type of sentence is called a **periodic sentence**. For more on this style, see Lopez's "Children in the Woods."

PRACTICE   Fill in the blanks with two sets of words ending with *ing*.

_____ and _____, _____ and _____, the cat tortured the mouse.

_____ and _____, _____ and _____, the dancer charmed the audience.

YOU TRY IT   Now write three sentences of your own in the above style. Use this technique in your next essay.

Teaming Up

1. **Photo Connection:** Form groups of three to five students and study the pictures. Choose one you're all familiar with or find intriguing. Brainstorm a list of characteristics unique to that creature. For ideas, reread Ackerman's piece or visit the Natural History Museum Web site and click on *Amazing Facts*. Next, co-write a riddle paragraph, using the characteristics as clues, saving the more obvious hints for the end. You can write from the first person point of view—*I*—or the third person—*he, she, it*. Here's an example of a riddle by bird writer George Hollister:

   > He's half tail and half feet. The rest of him is head and beak. When he runs, he moves on blurring wheels. He can turn on a dime and leave change. He doesn't need to fly because he can run faster. He kicks dirt in a snake's face, and then eats the snake.

   You'd want to reveal the answer—a roadrunner—at the end of the riddle. Notice that Hollister uses short sentences and metaphoric language while saving the more obvious clue—he doesn't need to fly because he can run faster—for near the end.

   After you've written your riddle, read it to the rest of the class and let them guess. Use this technique in one of the Writing Ideas below. Riddles work nicely as introductions to essays. (For more on how to write riddles, see the "Masquerading" section in *Adios, Strunk and White*—where the roadrunner riddle appears—by Gary and Glynis Hoffman, available through Amazon.com.)

2. In your group, discuss the controversy surrounding animals and emotions: to what extent do animals have feelings? What is your own experience? If there are any vegetarians in the group, have their experiences with animals influenced their decision to give up meat?

Writing Ideas

1. Observe an animal closely—a bird, an insect (you can sometimes buy a praying mantis at the local plant nursery), an animal at a zoo—and take notes about the animal's behavior. Write an essay explaining how to watch this animal. If necessary, look up information about the creature's behavior.

2. Choose a bird you think interesting or unusual. Research and write an essay which attempts to answer this question: what problem or problems did adaptation or evolution help the bird solve? For example,

Ackerman explains how hummingbirds solved the problem of being mute (see paragraph #14). Use a riddle introduction (see Teaming Up activity #1) to hook the reader.

3. Ackerman mentions that hummingbirds are often depicted as resurrection birds in mythology. Explore another animal that's often represented in myth or legend. For example, Native American myths and legends often depict eagles and wolves. Read the myth and then look up scientific information on the animal. Write an essay which attempts to explain—as Ackerman does—why the animal achieved its mythic or legendary status.

Essay and Film Connections

Several animal-themed essays are included in this book: "The Courage of Turtles" by Edward Hoagland; "Black Widow" by Gordon Corice; "Joyas Voladoras" by Brian Doyle. My film recommendations would be *Grizzly Man* and *Winged Migration.* In his book *When Elephants Weep,* Jeffrey Masson explores the emotional lives of animals.

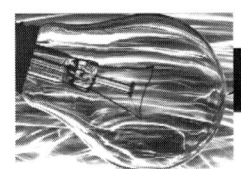

ROLL OVER BACH, TOO!

Jack Kroll

Jack Kroll was an award-winning journalist and drama critic for Newsweek. He died at age 74 on June 8, 2000. This essay on the Beatles attempts to explain the group's special appeal, claiming, "For many, Sgt. Pepper was an epochal event, the matriculation of rock into high art."

DUSTBIN OF HISTORY AND CULTURE

BUSTER KEATON: (1895–1966) An American silent film star and popular comic actor.
CHARLIE CHAPLIN: (1889–1977) Actor, director, producer, mostly of silent films. Though English, he moved to America, where he got his start in film.
DUKE ELLINGTON: (1899–1974) American jazz musician, credited with bringing jazz into concert halls.
LOUIS ARMSTRONG: (1900–1971) Also known as Satchmo. American jazz musician who often performed in films and was an international celebrity.
T. S. ELIOT: (1888–1965) One of the most influential poets of the 20th century; his most famous and controversial work is "The Waste Land."

1   Were you there? If not, you really can never know. Amazement must be experienced first-hand, and the coming of the Beatles was an amazement. Girls screamed; the captions in *Newsweek*'s Feb. 24, 1964, cover story read: "eeeeeeeeeeee . . . E E E E E E E E E E E E . . . EEEEEEEEEEEE!" and the London *Times* music critic praised the Beatles' "pandiatonic clusters" and "flat-submediant key-switches." Both reactions were perfectly appropriate; the Beatles were blowing minds and nervous systems. And cash registers. On their first U.S. tour, two entrepreneurial types bought the pillowcases on which the four mop-tops had reposed in a Kansas City hotel and sliced them into 160,000 tiny squares, which they sold for a dollar each.

2   The girls were screaming not at key-switches (which the Beatles, who could not read music, arrived at instinctively) but at things like the "Yeah, yeah, yeahs," in "She Loves You," delivered by Paul McCartney

"Roll Over Bach, Too!" by Jack Kroll from *Newsweek*, October 23, 1995. © 1995 Newsweek, Inc. All rights reserved. Used by permission and protected by the Copyright Laws of the United States. The printing, copying, redistribution, or retransmission of the Material without express written permission is prohibited.

and George Harrison. But what linked the screechers and the scholars was a sense of something new, an absolute freshness that the Beatles manifested musically and personally. Those early songs—"I Want to Hold Your Hand," "Please Please Me"—were both sexy and innocent. Like those two "pleases," the first a polite supplication, the second a verb vibrating with sexual possibility. A British writer described the band as "beat-up and depraved in the nicest possible way."

3   That's a perfect description of rock-and-roll charisma. But what made the Beatles the key pop artists of the '60s was the synthesis that they made out of almost every conceivable pop element. Both John Lennon and Ringo Starr hailed their hometown of Liverpool as a crucible, a port city that brought together Irish, blacks, Chinese and sailors coming from America with blues records. Clubs and pubs jumped with the sounds of country and Western, British music-hall songs and rural folk tunes. The classical composer and critic Wilfrid Mellers said that the Beatles, like "other geniuses such as Bach, Mozart and Beethoven, knew the right time and place to be born."

4   Out of all these elements, plus the influence of pioneer rockers like Chuck Berry and Little Richard, the Beatles created a unique multifaceted music. It rocked hard, it glinted with irony, it sang with poignant melancholy, as in "Yesterday," McCartney's anthem of loss, in which he sings solo and turns his guitar into the heart-strings of loneliness. The Lennon-McCartney songs were minidramas that evoked a wide spectrum of emotion. McCartney's "Penny Lane" and Lennon's "Strawberry Fields Forever" (coupled on one amazing single) conjured up their lost worlds of childhood, Paul's a "very strange" Utopia, John's a place where "nothing is real / and nothing to get hungabout."

5   In less than five years the Beatles produced a series of albums of increasing complexity, notably *A Hard Day's Night, Rubber Soul, Revolver* and *Sgt. Pepper's Lonely Hearts Club Band*. The album's climactic number, "A Day in the Life," is the Beatles' peak achievement. "I read the news today oh boy," sings Lennon, with a sweet hopelessness. Recounting news items of death, war and absurdity, John's refrain, "I'd love to turn you on," fuses the Beatles' drug experience with the desire to transcend the horrors of a foundering civilization. The number ends with the now legendary gigantic crescendo, played by a 41-piece orchestra, that wells up like a groan from the anguished heart of the city.

6   For many, *Sgt. Pepper* was an epochal event, the matriculation of rock into high art. Kenneth Tynan called it a decisive moment in the

history of Western civilization. But some critics thought that high art was exactly what rock shouldn't be. "What's so great about Art?" demanded critic Nik Cohn, insisting that the Beatles "have flown away into limbo." In a review I compared "A Day in the Life" to T. S. Eliot's apocalyptic poem "The Waste Land." In his illuminating survey of the Beatles' career, *Revolution in the Head,* Ian MacDonald rejects the comparison. He says of "A Day in the Life": "The fact that it achieves its transcendent goal via a potentially disillusioning confrontation with the 'real' world is precisely what makes it so moving." But that splendid sentence is also a succinct summation of "The Waste Land."

7   What the Beatles did in the '60s remains the most thrilling surge of creativity in the history of pop culture. They obliterated distinctions of high and low, like Chaplin, like Buster Keaton, like Louis Armstrong and Duke Ellington. They made it clear that if art is to survive in the techno-millennium that looms ahead, it must be hooked into the realities and redemptions in the days of our lives.

FOLLOW UP: ROLL OVER BACH, TOO!

Exploring Language

apocalyptic: prophetic of the world's future, usually a doomed or threatened vision.

crucible: a melting pot; in this context, a place where those of different backgrounds and styles meet, influencing change.

entrepreneurial: striking out on one's own in business or other ventures.

epochal: memorable or very significant.

matriculation: enrollment or signing up; admission to a group.

multifaceted: having many sides or appearances.

poignant: touching or moving, as in "The film had a poignant scene, moving Nam to tears."

redemption: atonement or making up for something.

succinct: brief, compact.

supplication: a plea or request.

synthesis: a blend or fusion.

transcend: to rise above, often used in a spiritual context.

USAGE Look up *crucible* in the dictionary and notice its different meanings. Use the word in at least two sentences, each with a different meaning.

Thinking and Talking Points

1. What is Kroll's thesis? Examine the examples Kroll uses to support each of his paragraphs. How well does he support his point? How does he explain his examples and tie them back to his thesis?

2. Kroll, in paragraph #6, quotes critics who disagree with his comparison of the Beatles' work to high art and comparison of "A Day in the Life" to a famous poem by T S. Eliot, "The Waste Land." Why does he bring in critics who disagree with him?

3. Read the section in paragraph #3 where Kroll quotes critic Mellers comparing the Beatles to famous classical composers. Do you agree with this assessment? Can you think of other music groups that might be compared to classical "geniuses"?

4. Kroll writes in paragraph #4, "The Lennon-McCartney songs were minidramas that evoked a wide spectrum of emotion." Listen to one of the songs he discusses—or find the lyrics on the Beatles Lyrics database—and explain how the song is a minidrama.

Styling

An opening that hooks the reader is an important ingredient in college-level writing. Jack Kroll opens his essay with a simple question, "Were you there?" Asking a question arouses the reader's curiosity. He or she usually wants an answer. In her essay "No Wonder They Call Me a Bitch," Ann Hodgman spends the entire introduction—with the exception of the first line—asking questions. When you're stuck for a good opening line, think about your essay, what questions you address, and try to come up with a short question.

PRACTICE Write a short question for each of these topics: hockey, hunting, jazz, snakes, art.

YOU TRY IT Open your next essay with a question or series of questions.

Teaming Up

1. **A Good Warm-up for Writing Idea #1.** Have someone in the group bring in the lyrics to "A Day in the Life" by the Beatles (available with the CD *Sgt. Peppers Lonely Hearts Club Band*). Now compare the verses from "The Waste Land" (the entire poem is too long to reprint here). What similarities in theme do you notice? What makes both of these pieces "apocalyptic"? How are they "hooked into the realities and redemptions in the days of our lives"?

2. **A Good Warm-up for Writing Idea #2.** Bring in lyrics to a song you think is "hooked into the realities and redemptions in the days of our lives." Compare in your group, explaining why your choice is a minidrama, how it fits Kroll's quote above. Now you have a start on Writing Idea #2.

Writing Ideas

1. Find the lyrics to another Beatles' song Kroll mentions in paragraph #4. Analyze the lyrics, and write an essay explaining how the song is a mini-drama, how it's "hooked into the realities and redemptions in the days of our lives."

2. Analyze a song of your own choice, possibly from Teaming Up #2, and write an essay comparing it to one of the Beatles' songs, explaining how both are "apocalyptic."
3. Research photos of the Beatles, one from their early days when Kroll says their music was "both sexy and innocent" and the other from the later years when Kroll says "the Beatles produced a series of albums of increasing complexity." Now listen to songs from both periods. Compare. Write an essay that attempts to answer this question: what does the change in appearance and the change in tone of the lyrics and music say about changes in our culture?

Essay and Film Connections

The essay "Musical Awakenings" by Clayton S. Collins examines music's ability to heal; in "A Voice for the Lonely," Stephen Corey writes a memoir about music's impact on the senses while paying a tribute to singer Roy Orbison of "Pretty Woman" fame. The essay "Prince" by Chuck Klosterman praises him as a genius. The film *Once* (2007) follows the trials and tribulations of a band trying to make it in the volatile music industry.

From "The Waste Land" by T. S. Eliot

> April is the cruellest month,
> breeding Lilacs out of the dead land, mixing
> Memory and desire, stirring
> Dull roots with spring rain.
> Winter kept us warm, covering
> Earth in forgetful snow, feeding
> A little life with dried tubers.
>
> * * *
>
> Unreal City,
> Under the brown fog of a winter dawn,
> A crowd flowed over London Bridge, so many,
> I had not thought death had undone so many.
> Sighs, short and infrequent, were exhaled,
> And each man fixed his eyes before his feet.
> Flowed up the hill and down King William Street,
> To where Saint Mary Woolnoth kept the hours
> With a dead sound on the final stroke of nine.
> There I saw one I knew, and stopped him, crying: "Stetson!
> "You who were with me in the ships at Mylae!
> "That corpse you planted last year in your garden,
> "Has it begun to sprout? Will it bloom this year?
> "Or has the sudden frost disturbed its bed?
> "O keep the Dog far hence, that's friend to men,
> "Or with his nails he'll dig it up again!"

MYLAE: where a battle was fought between Rome and Carthage in 260 B.C. Rome won.
SAINT MARY WOOLNOTH: a church in London.

Questions for Interpretation

1. April is springtime, a time of rebirth and resurrection. Why, then, does Eliot call it the "cruellest month"?
2. What does the brown fog represent?
3. People are walking across the London Bridge like the living dead, eyes fixed and staring, uttering sighs. Why does Eliot present such a picture of humans? What's wrong with these people?
4. What commentary is Eliot making about war?

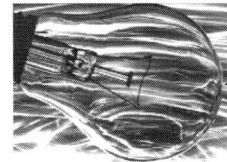

PRINCE

The Fargodome
Fargo, North Dakota
December 8, 1997

Chuck Klosterman

Chuck Klosterman's work has appeared in Esquire, GQ, Spin, New York Times Magazine, and The Washington Post. He's the author of several essay collections, including Fargo Rock City, Sex, Drugs, and Cocoa Puffs, and Killing Yourself to Live. The essay "Prince" appears in "The Show I'll Never Forget: 50 Writers Relive Their Most Memorable Concertgoing Experience," where he expresses his admiration of Prince as a genius, which he defines as "considerably more gifted and creative than almost everyone else who aspires to do the things he does best."

DUSTBIN OF HISTORY AND CULTURE

BYZANTINE: Eastern half of the Roman empire, which survived after the rest of Rome fell; it was eventually overrun by the Ottomans in 1453.

CORINTHIANS (Paul's first letter to): Also known as the Epistle of St. Paul (first and second letters are now the seventh and eighth books of the New Testament). The first letter was written about 53 or 54 CE, addressed to the Christian community of Corinth, Greece, which he had founded; it deals with the problems of the early church.

BIOSPHERE II: A self-contained ecological system in Arizona; Biosphere I is the earth.

1   I loved Prince when I was thirteen, and that was humiliating. It was among my darkest secrets. Seven hours before the first day of junior high, I laid in bed and listened to my sister's *Purple Rain* cassette, mortified by my own womanliness. "This will destroy me," I privately thought. "People will see right through me. I am a pussy." At the time, the only other artists I loved were Mötley Crüe, Ratt, KISS, and Ozzy. As far as I could tell, these were the only artists any intelligent, heterosexual male could (or would) love. While much of

"Prince, The Fargodome, Fargo, North Dakota, December 8, 1997" by Chuck Klosterman excerpted from *The Show I'll Never Forget: 50 Writers Relive Their Most Memorable Concertgoing Experience,* edited by Sean Manning, (Da Capo, 2007). Reprinted by permission of Chuck Klosterman.

1985 America may have secretly appreciated "Round and Round," I was a deeply closeted Prince fanatic, unwilling to tell even my friends and family. I listened to the solo on "Let's Go Crazy," and my creeping fears were instantaneously validated: Prince was a better guitar player than Warren DeMartini. It was true, and I could not deny it. When I watch *Before Stonewall,* this is the experience I relate to.

2   Twelve years later, I had to review a Prince concert for the *Forum* newspaper in Fargo, North Dakota. By then, I had been "out" as a Prince person for seven or eight years. The only problem was that I didn't really care anymore: Prince was working through his preposterous TAFKAP period and was slowly releasing long-awaited records that mostly sucked. Oddly, I found myself lying about Prince again, but now the context was reversed: I kept finding myself saying things like, "A bad record by Prince is still better than 90 percent of the albums that will come out this year, because he is a genius. A bad Prince record is still better than anything by the Crystal Method." Which was true, I suppose, but really only proved that MTV's *Amp* appeared to be inventing a dystopic future.

3   So ANYWAY, I went to this show cautiously pessimistic. I suspected it might be embarrassing, or devoid of familiar material, or punctuated by Prince walking onto the stage and wordlessly holding up four inexplicable fingers for the duration of the evening. However, my main trepidation involved time: I had to file my review by 11:10 P.M. that night, and that deadline was inflexible. The site of the concert (the Fargodome!) was a ten-minute drive from the *Forum* office, and this was the pre-laptop era. All the radio stations claimed the show would begin at eight, but everybody knew Prince usually played long and never played on time; at his club in Minneapolis, he would (supposedly) begin impromptu rock sets at 3:45 A.M. in the middle of the week. Nonetheless, I would need to exit the Dome parking lot by 10:15—this would give me fifty minutes to write a fifteen-inch, seven hundred-word review (plus or minus five minutes to self-edit the copy before sending it to the Night Desk). If Prince played two hours, I would almost certainly miss the encore; this is a common problem for anyone who has ever covered music for a daily newspaper. I think I saw three encores in eight years.

4   I arrived at the Dome around 7:30, pleasantly surprised to find I was directly in front of the stage (reviewers are usually relegated to the side of the arena, but not tonight). My friend Ross and I idly chatted about which songs might or might not be performed. (Ross was pulling hard for "Housequake" and "Pussy Control," if I recall correctly.) We

also snickered about the smallness of the crowd; while more than twenty thousand people had showed up to the Dome for Elton John, there were only 7,114 people in the building for TAFKAP. Prince had implemented a Byzantine anti-scalping policy where he would only announce a show two weeks before the actual date, and then everyone had to purchase vouchers that could only be exchanged for tickets at the door; I believe it was modeled after the method in which citizens of communist Russia were able to attain bread. Prince has been a goofball his entire life, but the middle nineties were truly the apex of his insanity. He was so crazy in 1997 that most people didn't even notice.

5   So . . . 7,114 of us sat there and waited. And waited. I was not surprised Prince didn't go on at eight, but I grew a little irritated at 8:30. And then—off in the distance, at the rear of the auditorium—there emerged the sound of a bass drum. "Aha!" we collectively thought. "This is it. Prepare for Prince!" The drum grew louder as it moved toward the stage; the beat emanated from (what looked like) a substantial marching band (the kind of band that might perform at halftime during the annual Grambling/Southern football game). We all searched for rock's purple elf within the melee. Was he leading the pack? No. Was he hidden among their broad shoulders and flamboyant outfits? No. Was he inside the bass drum, like the Lucky Charms leprechaun? Nay.

6   He was not there.

7   He was not there, because this was actually Larry Graham and Graham Central Station. Now, I have attended many shows where the audience was unfamiliar with the opening act. However, this was the only major concert I've ever attended where every single member of the audience was completely unaware that an opening act was appearing. There had been no publicity about this whatsoever. Everybody—including myself—immediately assumed this had to be Prince's entourage. I mean, I had no fucking idea what Larry Graham looked like; I hadn't seen a picture of him since the seventies. They took the stage and tried to bury us with funk, but we all kept waiting for Prince to come out. "This is rather curious," I thought. "Why is the backing band performing 'Thank You (Falettin Me Be Mice Elf Agin)' in its *totality*?" Twenty minutes passed before we finally concluded that this was, in fact, a group relatively unrelated to Prince. And they were excellent, but they played a long time; their set was over an hour. It was now 9:45, and—for all I knew—Prince wasn't even in Fargo. He was probably sitting inside Biosphere II, talking to a puppet and thinking about Paul's First Letter to the Corinthians.

8   It now seemed plausible that this concert might not begin before eleven, which would turn my seven hundred-word review into a less-nuanced four-word review: "Prince is a jerk." This was a real problem; there are no journalistic alternatives for covering an event that doesn't exist. Ross found this scenario increasingly comical. But then—at 9:59—a certain kind of existence began; this tiny, capricious freak walked onstage and started making rock music. And it was so goddamn mesmerizing that I remember almost none of it.

9   In my mind, I initially recall thinking, "Okay, I can maybe watch five songs, and then I have to go write this stupid story." But I have no idea how many songs I experienced, or what most of these songs were, or if any of them were "Housequake" or "Pussy Control." I had a notebook, but I didn't take any notes. There may have been a medley that included "Little Red Corvette," "Raspberry Beret," and "I Could Never Take the Place of Your Man," but that might have actually occurred at a Prince concert I would see in Cleveland three years later. He was just so amazingly good at *everything*. There was a sixty-second span where he played a keyboard, a bass, and a guitar in immediate succession, and I think he played each individual instrument better than anyone ever had played them before, anywhere, during any historical period over the past eleven thousand years. *And Prince didn't even care.* He didn't look happy, and he didn't look bored. He didn't even look focused. It seemed completely spontaneous, yet it wouldn't have mattered if he had rehearsed those specific sixty seconds for eight or nine months; the experience would have been exactly the same. And what I learned at this concert—and what I suspect can only be learned through seeing Prince live—is that all the moronic bullshit I made up about Prince's bad records and the Crystal Method was completely true: Prince is a genius. I was completely right. I just didn't know what "being right" meant.

10   Prior to this concert, what I actually meant when I said, "Prince is a genius," was that, "Prince is considerably more gifted and creative than almost everyone else who aspires to do the things he does best." By this criteria, there are a handful of other musicians who would qualify as geniuses: John Lennon and Paul McCartney, Jimmy Page, Donald Fagan and Walter Becker, Tony Iommi, Ike Turner, Lindsey Buckingham, Kevin Shields, and probably twenty-five other very famous people I can't recall at the moment I'm writing this particular sentence. For anecdotal purposes, this definition of "genius" is usually acceptable. But those artists are not geniuses; they are simply very,

very, very good at a vocation they have selected. That difference became weirdly lucid whenever Prince did anything onstage, including his attempt to have sexual intercourse with a piano. Eddie Van Halen plays guitar like a genius, but that is something he *figured out* how to do. He *turned himself into a genius,* and that isn't the same thing.

11   I suppose it's possible that Prince has worked harder at his music than any of his peers; I know almost nothing about his life that hasn't been fictionalized for his semi-autobiographical movies. This is not an attempt to discredit his work ethic, or to suggest he's lazy. However, this singular Fargo concert forces me to believe that the degree to which he has (or hasn't) worked on his craft is almost completely irrelevant. Prince doesn't really deserve credit for being a genius because he is not a normal human. His ability to create and perform music is so inherent and instinctual that it cannot really be measured against normal criteria; the only other rock musicians in this class are Jimi Hendrix and (maybe) Bob Dylan. And I only realized this by *seeing* Prince from a distance of twenty-five feet. His transcendence is not accurately felt through his songs or his albums, because a lot of those songs and records aren't especially good. Some of them are semi-terrible. But bad Prince records are still valuable because *he made them.* They are like triptychs from Stonehenge.

12   I do not know what time I exited the show, but it was not even half over. I know I arrived at the *Forum* office at 10:50 and wrote 492 bland words that did not reflect the experience in any meaningful way (and this review does not mention any specific song Prince played). According to my best calculations, I probably saw forty minutes of that concert. Which were thirty-nine more than I needed.

Exploring Language

apex: top or highest point.
capricious: given to sudden and/or unpredictable changes in mood or behavior.
dystopic: imaginary place or society where everything is bad; opposite of utopia.
emanate: radiate or spread out from.
entourage: a group of people who follow around and/or assist an important or famous person.
inexplicable: unexplainable.
melee: a mass of disorderly or unruly people; a group of people in a confused fight.
nuance: a slight difference, especially in sound or meaning.
transcendence: rising above the ordinary, often associated with a spiritual experience.
trepidation: fear or nervousness.
triptychs: three paintings or carved panels hinged together; or hinged tablet made of three leaves, used in ancient Rome.

USAGE Write a sentence containing three of the above words.

Thinking and Talking Points

1. What is Klosterman's main point or thesis? What evidence does he use to support his view?
2. Usually, students are taught to avoid repetition, but sometimes repetition creates style. Notice at the end of paragraph five, "He was not there," is set off as its own paragraph, and then repeated in the first line of the next paragraph. What effect is Klosterman trying to achieve?
3. The essay contains so-called "cuss" words and slang. Why might this language be appropriate in the context of this piece of writing? Can you think about other writing situations where it might be necessary and acceptable? In what writing situations would it not be appropriate?

4. Find areas in the essay where the writer uses exaggeration. How is this technique used to his advantage?
5. Klosterman makes a distinction between being a genius and turning yourself into one. What is that distinction? What is his definition of a genius?

Styling

One style technique you might be familiar with is **alliteration**, the repetition of sounds close to one another, creating rhythm. Some examples from Klosterman's essay include "specific sixty seconds" (s), "Prepare for Prince" (p), and "preposterous period"(p).

PRACTICE Find at least three other pairs of words close together that create alliteration in Klosterman's essay.

YOU TRY IT Choose a topic and brainstorm five pairs of words that contain alliteration. Some ideas for topics might be candy (jelly beans and juju bees), descriptions of your favorite meal (simply sublime salmon), your pet (perky poodle) or favorite song or poet (melancholy musician). Using your brainstorming list, write five sentences containing alliterations.

Teaming Up

1. The "You Try It" in the "Styling" section easily adapts to a group activity. It can be done as a round robin exercise, where each person writes down an object (like the ones above), passes it to the right, and then the next person must tag on another word, perhaps an adjective, that contains alliteration. If done in groups of three, then each word winds up with two tagged on alliterations. The best of the bunch can be made into sentences.
2. **A Good Warm-up for Writing Idea #3.** Bring in lyrics to a song you thinks stands up to the elements of poetry: imagery, tone and rhythm (for example **alliteration** and **assonance**), **symbol** and/or **allegory**, figurative language (**metaphor**, **simile**, **personification**). Read each set of lyrics and choose the one that best exemplifies poetry.

Writing Ideas

1. Write an essay about the best (or worst) live show you've ever attended. It can be a concert, play, musical—as long as it was live. Describe when and where it took place and what was going on in your life during that time. Use sensory detail to describe the surroundings, the crowd, the music. Your essay should reflect the tone of the show being the best or worst in your experience.
2. Compare and/or contrast two music concerts in the same genre (either ones you have attended or seen on DVD). Examples of genres might be country western, classical, rock, hip-hop, or rap. Argue for one artist being superior to the other in that genre. Be specific about what areas the artist excels. Reread Klosterman's essay for ideas.
3. Compare the theme in a song that you think qualifies as poetry to a poem of the same theme. Consider researching a literature data base in your school library (if available or try your public library) and type in search terms like "poetry themes." Write an essay comparing the themes as well as other literary devices, illustrating the universality of such themes. Some themes to consider might be teen depression, anger, war, suffering, guilt, betrayal, love, philosophy, politics, jealousy, solitude, nature. For comparing elements of poetry, here is a list to consider: imagery, tone and rhythm (alliteration, assonance), symbol and/or allegory, figurative language (metaphor, simile, personification).

Essay and Film Connections

Other essays in this book with music themes include "Monster Mash" by Jack Kroll and "Fiddling While Africa Starves" by P.J. O'Rourke. Music videos abound, but a critical comparison of the 1970 film *Woodstock* directed by Michael Wadleigh to the *Gimme Shelter* Maysles brothers documentary coupled with the O'Rourke piece might make for lively debate or essay writing.

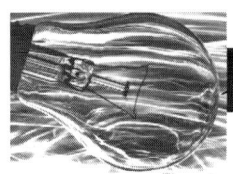

A BOX FILLED WITH MAGIC

Martin Scorsese

> Film director Martin Scorsese has to his credit such films as Cape Fear, The Age of Innocence, The Departed, and Goodfellas. He wrote this essay for Newsweek (summer 1999), which chronicles how his film making was influenced by going to church and the movies with his family.

DUSTBIN OF HISTORY AND CULTURE

SAINT TERESA OF AVILA: A Spanish mystic who suffered serious illnesses and claimed to see visions of Christ, hell, angels, and demons, professing that the pain she suffered was caused by the tip of an angel's spear in her heart.

SAINT ROCCO: Patron saint of pestilence who suffered from the plague. Revered in the Catholic Church as the protector against contagious disease.

1   I've always linked my moviegoing experiences to my family. My parents weren't educated. There were no books in our house. I was constantly ill with asthma, and the only activity we could share was going to the movies. We lived in Little Italy in downtown Manhattan, and I remember the neighborhood movie theaters well, with their tantalizing posters promising dreams, and a rich array of second- and third-run movies. Admission was 18 cents for children. The first film I remember seeing by title was *Duel in the Sun*. I was 4 years old. My mother said she took me to see it because I liked Westerns, but actually it had been condemned by the church, and I suspect that's the real reason she took me. The movie was overpowering with its hallucinatory color imagery, violent music, hysterical melodrama and intense sexuality. I wasn't ever the same after that.

See "Teaming Up" #1.

© Nikita Rogul, 2009. Used under license from Shutterstock, Inc.

"A Box Filled with Magic" by Martin Scorsese from *Newsweek*, June 22, 1998. © 1998 Newsweek, Inc. All rights reserved. Used by permission and protected by the Copyright Laws of the United States. The printing, copying, redistribution, or retransmission of the Material without express written permission is prohibited.

2   When I was a boy, there wasn't much direct communication between my father and me. But at the movie theater, the two of us shared the remarkable images and strong emotions that emanated from the giant screen, emotions we couldn't otherwise articulate to each other. Together we saw such pictures as *The Red Shoes, I Shot Jesse James, Rear Window, The Thing, The Day the Earth Stood Still, The Bad and the Beautiful,* Jean Renoir's *The River Sunset Boulevard, The Greatest Show on Earth,* a re-release of *The Public Enemy, War of the Worlds, The Heiress* and *Shane.* They left such an impression on me that today, much of the desire and need to express myself on film comes from that early loving experience with my father. Movies fulfilled a desire to communicate with those I loved.

3   The impulse to make movies began in 1951 when my father took me to see a British film, *The Magic Box,* directed by John Boulting. It starred the wonderful actor Robert Donat as William Friese-Greene, one of the unsung pioneers of the invention of cinema. A photographer at the turn of the century, Friese Greene was obsessed with making pictures move. In a scene that was pivotal to my life, he demonstrates the concept of moving pictures to his girlfriend, played by Maria Schell. He picks up a book she's reading in the garden and flips through its pages. On each page is a drawing of stick figures he'd made in the margins. The images of a little girl and a dog were static when seen separately, but when he flipped the pages, they moved. This was miraculous to me as a child. Friese-Greene explained that this phenomenon was called "the persistence of vision." Through this principle an optical illusion is created that makes the pictures appear to move. I went home and tried it myself with telephone books. I was transfixed. I wanted to make movies.

4   I wanted to create images that reflected the life around me: what I saw in the streets, at home and, in particular, in my church. There I found the images very powerful, transcendent and, at times, lurid and erotic. The church in my neighborhood was a historic one: the first Catholic cathedral in New York, St. Patrick's Old Cathedral, built in 1809. Imposing and grand, it provided a refuge from the streets. And it was, in its own way, a very theatrical place. Light coming through the stained-glass windows created color and drenched the atmosphere. Gilded chalices and monstrances and incense added to the effect. I was fascinated by the plaster statues of Saint Teresa of Avila and Saint Rocco, and by the giant crucifix over the altar. Candles were lit in front of two large plaster tableaux. One of them depicted souls in purgatory, naked bodies caressed by bright orange and yellow

flames, looking up to heaven where angels were dripping the most precious blood of the crucified Jesus from a golden chalice. The other tableau was a life-size figure of Jesus, his body wounded and broken, lying dead in his sepulcher.

5   There was also a statue of Saint Lucy, my father's favorite saint—he had eye ailments and she was the patron saint of eyes. My mother told the story of Saint Lucy this way: a young girl with beautiful eyes was pursued by a man who was obsessed with her to the point of violence. But her virtue was so great that she plucked out her eyes and defiled her beauty to put an end to his pursuit. God rewarded her by giving her back her eyes. The statue showed Lucy's beautiful face with her wonderful, innocent eyes gazing up to heaven. In her outstretched hand was a gilded plate, and on it were two human eyes. These images, as well as those from my home and my neighborhood, all found their way into the drawings I had started to make, drawings that—only in my imagination—moved. Later they found their way into my movies.

6   After going to the movies, I'd listen to my family talk about what we had seen together. Often I'd hear them say, "It was good, but you know what would've really happened in that story . . ." And they'd discuss what they thought would have been a more interesting scenario, usually a much more realistic one. Then my father would add, resignedly, "But they can't do that in movies." I often thought, "What if they could?" And as I got older; I wondered, "What if I could?" That impulse was so strong that I secretly drew my own movies after school. They were series of frames—like comic strips or storyboards—with opening credits and stories that were inspired by different Hollywood genres, including epics.

7   Years later, when I started to make movies for real, I found I couldn't be a part of the cinema that created that strong emotional bond between my father and me—entertainment from the "golden age" of Hollywood. The studio system had started to fall apart in the 1950s and had completely disintegrated by the time I began making movies in the '70s. So even though I thought along the lines of the movies I'd loved as a child, the movies I made came from a different place. Entertainment became secondary. (Even when I tried to make a film like those of the great era—New York, New York in 1977—it turned out quite differently.) When I accepted the fact that I wouldn't make old-style movies, I reconciled the situation by having my father and mother become a part of my films. My mother cooked for the

cast and crew, my father helped out in the costume department and often they both played small parts.

8   The 1950s, when the old system was changing, had a strong artistic impact on me. Something new was happening in the movies. Censorship broke down with the films of Otto Preminger, Fred Zinnemann, Billy Wilder, Stanley Kramer and others. They attacked the taboos. I think what struck me most in these movies was a new emotional power and honesty. And of foremost importance, the fourth wall between the audience and the camera was knocked down by the films of Ella Kazan. The acting of Marlon Brando, Montgomery Clift, James Dean was revelatory in its naturalness. I was mesmerized by *On the Waterfront*. For the first time I saw on the screen people I knew in real life, similar to those in my world of the Lower East Side. They reflected emotions and realities I knew intimately. At the end of the '50s, I thought if I were ever to make movies, I would want to create scenes as emotionally powerful and memorable as those in Kazan's films.

9   By 1960 my film viewing changed. I had seen foreign films on TV, particularly Italian films by Roberto Rossellini and Vittorio De Sica. A new cinema was being created abroad, by Ingmar Bergman and Andrzej Wajda and, of course, in the New Wave works coming from Italy, France and England. Add to that the "discovery" of Japanese cinema in the West, and the new American cinema shepherded by critic Jonas Mekas—experimental cinema and the new narrative films of Shirley Clarke and John Cassavetes. When I look back now, I realize that it was seeing Cassavetes's *Shadows* and a re-release of Orson Welles's *Citizen Kane* at the same time that were the defining moments for me. Over coffee afterward with fellow film students at New York University, I knew I really had to make movies. And today the impact both films made on me is still powerful. In a way I think some of the approaches in my own films are attempts to reconcile the disparate styles of those two seminal filmmakers. At the same time, I found I had one foot in European cinema and still can't seem to retract it.

10   Up to now I have not lost the intense desire to say something in film or, at times, the sheer exhilaration of working in the medium; nor have I lost the sense of challenging myself against the work of the great masters. From working on the script and designing shots in preproduction to mixing the score in postproduction, each stage of moviemaking is a collaborative process. On the set itself, there's an excitement that comes from working with great collaborators. It

ranges from raucous fun in scenes where actors perform freely, playing off each other like musicians in a band, to moments of almost religious serenity. In a sense, I've been able to re-create my early movie-viewing experience by making movies with a film family.

11   But the quiet concentration and sense of fulfillment I felt drawing my own movies as a child I can now find only in the editing room. It's where you deal with the very essence of film. When you take two pieces of film, one piece moves and the other piece moves, and when they are cut together, the cut itself creates another kind of movement—an emotional and psychological movement in the mind's eye that creates an emotional and psychological reaction, shared by the filmmaker and the audience. After 25 years, I think of each film as a new chance, an opportunity to explore new and different ways of expression. Still, I may never entirely get beyond the simple amazement of watching still pictures move and come to life.

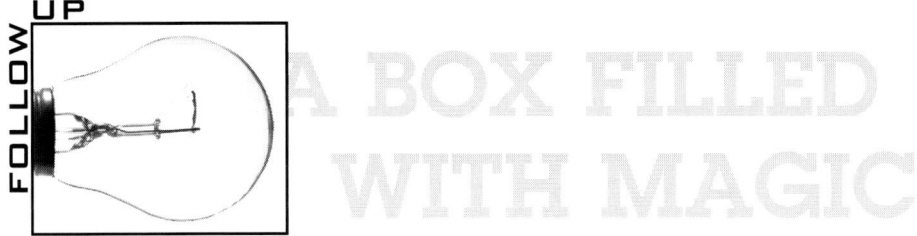

Exploring Language

disparate: different; not alike.
emanate: to radiate or flow from, as in "light *emanated* from beneath the chamber door."
genre: a category; for example, film genres include romance, western, drama, comedy, film noire.
mesmerized: fascinated or enthralled.
pivotal: critical or vital, usually referring to change.
raucous: loud, noisy, chaotic, shrill.
reconcile: to settle or resolve, as in "resolve differences."
revelatory: revealing something.
seminal: contributing to the later development of something. Scorsese is saying that Cassavetes and Welles provided a new approach to film that he built on, made his own.
sepulcher: a tomb, place of burial, or place for religious relics.
tableaux: representations, illustrations, scenes.
transfixed: impaled or held motionless.

USAGE In one of the Writing Ideas below, use either *mesmerized, transfixed,* or *pivotal.* What movie mesmerized or transfixed you as a child? What film do you remember seeing at a pivotal point in your life?

Thinking and Talking Points

1. In his introductory paragraph, Scorsese writes that his mother took him to see the film *Duel in the Sun* "because I liked Westerns, but actually it had been condemned by the church, and I suspect that's the real reason she took me." Find evidence in the essay of Scorsese's religious upbringing. Why—if religious—would his mother take her young son to see a film condemned by the church?
2. Scorsese writes that religious imagery had a powerful influence on his film making. Study his descriptions in paragraph #4. Look up the words *lurid* and *erotic.* In what way do these words fit his descriptions?

3. Scorsese says that watching movies gave him a way to connect with his father. How does Scorsese support this statement? How do films open communication? Or do you think watching movies can shut down communication?
4. Why does Scorsese go into such great detail about Saint Lucy when he only mentions Saint Teresa and Saint Rocco? The simple answer would be because it was his father's favorite, but is there another reason why he describes this saint so graphically?
5. Study the structure of Scorsese's essay, how it's organized. What pattern of organization do you notice? What **transitional** words or phrases does he use?

Styling

Writers often use lists as a gathering-the-evidence tool. Reread paragraph #2 and study the list of films. Listing several specific films is more effective than mentioning only one or two because the reader can see the importance of film in the writer's early life rather than just being told, "I saw a lot of films." The detailed list underscores his point.

PRACTICE Make a list of films you remember from childhood (if you didn't see many films when you were a child, you can either list TV shows or films you've seen as an adult). Don't stop to think about it. Just list whatever pops into your head. Now think about the films and what you remember about watching them, jotting down notes as ideas occur to you.

YOU TRY IT Look over your notes to find an idea for a topic sentence about films and their impact on you. You might begin your sentence, "Films influenced the way I . . ." Modeling Scorsese, write a paragraph using your topic sentence and list of films for support. Next, finish your paragraph with a closing statement. For example, Scorsese writes "Movies fulfilled a desire to communicate with those I loved." You can use your paragraph in one of the Writing Ideas.

Teaming Up

1. **Photo Connection:** Have each member in your group study the photo of the cathedral and jot down some description. What mood or emotion does the picture evoke? Next, co-write a paragraph combining the best of your descriptions. Create a clear topic sentence and set a tone as well as providing vivid details.

2. Imagine you are a filmmaker. What images would find their way into your movies? Have each member in your group write down an answer to this question and make a list of specific images. For example, Scorsese uses religious imagery, listing images from his church that influenced him. Discuss your writing. What did you learn about each other in your discussion?

Writing Ideas

1. Find a review of one of the movies mentioned in the essay and then view the film. Write an essay that either agrees or disagrees with the critic.
2. In paragraph #8 Scorsese writes that several films he saw in the 1950s "reflected emotions and realities I knew intimately." Write an essay about the films that reflect your emotions and realities, that have characters like the people in your own life.
3. Watch several Martin Scorsese films and study the religious images. Write an essay that analyzes the images as they relate to the childhood Scorsese describes in his essay.

Essay and Film Connections

Two other essays in this book concern film: Pauline Kael's "The Little Mermaid and Jack Kroll's "Monster Mash." Scorsese mentions enough films to keep us all busy for a while.

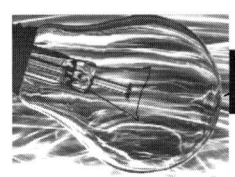

MONSTER MASH

Jack Kroll

Jack Kroll was an award-winning journalist and drama critic for Newsweek. He died at age 74 on June 8, 2000. This article appeared in a special edition of Newsweek (summer 1998). Kroll explores our fascination with horror, chronicling the development of the genre, lamenting the newer horror films like Scream that "[make] the genre seem to be regressing."

DUSTBIN OF HISTORY AND CULTURE

IONIANS: Greeks who lived toward the end of the second millennium B.C., some emigrating to what is now Turkey and the west coast of Asia Minor, giving the region the name Ionia.

1   "Then his teeth flew out; from two sides, blood came to his eyes; the blood that from lips and nostrils he was spilling, open-mouthed; death enveloped him in its black cloud."

2   Is this from the script for *The Texas Chain Saw Massacre? Friday the 13th, Part VIII?* No, it's from Homer's *Iliad,* which opened 3,000 years ago, performed to a preliterate audience by bards who were the ancestors of theater and film. The terror inspired in those ancient Ionians by such passages must have been something to see.

3   Terror may have been the first feeling that human beings ever experienced, in a world that threatened their very survival. The horror genre is a way for humans to revisit that primal fear, to turn it into pleasure, the pleasure of being safely scared. Horror lets us die vicariously, producing an artificial orgasm of mortality. Horror films came in with the very birth of the movies. Thomas Edison couldn't wait to get *Frankenstein* into his newly invented medium, turning out a 16-minute version of Mary Shelley's novel in 1910. Frankenstein's monster, Dracula and the Wolf Man are the unholy three of horror movies. Frankenstein's collage of body parts is the embodiment of man's arrogant desire to write his own Book of Genesis. The monster has new meaning in our age of genetic splicing and artificial intelligence. Dracula is Death as seducer; he sucks our blood to take us to a

"Monster Mash" by Jack Kroll from *Newsweek,* June 1, 1998. © 1998 Newsweek, Inc. All rights reserved. Used by permission and protected by the Copyright Laws of the United States. The printing, copying, redistribution, or retransmission of the Material without express written permission is prohibited.

perverse immortality. The Wolf Man wrenches us back to our origins in the animal world of pure instinct, reversing evolution with its burden of consciousness and responsibility.

4   Boris Karloffs burlap-suited, screw-necked creature in James Whale's 1931 *Frankenstein* is still the greatest of all incarnations of monsterhood, an amazing blend of bewilderment, despair and savage rage beyond anything human. Bela Lugosi, a much more limited actor, nonetheless achieved vampiric perfection in Tod Browning's *Dracula* (also 1931). The best-dressed of all monsters, Lugosi's Dracula is also the most erotic, surveying the necks of various lily-skinned maidens with a connoisseur's libidinous leer before puncturing them with his miniphalic incisors. Lon Chaney Jr. as the Wolf Man (1941) is such a clumsy galoot of an actor that he is believably hapless in his vulpine transformation, giving his soul-saving death at the hands of his father an affectingly Freudian pathos.

5   The '30s were a golden age for horror movies: Fredric March convulsing between virtue and vice as Dr. Jekyll and Mr. Hyde (1932), mad scientist Charles Laughton turning innocent animals into screwed-up humans in *The Island of Lost Souls* (1932) and, perhaps the most nightmarish of all horror films, Tod Browning's *Freaks,* in which a troupe of real sideshow freaks takes revenge on a beautiful trapeze artist and turns her into a monstrous half-human, half-bird. These films had a special resonance in the Depression, especially *King Kong,* in which the giant ape rampaging in a New York split between bread lines and skyscrapers seemed to symbolize a society at the mercy of Darwinian forces.

6   When men went off to war in the '40s, horror movies gave equal time to the unconscious sado-sexual yearnings of women in Jacques Tourneur's *Cat People* movies, with the enigmatic Simone Simon playing a feline version of the Wolf Man. The postwar '50s closed with a masterpiece, Alfred Hitchcock's *Psycho,* the *Citizen Kane* of horror movies in its far-ranging influence. Hitchcock's ironic genius mixed themes of cross-gendering, straightforward and perverse sexuality, Oedipal conflict and schizophrenia. Janet Leigh's last moments of life in the shower turned a bathtub into a mini-Transylvania of ordinary life. Horror provided a counterpoint to the disruptions of the '60s when George Romero created splatter movies with *Night of the Living Dead* (1968), in which a militia of corpses left their graves to attack those who dared to live. Splatter pics mutated like killer amoebas, targeting young people as both protagonists and audiences. In endlessly sequeled series like *Halloween* and *Nightmare on Elm Street,*

the hockey-masked Jason and razor-gloved Freddy were like demonized parental surrogates punishing kids for their newfound sexual freedom.

7   But the flood of teen horror makes the genre seem to be regressing. In Wes Craven's recent box-office smashes, *Scream* and *Scream 2,* it's as if the horror movie were engaged in autoerotic worship of itself. The kids in *Scream* talk incessantly about horror flicks, with a faux hipness that makes you wish all of them would be killed by some self-respecting monster. Horror movies need to return to good old guilt-ridden grown-up panic. The apocalyptic dangers in our time should give new life to the pure horror film. It's doubtful that the Americanization of Godzilla will do the job.

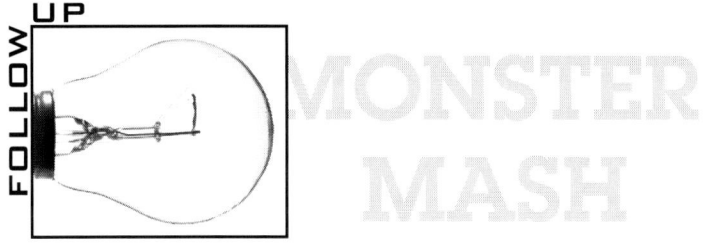

Exploring Language

autoerotic: self-satisfaction of sexual desire.
connoisseur: an expert or judge of taste, usually in a specific area, like a wine connoisseur.
enigmatic: puzzling or paradoxical (contradictory).
galoot: a clumsy person.
hapless: unfortunate or unlucky.
libidinous: lustful.
pathos: pity, sympathy.
preliterate: a culture that hasn't developed writing.
vicariously: through the experience of another. Kroll means that moviegoers experience death through the characters in horror films.
vulpine: resembling a fox; crafty. Which definition do you think Kroll means?

USAGE Write a sentence or two explaining how you (or someone you know) live vicariously, either through films, reading, or television.

Thinking and Talking Points

1. How does Kroll organize the essay?
2. What point does he make about modern horror films? If you've seen any of the films he mentions, do you agree with him?
3. Kroll comments, "Horror movies need to return to good old guilt-ridden grown-up panic." What does he mean? Why does he think guilt-ridden films offer more to the viewer?
4. "The monster has new meaning in our age of genetic splicing and artificial intelligence." In what way? Can you think of examples from film and life that support Kroll's observation?
5. How is the horror genre "a way for humans to revisit that primal fear, to turn it into pleasure, the pleasure of being safely scared"? How does horror let us "die vicariously"?

Styling

Jack Kroll knew that hooking the reader with a spirited title is a valuable tool, and he often uses lines or titles from old rock and roll songs. His essay "Roll Over, Bach, Too" borrows its title from a Beatles song titled "Roll Over, Beethoven." He lifts "Monster Mash" from another old rock and roll song of the same title. Many writers borrow from music, literature, and pop culture for lively titles (see Titles, Introductions, Conclusions in the Writing Basic College Essays section for more examples).

PRACTICE   Think of a possible essay topic for each of the following song titles (or brainstorm your own list of song titles to practice with):

"Mr. Pitiful" (from the soundtrack of the film *The Commitments*).

"Cupid's Dead" (from the CD *III Sides to Every Story* by Extreme).

"Only the Lonely" (Roy Orbison).

YOU TRY IT   For your next essay, find a title off a CD or a line from a song to use as your essay title.

Teaming Up

1. Brainstorm favorite movies scenes from a genre like action/adventure (for example, the Indiana Jones series, *Star Wars*, or *Iron Man*), drama, or science fiction (or other genres), and discuss why you like the films. Have each person in the group choose their favorite from the list and write an individual paragraph explaining how someone lives or dies vicariously through that type of character, perhaps a former jock who relives his or her glory day vicariously through armchair football or sports films. You may use yourself as an example or someone you know.

Writing Ideas

1. Watch two horror films, one old and one new, and write an essay arguing whether or not Kroll's assessment of modern teen horror movies is true: "But the flood of teen horror makes the genre seem to be regressing."
2. Write an essay comparing Dracula—perhaps Bela Lugosi's portrayal (or Bram Stoker's book)—to the modern vampire Edward Cullen in

the book (or film) *Twilight*. How has the image of the vampire changed to reflect modern culture?

3. Watch one of the films discussed in "Monster Mash" and write an essay analyzing the film and its "good old guilt-ridden, grown-up panic." Quote from Kroll's essay to make your points. Use strong description of film scenes.

Essay and Film Connections

Two other film essays or reviews appear in this book: "The Little Mermaid" by Pauline Kael (a scathing review of the Disney film); and Martin Scorsese's "A Box Filled with Magic," which recounts his early experience of film and its influence on himself and his family. Kroll mentions several horror films, but here are my recommendations: Hitchcock's 1960 film *Psycho;* either version of *Cape Fear:* J. Lee Thompson's 1962 version or Martin Scorsese's 1991 film; *The Innocents,* a classic ghost story based on the Henry James novel *The Turn of the Screw,* directed by Jack Clayton, starring Deborah Kerr.

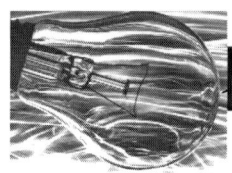

CITY OUT OF BREATH

Ken Chen

Ken Chen—poet, law school graduate, critic, essayist—has published work in Best American Essays 2006, Boston Review of Books, Satellite: The Berkeley Magazine of News and Culture (which he founded), and Arts and Letters Daily. "City Out of Breath," first published in Mānoa 2005, describes the author's impressions of Hong Kong on a visit there with his father, a Taiwanese immigrant, in 2000.

DUSTBIN OF HISTORY AND CULTURE

FILM NOIR: A film genre with usually dark lighting and bleak, cynical, shady characters; the term used by the French critics in the 1940s to describe certain American detective films or thrillers.

MILTONIC: Refers to the writing style or themes of John Milton (1608–1674); considered one of the greatest of English poets, Milton, a Puritan, wrote his epic *Paradise Lost*, while blind, dictating to his daughter.

SAMUEL JOHNSON (1709–1784): Also known as Dr. Johnson, a prominent English figure of the 18th century; poet, essayist, critic, biographer.

1   So all night, we walk in one direction: up.

2   This is really the only direction you can go in Hong Kong, a direction hinted at by skyscrapers and aspired to by the Hong Kong Stock Exchange. By "we," I mean my father, myself, and our guide—my stepgrandmother-to-be—who somehow possesses both our combined age and our combined speed. Trudging up the stairs behind her, my father and I are already panting. We stop and laugh—really only an excuse to catch our breath— but by the top of the stairs we're bent and sagging, our hands on our knees. And there, at the end of the street,

See "Teaming Up" #1.

© Kenneth Sponsler, 2009. Used under license from Shutterstock, Inc.

"City Out of Breath" by Ken Chen first published in *Mānoa*, Vol 17, No. 1, 2005. Reprinted by permission of Ken Chen.

she's waving at us to hurry up, almost as if to fan away whatever remains of our quaint Californian version of walking. When we catch up with her, she says, in what seems like an especially Chinese blend of ridicule and public affection, that we walk too slowly.

3   If an American city at night is film noir, then Hong Kong is just a camera blur. The residents of Kowloon speed around with the same look on their faces, as if they're irked at their bodies for not being cars. You feel that if you stood still, the city would just rotate past you, as if you have no other choice but motion. Hong Kong accelerates as though located on another, faster-spinning earth. Anyone who has been there knows that time and space can flick off their objectivity and instead pulse and jump, symphonic rather than metronomic. In Hong Kong the world stretches time until time—along with space and language— goes elastic. It's like a Chinese painting in which conflicting perspectives soak through the landscape like radiation. A McDonald's sits next to a vegetable cart tended by a woman who looks about five hundred years old. The all-Chinese police band plays bagpipes and marches in kilts for the St. Patrick's Day parade. Street markets are the opposite of flowers: opening up at night and closing at day. In Hong Kong, all times are contiguous. All times are simultaneous. This essay is an attempt to describe a city that is itself already a description—Hong Kong is a description of time. This essay is also an experiment in time travel—an artifact of memory from July 2000. Hong Kong is now the same city but a different place. Prosperity—once the city's one-word gloss—is slowly becoming synonymous with Shanghai. "I hear everyone's real depressed over there," I say at dinner to the mother of a friend of mine from Hong Kong. "That they're jealous, with all the jobs heading over to the mainland and all." She chews on a piece of lettuce and says, "Yes, they are jealous. But they have a right to be."

4   Five years later, we spend the next half-hour taking elevators that lead to stairs that lead to elevators. I don't have any idea where we're going and just follow my father, an immigrant from Taiwan whose Mandarin, I realize, makes him only a third less lost than I am. He's following our guide, who, like Hong Kong itself, is all energy and no conversation. "We're headed for Victoria Peak today," my dad announced this morning. The touristy lookout could be the only spot where Hong Kong can be made comprehensible.

5   Suddenly our guide stops. Are we lost? This possibility is not surprising. It feels like we've been going in spirals, victims of some kind of geographic hoax. Our guide decides to ask for directions in Cantonese. She stops a man with a dark complexion who reminds

me of the vendors at the Taipei night market. He has short, wiry hair that resembles a scouring pad and is wearing a security guard's uniform. Chinese—I think—obviously. Probably a migrant from the mainland. "Where is Victoria Peak?" she asks him in Cantonese. The security guard looks at her and says, "Do you speak English?"

6   Dad and I look at each other. He says, "This is a strange city," and I start laughing, relieved that I'm not the only one who thinks so. We seem to be fumbling through different languages, shifting, testing, trying to find one we can all stand in. A bus rocking through the northern hills speaks to its passengers in Miltonic English: *Do not board or alight whilst bus is in motion.* (Lucifer alights. Buses throttle.) And a week ago in Taiwan, my father had shed the most mundanely engrossing fear of any Chinese immigrant to America: his accent. He became a master of languages, all traces of self-consciousness suddenly gone from his voice. He chatted with taxi drivers and strangers about the drenching humidity or about which restaurants were good, casually code-switching to Taiwanese for jokes, Mandarin for information, and English for translation and one-word exclamations. When we showed up at the desk of the Taipei Hilton, the girls on staff spotted my dad and approached him in nervous English. He paused, got an odd look on his face—the fuzzy expression that Looney Tunes characters have when they're suspended in midair and about to fall—and said in Mandarin: "I'm Chinese!"

7   Back to searching for Victoria Peak, my father starts to ask the question in English, but someone interrupts. A Hong Kong yuppie standing thirty feet away muffles his cell phone in his blazer lapel and tells us the answer in rushed Cantonese. Some men in black blazers walk by, and some teens with blond spiky hair walk by, and some middle-aged men with grimy white aprons walk by—mostly Chinese, but otherwise unidentifiable. Indian? Polynesian? British? Hong Kong is an intensely international city. Every street in Kowloon is an intersection, not only of wet-walled alleys and futuristic buildings of glass, but also of the more transparent rays of cultures.

8   Somehow you are supposed to teach yourself how to comprehend Hong Kong's energy and flashy contradictions: Asian and Western; the encroaching Chinese mainland and the remnants of England; the greasy night markets of sticky-rice tamales and knock-off leather boots that slouch right across from Tiffany, Chanel, and Prada. The only things common to these are the offices sending air-conditioned blasts into the street, a kind of longing for money, and, most important, the sense of storytelling that the city seems to

require as a visitor's pass. Hong Kong has a way of turning on your internal monologue. Walking becomes an act of silent storytelling, figuring people out. You feel like you are lost in some prelapsarian novel in which the plot has begun but the characters wait for you to name them. In some time, at some place, we step into an underground Cantonese restaurant and I see a gray-suited, red-tied man act like a parody of the States. American, I say, with an American accent: good-natured smiles, occasionally the slow English dispatched on foreigners and children, and a slightly uncomfortable look, as though he's worried he's outnumbered.

9   Finally we find Victoria Peak, by which I mean that we find the gondola to get us there. We buy tickets and step in, waiting to be hoisted up into the humid nighttime atmosphere. The cab starts moving, At first, nothing in the windows but the ads on the sides of the tunnel, and then suddenly the city. Our gondola windows have become postcards. Hong Kong poses before us, bright, earnestly capitalist, electric, multiplying. A concrete wall blocks the view, and then the city is back again. Under us, a small red house sits on the cuff of the panorama. Light drops out of a pair of shutters, a door or window is open; someone is home. More stone, more wall. We hit the crest, reach our destination: Victoria Peak, the highest spot in Hong Kong and, for a tourist, the best. We have a God's-eye view of the skyline. The buildings shine yellow, white, orange, blue, all reflected in the dark bay waters; giant corporate logos shrink, sky-scrapers huddle, and the city glows with a brilliant coolness. My eye seems too small to hold it all in.

10   We take the bus back. I sit on the top of a double-decker bus, on the left side, in a city where they drive on the left side of the road. As we shake downhill, making acute turns, I begin to regret my seating preference: the wobbly tourists' corner. The bus hits a few branches, careens over double yellow lines, winds downhill. Whipped by full-motion vertigo, I grope for the metal railing, squeezing it as if for juice, and then laugh at my own cowardice. I gasp, then yawn in a slow, measured sort of panic, a civilized form of suffocation. Hong Kong—a city out of breath.

11   After we've been back from Victoria Peak for a few hours, I go to the front desk of the hotel. A Hong Kong–Chinese woman in her mid-twenties looks up the Internet rates for me. She reads the per-minute charges off a small white card, and her voice compresses Mandarin, English, and Cantonese into a linguistic diamond: the Chinese-British accent. There's the Merchant-Ivory sound, the lilt that movies tell us

is cultured but that also seems austere and imperial, the way Chinese period films do. Yet the sound is also familiar, humble, and awkward: a Chinese voice wandering inside the English language. The sound of it reminds me of my parents. I can't get enough of it.

Exploring Language

acute: serious or critical; intense; also a geometry term for angles less than 90 degrees.
careen: to rush carelessly.
contiguous: connected in space or time.
irked: irritated or annoyed.
linguistic: the study of language.
mundane: ordinary; unimaginative, common.
prelapsarian: relating to a time before the fall of Adam and Eve.
vertigo: dizziness; confusion.

USAGE Make a list of mundane situations or thinking. Write three sentences using *mundane* and at least one other word from the list.

Thinking and Talking Points

1. Search through the essay for Chen's descriptions of people. What do you notice? How do these descriptions underscore his point about Hong Kong?
2. Study Chen's use of dashes. He could use commas. Why the choice to use dashes instead? Explain each instance, why it might be a stronger choice than commas.
3. Chen describes American cities at night as film noir. Explain what you think he means. What evidence does he use as support for Hong Kong as "a camera blur?"
4. Find additional metaphors and similes and explain how they clarify a point or help the reader visualize a person or situation. Also consider the title and what it conveys about the essay's meaning.
5. Chen writes, "In Hong Kong, all times are contiguous. All times are simultaneous." He goes on to make other references to time. What's his purpose? How do his comments on time help explain a city that he says is "out of breath?"

Styling

Most students know how to use a colon with a simple list, but when that list becomes complicated with details that might require commas, then the list can get confusing. Such lists require more sophisticated punctuation. Chen uses semi-colons to separate pairs when describing the contradictions in Hong Kong. In paragraph #8, he writes, "Somehow you are supposed to teach yourself how to comprehend Hong Kong's energy and flashy contradictions: Asian and Western; the encroaching Chinese mainland and the remnants of England; the greasy night markets of sticky-rice tamales and knock-off leather boots that slouch right across from Tiffany, Chanel, and Prada." Each semi-colon signals a new set of items that seem at odds with each in this eclectic city.

PRACTICE   Write a complete sentence that makes a statement about the contradictions in a city you are familiar with and add a colon. Next, make a list of contradictions and pair them up. Is there a modern glass and metal building next to an old, crumbling brick structure? Mansions next to shacks? An outdoor market next to a gleaming, modern mall? Be specific and detailed.

YOU TRY IT   Now arrange each set of contradictions after your sentence with the colon. Add a semi-colon after each set. Write three more sentences in this style, about any topic you think is rich with contradictions.

Teaming Up

1. **Photo Connection and a Good Warm-up for Writing Idea #1:** Each member of the group write a description of the town in the photo, focusing on the mood the picture conveys and any details that would help the reader visualize the town without the photo. Read each other's descriptions. Are their contradictory opinions of the town? Discuss any disparities in views. Choose one to read to the class.

2. **A Good Warm-up for Writing Ideas #1 and #3:** Similar to Teaming Up #1, only this time describe the town or city where you are attending college. Share your impressions. If there are contradictions in views, discuss them and then write an argument against the views that differ from your own, attempting to convince your peers that they've misjudged the town, but be open to others' impressions. This activity also makes a good class brainstorm, with the teacher writing conflicting impressions on the board for discussion and writing possibilities.

Writing Ideas

1. Describe another city, one you're familiar with, describing its tone: is it rural, suburban, or urban? Naive or cynical? Snobby or friendly? Be specific, describing types of people, geography, buildings, the pace.
2. Compare two cities or towns that have something in common, but also exude different tones. For example, you might compare two small towns, one that's friendly, content, accepting; another that's nosey, judgmental, snobby. Use **personification**, describing each town as if it's a person.
3. Write an essay about the contradictions within a city, perhaps describing it during the day versus night, or consider contradicting the media's view of a particular city.

Essay Connections

Other essays in this book that analyze culture are "Naps" by Barbara Holland," "The Indian With a Camera " by Leslie Marmon Silko, "About Men" by Gretel Ehrlich, "The Culture of Celebrity" by Joseph Epstein, and "Toys" by Roland Barthes.

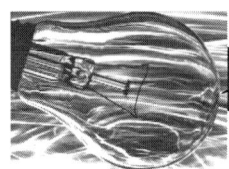

HAIR

Diane Ackerman

This essay is an excerpt from Diane Ackerman's book *The Natural History of the Senses*, which was made into a PBS special. Ackerman gives some fascinating facts and history about hair, as well as its connection with personal and group identity. She opens with the line, "Hair deeply affects people, can transfigure or repulse them."

DUSTBIN OF HISTORY AND CULTURE

GILGAMESH: An epic literary work from the Middle East written on clay tablets dating to about 2000 B.C. Gilgamesh is the name of the hero.
HAIR: A 1960s hippie musical.
RASTAFARIANS: People belonging to a Jamaican religious cult that forbids cutting off hair.

1 Hair deeply affects people, can transfigure or repulse them. Symbolic of life, hair bolts from our head. Like the earth, it can be harvested, but it will rise again. We can change its color and texture when the mood strikes us, but in time it will return to its original form, just as Nature will in time turn our precisely laid-out cities into a weedway. Giving one's lover a lock of hair to wear in a small locket around his neck used to be a moving and tender gesture, but also a dangerous one, since to spell-casters, magicians, voodooers, and necromancers of all sorts, a tuft of someone's hair could be used to cast a spell against them. In a variation on this theme, a medieval knight wore a lock of his lady's pubic hair into battle. Since one of the arch-tenets of courtly love was secrecy,

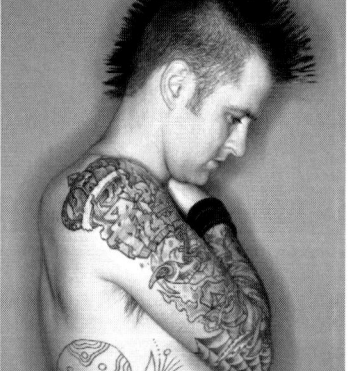

See "Teaming Up" #1.

© iofoto, 2009. Used under license from Shutterstock, Inc.

"Hair" from *A Natural History of the Senses* by Diane Ackerman, copyright © 1990 by Diane Ackerman. Used by permission of Random House, Inc.

choosing this tiny memento instead of a lock of hair from her head may have been more of a practical choice than a philosophical one, but it still symbolized her life-force, which he was carrying with him. Ancient male leaders wore long flowing tresses as a sign of virility (in fact, "kaiser" and "tsar" both mean "long-haired"). In the biblical story of Samson, the hero's loss of hair brings on his weakness and downfall, just as it did for the hero Gilgamesh before him. In Europe in more recent times, women who collaborated with the enemy in World War II were humiliated by having their hair cut short. Among some orthodox Jews, a young woman must cut off her hair when she marries, lest her husband find her too attractive and wish to have sex with her out of desire rather than for procreation. Rastafarians regard their dreadlocks as "high-tension cables to heaven." These days, to shock the bourgeoisie and establish their own identity, as every generation must, many young men and women wear their hair as freeform sculpture, with lacquered spikes, close-cropped patterns that resemble a formal garden maze, and colors borrowed from an aviary or spray-painted alley. The first time a student walked into my classroom wearing a "blue jay," it *did* startle me. Royal-blue slabs of hair were brushed and sprayed straight up along the sides of his head, a long jelly roll of white hair fell forward over his eyebrows, and the back was shiny black, brushed straight up and plastered close to the head. I didn't dislike it, it just seemed like a lot to fuss with each day. I'm sure my grandmother felt that way about my mother's "beehive," and I know my mother feels that way about the curly weather system which is my own mane of long thick hair. One's hairstyle can be the badge of a group, as we've always known—look at the military's crew cut, or the hairstyles worn by some nuns and monks. In the sixties, wearing long hair, especially if you were a man, often fetched a vitriolic outburst from parents, which is why the musical *Hair* summed up a generation so beautifully. The police, who seemed so clean-cut and cropped then, were succeeded by a generation of police in long sideburns and mustaches. But I remember at

See "Teaming Up" #1.

© R. Gino Santa Maria, 2009. Used under license from Shutterstock, Inc.

the Boston Love-in in 1967, my first year away at college, hearing one young man say to a passing couple who ridiculed his ponytail: "Fuck you and fuck your hairdressers." I also remember, in the fifties, walking out of my bathroom with my hair sprayed into a huge bubble. "What have you done to your hair?" my father demanded. "I've just teased it," I said. To which he replied: "Teased? You've driven it insane." I wear my curly hair au naturel these days, in a shag cut the French call *la coupe sauvage* ("the savage cut"), but its volume and faintly erotic unruliness bother my mother's sense of propriety. To her generation, serious women have serious hairdos that are formal, sprayed, and don't move. A few weeks ago, she phoned to warn me that professional women aren't taken seriously if they don't have a "wet set" (rollers, hair dryer, setting lotion, hair spray). Loose ends on one's head signal loose ends in one's life. From this point of view, which has been popular for ages, a woman grows her hair long but keeps it tightly controlled in a bun, under a hat or scarf, or with hair spray, and lets her hair down only in private at night.

2   Most people have about 100,000 hair follicles on their head, and lose between fifty and a hundred hairs a day through normal combing, brushing, or fussing. Each hair grows for only about two to six years, at about five or six inches a year, and then its follicle rests for a few months, the hair falls out, and is eventually replaced by a new hair.

See "Teaming Up" #1.

© Laurin Rinder, 2009. Used under license from Shutterstock, Inc.

So when you see a beautiful head of hair, you're looking at hairs in many different stages in a complex system of growth, death, and renewal. Fifteen percent of it is resting at any one time, the other 85 percent growing; many dozens of hairs are all set to die tomorrow, and deep in the follicles new hairs are budding.

3   Hair has a tough outer coating called the cuticle, and a soft interior called the cortex. People with coarse hair have larger follicles, and also a thin outer coat (10 percent of the hair) with a large inner cortex (90 percent). People with fine hair have smaller follicles, and almost the same amount of cuticle (40 percent) as cortex (60 percent). If the follicle cells grow in an even pattern, the hair will be straight; if they grow irregularly, the hair will be curly. Lice have a

hard time attaching to thick hair, which is why black schoolchildren don't succumb to epidemics of head lice as often as their white classmates. Besides being sexy to most people, head hair protects the brain from the sun's heat and ultraviolet rays, helps to insulate the skull, softens impact, and constantly monitors the world only a hair's breadth away from our body, that circle of danger and romance we allow few people to enter.

4   Of course, hairs grow in many places around the body, even on the toes and inside the nose and ears. The Chinese, the American Indian, and some other peoples have very little hair on their face and body; those of Mediterranean descent can be so woolly and thickly haired they seem only a step away from our ape-man ancestors. Bald men are sexy men; they go bald from a high level of testosterone in the blood, which is why you don't see bald castrati or eunuchs. Men with thick mats of hair on their shoulders and backs used to scare me. A word like "carnivore" would form in my mind when I passed them on beaches. Women tend to be smoother-fleshed than men, so it makes sense that we would shave our legs and apply lotions to accentuate the gender difference. But despite efforts to remove hair from our bodies, quite a lot remains on the arms, faces, and heads of women, and the chest, arms, and legs of men, to do what it was intended to do.

5   Hair is special to mammals, although reptiles do form scales, which are related. Each hair grows from the papilla, a wad of tissue at the base of a follicle, where there is a nerve ending, and there may be a group of other nerve endings nearby. The average body has about five million hairs. Because hairy skin is thinner, it's more sensitive than smooth skin. One hair can be easily triggered: If something presses it or tugs at it, if its tip is touched, if the skin around it is pressed, the hair vibrates and sparks a nerve. Down is the most sensitive hair of all and only has to move 0.00004 of an inch to make a nerve fire. Still, it can't be firing all the time, or the body would go into sensory overload. There is an infinitesimally small realm in which nothing at all seems to be happening, a desert of sensation. Then the merest breeze starts to blow, nothing like a real disturbance. When it grows just strong enough to reach an electrical threshold, it fires an impulse to the nervous system. Hairs make wonderful organs of touch. "Breeze," our brain says without much fanfare, as a few hairs on our forearms lift imperceptibly. If a dust mote or insect brushes an eyelash, we know at once and blink to protect the eye. Though hairs can take shapes as various as down or antennae, some especially

useful ones are *vibrissae*—the stiff hairs cats have as whiskers—which adorn many mammals, including whales and porpoises. A cat without its whiskers bumps into things at night, and can get its head caught in tight spaces. As we can. If we ever get a say-so in evolution, one of the things I'd vote for is whiskerlike feelers to keep us from bumping into furniture, friends, or raccoons in the dark.

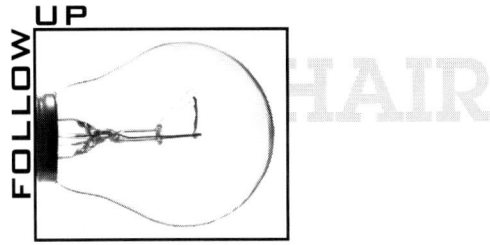

Exploring Language

aviary: a place to keep birds confined.
bourgeoisie: middle class.
castrati: those who have been castrated (had testicles or ovaries removed).
eunuch: a castrated man; usually refers to one put in charge of a harem.
infinitesimally: immeasurably small.
necromancers: those who practice magic or sorcery, often referring to raising dead spirits for the purpose of telling the future or influencing events.

Thinking and Talking Points

1. Ackerman writes that "one's hairstyle can be a badge of a group" and gives some examples. Think of other examples of a hairstyle being a badge of a group.
2. Ackerman makes good use of strong word choices. For example, she writes that hair "bolts" from the head. Find other strong word choices in the essay.
3. Ackerman writes, "Hair deeply affects people, can transfigure or repulse them." What does she mean? How is hair "symbolic of life"?
4. What does letting down one's hair symbolize? Find passages in the first paragraph where Ackerman discusses confining or loosening one's hair. Can you think of phrases from popular culture or literature that hint at this idea?
5. Reread paragraph #2. What might the "complex system of growth, death, and renewal" symbolize? Is she referring to more than just hair growth?

Styling

One way to create sentence variety is to use semicolons to connect two sentences (**independent clauses**). Ackerman writes:

> If the follicle cells grow in an even pattern, the hair will be straight; if they grow irregularly, the hair will be curly.

She could use a semicolon, a period, or a comma and conjunction:

> If the follicle cells grow in an even pattern, the hair will be straight. If they grow irregularly, the hair will be curly.

> If the follicle cells grow in an even pattern, the hair will be straight, but if they grow irregularly, the hair will be curly.

She chose the semicolon because the two sentences share the same structure and are closely related in thought. Each sentence contains an **introductory clause** followed by a comma and complete sentence.

> *If the follicle cells grow in an even pattern* (introductory clause)
> *If they grow irregularly* (introductory clause)

These clauses are introductory because they introduce the main sentences. These two sentences balance each other like two children of equal weight on either side of a teeter-totter. Connecting them with a semicolon emphasizes that balance.

PRACTICE For each of the following sentences, replace the period with a semicolon and add a complete sentence with an introductory clause.

> When Julia feeds her dachshund a Milk Bone treat, he rolls on the floor in ecstasy.

> If you feed and water orchids properly, they're easy to grow.

YOU TRY IT Write three sentences following the above pattern. Try this style in one of the Teaming Up activities or Writing Ideas.

Teaming Up

1. **Photo Connection:** Choose one of the photos and have each member of the group write a paragraph describing the hairdo and what it says about the person. Compare responses. Did you agree? What assumptions did you make about the person? What might be wrong with your assumptions?

2. **A Good Warm-up for Writing Idea #3.** Have each member of the group bring in information on hairstyles from another culture. You will probably need to go to the library. Try search terms like "hair and culture" or "hair and history." One example of a source would be *Hair: Its Power and Meaning in Asian Cultures* edited by Alf Hiltebeital et al. Share what you learned about the culture from your research. Write

down the source information from each member. Now you have a start on Writing Idea #2.

Writing Ideas

1. Write an essay that describes your own hairstyle and how it reflects your identity. Consider how your hair has changed over the years—or not—and what those changes (or lack of) say about you.
2. Like hair, clothing can also reveal culture or personality. Visit your college or local library and use both an online database such as Infotrac and the book catalogue to research clothing from another time or culture; then, write an essay that explains how clothing reflects the cultural values.
3. Visit your college or local library and use both an online database such as Infotrac and the book catalogue to research hairstyles from another country. Write an essay comparing hairstyles from your own culture and the one you researched. What did you learn about each culture?

Essay and Film Connections

"In the Kitchen" by Henry Louis Gates Jr. (not in this book, but available in *Best American Essays* college edition) explores the meaning of hair to the African Americans from his childhood. Ackerman's book, *The Natural History of the Senses,* was made into a 1995 PBS special. The musical *Hair,* while a bit outdated, gives a glimpse into the meaning of hair to the hippie culture of the 1960s.

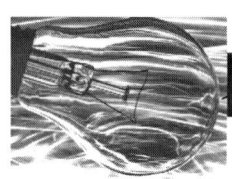

THE INDIAN WITH A CAMERA

Leslie Marmon Silko

In "The Indian With a Camera," Leslie Marmon Silko explores Native American views on visual images, and their spiritual significance, as well as the clash with the whites and their "intrusive vulgarity" when photographing Native American ceremonies. Silko has published several acclaimed novels, including Ceremony, Almanac of the Dead, and Gardens in the Dunes. This essay appears in her essay collection, Yellow Woman and the Beauty of the Spirit: Essays on Native American Life Today.

DUSTBIN OF HISTORY AND CULTURE

PETROGLYPHS: A carving or drawing on rock, especially by native people.
KIVA: An underground chamber in a Pueblo village used for ceremonies, councils, and other purposes.
KACHINA DANCES: Religious dances where the performer wears a mask depicting a sacred spirit or ancestor; the performer is thought to embody the spirit or ancestor while wearing the mask.
CACIQUE: Chieftain or leader.
QUETZALCOATL: A god of the Aztecs and Toltecs, depicted as a plumed serpent.

1   Petroglyphs on rock outcrops along the San Jose River suggest that the paleo-Indian ancestors of the Pueblos had already begun to make images of spiritual significance on the sandstone eighteen thousand years ago. Pueblo kivas have stylized abstract designs painted on the walls and altarpieces. The Pueblo people had long understood that certain manmade visual images were sacred and were necessary to Pueblo ceremony.

2   The Pueblo people did not fear or hate cameras or the photographic image so much as they objected to the intrusive vulgarity of the white men who gazed through the lens. My grandfather Henry Marmon attended Indian school in Riverside, California, which might explain his fascination with and purchase of a snapshot camera in the 1920s. As a child in the 1950s, I remember the delight of bringing out the old Hopi basket with the grasshopper-man design, because

"The Indian With a Camera" by Leslie Marmon Silko. Reprinted with the permission of Simon & Schuster, Inc., from *Yellow Woman and a Beauty of the Spirit* by Leslie Marmon Silko. Copyright © 1996 by Leslie Marmon Silko. All rights reserved.

Grandma Lily kept all of Grandpa Hank's snapshots and all the other family snapshots in the tall Hopi basket.

3   My sisters and cousins and I were too young to recognize the old-time people in the photographs, although we often recognized mesas and hills and certain houses. And so it was necessary that any viewing of the old snapshots in the Hopi basket be accompanied by a running commentary by my father and Grandma Lily, although they sometimes had to ask Grandpa Hank to help identify the really old Laguna people long dead and gone. The identification of the faces and the places in the photographs never failed to precipitate wonderful stories about the old days, which in turn brought out even older stories that stretched far beyond the confines of the snapshots in the grasshopper basket.

4   Our family is of mixed Laguna and white ancestry, but as a child I saw that many of the homes of the most traditional and conservative Laguna people included a great many photographs of family members.

5   At first, white men and their cameras were not barred from the sacred kachina dances and kiva rites. But soon the Hopis and other Pueblo people learned from experience that most white photographers attending sacred dances were cheap voyeurs who had no reverence for the spiritual. Worse, Pueblo leaders feared the photographs would be used to prosecute the caciques and other kiva members, because the United States government had outlawed the practice of the Pueblo religion in favor of Christianity exclusively.

6   Pueblo people may not believe that the camera steals the soul of the subject, but certainly the Pueblo people are quite aware of the intimate nature of the photographic image. Because Pueblo people appreciate so deeply the power and significance of the photographic image, they refuse to allow strangers with cameras the outrages to privacy that had been forced upon Pueblo people in the past.

7   Pueblo cultures seek to include rather than exclude. The Pueblo impulse is to accept and incorporate what works, because human survival in the southwestern climate is so arduous and risky. Before the Europeans appeared, the cultures of the Americas had vast networks of trade and commerce: during times of famine, trade partners sent food. Guatemalan macaw feathers went to Taos, and Minnesota pipestones to Honduras.

8   Europeans were shocked at the speed and ease with which Native Americans synthesized, then incorporated, what was alien and new. Mexican Indians had embraced Jesus, Mary, Joseph, and the saints almost at once; the Indians had happily set the Christian gods on

their altars to join the legions of older American spirits and gods. The Europeans completely misread the inclusivity of the Native American worldview, and they were disgusted by what they perceived to be weakness and disloyalty by the Indians to their Indian gods. For Europeans, it was quite unimaginable that Quetzalcoatl might ever share the altar with Jesus.

9 Euro-Americans project their own fears and values in their perception of a conflict between Native American photographers and traditional native artists. Traditional artists reassure the Euro-Americans that, while not extinct, Native Americans are not truly part of American society. The Indian with a camera is frightening for a number of reasons. Euro-Americans desperately need to believe that the indigenous people and cultures that were destroyed were somehow less than human; Indian photographers are proof to the contrary.

10 The Indian with a camera is an omen of a time in the future that all Euro-Americans unconsciously dread: the time when the indigenous people of the Americas will retake their land. Euro-Americans distract themselves with whether a real, or traditional, or authentic Indian would, should, or could work with a camera. (Get those Indians back to their basket making!)

11 Euro-Americans desperately try to deny what has already begun, that inexorable force which has already been set loose in the Americas. Hopi, Aztec, Maya, Inca—these are the people who would not die, the people who do not change, because they are always changing. The Indian with a camera announces the twilight of Eurocentric America.

12 Pueblo people today are quite sophisticated about film and video technology. Like all human beings they are concerned with their continued survival as the people *they believe themselves to be.* What is essential to all Pueblo people is that generation after generation will continue to remember and to tell one another who they are, who they have been, and who they may become.

13 Pueblo narratives are not mere bedtime stories or light entertainment. Through the narratives Pueblo people have for thousands of years maintained and transmitted their entire culture; not all the strategies and beliefs necessary to Pueblo survival are written, but they are remembered and repeated generation after generation. Even the most ordinary deer-hunting story is dense with information, from stalking techniques to weather forecasting and the correct rituals to be performed in honor of the dead deer. In short, the stories and reminiscences that enliven all Pueblo social gatherings are densely encoded with expression and information.

14   When the United States government began to forcibly remove Pueblo children to distant boarding schools in the 1890s, the Pueblo people faced a great crisis. Like the slaughter of the buffalo, the removal of Native American children to boarding schools was a calculated act of cultural genocide. How would the children hear and see, how would the children learn and remember what Pueblo people, what Native Americans for thousands of years had known and remembered together?

15   But the calculations failed. Eventually the children were returned to their beloved sandstone and expanses of blue sky: again the place soaked them in, and they were reunited with what continues and what has always continued.

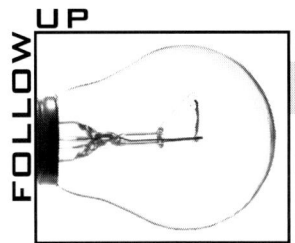

THE INDIAN WITH A CAMERA

Exploring Language

arduous: strenuous or difficult; requiring a lot of energy.
inexorable: adamant, obstinate; unmoved by pleas or reason.
omen: a sign of good or evil.
precipitate: to hasten (this word has many other connotations).
stylized: conform to a particular style.
synthesize: combine to create something new.
voyeur: someone who likes to observe private or intimate acts.

USAGE Look up "precipitate" and write a sentence for each connotation.

Thinking and Talking Points

1. What is Silko's main point? What examples does she use to support it?
2. In paragraph #2, Silko writes, "The Pueblo people did not fear or hate cameras or the photographic image so much as they objected to the intrusive vulgarity of the white men who gazed through the lens." What does she mean by "intrusive vulgarity?"
3. In what way do Pueblos "seek to include rather than exclude"? How does this tendency contribute to their survival?
4. How is the photographic image "intimate" for the Pueblos? How does this intimacy make "cheap voyeurs" of the whites behind the cameras?
5. In paragraph #11, Silko writes, "Pueblo people today are quite sophisticated about film and video technology. Like all human beings they are concerned with their continued survival as the people *they believe themselves to be.*" What do you think she means?

Styling

Sometimes writers will reverse an ordinary sentence structure for emphasis and sentence variety. You might be familiar with a listing sentence structure that uses a dash: complete sentence, followed by a dash and then a list. The dash will emphasize the list. But to emphasize the *sentence* or point rather than a list, a writer might *begin* the sentence with the list, creating suspense about the purpose of the list. Silko, in paragraph #10, writes:

> Hopi, Aztec, Maya, Inca—these are the people who would not die, the people who do not change, because they are always changing.

The list, occurring first, sets up the reader's mind to anticipate the purpose of the list; the sentence after the dash gets more attention, precisely as it should.

PRACTICE Brainstorm a list of items or ideas that go together. You might make a list of your favorite foods, politicians, films—almost anything. Next, write a sentence to follow the list, hopefully one with a significant point. Your list needs at least four items.

YOU TRY IT Create three more sentences with lists and significant points to emphasize. You might also want to attempt a more complex list like the one in the Styling with John Updike's "Disposable Rocket."

Teaming Up

1. Bring in a copy of an old family photo—the older the better. Do a quick freewrite of your impressions of the person. What is the **tone** of the picture? The time period? Describe the individual's expression and clothing, as well as any background that might be visible. Next, trade photos with someone in the group and write about that photo. Compare your impressions. Are they the same? If not, discuss why you had those impressions.

2. **A Good Warm-up for Writing Idea #2.** Have each person in the group bring in a Pueblo story. Read each story and analyze it for information about the culture. For ideas on what type of information to look for, see paragraph #13.

Writing Ideas

1. Read a Pueblo story and analyze it for information about the culture. Write an essay that explains how the story transmits different aspects of culture; think about the spiritual elements, food gathering or hunting, rituals or ceremonies, personal relationships, or moral lessons.
2. Compare the ideas on photography as well as the style in "The Indian With a Camera" and Saul Bellow's "Graven Images."

SECTION TWO   *Figuring It Out: Essays That Explain and Explore*   **137**

Essay and Film Connections

"Graven Images" by Saul Bellow explores photography. Other pieces that analyze images are "Museum Piece" by David Huddle and John Updike's "American Children." *Time Life* has a documentary on the disappearance of the Maya; the film *Smoke Signals*—written, directed, and produced by Native Americans—won awards at the 1998 Sundance film festival.

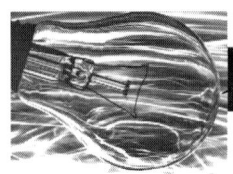

JOYAS VOLADORAS

Brian Doyle

Brian Doyle has several books of essays to his credit: Leaping: Revelations and Epiphanies, The Wet Engine: Exploring the Mad Wild Miracle of the Heart (where "Joyas Voladoras" appears), and Spirited Men. This essay also appeared in Best American Essays 2005. His collection of short stories is titled Epiphanies and Elegies.

1   Consider the hummingbird for a long moment. A hummingbird's heart beats ten times a second. A hummingbird's heart is the size of a pencil eraser. A hummingbird's heart is a lot of the hummingbird. *Joyas voladoras,* flying jewels, the first white explorers in the Americas called them, and the white men had never seen such creatures, for hummingbirds came into the world only in the Americas, nowhere else in the universe, more than three hundred species of them whirring and zooming and nectaring in hummer time zones nine times removed from ours, their hearts hammering faster than we could clearly hear if we pressed our elephantine ears to their infinitesimal chests.

2   Each one visits a thousand flowers a day. They can dive at sixty miles an hour. They can fly backward. They can fly more than five hundred miles without pausing to rest. But when they rest they come close to death: on frigid nights, or when they are starving, they retreat into torpor, their metabolic rate slowing to a fifteenth of their normal sleep rate, their hearts sludging nearly to a halt, barely beating, and if they are not soon warmed, if they do not soon find that which is sweet, their hearts grow cold, and they cease to be. Consider for a moment those hummingbirds who did not open their eyes again today, this very day, in the Americas: bearded helmetcrests and booted racket-tails, violet-tailed sylphs and violet-capped woodnymphs, crimson topazes and purple-crowned fairies, red-tailed comets and amethyst woodstars, rainbow-bearded thornbills and glittering-bellied emeralds, velvet-purple coronets and golden-bellied star-frontlets, fiery-tailed awlbills and Andean hillstars, spatuletails and pufflegs, each the most amazing thing you have never seen, each thunderous wild

"Joyas Voladoras" by Brian Doyle from *The American Scholar,* Volume 73, No. 4, Autumn 2004. Copyright © 2004 by the author. Used by permission.

heart the size of an infant's fingernail, each mad heart silent, a brilliant music stilled.

3   Hummingbirds, like all flying birds but more so, have incredible enormous immense ferocious metabolisms. To drive those metabolisms they have racecar hearts that eat oxygen at an eye-popping rate. Their hearts are built of thinner, leaner fibers than ours. Their arteries are stiffer and more taut. They have more mitochondria in their heart muscles—anything to gulp more oxygen. Their hearts are stripped to the skin for the war against gravity and inertia, the mad search for food, the insane idea of flight. The price of their ambition is a life closer to death; they suffer more heart attacks and aneurysms and ruptures than any other living creature. It's expensive to fly. You burn out. You fry the machine. You melt the engine. Every creature on earth has approximately two billion heartbeats to spend in a lifetime. You can spend them slowly, like a tortoise, and live to be two hundred years old, or you can spend them fast, like a hummingbird, and live to be two years old.

4   The biggest heart in the world is inside the blue whale. It weighs more than seven tons. It's as big as a room. It is a room, with four chambers. A child could walk around in it, head high, bending only to step through the valves. The valves are as big as the swinging doors in a saloon. This house of a heart drives a creature a hundred feet long. When this creature is born it is twenty feet long and weighs four tons. It is waaaaay bigger than your car. It drinks a hundred gallons of milk from its mama every day and gains two hundred pounds a day, and when it is seven or eight years old it endures an unimaginable puberty and then it essentially disappears from human ken, for next to nothing is known of the mating habits, travel patterns, diet, social life, language, social structure, diseases, spirituality, wars, stories, despairs, and arts of the blue whale. There are perhaps ten thousand blue whales in the world, living in every ocean on earth, and of the largest mammal who ever lived we know nearly nothing. But we know this: the animals with the largest hearts in the world generally travel in pairs, and their penetrating moaning cries, their piercing yearning tongue, can be heard underwater for miles and miles.

5   Mammals and birds have hearts with four chambers. Reptiles and turtles have hearts with three chambers. Fish have hearts with two chambers. Insects and mollusks have hearts with one chamber. Worms have hearts with one chamber, although they may have as many as eleven single-chambered hearts. Unicellular bacteria have

no hearts at all; but even they have fluid eternally in motion, washing from one side of the cell to the other, swirling and whirling. No living being is without interior liquid motion. We all churn inside.

6   So much held in a heart in a lifetime. So much held in a heart in a day, an hour, a moment. We are utterly open with no one, in the end—not mother and father, not wife or husband, not lover, not child, not friend. We open windows to each but we live alone in the house of the heart. Perhaps we must. Perhaps we could not bear to be so naked, for fear of a constantly harrowed heart. When young we think there will come one person who will savor and sustain us always; when we are older we know this is the dream of a child, that all hearts finally are bruised and scarred, scored and torn, repaired by time and will, patched by force of character, yet fragile and rickety forevermore, no matter how ferocious the defense and how many bricks you bring to the wall. You can brick up your heart as stout and tight and hard and cold and impregnable as you possibly can and down it comes in an instant, felled by a woman's second glance, a child's apple breath, the shatter of glass in the road, the words "I have something to tell you," a cat with a broken spine dragging itself into the forest to die, the brush of your mother's papery ancient hand in the thicket of your hair, the memory of your father's voice early in the morning echoing from the kitchen where he is making pancakes for his children.

FOLLOW UP: JOYAS VOLADORAS

Exploring Language

inertia: resistance to motion, action, or change.
infinitesimal: extremely small; too small to be measured.
ken: knowledge or understanding.
mitochondria: simply put, it's part of the cell.

Thinking and Talking Points

1. Find several comparisons Doyle makes (like "heart the size of an infant's fingernail"). How do these comparisons help the reader visualize and/or relate to the animals he's describing?
2. How do the examples and points show our relationship to the creatures? What is Doyle's overall point?
3. Is the conclusion unexpected? If so, what is the expectation? How do the examples relate to the conclusion?
4. Usually, beginning writers are told not to repeat words too close together. How does Doyle use repetition to his advantage?
5. Other than comparison, what other style techniques liven up this essay? Examine the length of the sentences. What do you notice? Also consider punctuation in your examination.

Styling

In addition to brilliant and vivid comparisons (see the Styling with Hoagland's "The Courage of Turtles"), this essay's unexpected conclusion—shifting from the physical workings of hearts to the emotional—moves the reader in almost the same way as the specific heartbreaks he mentions. It's these powerhouse **specifics**—a woman's second glance, a child's apple breath, the shatter of glass in the road, the words "I have something to tell you," a cat with a broken spine dragging itself into the forest to die, the brush of your mother's papery ancient hand in the thicket of your hair, the memory of your father's voice early in the morning echoing from the kitchen where he is making pancakes for his children—that make this conclusion so utterly unforgettable.

Notice that these examples are detailed as well as specific: not just a cat with a broken spine, but dragging itself into the forest to die; instead of simply mother's hand, it's papery ancient hand; a child's *apple* breath. These details hammer the heart, right on target.

PRACTICE   Think of an issue that concerns you, whether personal, social, or political. For example, you might be concerned about the plight of abused and neglected children; the unnecessary deaths of pets at a local animal shelter that still kills for space; a politician's views; a relative's health, and so on. Brainstorm a list of at least ten specific, detailed examples.

YOU TRY IT   Make a point about the issue you brainstormed, and write a sentence modeled on Doyle's concluding sentence. Consider livening up the conclusion to your next essay with this technique.

Teaming Up

1. The above Styling technique works well as a group activity. Everyone contribute an idea; then vote on which idea to brainstorm. Decide which examples are the most vivid or memorable, and then co-write the sentence.

2. **A Good Warm-up for Writing Idea #1:** Break down the parts of a machine—an automobile, an oven, washer or dryer, a computer, anything—or the anatomy of a particular animal (bird, insect, mammal). Have one person in the group list each part on a piece of paper. Discuss how each part might be a metaphor for a human emotion or personality trait, something like this:

   > beak = nagging
   > claws = jealousy
   > feathers = mothering

(You can use a particular animal or machine for your brainstorm: duck instead of bird; Volkswagen rather than car). List as many parts and traits as you can. Now examine the list for a tone: are the qualities mostly bitter, joyful, philosophical, sad, mean, humorous? Choose items from the list that seem similar in tone. Now co-write a paragraph comparing the animal parts to human behavior.

Writing Ideas

1. Using the warm-up in Teaming Up #2, write an essay that compares a person to either the parts of a machine or an animal. The person can be someone you know personally (a friend or relative, for example) or a public figure.
2. Compare and/or contrast Doyle's style and tone to Diane Ackerman's "Mute Dancers: How to Watch a Hummingbird." You might discuss a different style element—figurative language, sentence variety, word choice, punctuation—in each paragraph. Consider concluding with a contemplation of tone.

Essay and Film Connections

See the Writing Ideas and Essay and Film Connections with Hoagland's "The Courage of Turtles"; Ackerman's "Mute Dancers: How to Watch a Hummingbird"; Gordon Grice's "Black Widow."

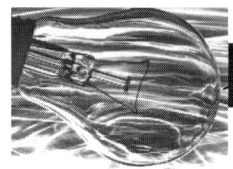

AMERICAN CHILDREN

John Updike

> John Updike was an American author of novels, poems, plays, essays, and frequent contributions to The New Yorker magazine. This essay, from his book Just Looking: Essays on Art, analyzes and compares two paintings of children, one by Winslow Homer and the other by John Singer Sargent. John Updike died in January, 2009.

DUSTBIN OF HISTORY AND CULTURE

WINSLOW HOMER: (1836–1910) Often considered one of the best 19th-century American naturalist painters.

JOHN SINGER SARGENT: (1856–1925) Primarily known for his portraits of wealthy and influential American families.

1   The boys and girls depicted here might not mix very well if they were released from their frames, but separately they compose two peaceful groups and two beautiful paintings. Winslow Homer's anonymous lads are taking their ease in a pasture; the daughters of the prosperous Edward Boit are scattered through two fine rooms, and all but one of them gaze with respectful curiosity at the busy bearded intruder into their home, the fashionable painter John Singer Sargent. The dashing impressionism of Sargent's technique carries a generation farther Homer's flickering grasses and dabs of sunny red, and the triangular pose of the little girl in the foreground mirrors the unified shape of the two country idlers. Both painters surround their childish subjects with large margins of environment. The effect is

See "Teaming Up" #1.

Daughters of Edward Boit by Singer Sargent.
Photograph © 2009 Museum of Fine Arts, Boston

"American Children," from *Just Looking* by John Updike, copyright © 1989 by John Updike. Used by permission of Alfred A. Knopf, a division of Random House, Inc.

SECTION TWO   *Figuring It Out: Essays That Explain and Explore*   **145**

See "Teaming Up" #1.

Boys in a Pasture by Winslow Homer.
Photograph © 2009 Museum of Fine Arts, Boston

of silence: silent vases, silent sky, silent carpet and turf underfoot. A great hushed world waits around these children to be tasted, explored, grown into.

2   They take themselves seriously, and are taken seriously. Homer gives his little subjects a monumental dignity; there is something of Greek drapery in the color-gouged fold of the sunlit white sleeve, and something angelically graceful in the extended, self-shadowed feet. And Sargent, catching his subjects where they have alighted like white butterflies, displays deep spaces about them, and permits them all the gravity their young femininity warrants. They recede, from youngest to oldest, toward a dark other room; beyond the toddler with her doll a girl no longer quite childish stands on the edge of shadow while her sister, a little taller and older still, is half-turned into it. The huge vase she leans against suggests a woman's shape. These young ladies are watching, not just the painter, but us, to see what we will do next, and whether what we do will be worthy of their responding. Like butterflies, they will elude us if we startle them.

3   Sargent's painting could have been a mere commission, an expert piece of toadying within the upper classes, but the jaunty eccentricity of its composition, and a daring within its deference, save it for art. Winslow Homer's could have been a bit of calendar art, falsely bucolic, but for the abstract power of a severe and stately composition that locks the barefoot pair as if forever into the center of the canvas and that lends solemn substance to a fleeting summer day. There is a mystery to the faces; the painter has declined all opportunity for easy anecdote within the ruddy shade of those hats.

4   Both artists have attempted honest portraits of children, as perhaps only Americans could have done. Though the Declaration of

Independence nowhere promises a better deal for children, the American child does appear freer than his European counterpart and is taken more seriously—as a source of opinion, as a market for sales, and as not just a future inheritor but an independent entity now, while still a child. Childhood and then youth are seen in our democracy as classes that cut across class distinctions. Within their frames these two sets of children are similarly pensive. Responsible but powerless, childhood does not smile; it watches and waits, amid shadows and sun.

Exploring Language

anecdote: a narrative account or story.
bucolic: relating to rural (country) life.
deference: respect or esteem for an elder or superior.
jaunty: carefree or high spirited.
pensive: thoughtful or meditative, in a dreamy sort of way, sometimes suggesting sadness.
toadying: brownnosing, flattering or, in modern slang, sucking up.

USAGE Practice using *pensive*; it's more descriptive than thoughtful. If friends or relatives accuse you of being distracted, you can say, "No, I'm just in a pensive mood today."

Thinking and Talking Points

1. What details in the essay help you understand the paintings or notice things you might otherwise have missed?
2. Updike comments that American children "appear freer" than European children, and are "taken more seriously—as a source of opinion, as a market for sales, and as not just a future inheritor but an independent entity now, while still a child." Do you agree or disagree that American children are taken seriously? Be ready to support your response with examples.
3. At the end of his essay Updike writes, "Responsible but powerless, childhood does not smile; it watches and waits, amid shadows and sun." What do you think he means? In what way is childhood "responsible but powerless"?
4. **Photo Connection:** Updike says of the children in the paintings that "there is a mystery to the faces" and "these two sets of children are similarly pensive." Study the paintings. What features—facial, posture—make them look this way?

Styling

Updike uses a colon to list silent objects in the painting, an effective way to create sentence variety, establish a mood, and gather supporting details. He writes:

> The effect is of silence: silent vases, silent sky, silent carpet and turf underfoot.

Use a colon only after a complete sentence.

Usually, you don't want to repeat a word as Updike does with silent, but sometimes it's an effective tool to make a point. Though we're mostly concerned with practicing using the colon, try his repetition technique as a style bonus. You wouldn't want to do this in a paper too frequently, but one sentence like this can make an impact.

PRACTICE Fill in the blanks with details that support the sentence. Here's an example:

> The concert radiated noise: *noisy drums, noisy bass,* and *noisy fans*.
>
> Jerry's bedroom oozed dust: _____, _____, and _____.
>
> After the storm, the old farmhouse leaked water: _____, _____, and _____.
>
> The items in the refrigerator were covered in mold: _____, _____, and _____.

YOU TRY IT Create five sentences of your own that begin with a complete sentence followed by a colon and a list of details. Try expanding your lists beyond three items.

Teaming Up

1. **Photo Connection:** In your group, study the two paintings. Discuss why you think Updike wrote that the children "might not mix very well if they were released from their frames." Co-write a dialogue between the two groups, what you imagine they would say to one another if they did meet.

2. Bring in a photograph of yourself (or someone else if you don't have a photo of yourself) as a child. Trade photos with another member of the group. Now write a description of the picture of your classmate,

describing the mood of the child by giving details of facial expression, setting, and clothing, and what you think he or she might have been thinking at the time of the photograph.

Writing Ideas

1. Write an essay about a time you felt powerless but responsible when you were a child.
2. Find a painting that moves you in some way. Write an essay describing the painting and the feelings it evokes.
3. Find two paintings or photographs by different artists of the same subject: two landscapes, two women, two men, two dogs, any subject. Write an essay comparing the two pieces of art.

Essay and Film Connections

Updike's book *Just Looking: Essays on Art* teems with essays full of style. David Huddle's essay "Museum Piece" is a delightful journey into the paintings of Jan Vermeer. The film *Artemisia* (1997), a historical drama set in 17th-century Italy, is based on the true story of the first woman to achieve success as an artist. The film gives a good look at the time period of Jan Vermeer—though Italian rather than Dutch. It's a bit immodest, rated R.

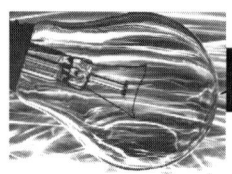

MUSICAL AWAKENINGS

Clayton S. Collins

This essay first appeared in Profiles: The Magazine of Continental Airlines. Clayton Collins discusses the work of neurologist and author Oliver Sacks, a strong believer in the healing power of music, and the essay contains fascinating case studies of people debilitated by stroke or other neurological diseases who are able to move once again when exposed to music.

DUSTBIN OF HISTORY AND CULTURE

FRIEDRICH NIETZSCHE: (1844–1900) A German philosopher, poet, and philologist (one who studies human speech, especially as it pertains to shedding light on culture). He coined the phrase "God is dead."

BIZET: (1838–1875) French composer best known for his operas, especially *Carmen*.

T. S. ELIOT: (1888–1965) British poet and critic. He won the Nobel prize for literature in 1948.

1   Oliver Sacks danced to the Dead. For three solid hours. At sixty. And with "two broken knees."

2   The Oxford-educated neurologist who likes to say, with an impish grin, that he doesn't like any music after Mozart's *Magic Flute,* wasn't particularly taken by the Grateful Dead concert in Friedrich Nietzsche's mnemonic sense, he explains (as only he would), "But in a tonic and dynamic sense they were quite overwhelming. And though I had effusions for a month after, it was worth it."

3   The power of music—not just to get an aging physician with classical tastes up and rocking, but also to "bring back" individuals rendered motionless and mute by neurological damage and disorders—is what's driving Sacks these days. The shyly brilliant and best-selling author of *The Man Who Mistook His Wife for a Hat* and *Awakenings*—the latter of which was made into a 1990 film starring Robin Williams—is working on another case-study book, one that deals in part with the role of music as a stimulus to minds that have thrown up stiff sensory barriers, leaving thousands of victims of stroke, tumors, Parkinson's

disease, Tourette's syndrome, Alzheimer's, and a wide range of less-publicized ailments alone, debilitated, and disoriented.

4   One sees how robust music is neurologically," Sacks says. "You can lose all sorts of particular powers, but you don't tend to lose music and identity." His conviction regarding the role of music in helping the neurologically afflicted to become mentally "reorganized" runs deep: "Whenever I get out a book on neurology or psychology, the first thing I look up in the index is music," he says. 'And if it's not there, I close the book."

5   Born in London in 1933 and a permanent resident of the United States for the past thirty-four years, Sacks is a frequent public speaker, careening from stories about great composers and poets to a report about goldfish dancing to a Strauss waltz. However, Sacks is a reluctant celebrity. The fourth son (three of them doctors) of two physicians, he preferred solitary research early in his career, far more comfortable extracting myelin from earthworms than working with humans. But when he misplaced a vial of the white fatty substance in 1966, he was banished, in effect, to the less-prestigious realm of clinical medicine. Since then, Sacks has burrowed deep into the illnesses and the lives of persons in his care, a miner in the catacombs of the catatonic, chipping away at the walls around their neurological cores. . . .

6   Much of what he has encountered, particularly in working with patients at Beth Abraham Hospital, in the Bronx, is startling. Much of it relates to music.

7   "One saw patients who couldn't take a single step, who couldn't walk, but who could dance," he says. "There were patients who couldn't speak, but who could sing. The power of music in these patients was instantaneous . . . from a frozen Parkinsonian state to a freely flowing, moving, speaking state."

8   Sacks remembers a woman with Parkinson's who would sit perfectly still until "activated" by the music of Chopin, which she loved and knew by heart. She didn't have to hear a tune played. "It was sometimes sufficient to give her an opus number," Sacks says. You would just say 'Opus 49,' and the F-minor *Fantasy* would start playing in her mind. And she could move."

9   Music is certainly cultural, acknowledges the doctor, but it is basically biological. "One listens to music with one's muscles," he says, quoting Nietzsche again. "The 'tonic' [the key] is mostly brainstem, an arousal response." The "dynamic"—how loud or forcefully the music is played—registers in the basal ganglia. And the "mnemonic"

aspect of songs speaks to the unique memories of individuals: from tribal chant to the blare of bagpipes to Bizet. The old cliché about music's universality, he says, has merit.

10 "Deeply demented people respond to music, babies respond to music, fetuses *probably* respond to music. Various animals respond to music," Sacks says. "There is something about the animal nervous system . . . which seems to respond to music all the way down."

11 "I don't know how it is with invertebrates. I think it's a desperately needed experiment to see how squids and cuttlefish respond," he says, his grin widening.

12 In 1974, Sacks was able to apply music therapy to himself to speed an orthopedic recovery. Hospitalized after a fall while climbing in Norway, he experienced neural damage and partial paralysis and sensed that he was, as a result, losing his "motor identity"—forgetting how to walk.

13 For weeks, flat on his back, he listened to a recording of a Mendelssohn violin concerto. One morning, awakened by the familiar piece, he got up and walked across the room to turn off the tape. He found that the concerto wasn't playing, except in his head. Then he realized he'd been walking, carried along by the tune. It was, he says, "the most dynamic experience in my life."

14 "I'm not normally all that fond of Mendelssohn," he jokes.

15 "I think the notion of music as being a prosthesis in a way, for neurological dysfunctions, is very fundamental," Sacks says, citing the case of a patient with damage to the frontal lobes of his brain.

16 "When he sings, one almost has the strange feeling that [music] has given him his frontal lobes back, given him back, temporally, some function that has been lost on an organic basis," Sacks says, adding a quote from T. S. Eliot: "You are the music, while the music lasts."

17 The key, says Sacks, is for patients to "learn to be well" again. Music can restore to them, he says, the identity that predates the illness. "There's a health to music, a life to music."

18 Those may not sound like the words of a typical clinician. But don't toss terms like "new age" and "holistic" at the good doctor. "I always tighten up a little bit when I hear the word 'holistic,'" he says, professing disdain for "Californian and Eastern" practices. For Sacks, who's been affiliated with a half-dozen neurological institutes and written dozens of seminal papers, medicine needs to be demonstrable, firmly grounded in physiology. Music's been healing for thousands of years, Sacks says. "It's just being looked at now more systematically and with these special populations."

19   So if the Grateful Dead moved Sacks to dance, it had been in the name of research. Seeking a clinical application, Sacks returned to Beth Abraham the next day and "kidnapped" one of his patients. "Greg" was an amnesiac with a brain tumor and no coherent memories of life since about 1969—but an encyclopedic memory of the years that came before, and a real love of Grateful Dead tunes.

20   Sacks took Greg to that night's show. "In the first half of the concert they were doing early music, and Greg was enchanted by everything," Sacks recalls. "I mean, he was not an amnesiac. He was completely oriented and organized and with it."

21   Between sets Sacks went backstage and introduced Greg to band member Mickey Hart, who was impressed with the depth of Greg's knowledge of the group but quite surprised when Greg asked after Pigpen. When told that the former band member had died twenty years before, "Greg was very upset," Sacks recalls. "And then thirty seconds later he asked, 'How's Pigpen?'"

22   During the second half, the band played its newer songs. And Greg's world began to fall apart. "He was bewildered and enthralled and frightened. Because the music for him—and this is an extremely musical man, who understands the idiom of the Grateful Dead—was both familiar and unfamiliar. . . . He said, 'This is like the music of the future.'"

23   Sacks tried to keep the new memories fresh. But the next day Greg had no memory of the concert. It seemed as if all had been lost. "But—and this is strange—when one played some of the new music, which he had heard for the first time at the concert, he could sing along with it and remember it."

24   It is an encouraging development. Amnesiacs have never been found capable of learning anything new. Children have been found to learn quickly lessons that are embedded in song. Sacks, the one-time quiet researcher, is invigorated by the possibilities. He wonders whether music could carry such information, to give his patient back a missing part of his life. To give Greg "some sense of what's been happening in the last twenty years, where he has no autobiography of his own."

25   That would have Sacks dancing in the aisles.

FOLLOW UP: MUSCIAL AWAKENINGS

Exploring Language

effusions: look up this word and decide which context Collins is using.
neurological: having to do with the nervous system.
mnemonic: assisting memory—like the childhood learning songs mentioned in Thinking and Talking Points #3. Those tools help you remember information.
myelin: a fatty white goo that helps protect nerves.
invertebrates: animals with no backbone (no spine).
orthopedic: having to do with the bones, or skeletal system.
prosthesis: artificial limb.
holistic: looking at the whole thing rather than its parts; when applied to medicine, it means treating the mind and body as one.
seminal: creative; contributing to later development. In other words, Sacks wrote papers that got people thinking and developing his ideas.
demonstrable: capable of being demonstrated.
invigorated: energized; renewed; restored.
enthralled: fascinated, absorbed.

USAGE Many of the words in the above list are medical and scientific terms which will be useful when reading and writing about those subjects. The words *effusions, invigorated, enthralled* beg to be used; they hop off the page. So in your essay, instead of writing "The song held my interest," write "The song enthralled me."

Thinking and Talking Points

1. According to Oliver Sacks, music is a powerful tool for healing. Go through the essay and list specific examples Sacks gives to support his view. What other powers can you attribute to music?
2. Collins writes that Sacks doesn't approve of "new age" or "holistic" therapies. But music therapy was once considered—and to some still is—quack medicine. What other once-considered-hogwash therapies

can you think of that have become mainstream? What is your opinion about some of these therapies? Do you base your view on personal experience or what you've read or heard from others?
3. Collins writes that "children have been found to learn quickly lessons that are embedded in song." Do you remember any of these learning songs from childhood?
4. Study the opening paragraph to this essay. How does it hook the reader's attention? Apply this technique of short, catchy sentences to your paragraph in Teaming Up #2.

Styling

In addition to a catchy opening and intriguing examples for support, Collins uses **metaphor** to spark life into his essay. He writes:

> Since then, Sacks has burrowed deep into the illnesses and the lives of persons in his care, a miner in the catacombs of the catatonic, chipping away at the walls around their neurological cores.

Collins compares Sacks to a miner and his patients' minds to catacombs. Look at this simple example from the Russell Sanders essay "Grub":

> Bloomington is ringed by the usual necklace of fast food shops.

The necklace image gives the reader a clearer picture of the town.
    Here's an example based on the Sanders model: *Laguna Beach is the McDonald's of the art world.*

PRACTICE (For another technique for creating figurative language, see Teaming Up #1.) Fill in the blanks below with your town or a nearby community and an appropriate metaphor. Try brainstorming lists of toys, brand name foods, or retail shops to get ideas for metaphors. For example, Barbie Doll becomes this sentence: *Beverly Hills is the Barbie Doll of Southern California.* Your metaphor should convey a recognizable attitude about the city. The Barbie Doll example works because Beverly Hills has a reputation for being full of affluent people who drive expensive cars, drink Evian water, and get a lot of plastic surgery; not everyone in Beverly Hills fits this stereotype, but enough do to make the metaphor appropriate. And let's face it, Barbie must have had breast implants, and she has everything.

_____ is the _____ of _____ .

YOU TRY IT Create three more sentences using metaphor. You can try this technique on other towns or cities you're familiar with, or describe friends or family members, your car, whatever sounds like fun: *My 1970 Chevy Vega is the Mr. Potato Head of the car world* (not very popular in our high-tech world, the Vega is seen as an oddity). Don't worry if some of the metaphors sound odd or silly. The idea is to practice creating metaphor.

Teaming Up

1. Here's a trick for creating a type of figurative language called **personification**. Form groups of three to five members and list some basic colors. Then list the various shades of that color. It helps if someone in the group has a set of colored pencils with various shades. Next, make a list of basic emotions. Think of as many words as you can that are similar for each emotion (synonyms). A thesaurus might help. Your lists might look like this:

Blue	*Happy*	*Sad*
navy	glad	unhappy
midnight	ecstatic	depressed
powder	cheerful	forlorn
peacock	delighted	melancholy
aquamarine	joyful	gloomy
royal	pleased	dejected

   Brainstorm other emotions. Now replace each shade of color with an emotion that you think describes that color. For example, peacock blue is a shocking color, so you might label it *ecstatic blue.* Midnight blue might become *melancholy blue.* Now attach each emotion/color combination to an object: melancholy blue recliner; forlorn pink ribbon. Finally, build sentences for each emotion/color/object combination:

   > The melancholy blue recliner sulked in the corner of the living room.
   >
   > My three-year-old sister's forlorn pink ribbon straggled limply through her tangled curls.

2. **A Good Warm-up for Writing Idea #1.** Have your group decide on a song that you all agree you like. I know this may be difficult with the diversity of tastes, but you can also use this activity to convince a dissenting member of the group that your song is worth listening to.

Have one member bring in the lyrics, and if possible, have everyone listen to the song before class and write down their reactions. In groups, read and analyze the lyrics. Compare reactions. Co-write a paragraph reporting your findings.

Writing Ideas

1. Think of a song that has an emotional impact on you—or simply a song you like. Listen to it several times and try to identify why the music moves you. Is it the tone? The rhythm? The way a particular instrument sounds? Try to describe the music for your reader. Study the lyrics. Does the song contain metaphor? Hidden meanings or allusions like a poem? Write an essay analyzing the song's impact through its music and message. Use at least one metaphor and one word from the vocabulary list.
2. Some music performers take on almost mythic status in our culture—the Beatles, Elvis, Tupac Shakur—while others burst onto the music scene and quickly fade. The Grateful Dead—while not exactly mythic—has quite a cult following. There are Dead Head clubs, Web sites—even the death of Jerry Garcia hasn't squashed the group's allure. Write an essay that attempts to explain the cult phenomenon that surrounds certain music groups, movies, or TV shows. Focus on one such group like the Grateful Dead's Dead Heads, *Star Trek* Trekkies, *Rocky Horror Picture Show* groupies. Try to find a photo to generate accurate description. Use at least one metaphor or personification in your essay.
3. Do some research on another area of unconventional medicine: acupuncture, chiropractic, herbal remedies, laugh therapy, meditation. Look at arguments from both sides of the issue. Your library should have books in the reference section that have articles on both sides of various arguments. Decide whether or not you think the therapy is credible. Provide numerous examples—as Collins does—to support your view. For tips on researching, see the Research section of this book.

Essay and Film Connections

"A Voice for the Lonely" by Stephen Corey also explores music's impact on mood and memory. You probably know more about music videos than I do, so I'm going to suggest a film related to music, *The Red Violin,* which traces the travels of a special violin throughout history, with a real surprise ending.

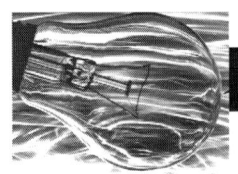

DISPOSABLE ROCKET

John Updike

John Updike was an American author of novels, poems, plays, essays, and frequent contributions to The New Yorker magazine. In "Disposable Rocket," Updike reflects on the male body, traveling through several stages in a man's life from boyhood to old age, comparing the male and female body, writing, "Inhabiting a male body is much like having a bank account; as long as it's healthy, you don't think much about it. Compared to the female body, it is a low-maintenance proposition." John Updike died in January, 2009.

DUSTBIN OF HISTORY AND CULTURE

BYRON: Lord George Gordon Byron (1788–1824). A prominent writer of the English Romantic Period.
DIANA: Roman goddess of the moon and hunting, also the protector of women.
DIONYSUS: Greek god—known by the Romans as Bacchus—of wine and revelry.
DON JUAN: An epic satirical poem by Lord Byron chronicling the adventures of the hero—Don Juan—who becomes Byron's mouthpiece for his views on wealth, power, society, sex, poets, and politicians in England. In the dedication of the work, Byron insults Coleridge and Wordsworth, two of his contemporaries, also renowned poets.
MARS: The Roman god of war. The Greeks identified him with their god Ares.
VENUS: Roman goddess of love and beauty. The Greeks identified her with their goddess Aphrodite.

1   Inhabiting a male body is much like having a bank account; as long as it's healthy, you don't think much about it. Compared to the female body, it is a low-maintenance proposition: a shower now and then, trim the fingernails every ten days, a haircut once a month. Oh yes, shaving—scraping or buzzing away at your face every morning. Byron, in *Don Juan,* thought the repeated nuisance of shaving balanced out the periodic agony, for females, of childbirth. Women are, his lines tell us,

> *Condemn'd to child-bed, as men for their sins*
> *Have shaving too entail'd upon their chins,—*

"The Disposable Rocket," from *More Matter: Essays and Criticism by John Updike,* copyright © 1999 by John Updike. Used by permission of Alfred A. Knopf, a division of Random House, Inc.

> *A daily plague, which in the aggregate*
> *May average on the whole with parturition.*

From the standpoint of reproduction, the male body is a delivery system, as the female is a mazy device for retention. Once the delivery is made, men feel a faint but distinct falling-off of interest. Yet against the enduring female heroics of birth and nurture should be set the male's superhuman frenzy to deliver his goods: he vaults walls, skips sleep, risks wallet, health, and his political future all to ram home his seed into the gut of the chosen woman. The sense of the chase lives in him as the key to life. His body is, like a delivery rocket that falls away in space, a disposable means. Men put their bodies at risk to experience the release from gravity.

2   When my tenancy of a male body was fairly new—of six or so years' duration—I used to jump and fall just for the joy of it. Falling—backwards, downstairs—became a specialty of mine, an attention-getting stunt I was practicing into my thirties, at suburban parties. Falling is, after all, a kind of flying, though of briefer duration than would be ideal. My impulse to hurl myself from high windows and the edges of cliffs belongs to my body, not my mind, which resists the siren call of the chasm with all its might; the interior struggle knocks the wind from my lungs and tightens my scrotum and gives any trip to Europe, with its Alps, castle parapets, and gargoyled cathedral lookouts, a flavor of nightmare. Falling, strangely, no longer figures in my dreams, as it often did when I was a boy and my subconscious was more honest with me. An airplane, that necessary evil, turns the earth into a map so quickly the brain turns aloof and calm; still, I marvel that there is no end of young men willing to become jet pilots.

3   Any accounting of male-female differences must include the male's superior recklessness, a drive not, I think, toward death, as the darker feminist cosmogonies would have it, but to test the limits, to see what the traffic will bear—a kind of mechanic's curiosity. The number of men who do lasting damage to their young bodies is striking; war and car accidents aside, secondary-school sports, with the approval of parents and the encouragement of brutish coaches, take a fearful toll of skulls and knees. We were made for combat, back in the post-simian, East African days, and the bumping, the whacking, the breathlessness, the pain-smothering adrenaline rush, form a cumbersome and unfashionable bliss, but bliss nevertheless. Take your body to the edge, and see if it flies.

4   The male sense of space must differ from that of the female, who has such interesting, active, and significant inner space. The space that interests men is outer. The fly ball high against the sky, the long pass spiraling overhead, the jet fighter like a scarcely visible pinpoint nozzle laying down its vapor trail at forty thousand feet, the gazelle haunch flickering just beyond arrow-reach, the uncountable stars sprinkled on their great black wheel, the horizon, the mountaintop, the quasar—these bring portents with them, and awaken a sense of relation with the invisible, with the empty. The ideal male body is taut with lines of potential force, a diagram extending outward; the ideal female body curves around centers of repose. Of course, no one is ideal, and the sexes are somewhat androgynous subdivisions of a species: Diana the huntress is a more trendy body-type nowadays than languid, overweight Venus, and polymorphous Dionysus poses for more underwear ads than Mars. Relatively, though, men's bodies, however elegant, are designed for covering territory, for moving on.

5   An erection, too, defies gravity, flirts with it precariously. It extends the diagram of outward direction into downright detachability—objective in the case of the sperm, subjective in the case of the testicles and penis. Men's bodies, at this juncture, feel only partly theirs; a demon of sorts has been attached to their lower torsos, whose performance is erratic and whose errands seem, at times, ridiculous. It is like having a (much) smaller brother toward whom you feel both fond and impatient; if he is you, it is you in curiously simplified and ignoble form. This sense, of the male body being two of them, is acknowledged in verbal love play and erotic writing, where the penis is playfully given its own name, an individuation not even the rarest rapture grants a vagina. Here, where maleness gathers to a quintessence of itself, there can be no insincerity, there can be no hiding; for sheer nakedness, there is nothing like a hopeful phallus; its aggressive shape is indivisible from its tender-skinned vulnerability. The act of intercourse, from the point of view of a consenting female, has an element of mothering, of enwrapment, of merciful concealment, even. The male body, for this interval, is tucked out of harm's way.

6   To inhabit a male body, then, is to feel somewhat detached from it. It is not an enemy, but not entirely a friend. Our essence seems to lie not in cells and muscles but in the traces our thoughts and actions inscribe on the air. The male body skims the surface of nature's deep, wherein the blood and pain and mysterious cravings

of women perpetuate the species. Participating less in nature's processes than the female body, the male body gives the impression—false—of being exempt from time. Its powers of strength and reach descend in early adolescence, along with acne and sweaty feet, and depart, in imperceptible increments, after thirty or so. It surprises me to discover, when I remove my shoes and socks, the same paper-white hairless ankles that struck me as pathetic when observed them on my father. I felt betrayed when, in some tumble of touch football twenty years ago, I heard my tibia snap; and when, between two reading engagements in Cleveland, my appendix tried to burst; and when, the other day, not for the first time, there arose to my nostrils out of my own body the musty attic smell my grandfather's body had.

7   A man's body does not betray its tenant as rapidly as a woman's. Never as fine and lovely, it has less distance to fall; what rugged beauty it has is wrinkle-proof. It keeps its capability of procreation indecently long. Unless intense athletic demands are made on it, the thing serves well enough to sixty, which is my age now. From here on, it's chancy. There are no breasts or ovaries to admit cancer to the male body, but the prostate, that awkwardly located little source of seminal fluid, shows the strain of sexual function with fits of hysterical cell replication, and all that beer and potato chips add up in the coronary arteries. A writer, whose physical equipment can be minimal, as long as it gets him to the desk, the lectern, and New York City once in a while, cannot but be grateful to his body, especially to his eyes, those tender and intricate sites where the brain extrudes from the skull, and to his hands, which hold the pen or tap the keyboard. His body has been, not himself exactly, but a close pal, pot-bellied and balding like most of his other pals now. A man and his body are like a boy and the buddy who has a driver's license and the use of his father's car for the evening; he goes along, gratefully, for the ride.

Exploring Language

aggregate: on the whole, or combined. Byron means that shaving for men—because it's a daily nuisance—on the whole may equal the agony of childbirth for women, which occurs less frequently.

androgynous: appearing partly male, partly female; of unclear gender.

chasm: a deep opening in the earth; sometimes refers to a wide difference in feelings, thoughts, or interests.

cosmogonies: theories about the origin of the universe.

ignoble: common, of low birth or origin; second rate; coarse; lacking refinement.

increments: stages of increasing number or value.

imperceptible: undetectable or unnoticeable; slight or minimal.

parturition: childbirth.

parapet: a balcony or low wall along the edge of a roof.

polymorphous: assuming or having many forms (*poly* means many or several).

portents: a sign of the future; an omen.

post-simian: after the apes (the prefix *post* means after).

tenancy: a tenant is someone who rents or occupies land or property, so tenancy means possession or status as a tenant.

quintessence: the most typical example or epitome; the purest or most perfect form.

USAGE Examine the passage where Updike uses the word *cosmogonies*. Why would he use this word in the same context with feminism?

Thinking and Talking Points

1. Updike writes, "The space that interests men is outer." How does he think it differs from female space? Do you agree or disagree? Why?
2. What other comparisons or contrasts—other than space—does Updike make between males and females? Do you agree with him? Explain.
3. Updike claims that "To inhabit a male body, then, is to feel somewhat detached from it." In what way does he mean that males are detached

from their bodies? How is that different from females' relationship with their bodies?
4. Look up information on the gods and goddess—Diana, Dionysus, Mars, and Venus—that Updike mentions, either on the Internet or in a dictionary of mythology. What point is he trying to make about our view of the human body? Think of the types of ads Updike mentions. Do you agree with his assertions?
5. In what way is a rocket "disposable"? What qualities does the male body share with a disposable rocket? What other metaphors does Updike use? Do they tie together a common theme or idea in the essay?
6. Updike writes that his subconscious was "more honest" with him as a child. What do you think he means? Is your subconscious less honest now than when you were younger?

Styling

Many writers use lists of specific examples beaded together in one long sentence to give a feeling of continuity or chaos, excitement or enormity. In "Disposable Rocket," Updike creates a vivid list to illustrate what he calls male "space":

> The space that interests men is outer. The fly ball high against the sky, the long pass spiraling overhead, the jet fighter like a scarcely visible pinpoint nozzle laying down its vapor trail at forty thousand feet, the gazelle haunch flickering just beyond arrow-reach, the uncountable stars sprinkled on their great black wheel, the horizon, the mountaintop, the quasar—these bring portents with them, and awaken a sense of relation with the invisible, with the empty.

Notice the structure of this sentence. Updike first makes his list—each item in the series separated with a comma—followed by a dash, followed by a complete sentence.

PRACTICE Fill in the blanks below with a list to go with each sentence. Don't resort to using all one-word objects. Notice that Updike sometimes describes or uses simile, "the jet fighter like a scarcely visible pin-point nozzle laying down its vapor trail at forty thousand feet."

_____, _____, _____, _____, _____, _____, _____—these are a few of my favorite things.

SECTION TWO *Figuring It Out: Essays That Explain and Explore* 165

_____, _____, _____,
_____, _____, _____,
_____—all of these annoyances I've learned to live with.

_____, _____, _____,
_____, _____, _____,
_____—that was the best summer of my life.

YOU TRY IT Based on the Updike model, write five sentences of your own containing long lists. Use this sentence style in your next writing assignment.

Teaming Up

1. **A Good Warm-up for Writing Idea #1.** Before class, do a quick freewrite or journal entry about a dream you had and what you think the dream means. You might consult a dream dictionary if you're stuck. In your group, describe your dream, and ask the other team members what they think it means. Discuss whether your analysis matches your classmates'. What did you learn about yourself or other group members?

2. **Photo Connection and Warm-up for Writing Idea #2.** Have each member of the group research the painting by Botticelli, *Birth of Venus* (available on the Internet), and do a freewrite describing her body type; then, write about what you think society considers the ideal female body type today. Compare your responses. Discuss how Botticelli's depiction of the ideal woman might differ from today's view. Who would be today's Venus?

Writing Ideas

1. Updike writes about the act of falling being prominent in his dreams when he was a boy. Think about a dream you had as a child—or maybe a more recent dream—and write an essay discussing what you think the dream meant, how it figured into events in your life. Explain in what way your subconscious might have been "more honest" with you as a child. You might compare a dream you had as a child to an adult dream.

2. Research visual depictions of the gods and goddesses Updike mentions in his essay—Venus, Diana, Mars, Dionysus. Write an essay comparing

each god and goddess to today's popular models. Is there a big change in our view of the ideal male and female image as Updike indicates? Why might we be moving toward a more androgynous ideal?

3. Think of an object that makes a good metaphor for a member of your family. Write an essay explaining how this person is like the object, but give at least three qualities that the person shares with the object, explaining in detail what they have in common. For example, if your mother is old fashioned in her views, has a tarnished halo—meaning you discovered something shocking about her—but puts on a respectable or prudish front, you might use an antique silver teapot as the metaphor, explaining how she holds old-fashioned—antiquated—notions about gender roles (girls cook, boys take out the trash, for example), but you found out she paid her way through college working in a strip joint when you thought she was above reproach (tarnished like silver), yet she seems prudish (gets offended at an off-color joke or won't let you wear a mini-skirt).

Essay and Film Connections

In "Graven Images," Saul Bellow writes about the power of the media over our self-image by the photos they choose to print, making us look glamorous or "worse than the Ruins of Athens." *In the Company of Men* delves into the darker world of male culture—it's a shocking film you won't soon forget. *The Deer Hunter* gives another peek into the tribe of men.

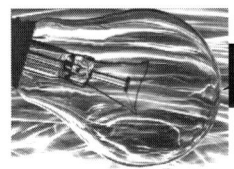

GRAVEN IMAGES

Saul Bellow

> One of America's most prominent writers of literature and nonfiction, Saul Bellow won the Nobel Prize in 1976 for his novel *Humboldt's Gift*. "Graven Images" first appeared in the periodical *News from the Republic of Letters* in 1997 and was chosen for the 1998 edition of *Best American Essays*. It also appears in *The Best American Essays of the Century*, edited by Joyce Carol Oates. In this essay, Bellow discusses the media's power to decide—through photography—"how you are to be seen publicly," to "bring you down when they think you have gotten ahead of yourself—when they suspect you of flying too high."

DUSTBIN OF HISTORY AND CULTURE

AMOUR PROPRE: A French term meaning love of oneself or self-esteem.
ANTONY AND CLEOPATRA: One of Shakespeare's historical plays.
ARISTOTLE: Greek philosopher who lived from 384–322 B.C.
WILLIAM BLAKE: (1757–1827) Considered the greatest visionary poet in English as well as an accomplished artist, Blake wrote numerous poems and critical essays, among them his famous collection of poems *Songs of Innocence and Experience*.
CORSICA: An island in the Mediterranean near Sardinia.
DIMITRI KARAMAZOV: A character in the Russian novel *The Brothers Karamazov* by Fydor Dostoyevsky (1821–1881).
FREUD: A 19th-century doctor who founded psychoanalysis and the theory called the Oedipus Complex, which says that children will have an erotic attachment to the parent of the opposite sex.
HARRY S. TRUMAN: (1884–1972) Thirty-third president of the United States (1948-1953); he ordered the atomic bombing of the Japanese cities Hiroshima and Nagasaki.
PABLO PICASSO: (1881–1973) Spanish painter and sculptor, known for his innovative styles, among them Cubism.
PYRENEES: Mountains along the French and Spanish border.

1   Harry S. Truman liked to say that as president of this country he was its most powerful citizen—but sometimes he added, smiling, the photographers were even more powerful. They could tell the

"Graven Images" by Saul Bellow as appeared in *News from The Republic of Letters*. Copyright © 1997 by Saul Bellow, reprinted with the permission of The Wylie Agency, Inc.

commander in chief where to go, make him move his chair, cross his legs, hold up a letter, order him to smile or to look stern. He acknowledged their power and, as a political matter, deferred to their judgment. What the people thought of their chief executive would to some extent be decided by the photographers and the picture editors. Photographers may claim to be a priesthood interpreting the laws of light, and light is a universal mystery that the picture takers measure with their light meters. "In nature's book of infinite mystery, a little I can read," says the Egyptian soothsayer in *Antony and Cleopatra*. Pictures taken in the light must be developed in the shallow mystery of darkrooms. But photographers have nothing in common with soothsayers. Their interests, apart from the technical one, are social and political. To some extent, it is they who decide how you are to be publicly seen. Your "visual record" is in their hands.

2   Broadly speaking, your *amour propre* is the territory invaded by the picture takers. You may wish or not wish to be in public life. Some people have not the slightest desire to be in the papers or on TV. Others feel that papers and TV screens confer immortality. TV crews on a city street immediately attract big crowds. The arrival of television cameras offers people the opportunity each and every one of them has dreamt of—a shot at eternity. Not by deeds, not by prayers, but solely by their faces, grinning and mugging.

3   But this aspect of modern image-making or idolatry is not, for me, the most interesting one. What I discover when I search my soul is that I have formed a picture of myself as I wish to be seen, and that while photographers are setting up their lights and cameras I am summoning up and fortifying that picture. My intent is to triumph over the photographers' vision of me—their judgment as to what my place in photographic reality is to be. They have *technics*—Science—on their side. On my side there is vanity and deceit—there is, as I have already said, *amour propre;* there is, moreover; a nagging sense that my powers of candor are weakening and sagging, and that my face betrays how heavily it is mortgaged to death. *Amour propre,* with all its hypocritical tricks, is the product of your bourgeois outlook. Your aim is to gain general acceptance for your false self, to make propaganda, concealing your real motives—motives of personal advantage. You persuade people to view you as you need to be viewed if you are to put it over on them. We all are, insofar as we live for our *amour propre,* loyal to nothing except our secret, crippled objectives— the objectives of every "civilized" man.

4   Et cetera.

5   Yes, we're all too familiar with *amour propre,* thanks to the great romantic writers of the nineteenth century. But give clever people something to understand and you can count on them to understand it. So in facing the photographers it's not the exposure of my *amour propie* that concerns me. What I feel in making innumerable last-minute ego arrangements is that the real me will decide to withhold itself. I know that the best picture instruments of Germany or "state-of-the-art" Japan are constructed for ends very different from mine. What need is there to bring these powerful lenses up to the very tip of my nose? They will meaninglessly enlarge the pores of my skin. You will supply them with shots that remind viewers of the leg of a mosquito photographed through a microscope. The truth about you is that you have lost more hair than you thought and that your scalp is shining through—the truth is that you have huge paisley-shaped bruises under your eyes and that your bridgework when you smile is far from "photogenic." You are not simply shown—you are exposed. This exposure cannot be prevented. One can only submit to the merciless cruelty of "pure objectivity," which is so hard on your illusions.

6   Then, too, from a contemporary point of view, the daily and weekly papers—to say nothing of television—do not feel that they are honoring the truth if they do not tear away the tatters of vanity that cover our imperfections. No one is safe from exposure except the owners, the main stockholders, and the leading advertisers of the great national papers. Things weren't always like this. The "gentlemen" described by Aristotle are immune to shame—they are made that way; nothing shameful can touch these aristocrats. But Adam and Eve, when they had eaten the apple of self-consciousness, sewed fig leaves together to cover their nakedness.

7   It is the (not always conscious) premise of the photographer that his is the art of penetrating your private defenses. We, his subjects, can learn not to care. But we are not by any means an Aristotelian class, trained in the virtues. We are democrats and lead our petty lives in the shadow of shame. And for this as for all our weaknesses and vices there arise, in all civilized countries, entire classes of people, categories of specialists who specialize in *discovery* and exposure.

8   Their slogan is: Let the Record Show. And what the record shows is, of course, change and decay, instability, weakness and infirmity, darkness as endless and winding as the Malabar Caves as E. M. Forster years ago described them in *A Passage to India.*

9   A photograph that made me look worse than the Ruins of Athens was published by *Time* together with a line from William Blake: "The lineaments of gratified desire." Nowhere in the novel *Time* was reviewing had I so much as hinted that my face, with its lineaments, was anything like the faces Blake had in mind (faces of prostitutes, as his text explicitly tells us). But there was my dreary, sullen, tired, and aging mug. I was brought low by Blake's blazing words. But it is the prerogative of the mass media to bring you down when they think that you have gotten ahead of yourself—when they suspect you of flying too high. It doesn't damage us to be exposed, to appear in distorted shapes on film or slick paper or newsprint. I often remember how at the age of ninety-nine Freud's grandmother complained that in the paper "they made me look a hundred years old."

10 But picture editors and journalists often seem to feel that they are the public representatives of truth, and even that they are conferring some sort of immortality on you by singling you out. But you had better be prepared for rough treatment. Often your "privacy" is to them a cover for the lies and manipulations of *amour propre*.

11 Who would have thought that minor vanities might lead to such vexations. Your secrets will die in the glare of publicity. When the police strip Dimitri Karamazov to his foul underpants, he says to them, "Gentlemen, you have sullied my soul."

12 But the world has undergone a revolutionary transformation. Such simple, romantic standards of personal dignity and of the respect due to privacy are to be found today only in remote corners of backward countries. Maybe in the Pyrenees or in the forgotten backlands of Corsica—places where I shouldn't care to live. Everywhere else, the forces of insight are on the lookout. The function of their insights is to make your secrets public, for the public has a right to know, and it is the duty of journalists to deliver the secrets of people "in the news" to their readers. For every story has a story behind it—which is to say that your face, in its own way a story, the story that you present, has another; sometimes very different story underlying it, and it is through the skill of the photographer that these layers of story are revealed.

13 Painters and sculptors, whose publics are smaller, also approach our heads and faces with insight. They class themselves as artists and are more intellectually sophisticated—better educated than photographers. They have generally absorbed a certain amount of twentieth-century psychology, and their portraits may be filled or formed by their ideas and they may have a diagnostic intent. Do you want to

know whether X, our subject, is a violent narcissist? Or whether his is a real, a human face, not a false ideological mask or disguise.

14   The photograph—to narrow it down—reduces us to two dimensions and it makes us small enough to be represented on a piece of paper or a frame of film. We have been trained by the camera to see the external world. We look *at* and not *into,* as one philosopher has put it. We do not allow ourselves to be *drawn* into what we see. We have been trained to go by the externals. The camera shows us only those, and it is we who do the rest. What we do this *with* is the imagination. What photographs have to show us is the external appearance of objects or beings in the real world, and this is only a portion of their reality. It is after all a convention.

15   I have known—and still know—many excellent photographers whose work I respect. There are demonic, sadistic camera technicians, too. All trades are like that. But neither the kindly nor the wicked ones can show us the realities we so hope—or long—to see.

16   Finally, there is the ancient Jewish rule forbidding graven images. My maternal grandfather refused to have his picture taken. But when he was dying my mother brought in a photographer and hid him behind the bushes.

17   This faded picture is one of my Old World legacies. I also inherited the brass family samovar and my mother's silver change purse. In this purse I now carry Betapace, Hytrin, and Coumadin tablets.

18   My grandfather's picture was taken in the late 1890s. He is sitting, dying in an apple orchard, his beard is spread over his upper body. His elbow rests on the top of his walking stick and his hand supports his head. His big eyes tell you that he is absorbed in *olam ha-bo*—the world to come, the next life. My mother used to say, "He would have, been very angry with me. To make pictures was sinful [an *averah*], but I took the *averah* on myself."

19   When we were very young, my parents told us that until we came of age they would be responsible for our transgressions. But that is an altogether different matter. What I am saying here is that nowadays not even the nobs have their portraits painted, and the masses preserve the faces of ancestors in daguerreotypes and Kodaks. The critical mind sees an insignificant photographer hidden in the bushes, inserting a plate and pulling the cloth over his head. Perhaps the old man knew perfectly well that his picture was being taken. My mother was then old enough to bear the burden of this sin. She committed it because she loved him and was afraid of forgetting what he had looked like.

20   In any case, I have been not only photographed but cast in bronze and also painted. Since I am too impatient to sit still, painters and sculptors have worked from photographs. The Chicago Public Library exhibits the busts of bookish local boys. The artist who did my head was obliged to measure it while I was watching the Chicago Bulls on television. It was an important game and I didn't intend to miss it.

21   Considering the bronze head on display in the Harold Washington Library, I think that Pablo Picasso would have done it better. He might perhaps have given me a third eye and two noses. I'd have loved two noses.

22   But for a one-nose job, the bust in the Chicago library isn't at all bad.

GRAVE IMAGES

Exploring Language

bourgeois: middle class.
candor: directness; honesty.
ideological: of beliefs or convictions, usually referring to political or economic viewpoints of a particular group.
idolatry: the worship of an idol or image.
narcissist: one in love with his or her own image or self (deriving from the Greek myth of a youth, Narcissus, who fell in love with his own image in a pool of water).
prerogative: privilege or right.
samovar: a Russian device that keeps water at the boiling point for tea; tea urn.
soothsayer: a prophet, or one who sees the future.
transgression: an offense or violation of a law, rule, command, or bounds of propriety.
vexation: irritation, annoyance.

Thinking and Talking Points

1. To what degree does Bellow's self-image hold up to the photographer's view? What is his how-he-wants-to-appear image vs. the photographer's depiction of him?
2. Bellow writes that photographers' interests are "social and political." What does he mean? Think of recent examples from the media.
3. Bellow writes, "For every story has a story behind it—which is to say that your face, in its own way a story, the story that you present, has another, sometimes very different story underlying it." What does he mean? Where else in the essay does he bring up this idea of illusion vs. reality?
4. Explain the references to Aristotle and Adam and Eve. Why does he compare them?
5. Are picture editors and journalists "public representatives of truth"? Explain and give examples, both from the essay and your own observations.

Styling

Go through Bellow's essay and pick out the sentences where he uses dashes. Notice that he uses them two ways: one dash to set off a clause or phrase at the end of a sentence, and a set of dashes to draw attention to an interrupter in the middle of a sentence. Let's focus on using the dash at the end of a sentence. Here's an example from the essay:

> Harry S. Truman liked to say that as president of this country he was its most powerful citizen—but sometimes he added, smiling, the photographers were even more powerful.

Examine the sentence. When writers use dashes, they do so to draw special attention to part of the sentence. In this case, Bellow wants to emphasize the power of the photographers, the subject of his essay. What comes after the dash does not have to be a complete sentence—it's the writer's choice.

Here's a student sample:

> My cat, Mozart, sleeps contentedly in the sun—until he hears the can opener.

Note: For practice using the dash with interrupting clauses, see the Styling section that accompanies David Huddle's "Museum Piece."

PRACTICE   Fill in the blanks after the dash in each sentence below with sentences or phrases that you think should have emphasis.

> *The Catcher in the Rye,* a popular novel read in high school, has been challenged over the years as unsuitable for teens—_____

> All my friends flocked to see the film *Pirates of the Caribbean* _____

YOU TRY IT   Modeling the above structure, write five sentences using dashes.

Teaming Up

1. **A Good Warm-up for Writing Idea #1.** Bring in two pictures of yourself: one you like and one you dislike. Before class, freewrite about each picture, discussing what formed your opinion. Don't tell your group which is which. Have each member of the group study

your photos and write what they think about each one. Do they like the same one as you? What formed their opinions? How does your private image of yourself and your group's view match your own or differ? Do this procedure for each member of the group.

Writing Ideas

1. Write an essay about the image you wish to portray to the public, your camera face. Describe the process you go through to prepare this image for the camera and your surprise when the picture doesn't turn out the way you expect. What did you learn about the mask you wear?
2. Find a photo—either by browsing through family albums or visiting the library photography section—that might be distorting reality. For example, a picture of two sisters linking arms portrays a picture of sisterly camaraderie, but in reality, the sisters might not be speaking to one another. Describe the photo and then bust the illusion, telling the story behind the story.
3. Visit an online database at a public or college library, one that has access to newspapers and magazines. Examine several newspaper articles, perhaps different views of the same story. Write an essay that discusses the media's distortion of reality, not only in images, but in articles as well. Using your research for examples and evidence, answer this question: Is the journalism of the main-stream media becoming nothing more than tabloid journalism?

Essay and Film Connections

"Burl's" by Bernard Cooper explores the things-aren't-always-what-they-seem topic. The films *The Crying Game* and *Desert Bloom* also explore the illusion vs. reality theme.

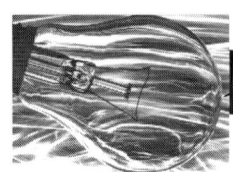

THE BLACK WIDOW

Gordon Grice

Professor of English and humanities, spirerololgist Gordon Grice eloquently explores the brutal world of the black widow spider, at the same time busting our misconceptions and urban legends about this misunderstood arachnid. His essays have been published in Harper's, High Plains Literary Review (the source of this essay), and Best American Essays 1996. He also has a book aptly titled The Red Hourglass.

DUSTBIN OF HISTORY AND CULTURE

BOUFFANT: A hairdo where the hair has been teased into a high, puffy dome on top of the head.

GARGOYLE: An architectural adornment that spouts water out of the rain gutters of buildings; the gargoyle, originally lion heads like those on the Parthenon in Athens, became associated with more grotesque beasts in the Middle Ages.

LYRE: A stringed instrument related to the harp, originating in ancient Greece.

1   I hunt Black Widow. When I find one, I capture it. I have found them in discarded wheels and tires and under railroad ties. I have found them in house foundations and cellars, in automotive shops and toolsheds, in water meters and rock gardens, against fences and in cinderblock walls. I have found them in a hospital and in the den of a rattlesnake, and once on the bottom of the chair I was sitting in.

2   Sometimes I raise a generation or two in captivity. The egg sacs produce a hundred or more pinpoint cannibals, each leaving a trail of gleaming light in the air, the group of them eventually producing a glimmering tangle in which most of them die, eaten by stronger sibs. Finally I separate the three or four survivors and feed them bigger game.

3   Once I let several egg sacs hatch out in a container about eighteen inches on a side, a tight wooden box with a sliding glass top. As I tried to move the box one day, the lid slid off and I fell, hands first, into the mass of young widows. Most were still translucent newborns, their bodies a swirl of brown and cream. A few of the females had eaten enough to molt; they had the beginnings of their blackness.

"The Black Widow" by Gordon Grice as appeared in *High Plains Review*. Used by permission of the author.

Their tangle of broken web clung to my forearms. They felt like trickling water in my arm hairs.

4   I walked out into the open air and raised my arms into the stiff wind. The widows answered the wind with new strands of web and drifted away, their bodies gold in the late sun. In about ten minutes my arms carried nothing but old web and the husks of spiderlings eaten by their sibs.

5   I have never been bitten.

6   The black widow has the ugliest web of any spider. The orb weavers make those seemingly delicate nets that poets have traditionally used as symbols of imagination, order, and perfection. The sheet web spiders weave crisp linens on the grass. But the widow makes messy-looking tangles in the corners and bends of things and under logs and debris. Often the web is littered with leaves. Beneath it lie the husks of insect prey, their antennae still as gargoyle horns, cut loose and dropped; on them and the surrounding ground are splashes of the spider's white urine, which looks like bird guano and smells of ammonia even at a distance of several feet. This fetid material draws scavengers—ants, sow bugs, crickets, roaches, and so on—which become tangled in vertical strands of silk reaching from the ground up into the web. The widow comes down and, with a bicycling of the hind pair of legs, throws gummy silk onto this new prey.

7   When the prey is seriously tangled but still struggling, the widow cautiously descends and bites the creature, usually on a leg joint. This is a killing bite; it pumps neurotoxin into the victim. The widow will deliver a series of bites as the creature dies, injecting substances that liquefy the organs. Finally it will settle down to suck the liquefied innards out of the prey, changing position two or three times to get it all.

8   Before the eating begins, and sometimes before the victim dies from the slow venom, the widow usually moves it higher into the web. It attaches some line to the prey with a leg-bicycling toss, moves up the vertical web strand that originally snagged the prey, crosses a diagonal strand upward to a higher point on a different vertical strand, and here secures the line. It has thus dragged the prey's body up off the ground. The whole operation is like that of a person moving a load with block and tackle. It occurs in three dimensions—as opposed to the essentially two-dimensional operations of orb weavers and sheet weavers.

9   You can't watch the widow in this activity very long without realizing that its web is not a mess at all but an efficient machine. It allows

complicated uses of leverage and also, because of its complexity of connections, lets the spider feel a disturbance anywhere in the web—usually with enough accuracy to tell the difference at a distance between a raindrop or leaf and viable prey.

10   The web is also constructed in a certain relationship to movements of air so that flying insects are drawn into it. This fact partly explains why widow webs are so often found in the face-down side of discarded car wheels—the wheel is essentially a vault of still air that protects the web, but the central hole at the top allows airborne insects to fall in. An insect that is clumsy and flies in random hops, such as a June beetle, is especially vulnerable to this trap. The widow often seems to choose her building sites according to indigenous smells rather than creating her own stinking waste pile from scratch. The webs turn up, for example, in piles of trash and rotting wood. A few decades ago, the widow was notorious for building its home inside the works of outdoor toilets. Scraping around with a stick before using the toilet was a common practice.

11   The architectural complexities of the widow web do not particularly impress the widows. They move around in these webs almost blind, yet they never misstep or get lost. In fact, a widow forcibly removed from its web and put back at a different point does not seem confused; it will quickly return to its habitual resting place. Furthermore, widows never snare themselves, even though every strand of the web is a potential trap. A widow will spend a few minutes every day coating the clawed tips of its legs with the oil that lets it walk the sticky strands. It secretes the oil from its mouth, coating its legs like a cat cleaning its paws.

12   The human mind cannot grasp the complex functions of the web but must infer them. The widow constructs it by instinct. A brain smaller than a pinhead contains the blueprints, precognitive memories the widow unfolds out of itself into actuality. I have never dissected with enough precision or delicacy to get a good specimen of the black widow brain, but I did glimpse one once. A widow was struggling to wrap a praying mantis when the insect's forelegs, like scalpels mounted on lightning, sliced away the spider's carapace and left exposed the clear droplet of bloody brain.

13   Widows reportedly eat mice, toads, tarantulas—anything that wanders into that remarkable web. I have never witnessed a widow performing a gustatory act of that magnitude, but I have seen them eat scarab beetles heavy as pecans; carabid beetles strong enough to

prey on wolf spiders; cockroaches more than an inch long; and hundreds of other arthropods of various sizes. Widows begin life by eating their siblings. An adult female will fight any other female; the winner often eats the loser. A popular game among Mexican children is to stage such fights and bet on the outcome. The children put the widows on a stick and pass it around so that everyone can see. Sometimes one female ties another up and leaves without killing her. I have come across such black pearls wrapped in silk and, upon peeling off the skin, seen the pearls unfold their legs and rush away.

14   The widow gets her name by eating her lover, though this does not always happen. He distinguishes himself from ordinary prey by playing her web like a lyre. Sometimes she eats him without first copulating; sometimes she snags him as he withdraws his palp from her genital pore. Sometimes he leaves unharmed after mating; in this case, he soon withers and dies on his own. I have witnessed male and female living in platonic relationships in one web. The males' palps, still swollen with sperm, proved that these relationships had not been sexual.

15   Many widows will eat as much as opportunity gives. One aggressive female had an abdomen a little bigger than an English pea. She snared a huge cockroach and spent several hours subduing it, then three days consuming it. Her abdomen swelled to the size of a largish marble, its glossy black stretching to a tight red-brown. With a different widow, I decided to see whether that appetite was really insatiable. I collected dozens of large crickets and grasshoppers and began to drop them into her web at a rate of one every three or four hours. After catching and consuming her tenth victim, this bloated widow fell from her web, landing on her back. She remained in this position for hours, making only feeble attempts to move. Then she died.

16   The first thing people ask when they hear about my fascination with the widow is why I am not afraid. The truth is that my fascination is rooted in fear.

17   I have childhood memories that partly account for my fear. When I was six my mother took my sister and me to the cellar of our farmhouse and told us to watch as she killed a widow. With great ceremony she produced a long stick (I am tempted to say a ten-foot pole) and, narrating her technique in exactly the hushed voice she used for discussing religion or sex, went to work. Her flashlight beam found a point halfway up the cement wall where two marbles hung together—one crisp white, the other a glossy black. My mother ran her stick

through the dirty silver web around them, and as it tore it sounded like the crackling of paper in fire. This sound is unique to the widow's powerful web—anybody with a little experience can tell a widow's work from another spider's by ear. The black marble rose on thin legs to fight off the intruder. As the plump abdomen wobbled across the wall, it seemed to be constantly throwing those legs out of its path. The impression it gave was of speed and frantic anger, but actually a widow's movements outside the web are slow and inefficient. My mother smashed the widow onto the stick and carried it up into the light. It was still kicking its remaining legs. Mom scraped it against the sidewalk, grinding it to a paste. Then she returned for the white marble—the widow's egg sac. This, too, came to an abrasive end.

18   My mother's stated purpose was to teach us how to recognize and deal with a dangerous creature we would probably encounter on the farm. But of course we also took the understanding that widows were actively malevolent, that they waited in dark places to ambush us, that they were worthy of ritual disposition, like an enemy whose death is not sufficient but must be followed with the murder of his children and the salting of his land and whose unclean remains must not touch our hands.

19   The odd thing is that so many people, some of whom presumably did not first encounter the widow in such an atmosphere of mystic reverence, hold the widow in awe. Various friends have told me that the widow always devours her mate, or that her bite is always fatal to humans—in fact, it almost never is. I have heard told for truth that goods imported from the Orient are likely infested with widows and that women with bouffant hairdos have died of widow infestation. Any contradiction of such tales is received as if it were a proclamation of atheism.

20   The most startling contribution to the widow's mythical status I have ever encountered was *Black Widow: America's Most Poisonous Spider,* a book that appeared in 1945. Between genuine scientific observations, the authors present the widow as a lurking menace with a taste for human flesh. They describe the experiments of other investigators; one involved inducing a widow to bite a laboratory rat on the penis, after which event the rat "appeared to become dejected and depressed." Perhaps the most psychologically revealing passage is the authors' quotation from another writer, who said the "deadliest Communists are like the black widow spider; they conceal their red underneath."

21 We project our archetypal terrors onto the widow. It is black; it avoids the light; it is a voracious carnivore. Its red markings suggest blood. Its name, its sleek, rounded form invite a strangely sexual discomfort; the widow becomes an emblem for a man's fear of extending himself into the blood and darkness of a woman, something like the legendary Eskimo vampire that takes the form of a fanged vagina.

22 The widow's venom is, of course, a soundly pragmatic reason for fear. The venom contains a neurotoxin that can produce sweats, vomiting, swelling, convulsions, and dozens of other symptoms. The variation in symptoms from one person to the next is remarkable. The constant is pain. A useful question for a doctor trying to diagnose an uncertain case: "Is this the worst pain you've ever felt?" A "yes" suggests a diagnosis of black widow bite. Occasionally people die from widow bites. The very young and the very old are especially vulnerable. Some people seem to die not from the venom but from the infection that may follow; because of its habitat, the widow carries dangerous microbes.

23 Some researchers hypothesized that the virulence of the venom was necessary for killing beetles of the scarab family. This family contains thousands of species, including the June beetle and the famous dung beetle the Egyptians thought immortal. All the scarabs have thick, strong bodies and unusually tough exoskeletons, and many of them are common prey for the widow. The tough hide was supposed to require a particularly nasty venom. As it turns out, the venom is thousands of times more virulent than necessary for this purpose. The whole idea is full of the widow's glamour: an emblem of eternal life killed by a creature whose most distinctive blood-colored markings people invariably describe as an hourglass.

24 No one has ever offered a sufficient explanation for the dangerous venom. It provides no evolutionary advantages: all of the widow's prey items would find lesser toxins fatal, and there is no particular benefit in killing or harming larger animals. A widow that bites a human being or other large animal is likely to be killed. Evolution does sometimes produce such flowers of natural evil—traits that are neither functional nor vestigial but utterly pointless. Natural selection favors the inheritance of useful characteristics that arise from random mutation and tends to extinguish disadvantageous traits. All other characteristics, the ones that neither help nor hinder survival, are preserved or extinguished at random as mutation links them with

useful or harmful traits. Many people—even many scientists—assume that every animal is elegantly engineered for its ecological niche, that every bit of an animal's anatomy and behavior has a functional explanation. This assumption is false. Nothing in evolutionary theory sanctions it; fact refutes it.

25   We want the world to be an ordered room, but in a corner of that room there hangs an untidy web. Here the analytical minds find an irreducible mystery, a motiveless evil in nature, and the scientist's vision of evil comes to match the vision of a God-fearing country woman with a ten-foot pole. No idea of the cosmos as elegant design accounts for the widow. No idea of a benevolent God is comfortable in a world with the widow. She hangs in her web, that marvel of design, and defies teleology.

THE BLACK WIDOW

Exploring Language

abrasive: in this context, harsh or rough.

archetypal: an archetype is a recurrent character type, plot, symbol, or theme of seemingly universal significance; Carl Jung believed human beings have a collective subconscious and therefore have similar dreams. For example, dreams of flying or falling occur in almost every culture, as do literary archetypes like "Cinderella," which has variants in virtually every culture, going back as far as 500 B.C. China.

arthropods: a scientific term for animals with jointed limbs, segmented bodies (think ants), and exoskeletons (instead of skeletons, a hard outer shell), which includes insects, mollusks (snails), and crustaceans (lobster, shrimp).

carapace: protective shell or shell-like covering.

fetid: having a bad odor.

gustatory: relating to the sense of taste.

indigenous: occurring naturally in a particular region or environment, as in "indigenous species."

irreducible: cannot be made smaller or simpler.

insatiable: impossible to satisfy.

malevolent: vicious ill-will.

neurotoxin: a toxin or poison that damages or destroys nerve tissue.

pragmatic: practical.

teleology: study of design in nature.

vestigial: body part left over from evolution that no longer has a purpose.

virulence: in this context, intensely poisonous.

voracious: eager to consume large quantities of food.

USAGE Look up "abrasive" for meanings other than the one in the Exploring Language list and use it in a sentence that implies one of those meanings.

Thinking and Talking Points

1. Reread the introduction to Grice's essay. Does the first sentence hook the reader? Why or why not? What is the effect of his listing all of the places where he has found black widows?
2. Find where the essay refutes our preconceived notions of the black widow. Did you hold these same ideas about the spider? How does Grice dispel these notions?
3. What is Grice's point in writing this essay? Is he trying to persuade you or merely inform? Defend your stand with evidence from the essay.
4. Hunt down the numerous **metaphors** and **similes** in this essay. How do they help convey an attitude about the black widow?
5. How does the essay provide information that helps the reader hunt for black widows (if desired)?
6. Grice writes in paragraph #22, "The whole idea is full of the widow's glamour: an emblem of eternal life killed by a creature whose most distinctive blood-colored markings people invariably describe an hourglass." What does he mean by glamorous? What does the hourglass have to do with glamour?

Styling

Many students—and non-students—think of punctuation as a mysterious code known only to English teachers that has very little purpose other than creating pause for the reader. While punctuation does create pause, it also helps strengthen your writer's voice, to say what you want to say, dramatically or demurely, simply or with complexity. Punctuation is style.

You might have noticed that Gordon Grice uses dashes in different ways for dramatic interruption or pause. Study the three ways he uses dashes: with a simple interruption, with a list that interrupts a sentence, and at the end of a sentence for emphasis.

Dashes with a simple interrupter:

> Many people—even many scientists—assume that every animal is elegantly engineered for its ecological niche, that every bit of an animal's anatomy and behavior has a functional explanation.

Notice that if you remove the words enclosed with dashes, the sentence still makes sense:

> Many people assume that every animal is elegantly engineered for its ecological niche, that every bit of an animal's anatomy and behavior has a function explanation.

When practicing the use of dashes with an interrupter, test the sentence to see if you can remove the material within the dashes and still have a complete, coherent sentence. You might choose to use commas with an interrupter, or parentheses, but dashes draw attention to the interrupter "even many scientists," alerting the reader to the fact that even scientists—usually credited with logical thinking—make wrong assumptions.

Hint: Avoid using dashes with simple adjectives or prepositional phrases.

Dashes with an internal list that interrupts the sentence:

> The fetid material draws scavengers—ants, sow bugs, crickets, roaches, and so on—which become tangled in vertical strands of silk reaching from the ground up into the web.

Again, you could take out the list and dashes and the sentence would still be grammatically correct and make sense: "The fetid material draws scavengers which become tangled in vertical strands of silk reaching from the ground up into the web."

CAUTION In the sentence above, dashes become essential; without the dashes, the word "scavengers" crashes into "ants," wreaking havoc with the sentence's meaning. If you use commas instead of dashes here, your reader might think "scavengers" is part of the list that includes ants rather than ants being an example of a scavenger in a list of other such bugs.

Dashes at the end for emphasis:

> Widows reportedly eat mice, toads, tarantulas—anything that wanders into that remarkable web.

> Then she returned for the white marble—the widow's egg sac.

> Various friends have told me that the widow always devours her mate, or that her bite is always fatal to humans—in fact, it almost never is.

> Her flashlight beam found a point halfway up the cement wall where two marbles hung together—one crisp white, the other a glossy black.

In these examples, Grice might have chosen to use a comma at the end of his sentence to connect non-essential or extra material, but the dash creates a bit of drama, a longer pause, lingering on those set-off words, both on the page and in the reader's mind.

PRACTICE In each of the sentences below, fill in the blanks with appropriate material.

Simple Interrupter
The bird—_____—cautiously flitted down to the bird feeder.

List That Interrupts
Those flowers—_____, _____, _____, and _____—do not grow well on that side of the house.

At the End for Emphasis
Hummingbirds will attack almost anything—_____

YOU TRY IT Write five of each type of dash sentence: five with simple interrupters, five with a list, and five with one dash at the end for emphasis.

Teaming Up

1. **A Good Warm-up for Writing Idea #2:** Brainstorm urban legends you've heard about or read on the Internet. What fear does each legend prey on? Do you find these hoaxes helpful or harmful?

2. **A Good Warm-up for Writing Idea #3:** Bring in a legend, fable, or story about an animal. Read all of the stories in your group and discuss what each story reveals about the culture. Choose one story to read to the rest of the class. Pick someone to read the story—or you can share the responsibility—and another member(s) to present your ideas.

Writing Ideas

1. Hunt another insect, perhaps one people usually think of as creepy or one that you fear: another type of spider, a preying mantis, a beetle, a centipede, or whatever you fancy. Be sure it's one that can be found in your immediate area. You might need to look up information on the creature's habits like what it eats, what habitat it likes, what time of year it can easily be located. Write an essay that attempts to persuade the reader of the creature's worthiness; maybe it's environmentally helpful or a friend to gardeners. Maybe it's simply fascinating. Use description, **figurative language**, and debunking of preconceived ideas about the critter.

2. A lot of urban legends get circulated on the Internet; you might have been victim to some of these untruths, usually sent as warnings to beware of some danger lurking around the next corner. Before the Internet, such stories circulated through word of mouth. Gather some of these myths, and write an essay that attempts to explain our fascination with these hoaxes and argues whether or not they're helpful, either warning of dangers that *could* occur or the opposite, that they incite fear and paranoia in an otherwise safe environment. Are they cautionary tales or fear-mongering?
3. Choose an animal and research myths and legends from different cultures about that animal. You might try Native American myths and legends, legends from around the world, *Aesop's Fables,* or a collection of animal myths from almost any country. Choose at least three different cultures and write an essay that explains how the culture views that creature and what that view reveals about the culture, its fears or hopes, its view about animals in general.

Essay and Film Connections

Several animal essays in Sparks include "Mute Dancers: How to Watch a Hummingbird" by Diane Ackerman, "The Courage of Turtles" by Edward Hoagland, and "Joyas Voladoras" by Brian Doyle. For films, consider *Grizzly Man, Winged Migration,* and, of course, *March of the Penguins.*

SECTION THREE

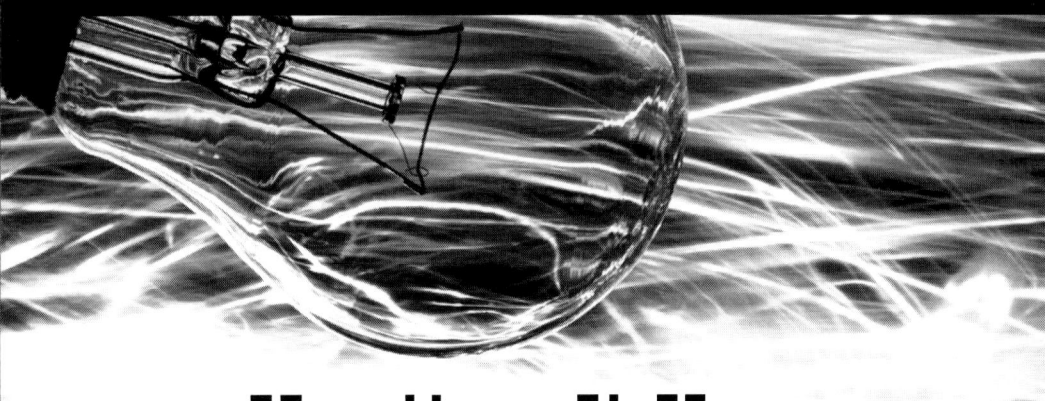

Heating It Up: Essays That Argue

INTRODUCTION

Did Disney butcher Hans Christian Andersen's original story "The Little Mermaid"? Should drugs be legalized? Do concerts that raise money for aid to Africa really help? Are cowboys tender-hearted rather than rough-and-tough like those Marlboro ads portray? The writers in this section address these questions, and more, attempting to lure you to their point of view.

That attempt can be subtle like Barbara Holland's "Naps," an argument in favor of taking an afternoon siesta like most of the rest of the world. In "Fiddling While Africa Starves," P. J. O'Rourke is more forthright and controversial, stating, "African famine is not a visitation of fate. It is largely man-made, and the men who made it are largely Africans." Joseph Epstein proclaims that our culture is too focused on celebrities in "The Culture of Celebrity." Whether argued gently or vehemently, an argument attempts to persuade the reader, or at least make them think.

An argument essay should provoke controversy and debate, get you thinking about two sides of an issue, help you consider angles of a topic you might not have contemplated (see Section Five for argument strategies).

I've tried to avoid the beat-into-the-ground issues like gun control, the death penalty, and mercy killing (with the exception of Gore Vidal's "Drugs" because he takes a different perspective, and the age of the essay illustrates that not much has changed in the drug war). You can't come up with anything new to say about such topics, and you're probably familiar with most of the arguments, so why bother?

When reading these essays, whether you agree or disagree, study how well the writers support their arguments, and how they refute the opposing side. Do you find it hard to refute the points in the essays or can you easily find areas that haven't been addressed?

So read on, analyze, and find a topic that fires you up, that moves you to speak out. Then you'll know you have something worth writing about and be on your way to a good argument paper.

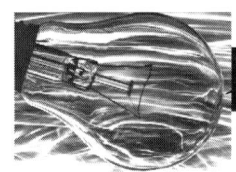

THE LITTLE MERMAID

Pauline Kael

> Pauline Kael wrote film reviews for the The New Yorker magazine from the 1960s until her retirement in 1991. For a collection of her reviews, see the book For Keeps. In this short review, Kael lambastes Disney for turning Hans Christian Andersen's The Little Mermaid into "a bland reworking of old Disney fairy tales, featuring a teen-age tootsie in a flirty seashell bra."

DUSTBIN OF HISTORY AND CULTURE

HANS CHRISTIAN ANDERSEN: A Danish writer (1805–1875) credited with the creation of modern children's stories. He gained popularity writing literary fairy tales, *The Little Mermaid* being the original story that Disney "borrowed."

ROALD DAHL: A writer of children's books, *James and the Giant Peach* and *Charlie and the Chocolate Factory* two of his most popular.

THE DARK CRYSTAL: A fantasy film for children, exploring the dark side of the soul.

KITSCH: A German word for tasteless or sentimental junk-art (sources: *The Concise Oxford Dictionary*, Ninth Edition, and *Merriam Webster's Collegiate Dictionary*, Tenth Edition).

FAUST: A man who sells his soul to the devil, in an old story made most famous by German poet and playwright Johann Wolfgang Goethe.

THE SECRET OF NIMH: A film based on the children's fantasy book *Mrs. Frisby and the Rats of Nimh* by Robert O'Brien.

WHERE THE WILD THINGS ARE: Children's fantasy picture book by Maurice Sendak about a boy named Max—angry at his mother and banished to his room without supper—who fantasizes sailing across the sea to a land of wild beasts.

1   Hans Christian Andersen's tear-stained *The Little Mermaid* is peerlessly mythic. It's the closest thing women have to a feminine Faust story. The Little Mermaid gives up her lovely voice—her means of expression—in exchange for legs, so she'll be able to walk on land and attract the man she loves. If she can win him in marriage, she will gain an immortal soul; if she can't, she'll be foam on the sea.

2   I didn't expect the new Disney *The Little Mermaid* to be Faust, but after reading the reviews ("everything an animated feature should be," "reclaims the movie house as a dream palace," and so on) I

"The Little Mermaid" by Pauline Kael. Copyright © 1989 by Pauline Kael. Reprinted by permission of Curtis Brown, Ltd.

expected to see something more than a bland reworking of old Disney fairy tales, featuring a teen-age tootsie in a flirty seashell bra. This is a technologically sophisticated cartoon with just about all the simpering old Disney values in place. (The Faust theme acquires a wholesome family sub-theme.) The film does have a cheerful calypso number ("Under the Sea"), and the color is bright—at least, until the mermaid goes on land, when everything seems to dull out.

3   Are we trying to put kids into some sort of moral-aesthetic safe house? Parents seem desperate for harmless family entertainment. Probably they don't mind this movie's being vapid, because the whole family can share it, and no one is offended. We're caught in a culture warp. Our children are flushed with pleasure when we read them *Where the Wild Things Are* or Roald Dahl's sinister stories. Kids are ecstatic watching videos of *The Secret of Nimh* and *The Dark Crystal.* Yet here comes the press telling us that *The Little Mermaid* is "due for immortality." People are made to feel that this stale pastry is what they should be taking their kids to, that it's art for children. And when they see the movie they may believe it, because this *Mermaid* is just a slightly updated version of what their parents took them to. They've been imprinted with Disney-style kitsch.

Exploring Language

aesthetic: pleasing to the senses; often refers to artistic taste.
peerlessly: peerless means unrivaled, unequaled, unmatched.
simpering: smiling in a silly way.
tootsie: slang for female, akin to cutie-pie, but can also imply a woman of ill repute (prostitute).
vapid: dull, flat, boring, unimaginative.

USAGE Use at least one of the Exploring Language words in your next writing assignment, or look one up in a thesaurus and choose a lively substitute.

Thinking and Talking Points

1. Kael writes that in the original version of *The Little Mermaid*, the mermaid will gain an immortal soul if she marries the prince, a detail Disney left out. Even though you may not have read the original story or seen the film, what do you think might be lost in the story by omitting the idea of gaining an immortal soul?
2. How convincing is Kael's review? List specific evidence in the review that did or did not convince you.
3. Kael writes, "This is a technologically sophisticated cartoon with just about all the simpering old Disney values in place." What values do you think she means? How are they simpering?
4. Kael asks, "Are we trying to put kids into some sort of moral-aesthetic safe house?" What do you think? Are parents "desperate for harmless family entertainment"? Do children lose out, as Kael indicates, by being shielded from the classics in favor of blander cartoon versions?

Styling

A Good Warm-up for Writing Idea #1. Specific examples are necessary in any essay; if you don't support your point with specific examples, your reader will think you don't know your subject. Kael cites several children's books and films, holding them up as standards, comparing them to Disney, illustrating Disney cartoons' inferiority. She didn't just write, "Other books and films are better." Instead, she reminds us of specific children's stories, hoping we'll remember and think, "I loved *Where the Wild Things Are* when I was a kid."

If you tell a friend, "I couldn't sleep all night because of the noises," your friend will mostly likely sympathize and ask, "What noises?" You would then proceed to give specific examples: somebody snoring, a barking dog, dripping faucet. Here's a paragraph from F. Scott Fitzgerald's *The Great Gatsby*:

> I couldn't sleep all night; a fog-horn was groaning incessantly on the Sound, and I tossed half sick between grotesque reality and savage frightening dreams. Toward dawn I heard a taxi go up Gatsby's drive and immediately I jumped out of bed and began to dress—I felt that I had something to tell him, something to warn him about and morning would be too late.

The groaning fog-horn, the frightening dreams, and the taxi breathe life into the paragraph.

PRACTICE Think of a genre of films—action/adventure, comedy, science fiction, horror, drama—and make a list of titles from that genre.

YOU TRY IT Using three or four of the items from your above list—you may have to alter the list to fit the **topic sentence**—write a paragraph with a topic sentence that makes a claim about that genre (something like "Most horror films attempt to scare the viewer with cheap gore-and-guts rather than a strong plot"). In a sentence or two, explain why each film title you chose from the list supports that topic sentence.

Teaming Up

1. In your group, discuss the children's literature and film examples Kael mentions in her essay, or other childhood favorites. What do you remember about the stories? What makes them literature rather than kitsch? If you have time, read one of these stories before discussion.

2. Kael writes, "They've been imprinted with Disney-style kitsch." In your group, make a list of all the places in our culture where you see Disney products or images and list companies you know Disney owns. Discuss in what ways a company like Disney might influence society. Use your list and discussion to co-write a paragraph. Be sure

your topic sentence expresses an opinion; you might attempt to answer this question: have we been "imprinted with Disney-style kitsch"? Explain how the examples you use from the list support your opinion. If your group disagrees, it's okay to split up and write two paragraphs with different opinions.

Writing Ideas

1. Use your paragraph from the Styling section as a supporting paragraph of a larger essay.
2. Almost every culture has a version of the "Cinderella" fairy tale. Read several Cinderella versions. Choose two of the stories from different cultures and write a comparison/contrast essay. What do the differences tell us about the culture?
3. Watch another Disney fairy tale film and read the older version of the story—many of the written stories are from Grimms' fairy tales. Write an essay comparing the two, making a judgment about which story is more meaningful and why. Or read the original *The Little Mermaid* by Hans Christian Andersen and do a more in-depth comparison of it to the Disney version.

Essay and Film Connections

Other essays critiquing culture include "The Celebrity of Culture" by Joseph Epstein and "Toys" by Roland Barthes. Davenport films has a series of fairy tales—though set in rural America in different time periods—that keep the flavor and integrity of the original Grimms'. My favorites: *Willa: An American Snow Write, Bearskin,* and *Bristlelip,* available from Davenport Films, Delaplane, Virginia. *Pan's Labyrinth* is another favorite.

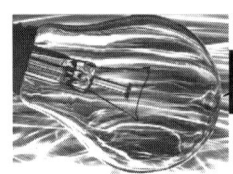

DRUGS

Gore Vidal

> Gore Vidal has written essays and novels, among them Myra Breckenridge (1968), one of his most famous. More recent works include The Golden Age, a novel, and The American Presidency, Vidal's view of the history of this highest office and the men who have served in it. In this essay, Vidal argues that we should legalize all drugs and provide warning labels, as we do for cigarettes. He states, "This will require heroic honesty. Don't say that marijuana is addictive or dangerous when it is neither, as millions of people know—unlike 'speed,' which kills most unpleasantly, or heroin, which is addictive and difficult to kick."

DUSTBIN OF HISTORY AND CULTURE

Fu Manchu: A Chinese villain with a long mustache who appears in stories by Sax Rohmer, later made into films—the character was usually played by a white man.

GNP: Gross National Product.

Dr. Spock: Benjamin Spock, child pediatrician who wrote *The Common Sense Book of Baby and Child Care* (1946), a controversial book which advocated affection and more permissiveness toward children, and is believed to have had a major impact on child rearing.

Dr. Leary: Timothy Leary, identified with the hippie subculture. In a 1967 speech, he coined the phrase "you must turn on, tune in, and drop out."

1   It is possible to stop most drug addiction in the United States within a very short time. Simply make all drugs available and sell them at cost. Label each drug with a precise description of what effect—good and bad—the drug will have on the taker. This will require heroic honesty. Don't say that marijuana is addictive or dangerous when it is neither, as millions of people know—unlike "speed," which kills most unpleasantly, or heroin, which is addictive and difficult to kick.

2   For the record, I have tried—once—almost every drug and liked none, disproving the popular Fu Manchu theory that a single sniff of opium will enslave the mind. Nevertheless, many drugs are bad for certain people to take and they should be told why in a sensible way.

"Drugs" by Gore Vidal, copyright © 1970 by Gore Vidal, from *Homage to Daniel Shays: Collected Essays 1952–1972* by Gore Vidal. Used by permission of Random House, Inc.

3   Along with exhortation and warning, it might be good for our citizens to recall (or learn for the first time) that the United States was the creation of men who believed that each man has the right to do what he wants with his own life as long as he does not interfere with his neighbor's pursuit of happiness (that his neighbor's idea of happiness is persecuting others does confuse matters a bit).

4   This is a startling notion to the current generation of Americans. They reflect a system of public education which has made the Bill of Rights, literally, unacceptable to a majority of high school graduates (see the annual Purdue reports) who now form the "silent majority"—a phrase which that underestimated wit Richard Nixon took from Homer, who used it to describe the dead.

5   Now one can hear the warning rumble begin: if everyone is allowed to take drugs everyone will and the GNP will decrease, the Commies will stop us from making everyone free, and we shall end up a race of Zombies, passively murmuring "groovy" to one another. Alarming thought. Yet it seems most unlikely that any reasonably sane person will become a drug addict if he knows in advance what addiction is going to be like.

6   Is everyone reasonably sane? No. Some people will always become drug addicts just as some people will always become alcoholics, and it is just too bad. Every man, however, has the power (and should have the legal right) to kill himself if he chooses. But since most men don't, they won't be mainliners either. Nevertheless, forbidding people things they like or think they might enjoy only makes them want those things all the more. This psychological insight is, for some mysterious reason, perennially denied our governors.

7   It is a lucky thing for the American moralist that our country has always existed in a kind of time-vacuum: we have no public memory of anything that happened before last Tuesday. No one in Washington today recalls what happened during the years alcohol was forbidden to the people by a Congress that thought it had a divine mission to stamp out Demon Rum—launching, in the process, the greatest crime wave in the country's history, causing thousands of deaths from bad alcohol, and creating a general (and persisting) contempt among the citizenry for the laws of the United States.

8   The same thing is happening today. But the government has learned nothing from past attempts at prohibition, not to mention repression.

9   Last year when the supply of Mexican marijuana was slightly curtailed by the Feds, the pushers got the kids hooked on heroin

and deaths increased dramatically, particularly in New York. Whose fault? Evil men like the Mafiosi? Permissive Dr. Spock? Wild-eyed Dr. Leary? No.

10   The Government of the United States was responsible for those deaths. The bureaucratic machine has a vested interest in playing cops and robbers. Both the Bureau of Narcotics and the Mafia want strong laws against the sale and use of drugs because if drugs are sold at cost there would be no money in it for anyone.

11   If there was no money in it for the Mafia, there would be no friendly playground pushers, and addicts would not commit crimes to pay for the next fix. Finally, if there was no money in it, the Bureau of Narcotics would wither away, something they are not about to do without a struggle.

12   Will anything sensible be done? Of course not. The American people are as devoted to the idea of sin and its punishment as they are to making money—and fighting drugs is nearly as big a business as pushing them. Since the combination of sin and money is irresistible (particularly to the professional politician), the situation will only grow worse.

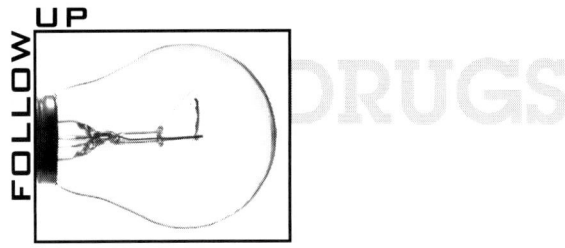

Exploring Language

exhortation: language intended to encourage, excite, or provoke.
perennially: permanently, enduringly, constantly.

USAGE Locate *exhortation* in the essay and then look up synonyms. In what context does Vidal use the word? Now use the word in another context.

Thinking and Talking Points

1. Where in the essay does Vidal address and refute his opponents' views (those against drug legalization)? How well does he support his argument? Are there arguments from the other side he hasn't considered?
2. Reread paragraph #6. Do you think "forbidding people things they like or think they might enjoy only makes them want those things all the more"? Think of examples other than drugs.
3. Reread paragraphs #9 and #10. Explain what Vidal means by his statement, "The Government of the United States was responsible for those deaths." Do you agree or disagree with his reasoning? How does comparing the Bureau of Narcotics and the Mafia work in his favor?
4. Vidal writes, "The American people are as devoted to the idea of sin and its punishment as they are to making money—and fighting drugs is nearly as big a business as pushing them." Where in the essay does he support these statements? Do you agree or disagree with these ideas? Can you think of other examples that illustrate Americans are devoted to sin and its punishment?
5. What do you think Vidal means by his statement "we have no public memory of anything that happened before last Tuesday"? Can you think of examples?

Styling

You can use a colon to list items following a complete sentence or to give an explanation. Here's an example from Vidal's essay:

It's a lucky thing for the American moralist that our country has always existed in a kind of time-vacuum: we have no public memory of anything that happened before last Tuesday.

Notice that the phrase before the colon is a **complete sentence.** The phrase after the colon explains something in the complete sentence, in this instance, the time-vacuum. Although the sentence before the colon must be complete, what follows the colon can be either a complete or **incomplete sentence**. Here's another example of a sentence that uses a colon with an explanation; this is from Jamaica Kincaid's essay "On Seeing England for the First Time" (not in this book):

> I did not know then that this statement was meant to make me feel awe and small whenever I heard the word "England": awe at its existence, small because I was not from it.

Although the part before the colon forms a complete sentence, the phrase after the colon is incomplete, explaining "awe" and "small."

PRACTICE Fill in the blanks below with a phrase or sentence that explains.

Sasha was the Joan of Arc of her high school: _____

The Doberman diligently protected its puppies: _____

YOU TRY IT Create five sentences about your life—family members, hobbies, job—that use the colon with an explanation. Use this technique in your next writing assignment.

Teaming Up

1. Before coming to class, have each group member look up information on the Volstead Act. Share your information, and then compare what you've learned with the argument Vidal makes for legalizing drugs. Does he have a valid point? Can your group think of ways to refute him?

2. **A Good Warm-up for Writing Idea #1.** Divide your group into two teams: one for legalizing drugs and one against. Don't worry about what side you really agree with. For critical thinking, you should be able to argue either side whether or not you agree. Do some research and prepare a debate. In class, debate the issue. Have an impartial judge—the teacher or another classmate—judge which side presents the strongest argument.

Writing Ideas

1. Gather information on the cost of the drug war—both economic and human—and write an essay that argues whether or not the Drug War is worth it. (See the Writing Strategies for Arguing section in this book.)
2. Throughout his essay, Vidal blames the government for the drug problem in America. Since this essay was written—1970—the drug war has raged on. Do some research to determine whether or not the drug problem has improved. Also gather information on the Iran-Contra affair. Write an essay that argues whether or not the drug situation in America has improved and to what degree the Iran-Contra affair supports Vidal's blaming the government.

Essay and Film Connections

A more benign topic on America's "devotion to sin and its punishment" is "Naps" by Barbara Holland. P. J. O'Rourke's "How to Drive Fast" satirizes drinking and driving. The film *Traffic* brutally depicts the drug problem in the United States.

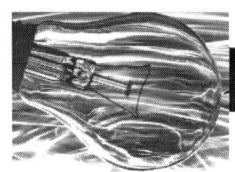
NAPS

Barbara Holland

Barbara Holland has written several books, including Bingo Night at the Fire Halls, Wasn't the Grass Greener?, The Joy of Drinking, When All the World Was Young: A Memoir, and Endangered Pleasures: In Defense of Naps, Bacon, Martinis, Profanity, and Other Indulgences where this essay, "Naps," appears. In "Naps," Holland argues for our right to take an afternoon nap like most of the rest of the "civilized" world, claiming "Americans are afraid of naps."

DUSTBIN OF HISTORY AND CULTURE

L'ÉCLUSIÈRE: Ecluse is French for lock.
COOLIDGE: Calvin Coolidge, 30th president of the United States (1923–1929).
MILTON: John Milton (1608–1674): considered one of the greatest of English poets, Milton, a Puritan, wrote his epic *Paradise Lost*, while blind, dictating to his daughter.
WINSTON CHURCHILL: Sir Winston Churchill (1874–1965) was prime minister (1940–1945 and 1951–1955) of Britain during WWII (1939–1945).
MORPHEUS: God of dreams, son of Sleep.

1   In France, on a rented canal boat, my friends and I gazed in despair at the closed oaken gates of the lock. We'd come to them only seconds after the witching hour of noon, but we were too late. There was no one to open the lock for us; *l'éclusière* was at lunch, and after lunch she would lay herself down, close her eyes, and nap. At two, but not before, she would emerge refreshed from her square granite house and set the great cogs in motion.

2   We tied the boat up to a spindly bush beside the towpath and waited. And waited. It was high haying season, but the fields lay empty of farmers. The roads lay empty of trucks. France lunched, and then slept. So did Spain. So did much of the civilized world.

3   If we'd been differently nurtured we too would have taken a nap, but we were Americans, condemned from the age of four to trudge through our sleepless days. Americans are afraid of naps. Napping is too luxurious, too sybaritic, too unproductive, and it's free; pleasures for which we don't pay make us anxious. Besides, it seems to be a

"Naps" from *Endangered Pleasures* by Barbara Holland. Copyright © 1995 by Barbara Holland. By permission of Little, Brown & Company.

natural inclination. Those who get paid to investigate such things have proved that people deprived of daylight and their wristwatches, with no notion of whether it was night or day, sink blissfully asleep in midafternoon as regular as clocks. Fighting off natural inclinations is a major Puritan virtue, and nothing that feels that good can be respectable.

4   They may have a point there. Certainly the process of falling asleep in the afternoon is quite different from bedtime sleep. Whether this is physiological or merely a by-product of guilt, it's a blatantly sensual experience, a voluptuous surrender, akin to the euphoric swoon of the heroine in a vampire movie. For the self-controlled, it's frightening—*how far down am I falling? will I ever climb back?* The sleep itself has a different texture. It's blacker, thicker, more intense, and works faster. Fifteen minutes later the napper pops back to the surface as from time travel, bewildered to find that it's only ten of two instead of centuries later.

5   Like skydiving, napping takes practice; the first few tries are scary.

6   The American nap is even scarier because it's unilateral. Sleeping Frenchmen are surrounded by sleeping compatriots, but Americans who lie down by day stiffen with the thought of the busy world rushing past. There we lie, visible and vulnerable on our daylit bed, ready to cut the strings and sink into the dark, swirling, almost sexual currents of the impending doze, but what will happen in our absence? Our stocks will fall; our employees will mutiny and seize the helm; our clients will tiptoe away to competitors. Even the housewife, taking advantage of the afternoon lull, knows at the deepest level of consciousness that the phone is about to ring.

7   And of course, for those of us with proper jobs, there's the problem of finding a bed. Some corporations, in their concern for their employees' health and fitness, provide gym rooms where we can commit strenuous exercise at lunchtime, but where are our beds? In Japan, the productivity wonder of the industrialized world, properly run companies maintain a nap room wherein the workers may refresh themselves. Even in America, rumor has it, the costly CEOs of giant corporations work sequestered in private suites, guarded by watchpersons, mainly so they can curl up unseen to sharpen their predatory powers with a quick snooze. A couple of recent presidents famous for their all-night energies kept up the pace by means of naps. Other presidents, less famous for energy, slept by day *and* night; woe to the unwary footstep that wakened Coolidge in the afternoon.

8   This leaves the rest of us lackeys bolt upright, toughing it out, trying to focus on the computer screen, from time to time snatching our chins up off our collarbones and glancing furtively around to see if we were noticed. The modern office isn't designed for privacy, and most of our cubicles have no doors to close, only gaps in the portable partitions. Lay our heads down on the desk at the appropriate hour and we're exposed to any passing snitch who strolls the halls enforcing alertness. It's a wonder they don't walk around ringing bells and blowing trumpets from one till three. American employers do not see the afternoon forty winks as refreshing the creative wellsprings of mere employees. They see it as goofing off.

9   Apparently most of us agree. Large numbers of us are, for one reason or another, home-bound, but do we indulge in the restorative nap? Mostly not. Even with no witness but ourselves, we're ashamed to. It would mean we weren't busy. We tell ourselves we have a million urgent things to do and our lives are so full and exciting we couldn't possibly lie down by daylight. Never mind that our heads are no particular use in midafternoon and half the work we do may need to be redone in the cold light of tomorrow morning. Oozing virtue and busyness, we flog ourselves on till evening.

10 In the evening, at least according to the cartoons, American men fall asleep on the couch, after dinner, a-flicker with light from the television screen. They are home from work, the day's toil accomplished, and they're free to doze, though if they'd napped at the biologically appointed time they wouldn't need to now, and at this hour it's not so much a nap as an awkward preview of the night's sleep, possibly leading to four-a.m. insomnia. Women, on the other hand, are never home from work unless it's someone else's home; home for them is simply different work, and naps are not an option.

11 It's time to rethink the nap from both the corporate and the personal viewpoint.

12 Those CEOs who find their own naps such an asset to productivity might consider what they'd do for the rest of us. They could hire consultants to conduct productivity studies, dividing us into teams of sleepers and wakers. When the results were in, they might even decide to mandate naps, as naps were mandated in nursery school, when we each unfolded a name-tagged blanket and spread it on the floor and lay down and shut up for a while. Granted we can't all have office suites, or even couches, and it would be unseemly to have us stacked up like firewood on the conference table, but we could

use futons, stored discreetly under the desk, or folding cots, or sleeping bags. The phones could be left to their answering devices, the faxes could pile up in the hopper, and the sales reps could pound in vain on the door as they'd find themselves doing in France.

13   Those of us at home, with beds at hand, should take pleasure as well as productivity into account. Consider the cat. A perfectly healthy cat can nap through the entire month of February and wake feeling all the better for it. The house may be simply pattering with uncaught mice, but no twitch of guilt quivers the whiskers of the napping cat. In summer he stretches out to full length, preferably in a breezy doorway where he's rather in the way, and sometimes on his back, looking dead enough to alarm the chance visitor, and drapes his arm over his eyes. Swiftly and easily he lowers himself into sleep, sensuous, fur-lined sleep, the sleep of the untroubled conscience. Nothing tells him he ought to be rushing about his various occupations. Sleep, for a cat, is a worthy occupation in itself.

14   Let us consider the cat and go to bed. Bed the haven, the motherly lap, the downy nest. Bed, from which Earth with its fuss and fidgeting shrinks to the size of Pluto, visible only by telescope. We should loosen or remove some of our clothing, close the curtains, and lie down flat, allowing the vital forces to circulate through the brain and restore its muscle tone.

15   Bed is *not* a shameful, shiftless place to be by day, nor is it necessary to run a fever of 102 to deserve it. Bed can even be productive. The effortless horizontal body and the sensory deprivation of the quiet bedroom leave the mind free, even in sleep, to focus, to roam, sometimes to forge ahead. Knotty problems can unknot themselves as if by magic. Creative solutions can tiptoe across the coverlet and nestle onto the pillow of the napper, even while the black velvet paws of Morpheus lie closely over his eyes. He may wake half an hour later with the road ahead laid clear.

16   Creativity doesn't come a-running to those who toil and slave for her; she's as much the daughter of rest and play as of effort; just because we're uncomfortable doesn't mean we're productive; just because we're comfortable doesn't mean we're lazy. Milton wrote *Paradise Lost* in bed. Winston Churchill, a prodigious producer, wrote all those large important histories in bed, brandy bottle at the ready. No doubt when inspiration flagged and his thoughts refused to marshal, he took a nip and a nap. Now, there was a man who knew a thing or two about a good day's work.

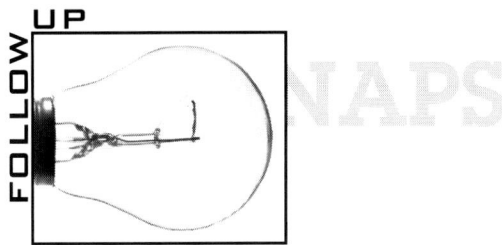

Exploring Language

compatriot: a person from your own country.
euphoric: a feeling of great happiness, joy, ecstasy, well-being.
furtively: slyly or secretively.
lackey: servant; footman.
mandate: command or authorize.
prodigious: extraordinary in size; enormous, huge.
spindly: long, thin, and frail.
sybaritic: luxurious.
unilateral: one-sided.

Thinking and Talking Points

1. Are Americans—in general—afraid of naps, as Holland claims? Is there a prejudice against naps? What evidence does she present for this claim? What is your experience with nap prejudice?
2. Holland claims that "pleasures for which we don't pay make us anxious." Do you agree? Can you think of examples? How does she defend this statement?
3. Holland uses a light-hearted tone in her essay. What word choices convey this tone? How do we know she is serious about her topic?
4. Examine phrases like "civilized world" (paragraph #2), "proper jobs," and "properly run companies" (paragraph #8). What are the underlying implications of these statements? What do they tell us about her opinions?
5. Examine the last and first sentences of each paragraph, and discuss how Holland links the essay through strong **transitions**, tying each paragraph to the next with careful word choices.

Styling

One style technique you might be familiar with is **alliteration**, the repetition of sounds close to one another, creating rhythm. Some examples from Holland's essay include "consider the cat," "deprived of daylight" and "snitch who strolls." Notice that the words in each pair begin with the same letter or sound.

PRACTICE First, find at least three other pairs of words close together that create alliteration in Holland's essay.

YOU TRY IT Choose a topic and brainstorm five pairs of words that contain alliteration. Some ideas for topics might be candy (jelly beans and juju bees), descriptions of your favorite meal (simply sublime), your pet (perky poodle), favorite song or poet (melancholy musician). Using your brainstorming list, write five sentences. Apply this technique to your next essay.

Teaming Up

1. **A Good Warm-up for Writing Ideas #1 and #2.** Everyone in the group jot down a list of jobs they've had (even babysitting or mowing lawns), and then under each job, list the positives and negatives. Compare lists. Co-write a paragraph that discusses what benefits would be available in the ideal job.

2. **A Good Warm-up for Writing Idea #3.** Brainstorm your guilty pleasure, what it is and why you like it. Everyone pass their paper to their right. On your peer's paper, brainstorm all the reasons why the activity might be objectionable to others (or yourself). After you get your paper handed back to you, write a defense next to each objection. Now you have a good start on Writing Idea #3.

Writing Ideas

1. Research companies in another country and their work habits. How much vacation time is typical? What about overtime? Do they provide child care? Exercise rooms? Meals? Nap rooms? What other perks might be offered? Write an essay that compares those benefits to a typical benefit package in the United States.

2. Research two companies in the same field, perhaps Microsoft and Google. What benefits do they offer employees? Which company seems more progressive in providing for employees? Which one needs to improve? You might write your essay in letter format to the company you think needs improvement, comparing them to the superior company, questioning and advising them on their practices.

3. Everyone has a guilty or "endangered" pleasure, an innocent pastime (not illegal) that others complain or nag about, or frown upon. Write an essay that defends your innocent pleasure. Some ideas might be shopping, eating junk food, playing video games, chocolate, reading silly novels, or watching mindless television shows.

Essay Connections

Essays that analyze culture include an excerpt from "The Culture of Celebrity" by Joseph Epstein, "Toys" by Roland Barthes, and "About Men," by Gretel Ehrlich.

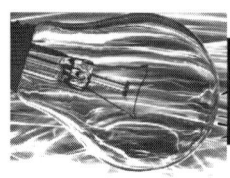

FROM THE CULTURE OF CELEBRITY

Joseph Epstein

Among Joseph Epstein's (former editor of American Scholar) books are Snobbery: The American Version, Friendship: an Expose, and In a Cardboard Belt!: Essays Personal, Literary, and Savage. His essays have appeared in Harper's, Atlantic Monthly, The New Yorker, and Best American Essays. This excerpt from "The Culture of Celebrity" appeared in Best American Essays 2006; it reflects on our obsession with the lives of famous people simply because they are famous.

DUSTBIN OF HISTORY AND CULTURE

FLAUBERT, GUSTAVE (1821–1880): French writer best known for *Madame Bovary;* the French government charged Flaubert with immorality because of the novel's content.

MACHIAVELLIAN: Refers to Niccolo Machiavelli (1469–1527), an Italian Renaissance statesman and writer of *The Prince*, among other works; the term *Machiavellian* has come to be associated with deception and dishonesty.

ANDY WARHOL (1928–1987): American pop artist who painted mundane objects like Campbell's soup cans and Coca-Cola bottles, as well as portraits of celebrities.

SID AND MERCEDES BASS: Wealthy oil tycoons known for lavish parties; in 2006 they donated $25 million to The Metropolitan Opera.

AHMET AND MICA ERTEGUN: Ahmet Ertegun, son of a Turkish diplomat, founder and former chairman of Atlantic records, died in 2006; Mica is his widow.

TED WILLIAMS (1918–2002): Played with the Boston Red Sox from 1939–1960.

ADONIS: In mythology, a handsome young man loved by Venus; when he is killed by a wild boar, she changes his blood into a flower.

OLIVER GOLDSMITH (1730–1774): Irish born novelist, essayist, poet, and dramatist, best known for his humorous and bawdy—and still popular—play, *She Stoops to Conquer.*

FRANK MUIR (1920–1998): British writer and broadcaster of radio and television shows like *Till Death Do Us Part* and *Steptoe and Son.*

From "The Culture of Celebrity" by John Epstein as appeared in *The Weekly Standard*, October 17, 2005, Vol. 11, Issue 5. An earlier version of this essay was published in "Celebrity Culture" the Spring 2005 issue of *The Hedgehog Review: Critical Reflections on Contemporary Culture*, published by the Institute for Advanced Studies in Culture at the University of Virginia (www.virginia.edu/iasc/).

SECTION THREE *Heating It Up: Essays That Argue*

MARCEL PROUST (1871–1922): French novelist, his best known work being *Swann's Way.*

W. H. AUDEN (1907–1973): British born poet and critic who became a U.S. citizen in 1939; poems include "The Unknown Citizen," "Lullaby," and "In Memory of W.B. Yeats."

PHILIP LARKIN (1922–1985): British poet whose collections include *The Whitsun Weddings* and *High Windows;* a novel (*Jill* and *A Girl in Winter*); he was also a jazz critic.

LENNY BRUCE (1925–1966): Comedian whose comedy was seen as obscene and outrageous; Bruce was arrested, but his controversial comedy act is seen to have been groundbreaking, opening the way for those who followed.

1   Celebrity at this moment in America is epidemic, and it's spreading fast, sometimes seeming as if nearly everyone has got it. Television provides celebrity dance contests, celebrities take part in reality shows, perfumes carry the names not merely of designers but of actors and singers. Without celebrities, whole sections of the *New York Times* and the *Washington Post* would have to close down. So pervasive has celebrity become in contemporary American life that one now begins to hear a good deal about a phenomenon known as the Culture of Celebrity.

2   The word "culture" no longer, I suspect, stands in most people's minds for that whole congeries of institutions, relations, kinship patterns, linguistic forms, and the rest for which the early anthropologists meant it to stand. Words, unlike disciplined soldiers, refuse to remain in place and take orders. They insist on being unruly, and slither and slide around, picking up all sorts of slippery and even goofy meanings. An icon, as we shall see, doesn't stay a small picture of a religious personage but usually turns out nowadays to be someone with spectacular grosses. "The language," as Flaubert once protested in his attempt to tell his mistress Louise Colet how much he loved her, "is inept."

3   Today, when people glibly refer to "the corporate culture," "the culture of poverty," "the culture of journalism," "the culture of the intelligence community"—and "community" has, of course, itself become another of those hopelessly baggy-pants words, so that one hears talk even of "the homeless community"—what I think is meant by "culture" is the general emotional atmosphere and institutional character surrounding the word to which "culture" is attached. Thus, corporate culture is thought to breed selfishness practiced at the Machiavellian level; the culture of poverty, hopelessness and despair;

the culture of journalism, a taste for the sensational combined with a short attention span; the culture of the intelligence community, covering-one's-own-behind viperishness; and so on. Culture used in this way is also brought in to explain unpleasant or at least dreary behavior. "The culture of NASA has to be changed" is a sample of its current usage. The comedian Flip Wilson, after saying something outrageous, would revert to the refrain line "The debbil made me do it." So, today, when admitting to unethical or otherwise wretched behavior, people often say, "The culture made me do it."

4   As for "celebrity," the standard definition is no longer the dictionary one but rather closer to the one that Daniel Boorstin gave in his book *The Image; or, What Happened to the American Dream:* "The celebrity," Boorstin wrote, "is a person who is well-known for his well-knownness," which is improved in its frequently misquoted form as "A celebrity is someone famous for being famous." The other standard quotation on this subject is Andy Warhol's "In the future everyone will be world-famous for fifteen minutes," which also frequently turns up in an improved misquotation as "Everyone will have his fifteen minutes of fame."

5   But to say that a celebrity is someone well known for being well known, though clever enough, doesn't quite cover it. Not that there is a shortage of such people who seem to be known only for their well-knownness. What do a couple named Sid and Mercedes Bass do, except appear in boldface in the *New York Times* Sunday Styles section and other such venues (as we now call them) of equally shimmering insignificance, often standing next to Ahmet and Mica Ertegun, also well known for being well known? Many moons ago, journalists used to refer to royalty as "face cards"; today celebrities are perhaps best thought of as bold faces, for as such do their names often appear in the press (and in a *New York Times* column with that very name, "Bold Face").

6   The distinction between celebrity and fame is one most dictionaries tend to fudge. I suspect everyone has, or prefers to make, his own. The one I like derives not from Aristotle, who didn't have to trouble with celebrities, but from the career of Ted Williams. A sportswriter once said that he, Williams, wished to be famous but had no interest in being a celebrity. What Ted Williams wanted to be famous for was his hitting. He wanted everyone who cared about baseball to know that he was—as he believed and may well have been—the greatest pure hitter who ever lived. What he didn't want to do was to take

on any of the effort off the baseball field involved in making this known. As an active player, Williams gave no interviews, signed no baseballs or photographs, chose not to be obliging in any way to journalists or fans. A rebarbative character, not to mention often a slightly menacing s.o.b., Williams, if you had asked him, would have said that it was enough that he was the last man to hit .400; he did it on the field, and therefore didn't have to sell himself off the field. As for his duty to his fans, he didn't see that he had any.

7   Whether Ted Williams was right or wrong to feel as he did is of less interest than the distinction his example provides, which suggests that fame is something one earns—through talent or achievement of one kind or another—while celebrity is something one cultivates or, possibly, has thrust upon one. The two are not, of course, entirely exclusive. One can be immensely talented and full of achievement and yet wish to broadcast one's fame further through the careful cultivation of celebrity; and one can have the thinnest of achievements and be talentless and yet be made to seem otherwise through the mechanics and dynamics of celebrity creation, in our day a whole mini- (or maybe not so mini) industry of its own.

8   Or, another possibility, one can become a celebrity with scarcely any pretense to talent or achievement whatsoever. Much modern celebrity seems the result of careful promotion or great good luck or something besides talent and achievement: Mr. Donald Trump, Ms. Paris Hilton, Mr. Regis Philbin, take a bow. The ultimate celebrity of our time may have been John F. Kennedy Jr., notable only for being his parents' very handsome son—both his birth and good looks factors beyond his control—and, alas, known for nothing else whatsoever now, except for the sad, dying-young-Adonis end to his life.

9   Fame, then, at least as I prefer to think of it, is based on true achievement; celebrity on the broadcasting of that achievement, or the inventing of something that, if not scrutinized too closely, might pass for achievement. Celebrity suggests ephemerality, while fame has a chance of lasting, a shot at reaching the happy shores of posterity.

10   Oliver Goldsmith, in his poem "The Deserted Village," refers to "good fame," which implies that there is also a bad or false fame. Bad fame is sometimes thought to be fame in the present, or fame on earth, while good fame is that bestowed by posterity—those happy shores again. (Which doesn't eliminate the desire of most of us, at least nowadays, to have our fame here and hereafter, too.) Not false but wretched fame is covered by the word "infamy"—"Infamy, infamy,

infamy," remarked the English wit Frank Muir, "they all have it in for me"—while the lower, or pejorative, order of celebrity is covered by the word "notoriety," also frequently misused to mean noteworthiness.

11   Leo Braudy's magnificent book on the history of fame, *The Frenzy of Renown*, illustrates how the means of broadcasting fame have changed over the centuries: from having one's head engraved on coins, to purchasing statuary of oneself, to (for the really high rollers—Alexander the Great, the Caesar boys) naming cities or even months after oneself, to commissioning painted portraits, to writing books or having books written about one, and so on into our day of the publicity or press agent, the media blitz, the public relations expert, and the egomaniacal blogger. One of the most successful of public relations experts, Ben Sonnenberg Sr., used to say that he saw it as his job to construct very high pedestals for very small men.

12   Which leads one to a very proper suspicion of celebrity. As George Orwell said about saints, so it seems only sensible to say about celebrities: they should all be judged guilty until proven innocent. Guilty of what, precisely? I'd say of the fraudulence (however minor) of inflating their brilliance, accomplishments, worth, of passing themselves off as something they aren't, or at least are not quite. If fraudulence is the crime, publicity is the means by which the caper is brought off.

13   Is the current heightened interest in the celebrated sufficient to form a culture—a culture of a kind worthy of study? The anthropologist Alfred Kroeber defined culture, in part, as embodying "values which may be formulated (overtly as mores) or felt (implicitly as in folkways) by the society carrying the culture, and which it is part of the business of the anthropologist to characterize and define." What are the values of celebrity culture? They are the values, almost exclusively, of publicity. Did they spell one's name right? What was the size and composition of the audience? Did you check the receipts? Was the timing right? Publicity is concerned solely with effects and does not investigate causes or intrinsic value too closely. For example, a few years ago a book of mine called *Snobbery: The American Version* received what I thought was a too greatly mixed review in the *New York Times Book Review*. I remarked on my disappointment to the publicity man at my publisher's, who promptly told me not to worry: it was a full-page review, on page 11, right-hand side. That, he said, "is very good real estate," which was quite as important as, perhaps more important than, the reviewer's actual words and final judgment. Better

to be tepidly considered on page 11 than extravagantly praised on page 27, left-hand side. Real estate, man, it's the name of the game.

14   We must have new names, Marcel Proust presciently noted—in fashion, in medicine, in art, there must always be new names. It's a very smart remark, and the fields Proust chose seem smart, too, at least for his time. (Now there must also be new names, at a minimum, among movie stars and athletes and politicians.) Implicit in Proust's remark is the notion that if the names don't really exist, if the quality isn't there to sustain them, it doesn't matter; new names we shall have in any case. And every sophisticated society somehow, more or less implicitly, contrives to supply them.

15   I happen to think that we haven't had a major poet writing in English since perhaps the death of W. H. Auden or, to lower the bar a little, Philip Larkin. But new names are put forth nevertheless—high among them in recent years has been that of Seamus Heaney—because, after all, what kind of a time could we be living in if we didn't have a major poet? And besides there are all those prizes that, year after year, must be given out, even if so many of the recipients don't seem quite worthy of them.

16   Considered as a culture, celebrity does have its institutions. We now have an elaborate celebrity-creating machinery well in place—all those short-attention-span television shows (*Entertainment Tonight, Access Hollywood, Lifestyles of the Rich and Famous*); all those magazines (beginning with *People* and far from ending with the *National Enquirer*). We have high-priced celebrity-mongers—Barbara Walters, Diane Sawyer, Jay Leno, David Letterman, Oprah—who not only live off others' celebrity but also, through their publicity-making power, confer it and have in time become very considerable celebrities each in his or her own right.

17   Without the taste for celebrity, they would have to close down the whole Style section of every newspaper in the country. Then there is the celebrity profile (in *Vanity Fair, Esquire, Gentlemen's Quarterly;* these are nowadays usually orchestrated by a press agent, with all touchy questions declared out-of-bounds), or the television talk-show interview with a star, which is beyond parody. Well, *almost* beyond: Martin Short in his parody of a talk-show host remarked to the actor Kiefer Sutherland, "You're Canadian, aren't you? What's that all about?"

18   Yet we still seem never to have enough celebrities, so we drag in so-called It Girls (Paris Hilton, Cindy Crawford, other super-models),

tired television hacks (Regis Philbin, Ed McMahon), back-achingly boring but somehow sacrosanct news anchors (Walter Cronkite, Tom Brokaw). Toss in what I think of as the lower-class punditi, who await calls from various television news and chat shows to demonstrate their locked-in political views and meager expertise on major and cable stations alike: Pat Buchanan, Eleanor Clift, Mark Shields, Robert Novak, Michael Beschloss, and the rest. Ah, if only Lenny Bruce were alive today, he could do a scorchingly cruel bit about Dr. Joyce Brothers sitting by the phone wondering why Jerry Springer never calls.

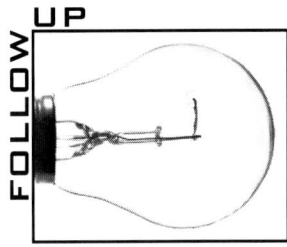

THE CULTURE OF CELEBRITY

Exploring Language

congeries: a collection or mass.
ephemerality: short-lived; lasting only a short period of time.
glibly: offhand; without thought or preparation; with ease.
inept: awkward or clumsy; without skill.
pejorative: belittling or derogatory.
posterity: future generations.
presciently: to know things before they happen; foresight.
pundit: an authority or expert; a critic; Epstein created his own word with punditi.
sacrosanct: sacred; above criticism.

USAGE Reread paragraph three. Which definition of "glibly" is Epstein using? Write two sentences, one using glibly as meaning without thought or preparation and the other meaning with ease.

Thinking and Talking Points

1. What evidence does Epstein use for his comment, "Celebrity at this moment in America is epidemic . . ."? Do you agree? Why or why not?
2. How does the essay distinguish celebrity from fame?
3. How does Epstein define the word *culture,* the way it's used today versus the past?
4. What is the essay's main point? What is Epstein's view of "the culture of celebrity?" What are his objections to the use of the word *community?*
5. Epstein claims that celebrities are guilty of fraudulence. What does he mean? Do you agree? Why or why not?

Styling

Many good writer's create their own adjectives by hooking together words that are not always adjectives—perhaps nouns or verbs—with hyphens. You might be familiar with such words that have become standard, like deep-rooted, stay-at-home moms, or close-knit. The trick is to not rely on these standards but write fresh ones of your own.

Epstein uses this technique several times: "baggy-pants words," "covering-one's-own-behind viperishness," and "dying-young-Adonis end." **Notice that the noun being described is not connected to the new adjective.**

Until you master this technique, you might be more successful if you stick to using nouns and verbs in your hyphenated words to describe another noun. If, for example, you want to describe a cat's fur, you wouldn't hook together a string of adjectives like black-silky-shiny-gleaming fur. It doesn't quite work. Instead, write something like gleams-in-the-light fur. Here you've got the verb, (gleams), a preposition and an article (in, the) and a noun (light).

In "Bully Pulpit," Amy Dickinson could have written "the time I vomited on my sneakers," but instead chose to hyphenate, creating vomiting-on-my-sneakers incident.

Note: Be sure when you're typing to use **hyphens**, not **dashes**. Type one short line (-) for a hyphen, two (--) for a dash. Otherwise, you'll confuse your reader.

PRACTICE Rewrite the sentence below using new, hyphenated adjectives to describe the subject (noun).

> There was one time when I slipped in the cafeteria with a tray full of food and dumped it on a popular football jock.

YOU TRY IT Write three sentences of your own using hyphenated words to describe a subject.

Teaming Up

1. **A Good Warm-up for Writing Idea #1.** Make a list of words you think are overused (to save time, you can use the words in Writing Idea #1). Write at least three sentences for each overused word. Be specific so that the context is clear. Give a specific incident as an example.

2. **A Good Warm-up for Writing Idea #3.** Choose a category from Writing Idea #3 and list several examples. Next, describe three of the examples in some detail. Discuss why these shows (or the merchandise) are popular and why you think stars participate.

Writing Ideas

1. Write an essay tracing the history of a word that you think is overused. Discuss the origin of the word, its previous meaning, and how it is used today. See Writing Strategies for Defining Terms in Section Five. Some ideas might be the words miracle, awesome, or history (as in "That's ancient history").
2. Write an essay that analyzes the difference between the words *icon* and *celebrity*. Look up the origin of each word and their definitions. Use the Writing Strategies for Defining Terms in Section Five.
3. In his introduction, Epstein complains, "Television provides celebrity dance contests, celebrities take part in reality shows, perfumes carry the names not merely of the designers but of actors and singers." Choose one of these categories—dance contests, reality shows, or designer merchandise—and analyze the content. Describe each show or type of merchandise in detail. Attempt to answer why celebrities participate and why people watch these shows or buy these products. Does your analysis end up supporting or refuting Epstein's claim that celebrity is an epidemic?

Essay and Film Connections

Other essays that analyze culture include "About Men," by Gretel Ehrlich, "Indian With a Camera" by Leslie Marmon Silko, "Graven Images," by Saul Bellow, "Naps" by Barbara Holland, "Fiddling While Africa Starves" by P.J. O'Rourke, and "Toys" by Roland Barthes. The film *Thank You For Smoking* satirically examines cigarette advertising.

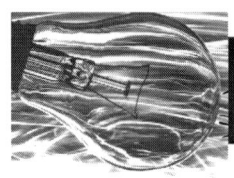

FIDDLING WHILE AFRICA STARVES

P. J. O'Rourke

P. J. O'Rourke is a humorist and former foreign correspondent for Rolling Stone. The following is an excerpt from an essay in his book Give War a Chance *(1992). O'Rourke, in this piece, is horrified by concerts that raise money for starving countries like Africa, comparing these events to mobs, stating, "An audience that's easily moved to tears is as easily moved to sadistic dementia. People are not thinking under such circumstances."*

DUSTBIN OF HISTORY AND CULTURE

HAILE MARIAM MENGISTU: President of Ethiopia from 1987 to 1991.
MARXIST: One who follows the political philosophies of German revolutionary Karl Marx (1818–1883), the co-founder (with Friedrich Engels) of scientific socialism—modern communism.

1   When the "We Are the World" video first slithered into public view, I was sitting around with a friend who himself happens to be in show business. The thing gave him the willies. Me too. But neither of us could figure exactly why. "Whenever you see people that pleased with themselves on a stage," said my friend, "you know you're in for a bad show." And the USA for Africa performers did have that self-satisfied look of toddlers on a pot. But in this world of behemoth evils, such a minor lapse of taste shouldn't have upset us. We changed the channel.

2   Half a year later; in the middle of the Live Aid broadcast, my friend called me. "Turn on your television," he said. "This is horrible. They're in a frenzy."

3   "Well," I said, "at least it's a frenzy of charity."

4   "Oh, no," he said, "it could be *anything*. Next time it might be 'Kill the Jews.'"

5   A mob, even an eleemosynary mob, is an ugly thing to see. No good ever came of mass emotion. The audience that's easily moved to tears is as easily moved to sadistic dementia. People are not thinking under such circumstances. And poor, dreadful Africa is something which surely needs thought.

From "Fiddling While Africa Starves" from *Give War a Chance* by P. J. O'Rourke. Copyright © 1992 by P. J. O'Rourke. Used by permission of Grove/Atlantic, Inc.

6   The Band Aid, Live Aid, USA for Africa concerts and records (and videos, posters, T-shirts, lunch buckets, thermos bottles, bath toys, etc.) are supposed to illuminate the plight of the Africans. Note the insights provided by these lyrics:

> *We are the world [solipsism], we are the children [average age near forty]*
> *We are the ones to make a brighter day [unproven]*
> *So let's start giving [logical inference supplied without argument]*
> *There's a choice we're making [true as far as it goes]*
> *We're saving our own lives [absurd]*
> *It's true we'll make a better day [see line 2 above]*
> *Just you and me [statistically unlikely]*

7   That's three palpable untruths, two dubious assertions, nine uses of a first-person pronoun, not a single reference to trouble or anybody in it and no facts. The verse contains, literally, neither rhyme nor reason.

8   And these musical riots of philanthropy address themselves to the wrong problems. There is, of course, a shortage of food among Africans, but that doesn't mean there's a shortage of food *in* Africa. "A huge backlog of emergency grain has built up at the Red Sea port of Assab," says the *Christian Science Monitor.* "Food sits rotting in Ethiopia," reads a headline in the *St. Louis Post-Dispatch*. And according to hunger maven William Shawcross, 200,000 tons of food aid delivered to Ethiopia is being held in storage by the country's government.

9   There's also, of course, a lack of transport for that food. But that's not the real problem either. The authorities in Addis Ababa have plenty of trucks for their military operations against the Eritrean rebels, and much of the rest of Ethiopia's haulage is being used for forcibly resettling people instead of feeding them. Western governments are reluctant to send more trucks, for fear they'll be used the same way. And similar behavior can be seen in the rest of miserable Africa.

10   The African relief fad serves to distract attention from the real issues. There is famine in Ethiopia, Chad, Sudan and areas of Mozambique. All these countries are involved in pointless civil wars. There are pockets of famine in Mauritania, Niger and Mali—the result of desertification caused mostly by idiot agricultural policies. African famine is not a visitation of fate. It is largely man-made, and the men who made it are largely Africans.

11   Enormous irrigation projects have been put onto lands that cannot support them and into cultures that cannot use them. Feeble-witted nationalism puts borders in the way of nomadic peoples who

used to pick up and move when things got dry. Rural poverty drives populations to African cities where governments keep food prices artificially low, thus increasing rural poverty. Bumbling and corrupt central planning stymies farm production. And the hideous regimes use hunger as a weapon to suppress rebellion. People are not just starving. They are *being* starved.

12   "Socialist" ideals infest Africa like malaria or dengue fever. African leaders, lost in the frippery of centrist thinking, fail to deal with market forces or any other natural phenomena. Leave it to a Marxist to see the world as the world is not. It's not unusual for African intellectuals to receive their education at such august bodies of learning as Patrice Lumumba U. in Moscow. That is, they are trained by a nation which intentionally starved millions of its citizens in order to collectivize farming.

13   Death is the result of bad politics. And the Aid concerts are examples of the bad logic that leads to bad politics. It's probably not going too far to say that Africa's problems have been produced by the same kind of dim, ignorant thinking found among American pop artists. "If we take, say, six months and not spend any money on nuclear weapons, and just spend it on food, I think we could make a big dent," says Waylon Jennings in the USA for Africa publicity packet. In fact, a small nuclear weapon placed directly under Haile Mariam Mengistu and his pals would probably make a more beneficial dent than a whole U.S. defense budget worth of canned goods.

14   Anyway, money is not going to solve the problem. Yet the concert nonsense is all put strictly in terms of cash. Perhaps it is the only thing the idiot famous understand.

15   Getting people to give vast amounts of money when there's no firm idea what that money will do is like throwing maidens down a well. It's an appeal to magic. And the results are likely to be as stupid and disappointing as the results of magic usually are.

16   But, say some, Live Aid sets a good example for today's selfish youth, reminding them to be socially concerned. Nonsense. The circus atmosphere of the Live Aid concerts makes the world's problems seem easy and fun to solve and implies that the solutions are naturally uncontroversial. As an example of charity, Live Aid couldn't be worse. Charity entails sacrifice. Yet the Live Aid performers are sacrificing nothing. Indeed, they're gaining public adulation and a thoroughly unmerited good opinion of themselves. Plus it's free advertising. These LPs, performances and multiform by-products have nothing in common with charity. Instead they levy a sort of

regressive alms tax on the befuddled millions. The performers donate their time, which is wholly worthless. Big corporations donate their services, which are worth little enough. Then the poor audience pledges all the contributions and buys all the trash with money it can ill afford. The worst nineteenth-century robber barons wouldn't have had the cheek to put forward such a bunco scheme. They may have given away tainted money, but at least they didn't ask you to give away yours.

17   One more thing, the music's lousy. If we must save the world with a song, what's the matter with the Metropolitan Opera Company?

18   Rock and roll's dopey crusade against African hunger has, I posit, added to the stock of human misery. And not just audibly. Any religious person—whether he worships at a pile of gazelle bones or in the Cathedral of St. Paul—will tell you egotism is the source of sin. The lust for power that destroys the benighted Ethiope has the same fountainhead as the lust for fame that propels the lousy pop band. "Not every one that saith unto me, Lord, Lord, shall enter into the kingdom of heaven." Let alone everyone that saith sha la la la la and doobie doobie do.

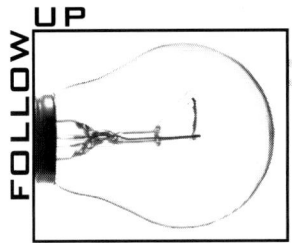

FIDDLING WHILE AFRICA STARVES

Exploring Language

BEFUDDLED: confused.
BEHEMOTH: huge or powerful.
ELEEMOSYNARY: related to charity or supported by it.
FRIPPERY: this word has more than one connotation; look it up to see which one O'Rourke means.
MAVEN: an expert or one experienced in a particular area.
SOLIPSISM: the philosophy that only the self exists and can be known.
STYMIE: to baffle or obstruct.

USAGE See *frippery*. Try using one of the following words in your next essay or conversation: *befuddled, behemoth, maven, frippery*.

Thinking and Talking Points

1. What is O'Rourke's argument and how does he support it? How well do you think he **refutes** the **opposition**?
2. O'Rourke sometimes calls his opposition names. Find examples. Do you think this name calling helps or hurts his argument?
3. O'Rourke claims that "charity entails sacrifice." What kind of sacrifice do you think O'Rourke means?
4. What is O'Rourke's reason for bringing up Russia?
5. "A mob . . . is an ugly thing to see," writes O'Rourke. Why is he so disturbed by these charity concerts? Do you agree with him about the dangers of mob mentality, or do you think he's overreacting?

Styling

O'Rourke writes, "When the 'We Are the World' video first slithered into public view, I was sitting around with a friend who himself happens to be in show business." *Slithered* stands out, making us think of a snake, a negative association for most people. It sounds dangerous, disturbing, setting the tone for the rest of the essay. Using descriptions of animal movements or sounds is a clever technique and easy to practice.

PRACTICE Make a list of animals, at least ten. Next to each one, write a sound or movement you associate with that animal. Here's an example:

elephants lumber

Next, replace the animal with another object or person:

the film lumbers

YOU TRY IT Choose five of your best word associations from the Practice and use them to write five sentences, using the sound or movement as a verb:

The film *Dances With Wolves* lumbers across the screen, a ponderous cliché of one man's enlightenment.

Teaming Up

1. **A Good Warm-up for Writing Idea #2.** Each member of the group brings in song lyrics that have a political or social message. Choose one and analyze the lyrics as O'Rourke does, pointing out absurdities, unproven arguments, and untruths.
2. **A Good Warm-up for Writing Idea #3.** Each group member brings in an article on United States foreign aid to Africa. Before class, summarize your article, and state whether or not the article supports O'Rourke's statements that most of the food and aid sent to Africa doesn't reach the people.

Writing Ideas

1. Watch a charity concert video (or several), perhaps one that O'Rourke mentions. Write an essay describing the concert, agreeing or disagreeing with O'Rourke's views that these events have an underlying sinister tone and mob mentality.
2. Write an essay that analyzes a song which supports a political, social, or charitable agenda, pointing out any absurdities, untruths, assumptions, or other logic errors.
3. Visit your library, log onto an online periodicals (newspapers and magazines) database, and research American charity aid to another country. You can type in "Foreign Aid" or "Aid to Africa" or another country and find out if charity reaches the people any better than it did when O'Rourke wrote his essay. Read several articles and write an essay that agrees or disagrees with sending charity to other countries.

Essay and Film Connections

In "Modern Times," Lawrence Weschler discusses another world issue, war and technology. O'Rourke mentions several foreign aid concerts that are available on video.

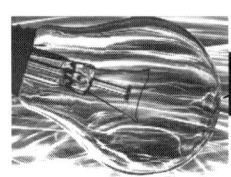

ABOUT MEN

Gretel Ehrlich

> Writer, rancher, documentary film maker, Gretel Ehrlich has several books to her credit, including This Cold Heaven, The Solace of Open Spaces, Questions of Heaven, John Muir: Nature's Visionary, and The Future of Ice. In "About Men," from Solace of Open Spaces, Ehrlich debunks the myth of the American cowboy, claiming that those Marlboro ads have it all wrong: "Instead of the macho, trigger-happy man our culture perversely wants him to be, the cowboy is more apt to be convivial, quirky, and softhearted."

DUSTBIN OF HISTORY AND CULTURE

CHISHOLM TRAIL: A cattle trail that ran between San Antonio, Texas and Abilene, Kansas (exact trail unknown); it was used for about twenty years after the Civil War (1861–1865) until the expansion of the railroad made it no longer useful.

HOBBLES: Restraints used mostly on horses (though sometimes on dogs or humans), placed on the front legs to restrict movement.

1   When I'm in New York but feeling lonely for Wyoming I look for the Marlboro ads in the subway. What I'm aching to see is horseflesh, the glint of a spur, a line of distant mountains, brimming creeks, and a re-minder of the ranchers and cowboys I've ridden with for the last eight years. But the men I see in those posters with their stern, humorless looks remind me of no one I know here. In our hellbent earnestness to romanticize the cowboy we've ironically disesteemed his true character. If he's "strong and silent" it's because there's probably no one to talk to. If he "rides away into the sunset" it's because he's been on horseback since four in the morning moving cattle and he's trying, fifteen hours later, to get home to his family. If he's "a rugged individualist" he's also part of a team: ranch work is teamwork and even the glorified open-range cowboys of the 1880s rode up and down the Chisholm Trail in the company of twenty or thirty other riders. Instead of the macho, trigger-happy man our culture has perversely wanted him to be, the cowboy is more apt to be convivial, quirky, and softhearted. To be "tough" on a ranch has nothing to do with conquests

"About Men," from *The Solace of Open Spaces* by Gretel Ehrlich, copyright © 1985 by Gretel Ehrlich. Used by permission of Viking Penguin, a division of Penguin Group (USA) Inc.

and displays of power. More often than not, circumstances—like the colt he's riding or an unexpected blizzard—are overpowering him. It's not toughness but "toughing it out" that counts. In other words, this macho, cultural artifact the cowboy has become is simply a man who possesses resilience, patience, and an instinct for survival. "Cowboys are just like a pile of rocks—everything happens to them. They get climbed on, kicked, rained and snowed on, scuffed up by wind. Their job is 'just to take it,'" one old-timer told me.

2 A cowboy is someone who loves his work. Since the hours are long—ten to fifteen hours a day—and the pay is $30 he has to. What's required of him is an odd mixture of physical vigor and maternalism. His part of the beef-raising industry is to birth and nurture calves and take care of their mothers. For the most part his work is done on horseback and in a lifetime he sees and comes to know more animals than people. The iconic myth surrounding him is built on American notions of heroism: the index of a man's value as measured in physical courage. Such ideas have perverted manliness into a self-absorbed race for cheap thrills. In a rancher's world, courage has less to do with facing danger than with acting spontaneously—usually on behalf of an animal or another rider. If a cow is stuck in a boghole he throws a loop around her neck, takes his daily (a half hitch around the saddle horn), and pulls her out with horsepower. If a calf is born sick, he may take her home, warm her in front of the kitchen fire, and massage her legs until dawn. One friend, whose favorite horse was tying to swim a lake with hobbles on, dove under water and cut her legs loose with a knife, then swam her to shore, his arm around her neck lifeguard-style, and saved her from drowning. Because these incidents are usually linked to someone or something outside himself, the westerner's courage is selfless, a form of compassion.

3 The physical punishment that goes with cowboying is greatly underplayed. Once fear is dispensed with, the threshold of pain rises to meet the demands of the job. When Jane Fonda asked Robert Redford (in the film *Electric Horseman*) if he was sick as he struggled to his feet one morning, he replied, "No, just bent." For once the movies had it right. The cowboys I was sitting with laughed in agreement. Cowboys are rarely complainers; they show their stoicism by laughing at themselves.

4 If a rancher or cowboy has been thought of as a "man's man"—laconic, hard-drinking, inscrutable—there's almost no place in which the balancing act between male and female, manliness and femininity, can be more natural. If he's gruff, handsome, and physically fit on the

outside, he's androgynous at the core. Ranchers are midwives, hunters, nurturers, providers, and conservationists all at once. What we've interpreted as toughness—weathered skin, calloused hands, a squint in the eye and a growl in the voice—only masks the tenderness inside. "Now don't go telling me these lambs are cute, one rancher warned me the first day I walked into the football-field-sized lambing sheds. The next thing I knew he was holding a black lamb. "Ain't this little rat good-lookin'?"

5   So many of the men who came to the West were southerners—men looking for work and a new life after the Civil War—that chivalrousness and strict codes of honor were soon thought of as western traits. There were very few women in Wyoming during territorial days, so when they did arrive (some as mail-order brides from places like Philadelphia) there was a stand-offishness between the sexes and a formality that persists now. Ranchers still tip their hats and say, "Howdy, ma'am" instead of shaking hands with me.

6   Even young cowboys are often evasive with women. It's not that they're Jekyll and Hyde creatures—gentle with animals and rough on women—but rather that they don't know how to bring their tenderness into the house and lack the vocabulary to express the complexity of what they feel. Dancing wildly all night becomes a metaphor for the explosive emotions pent up inside, and when these are, on occasion, released, they're so battery-charged and potent that one caress of the face or one "I love you" will peal for a long while.

7   The geographical vastness and the social isolation here make emotional evolution seem impossible. Those contradictions of the heart between respectability, logic, and convention on the one hand, and impulse, passion, and intuition on the other, played out wordlessly against the paradisical beauty of the West, give cowboys a wide-eyed but drawn look. Their lips pucker up, not with kisses but with immutability. They may want to break out, staying up all night with a lover just to talk, but they don't know how and can't imagine what the consequences will be. Those rare occasions when they do bare themselves result in confusion. "I feel as if I'd sprained my heart," one friend told me a month after such a meeting.

8   My friend Ted Hoagland wrote, "No one is as fragile as a woman but no one is as fragile as a man." For all the women here who use "fragileness" to avoid work or as a sexual ploy, there are men who try to hide theirs, all the while clinging to an adolescent dependency on women to cook their meals, wash their clothes, and keep the ranch

house warm in winter. But there is true vulnerability in evidence here. Because these men work with animals, not machines or numbers, because they live outside in landscapes of torrential beauty, because they are confined to a place and a routine embellished with awesome variables, because calves die in the arms that pulled others into life, because they go to the mountains as if on a pilgrimage to find out what makes a herd of elk tick, their strength is also a softness, their toughness, a rare delicacy.

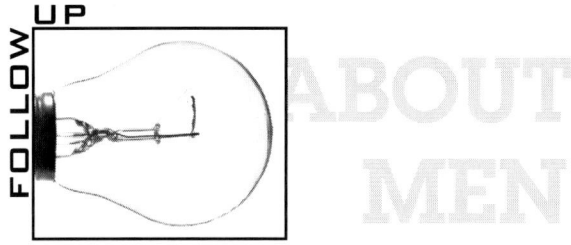

Exploring Language

androgynous: having both masculine and feminine characteristics.
convivial: friendly, agreeable.
disesteemed: made unfavorable.
evasive: avoiding a direct response to a verbal challenge; elusive is used when the avoidance is physical.
immutability: unchangeable.
inscrutable: not easily understood; mysterious.
laconic: using few words.
stoicism: repressing emotion and physical pain.

USAGE Write two sentences, one using *elusive* and the other *evasive*.

Thinking and Talking Points

1. How does Ehrlich debunk the myth of the American cowboy? Which examples best support her point? Do any weaken it? Which ones surprise you the most?
2. Examine the stories and quotes about and from cowboys. How does each one support a topic sentence in the paragraph?
3. What does Ehrlich's essay imply about stereotypes in general? What other not-so-obvious stereotypes exist in our culture?
4. How does Ehrlich use contrast to her advantage? Examine each one and comment on whether or not it works.
5. In paragraph #5, she examines the origins of the cowboy's standoffishness. What is the significance of her analysis? Does it adequately explain the cowboys' relationships with women?

Styling

If you've ever been told that your essay doesn't flow, the problem might be lack of **transitions**. Though many things contribute to flow in an essay—correct grammar and punctuation, sentence variety, organization—if proper transition doesn't exist between paragraphs, the piece will sound too abrupt, as if you're changing ideas without signaling your reader. You might have been taught simple transitions like however, therefore, first of all, secondly, and so on, but to bump your writing up to a more college-level style, transitions should be more subtle than these worn-out examples.

Examine the last and first sentences of each paragraph in Ehrlich's essay. You'll notice that she carefully shifts ideas by using the same word in a different form (*emotions* and *emotional* in paragraphs #6 and #7); words that have similar meanings or connotations (*job* and *work* in paragraphs #1 and #2); or seeming opposites (*compassion* and *physical punishment* in paragraphs #2 and #3). Though there are more sophisticated transitions, these three should get you started.

PRACTICE For each word in the list, think of a similar word, an opposite, or use the same word in a different form: friendly, melancholy, sincere, evil, cynical, water, writer, surfer, computer, plastic.

YOU TRY IT Examine an essay you have written to see if you've used strong transition. If not, edit the essay, using the above styles of transition.

Teaming Up

1. **A Good Warm-up for Writing Idea #3.** As a group, brainstorm ideas on other topics that are often advertised, and have each person bring in at least three ads so you'll have nine to twelve ads on the same topic. Some ideas might be pet food, blue jeans, surf wear, moms, make-up, toys. Examine the ads for stereotypes and list them. Discuss how each stereotype might be untrue.

2. Using the list from Teaming Up #1, co-write a paragraph using "if" to debunk the myths in one of the stereotypes. For help, examine paragraph #2 in the essay and use it for a model.

3. **A Good Warm-up for Writing idea #2.** Have each group member write down a figure from popular culture that he or she admires or loathes. The icon can be from the past or present as long as it fits the definition of an icon. An icon is a representative image, in this case a body of cultural assumptions; for example, Marilyn Monroe is seen as an icon of American beauty, and with that comes a set of assumptions about beauty in America. As a group, brainstorm the assumptions you make about what each image represents. Co-write a paragraph describing the icon and the assumptions you listed.

Writing Ideas

1. Write an essay that debunks a common misconception (or misconceptions) about a personality trait such as sentimentality, altruism, shyness, loneliness, individualism. Explain how there might be more sides to this character trait than our clichéd thinking usually allows. For example how might sentimentality be a negative quality? Is an individualist hiding a selfish nature? Does an altruist have an egoist alter ego? Follow the Writing Strategies for Defining Terms in Section Five.
2. The Marlboro Man might be seen as an American icon, embodying our cultural assumptions about the American cowboy. Explore another icon and write an essay that debunks our widely held assumption about that icon. You can choose from the art world, music, television, film, cereal boxes, advertising, Disney—almost anything is open for analysis.
3. Examine ads on another topic—blue jeans, toys, make-up, pet food, anything that's often advertised—and write an essay that explores the stereotypes hidden in these ads and debunk each stereotype. Be sure to describe each ad in detail for your reader.

Essay and Film Connections

The essay "Toys" by Roland Barthes examines French toys and what they say about French culture and assumptions of children. Ken Chen's "City Out of Breath" describes the contradictions in Hong Kong. The film *Thank You For Smoking* satirically examines cigarette advertising.

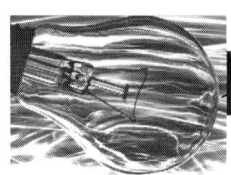

FOLKTALE LIBERATION

Alison Lurie

> Alison Lurie is a Pulitzer Prize-winning author and folklore historian/critic. This selection is from her book Don't Tell the Grownups: Subversive Children's Literature. Lurie promotes the use of original folk and fairy tales for developing children's minds and characters over literature that preaches straight lessons. Children like these dark tales and benefit from their subtle messages.

DUSTBIN OF HISTORY AND CULTURE

Dick and Jane: The main characters in a series of first grade readers from the 1950s and early 1960s. Dick and Jane were two white, middle-class children who—when outside playing—seemed dressed for church. The texts had such phrases as "See Dick. See Dick run. Run, Dick, run!"

Transactional Analysis: A method of psychotherapy (treatment of mental or emotional disorders) focusing on analyzing childhood events thought to contribute to behavior.

Structuralist: Relating to analysis that is focused on behavior patterns.

Maurice Sendak: Famous illustrator and author of children's picture books, among them *Where the Wild Things Are, In the Night Kitchen,* and *Outside, Over There.*

1   Folktales are the oldest and most widely known form of literature for children. "Beauty and the Beast" was told in classical Greece and ancient India; "Hansel and Gretel" has been collected in the West Indies, in African villages, and among the American Indians.

2   These tales also have another distinction: they are among the most subversive texts in children's literature. Often, though usually in disguised form, they support the rights of disadvantaged members of the population—children, women, and the poor—against the establishment. Law and order are not always respected: the master thief fools the count and the parson, and Jack kills the giant and steals his treasure. Rich people are often unlucky, afflicted, or helpless: kings and queens cannot have children or suffer from strange illnesses, while the poor are healthy and enterprising and fortunate.

"Folktale Liberation," from *Don't Tell the Grownups* by Alison Lurie. Copyright © 1990 by Alison Lurie. By permission of Little, Brown & Company.

3   As long as these stories remained part of an oral culture, related to small audiences of unimportant people, they were largely overlooked by the literary and educational establishment. But as soon as they began to surface in printed texts there were outcries of horror and disapproval; cries that have continued to this day.

4   The late-eighteenth-century author and educational authority Sarah Trimmer cautioned parents against allowing their children to hear or read fairy tales, which she considered immoral because they taught ambition, violence, a love of wealth, and the desire to marry above one's station. Cinderella, she wrote, "paints some of the worst passions that can enter into the human breast, and of which little children should, if possible, be totally ignorant; such as envy, jealousy, a dislike of step-mothers and half-sisters, vanity, a love of dress, etc." Other critics complained that these tales were unscientific and confused truth with fiction, and that they wasted time that would be better spent learning facts, skills, and good manners.

5   More than 150 years later it was still believed in high-minded progressive circles that fairy tales were unsuitable for children. "Does not 'Cinderella' interject a social and economic situation which is both confusing and vicious? . . . Does not 'Jack and the Beanstalk' delay a child's rationalizing of the world and leave him longer than is desirable without the beginnings of scientific standards?" as one child education expert, Lucy Sprague Mitchell, put it in the introduction to her *Here and Now Story Book,* which I received for my fifth birthday. It would be much better, she and her colleagues thought, for children to read simple, pleasant, realistic tales that would help to prepare us for the adult world.

6   Mrs. Mitchell's own contribution to literature was a squat volume, sunny orange in color, with an idealized city scene on the cover. Inside I could read about the Grocery Man ("This is John's Mother. Good morning, Mr. Grocery Man") and How Spot Found a Home. The children and parents in these stories were exactly like the ones I knew, only more boring. They never did anything really wrong, and nothing dangerous or surprising ever happened to them—no more than it did to Dick and Jane, whom I and my friends were soon to meet in first grade.

7   After we grew up, of course, we found out how unrealistic these stories had been. The simple, pleasant adult society they had prepared us for did not exist. As we had suspected, the fairy tales had been right all along—the world was full of hostile, stupid giants and perilous castles and people who abandoned their children in the

nearest forest. To succeed in this world you needed some special skill or patronage, plus remarkable luck; and it didn't hurt to be very good-looking. The other qualities that counted were wit, boldness, stubborn persistence, and an eye for the main chance. Kindness to those in trouble was also advisable—you never knew who might be useful to you later on.

8   The fairy tales were also way ahead of Mrs. Mitchell with respect to women's liberation. In her stories men drove wagons and engines and boats, built skyscrapers, worked in stores, and ran factories; women did nothing except keep house, look after children, and go shopping. Fairy tales, on the other hand, portrayed a society in which women were as competent and active as men, at every age and in every class. Gretel, not Hansel, defeated the witch; and for every clever youngest son there was a youngest daughter equally resourceful. The contrast continued in maturity, when women were often more powerful than men. Real help for the hero or heroine came most often from a fairy godmother or wise woman, and real trouble from a witch or wicked stepmother. With a frequency that recalls current feminist polemics, the significant older male figures were either dumb macho giants or malevolent little dwarfs.

9   Yet in spite of this, some contemporary feminists have joined the chorus of critics and attacked fairy tales as a male chauvinist form of literature: they believe that giving children stories like "Cinderella" and "Snow White" is a sort of brainwashing, intended to convince them that all little girls must be gentle, obedient, passive, and domestic while they wait patiently for their princes to come.

10   In a way these objections are understandable, since some of the tales we know best—those that have been popularized by Walt Disney, for instance—do have this kind of heroine. But from the point of view of European (and world) folklore, such stories are highly unrepresentative. The traditional tale, in fact, is exactly the sort of subversive literature of which a feminist should approve.

11   For one thing, these stories are in a literal sense women's literature. Charles Perrault, who was one of the first to write them down, called them "old wives' tales, governesses' and grannies' tales." Later, throughout Europe (except in Ireland), the storytellers from whom the Grimm brothers and their followers collected their material were most often women; in some areas, they were all women. For hundreds of years, while written literature was almost exclusively in the hands of men, these tales were being invented and passed on orally by women.

12   In content too fairy tales are women's literature. Writers like Robert Graves have seen them as survivals of an older, matriarchal culture and faith; but whether they are right or not, it is women who most often are the central characters in many of these stories, and women who have the supernatural power. In the Grimms' original *Children's and Household Tales* (1812), there are sixty-one women and girl characters who have magic powers as against only twenty-one men and boys: and these men are usually dwarfs and not humans.

13   Another thing that separates the folktale from the printed literature of its time is that it is a middle- and working-class genre. The world it portrays and the problems it deals with are those of farmers, artisans, shopkeepers, and the working poor: survival, employment, family unity. The heroes and heroines of these tales are often very badly off, while the supernatural villains—the giants and ogres and witches—are rich. "Kings" and "queens," who lack supernatural powers and have human problems—infertility, exterior enemies, serious illness—seem from internal evidence to be merely well-to-do farmers. Literary retellings of the tales, however, from Perrault to the present, usually give their royalty a convincingly aristocratic setting.

14   The handful of folktales that most readers today know are not typical of the genre. They are the result of a more insidious sort of critical attack than that mounted by Sarah Trimmer and her heirs: the skewed selection and silent revision of subversive texts. At first this selection and revision were open and acknowledged. Perrault rewrote the stories he had heard from his "old wives" in elegant seventeenth-century French, adding witty morals in verse and turning the wise women of folk tradition into pretty fairies in court dress with sparkling wands and butterfly wings. In mid-nineteenth-century England, George Cruikshank made his four favorite tales into temperance tracts—at Cinderella's wedding, he reported, a great bonfire was made of all the bottles of wine and spirits in the castle. Even the Grimm brothers openly bowdlerized their stories to make them "suitable for childhood," and, as time went on, altered them in other ways. In each subsequent edition of the tales, for instance, women were given less to say and do.

15   Most compilers of books of fairy tales, unfortunately, have been less direct. For nearly two hundred years tales have been omitted and unacknowledged changes made in the original texts. The stories we know best today reflect the taste of the literary men who edited the first popular collections of fairy stories for children during the nineteenth century. They read the hundreds of folktales that had been

gathered by scholars, chose the ones that most appealed to them as conventional upper-middle-class Victorians, and then rewrote these tales to make them suitable for Victorian children.

16   By the late nineteenth century a canon had been established, and the dozen or so tales these editors had liked best were reprinted again and again. "Sleeping Beauty" was retold over and over, always without its original ending, in which the heroine gives birth to two children as the result of the prince's passionate awakening of her. Meanwhile, "The Sleeping Prince," a parallel story about a passive hero rescued from enchantment by an active heroine, was forgotten.

17   Folktales recorded in the field are full of everything the Victorian editors left out: sex, death, low humor, and especially female initiative. In some more recent and comprehensive books of tales—as well as in Andrew Lang's famous fairy books named after colors, the later volumes of which were largely compiled and revised by his wife— there are more active heroines. They travel to the world's end, cross oceans on a wild goose's back, climb mountains of glass, enter giants' castles and steal magic objects, outwit false suitors, and defeat all kind of supernatural enemies. They work for years to release their lovers or relatives from enchantments and help them to escape from witches and ogres. They are in effect liberated women who have courage, intelligence, resourcefulness, endurance, and kind hearts.

18   Even in edited versions, fairy tales—as hostile critics have recognized—can be dangerous, and today bookstores are still full of bowdlerized and skewed volumes in which the energy and excitement and vivid detail of the stories are missing or watered down. Sometimes this is done through the illustrations, which are either artificially cute in a comic book style or sentimentally vague, muting the strong impact of events and characters under romantic watercolor washes of pink and blue. Such pictures are unpopular with children, who do not believe that the imaginative is identical with the vague; they notice and object when the witch's house is obviously not made of gingerbread. Even more depressing and inappropriate are pictures that derive from modern art and run to heavily patterned woodcuts or silk-screen prints in muddy shades of green and purple, in which it is impossible to tell the princess from the wallpaper.

19   A more serious problem in many of these collections is the stories themselves. Some of them lazily reprint the Victorian versions of the tales; but even when an editor has conscientiously gone back to the original, there are difficulties. Is one to reproduce the version collected in the field, or should one retell the story with the object of making it more literary, easier for children to understand, or less disturbing?

20   Fidelity to the original might seem at first the best choice, but it is not as easy as that. The semiliterate, elderly rural people who are folklorists' usual informants tend to speak in dialect; they repeat themselves and sometimes forget episodes. Perhaps as a result, Perrault's "Little Red Riding-Hood" ends with both the heroine and her grandmother eaten alive. No last-minute arrival of the woodsman, no miraculous surgical operation, no punishment of the wolf. The Grimms collected two different endings to the story: in one version the wolf is drowned, while in the other his belly is filled with stones and he falls down dead.

21   Even today sentimental editors still bowdlerize and rewrite, often without admitting it. They speed up the appearance of the woodsman so that he walks in just after the villain has growled his immortal last line, "The better to eat you with, my dear!" The wolf is chased out the door and disappears in the forest; Grandmother comes out of the closet, where she has been hiding, or returns home from the village. Nobody gets eaten, nobody gets rescued, nobody gets punished. This is supposed to make children feel safer—even though the wolf is still wandering around outside somewhere, waiting for the next little girl. Which is possibly truer to current social conditions—but hardly more reassuring.

22   In spite of all the damage that has been done by well-meaning editors, fairy tales continue to fascinate and haunt us; and they have their defenders as well as their critics. The psychoanalyst Bruno Bettelheim, in *The Uses of Enchantment,* set out to rescue the tales from what he saw as a horde of hostile and disapproving colleagues, who considered them unrealistic, immoral, and violent. In his view, this prejudice can have serious and destructive social effects:

> I have known many examples where, particularly in late adolescence, years of belief in magic are called upon to compensate for the person's having been deprived of it prematurely in childhood. . . . Many young people who today suddenly seek escape in drug-induced dreams, apprentice themselves to some guru, believe in astrology, engage in practicing "black magic," or who in some other fashion escape from reality into daydreams about magic experiences which are to change their life for the better, were prematurely pressed to view reality in an adult way.

23   Though some of Bettelheim's interpretations seem overdetermined by orthodox Freudianism, his approach is in the main thoughtful, humane, and sensitive. One of his most interesting insights is that the various protagonists of a story often represent conflicting motives or emotions within a single individual. The ambitious, single-minded

brother who has no time to waste on an old beggar woman or a wounded animal and the good-natured simpleton who shares his last piece of bread are the same fellow in different moods: the tale shows the consequences of different choices. The fairy godmother and the witch are two versions of the same woman, and the wicked stepmother is our own mother seen by black light after the blissful years of babyhood are over.

24   Another psychologist who has defended folktales is the transactional analyst Eric Berne (the author of *Games People Play*), who points out that folks remember the tales that matter most to them. He claims that your favorite fairy story is as much a giveaway of character and life history as your most recurrent dream. The boy who once admired Jack the Giant Killer has grown up to work for Ralph Nader; the girl who loved the tale "The Frog Prince" is married now to an ugly but very successful man, while the one who preferred "Little Red Riding-Hood" still keeps getting deceived and seduced, often with rather nasty consequences for her seducer.

25   But it is not necessary to be a psychologist to understand folktales. Often, the hidden messages lie just under the surface. "Snow White," for instance, could be seen as telling girls to beware of a mother or stepmother who is secretly competitive and envious of their youth and good looks. The gifts and advice of such a mother are poisonous and designed not to make you more attractive but to immobilize you in a kind of death in life. In extreme cases it might be best to run away and live with friends. Even the horrifying ending, in which the wicked queen dances in red-hot shoes till she drops, suggests a real-life equivalent: the middle-aged woman who exhausts herself by insisting on upstaging her daughter and being the life of the party. "Red Riding-Hood," in this reading, not only warns against predatory men but against the sort of grandmother who wants to devour her grandchild emotionally and announces her intent by crying, "You're so cute I could just eat you up!"

26   "Jack the Giant Killer" can be seen as a lesson about how to deal with the big, stupid, mean, and ugly people you are going to meet in life, a more useful lesson than that taught by video games. Jack doesn't zap the giant with a laser gun, because in real life when you meet a bully or an armed mugger or a boss who wants to push you around you probably won't have a laser gun. What Jack does is to defeat the giant by using his intelligence and powers of invention.

27   As with individuals, so with societies. Each nation and generation chooses its favorite stories from the hundreds available and alters

them to suit local beliefs and conditions. Cinderella appears as a ninth-century Chinese maiden, and her story is told today, anthropologists report, by the Arabs of North Africa and the Zuni Indians of New Mexico—where her fairy godmother is a wild turkey. In the Scottish High-lands, on the other hand, she is Cinderella's dead mother come back to life in the form of a wise old sheep.

28   Anthropologists of the structuralist school have noticed that almost every popular European fairy story begins with the description of a family situation. "Once upon a time there was a poor woodcutter who lived near the forest with his wife and two children . . ." or "Long ago there lived a king and queen who had a daughter as beautiful as the day . . ." The endings of these tales are often alike too: "So they were married, and lived happily ever after." The story itself is about the period of time between the hero's or heroine's leaving their family of origin and the establishment of a new family of procreation. Between these two events lie many adventures that are also tests—tests of virtue, courage, cleverness, patient endurance, or kindness of heart.

29   In another popular type of fairy story, such as "Hansel and Gretel," the hero and heroine remain children throughout. They too go through adventures and tests; they are lost in the forest, threatened by cannibalistic witches and giants. But their happy ending comes when they are restored to their family of origin. One purpose of such tales, according to a colleague of mine, is to express and relieve the two basic but opposed fears of all children (and a good many grown-ups): that they will be abandoned, and that they will be devoured. Adults who prefer these tales to the first type may still be stuck in their own childhood.

30   The structuralists have noticed, too, that the hero or heroine of a fairy tale usually cannot kill the dragon or marry the princess without help. This, of course, is contrary to the American tradition that if you go it alone and work hard enough, you will get to the top. In fairy tales, characters who refuse help, or refuse to help others, end up covered with tar or talking frogs and snakes. If the compiler of a book of fairy stories doesn't see things this way, he can edit out such tales in favor of ones like "The Gallant Tailor" or "Mollie Whuppie," in which the protagonists make it completely on their own.

31   The great distinction of the Grimm brothers was that though they altered their tales, they did not pick and choose; they printed almost everything they heard. The complete edition of their *Household Tales* contains two hundred stories and runs to nearly 650 pages of small

type in the standard American edition. Only about eighty of these tales involve magic—the rest are a mixed bag of jokes, fables, legends, comic anecdotes, and ghost stories. They were told not only to children but (as the name implies) to the whole family.

32   Though Christian saints appear in some of the stories, the Grimms' tales can also be seen as a kind of pagan Bible, garbled and altered by being passed down orally through many generations but still full of the half-animal gods and familiar spirits of pre-Christian Europe—the haunted wells and forests, the elves and witches, the ancient superstitions and rituals. As with the Bible, every reader or editor can take from it what suits him or her.

33   An excellent sampling of the unfamiliar *Household Tales* is contained in *The Juniper Tree and Other Tales from Grimm,* selected by Lore Segal and Maurice Sendak. They have included a few old favorites, but more are missing; and the stories that replace them are among the strangest, most grotesque, mysterious, and haunting in Grimm. Some are not fairy tales at all but half-comic, half-frightening realistic stories of violence, deception, and folly; and by no means all end happily.

34   Even the tales of magic, for a modern reader, have odd symbolic overtones. In "Hans My Hedgehog," for instance, a peasant's wife gives birth to a child who is a hedgehog from the waist up; he rides on a cock and can play the bagpipes better than any man in the country. His parents do not care much for him and make him sleep on a pile of straw behind the stove: "So there he lay behind the oven for eight years and his father got tired of him and thought, If he would only die! He did not die, however, but went on lying there."

35   In the tale "Godfather Death," Death takes his young godson into the woods and shows him an herb that grows there, saying,

> I shall make you into a famous doctor. When you are called to a patient's bedside I will appear and if I stand at the sick man's head you can boldly say that you will cure him and if you give him some of this herb he will recover. But if I stand at the sick man's feet, then he is mine, and you must say there is no help for him and no doctor on this earth could save him.

The godson becomes rich and successful; but finally he oversteps himself and angers Death—like some modern physicians—by keeping a patient alive when he knows she should die. He pays with his own life.

36   The same fantastic and haunting quality appears in the illustrations to *The Juniper Tree*. Like all Maurice Sendak's work, they are superb. But they come from a darker and stranger side of his genius than the pictures in *In the Night Kitchen* or *Where the Wild Things Are*. They are visions of another and in some ways realer world than this, a dream—or nightmare—world certainly, but one in which the dream gardens contain actual toads, complete to the last wart. They have beauty too, though it is a beauty that sometimes merges into the terrifying; skeletons appear, corpses, hooded ghosts, and a devil that makes the Wild Things look like stuffed toys.

37   The late J.R.R. Tolkien once wrote, "If fairy story as a kind is worth reading at all it is worthy to be written for and read by adults. They will, of course, put more in and get more out than children can." *The Juniper Tree* is for adults, who can read these strange old tales as if they had been written yesterday by Jorge Luis Borges, Italo Calvino, or I. B. Singer and who will, if they are fortunate, find them a way into a lost world, not only of childhood, but of universal power and meaning.

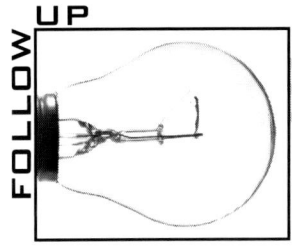

FOLKTALE LIBERATION

Exploring Language

anecdotes: stories or personal experiences illustrating a point.
aristocratic: of the higher social classes, like lords and nobles or high-society Americans who can trace their heritage back to the *Mayflower*. Often called *bluebloods*.
bowdlerized: modified to leave out or change, sometimes simplify, parts of the original that might offend current ideas of morality.
fidelity: faithfulness.
insidious: treacherous or deceitful.
interject: to interrupt or throw in your own ideas or information.
matriarchal: run by females. Elephants have a matriarchal society—they kick out the males as soon as they're old enough to fend for themselves. *Patriarchal* is the opposite, meaning run by males.
ogre: a monster or frightening giant in fairy tales that eats people; also used to refer to a mean person. An ogress is a female ogre.
orthodox: traditional or established.
perilous: dangerous or threatening.
polemics: argument or debate, usually the attack of the opponent.
procreation: having children, or in the case of animals, offspring.
rationalize: to explain or justify.
semiliterate: reading and writing on an elementary level; having limited knowledge.
skewed: slanted or distorted.
subversive: seeking to corrupt or overthrow. Lurie is saying that subversive children's literature is that which goes against what many parents think is proper.
temperance: restraint or self-control.

USAGE Language challenge: Use at least three of these Exploring Language words in one sentence.

Thinking and Talking Points

1. Examine the long quote by Bruno Bettelheim in paragraph #22. In your own words, summarize his point. What has your own experience been with fairy tales? Do you agree—at least in a general way—with his statement? Why or why not?
2. In paragraph #6, Lurie gives some examples of childhood stories and states, "The children and parents in these stories were exactly like the ones I knew, only more boring." Try to remember your favorite childhood story or picture book. Why did you like it? What makes the stories that Lurie mentions boring?
3. Reread paragraph #7. Can you think of examples from your experience or from the media that support the view that "the world was full of hostile, stupid giants and perilous castles and people who abandoned their children in the nearest forest"? Examine the list of qualities Lurie says fairy tales teach us we need in the world. Do you think there's some truth to these statements?
4. Reread paragraphs #9 and 10. How does Lurie **refute** the argument by some feminists that tales like Cinderella brainwash girls and are "intended to convince them that all little girls must be gentle, obedient, passive, and domestic while they wait patiently for their princes to come." How convincing is Lurie's argument?
5. In paragraph #34, Lurie gives a summary of a fairy tale called "Hans My Hedgehog," saying that it has "odd symbolic overtones." Read the passage and explain what you think she means.

Styling

Lurie, like most good writers, uses a variety of sentence styles. Here's one you can practice:

> In her stories, men drove wagons and engines and boats, built skyscrapers, worked in stores, and ran factories; women did nothing except keep house, look after children, and go shopping.

Lurie pulls together several details in one sentence to make her point: unlike fairy tales, the stories of Lucy Sprague Mitchell bored children and perpetuated gender stereotypes. Gathering several examples into one sentence creates stronger impact and sentence style. If Lurie just had one example in her sentence, it wouldn't be very convincing. Lurie has two complete sentences—one about men and one about women—

that she wants to link in thought, so she uses a semicolon. She gives a verb followed by objects. Look at the breakdown:

men *drove* wagons and engines and boats

built skyscrapers

worked in stores

ran factories

The statement after the semicolon does the same thing, creating a balance to the structure:

women did nothing but *keep* house

look after children

go shopping

PRACTICE Fill in the blanks below with objects that complete the thoughts. You can use more than one word for each blank.

Hummingbirds dive at _____, fight over the _____, build _____, and eat _____.

When Chester went hiking, he climbed _____, tore his _____, ran out of _____, and finally reached _____.

At the Wild Animal Park in San Diego, the keepers feed _____, clean up _____, walk _____, count _____, and enjoy _____.

YOU TRY IT For each of the above sentences, replace the period at the end with a semicolon and then add another statement that models the structure of the first; in the hummingbird example, you might want to write about another bird or animal.

Teaming Up

1. Bring in illustrations by Maurice Sendak that Lurie mentions in paragraph #36. Compare illustrations. Reread the paragraph and discuss whether or not the illustrations support her point.

2. A Good Warm-up for Writing Idea #3. Have each team member bring in a fairy tale either from Grimms or Hans Christian Andersen (this activity works best in small teams). Read the stories aloud in your group and discuss how they might teach lessons about real life and how to cope with problems. Now you have a start on Writing Idea #3.

Writing Ideas

1. Search online or in a library for annotated versions of fairy tales (*The Annotated Brothers Grimm* by Maria Tatar, published by Norton, is a good source). Choose one of the fairy tales Lurie mentions in her essay. Write an essay that explains how the annotations helped—or didn't help—you understand the story's meanings. Does the story help support any of Lurie's views?
2. Choose a favorite fairy tale (if you don't remember any from childhood, choose one you've heard about or get a copy of Grimms' fairy tales from your library). Write an essay that explains how the story reveals your character or life history. For examples, read paragraph #24 of Lurie's essay. Don't be tempted to watch the Disney version. It's very different!
3. Read a story from Grimms or Hans Christian Andersen. Write an essay explaining how the tale teaches life lessons like dealing with mean people or coping with sibling rivalry (jealousy among sisters and brothers).

Essay and Film Connections

Pauline Kael's review of Disney's *The Little Mermaid* also defends the traditional versions of fairy tales. In addition to the Davenport films recommended with the Kael article, I suggest another fantasy film based on an Irish folktale, *The Secret of Roan Inish* by director John Sayles. Another excellent film—with French subtitles—by Jean Cocteau superbly recreates *Beauty and the Beast*. Some of the special effects are quite remarkable for the day. The film is available in the foreign film section of many video stores.

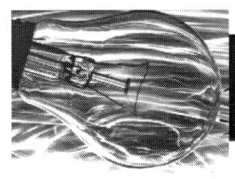

FROM THE CONTENT OF OUR CHARACTER

Shelby Steele

> Shelby Steele is a writer and educator who has many published essays and books to his credit. In this excerpt from his book, Steele argues that despite still-existing racism, overall, there is "a remarkable range of opportunity if we are willing to pursue it." African Americans, according to Steele, need to stop focusing on a victim-based identity and take advantage of what mainstream America has to offer.

DUSTBIN OF HISTORY AND CULTURE

JEAN-PAUL SARTRE: (1905–1980) French philosopher and writer and leading proponent of existentialism.
RALPH ELLISON: (1914–1994) American novelist and essayist who wrote *The Invisible Man*.
EXISTENTIAL: See "Thinking and Talking Points" #5

1   There are many profound problems facing black America today: a swelling black underclass; a black middle class that declined slightly in size during the Eighties; a declining number of black college students; an epidemic of teenage pregnancy, drug use, and gang violence; continuing chronic unemployment; astoundingly high college and high school dropout rates; an increasing number of single-parent families; a disproportionately high infant mortality rate; and so on. Against this despair it might seem almost esoteric for me to talk about the importance of individual identity and possibility. Yet I have come to believe that despite the existing racism in today's America, opportunity is the single most constant but unexploited aspect of the black condition. The only way we will see the advancement of black people in this country is for us to focus on developing ourselves as individuals and embracing opportunity.

2   I have come to this conclusion over time. In the late Sixties, I was caught up in the new spirit of black power and pride that swept over black America like one of those storms that change the landscape. I

From "The Content of Our Character" by Shelby Steele, *Harper's Magazine,* May, 1990. Copyright © 1990 by Harper's Magazine. All rights reserved. Reproduced from the May issue by special permission.

will always believe this storm was inevitable and, therefore, positive in many ways. What I gained from it was the power to be racially unapologetic, no mean benefit considering the long trial of patience that blacks were subjected to during the civil rights movement. But after a while, by the early Seventies, it became clear that black power did not offer much of a blueprint for how to move my life forward; it told me virtually nothing about who I was as an individual or how I might live in the world as myself. Of course, it was my mistake to think it could. But in the late Sixties, "blackness" was an invasive form of collective identity that cut so deeply into one's individual space that it seemed also to be an individual identity. It came as something of a disappointment to realize that the two were not the same, that being "black" in no way spared me the necessity of being myself.

3   In the early Seventies, without realizing it, I made a sort of bargain with the prevailing black identity—I subscribed in a general way to its point of view so that I could be free to get on with my life. Many blacks I knew did the same.

4   And what were we subscribing to? Generally, I think it was a form of black identity grounded in the spirit of black power. It carried a righteous anger at and mistrust of American society; it believed that blacks continued to be the victims of institutional racism, that we would have to maintain an adversarial stance toward society, and that a right racial unity was necessary both for survival and advancement. This identity was, and is, predicated on the notion that those who burned you once will burn you again, and it presupposes a deep racist reflex in American life that will forever try to limit black possibility.

5   I think it was the space I cleared for myself by loosely subscribing to this identity that ultimately put me in conflict with it. It is in the day-to-day struggle of living on the floor of a society, so to speak, that one gains a measure of what is possible in that society. And by simply living as an individual in America—with my racial-identity struggle suspended temporarily—I discovered that American society offered me, and blacks in general, a remarkable range of opportunity if we were willing to pursue it.

6   In my daily life I continue to experience racial indignities and slights: This morning I was told that blacks had too much musical feeling (soul, I suppose) to be good classical musicians; yesterday I passed two houses with gnomish black lawn jockeys on their front porches; my children have been called "nigger," as have I; I wear a tie and carry a briefcase so that my students on the first day of class will know I'm the professor; and so on. I also know that actual racial discrimination

persists in many areas of American life. I have been the victor in one housing-discrimination suit, as were my parents before me. My life is not immune to any of this, and I will never endure it with élan. Yet I have also come to realize that, in this same society, I have been more in charge of my fate than I ever wanted to believe and that though I have been limited by many things, my race was not foremost among them.

7   The point is that both realities exist simultaneously. There is still racial insensitivity and some racial discrimination against blacks in this society, but there is also much opportunity. What brought me into conflict with the prevailing black identity was that it was almost entirely preoccupied with the former to the exclusion of the latter. The black identity I was subscribing to in the Seventies—and that still prevails today—was essentially a "wartime" identity shaped in the confrontational Sixties. It saw blacks as victims even as new possibilities for advancement opened all around.

8   Why do we cling to an adversarial, victim-focused identity and remain preoccupied with white racism? Part of the reason, I think, is that we carry an inferiority anxiety—an unconscious fear that the notion that we are inferior may, in fact, be true—that makes the seizing of opportunity more risky for us, since setbacks and failures may seem to confirm our worst fears. To avoid this risk we hold a victim-focused identity that tells us there is less opportunity than there actually is. And, in fact, our victimization itself has been our primary source of power in society—the basis of our demands for redress. The paradoxical result of relying on this source of power is that it rewards us for continuing to see ourselves as victims of a racist society and implies that opportunity itself is something to be given instead of taken.

9   This leaves us with an identity that is at war with our own best interests, that magnifies our oppression and diminishes our sense of possibility. I think this identity is a burden for blacks, because it is built around our collective insecurity rather than a faith in our human capacity to seize opportunity as individuals. It amounts to a self-protective collectivism that focuses on black unity instead of individual initiative. To be "black" in this identity, one need only manifest the symbols, postures, and rhetoric of black unity. Not only is personal initiative unnecessary for being "black," but the successful exercise of initiative—working one's way into the middle class, becoming well-off, gaining an important position—may, in fact, jeopardize one's "blackness," make one somehow less black.

10   This sort of identity is never effective and never translates into the actual uplift of black people. Though it espouses black pride, it is actually a repressive identity that generates a victimized self-image, curbs individualism and initiative, diminishes our sense of possibility, and contributes to our demoralization and inertia. Uplift can only come when many millions of blacks seize the possibilities inside the sphere of their personal lives and use them to move themselves forward. Collectively we can resist oppression, but racial development will always be, as Ralph Ellison once put it, "the gift" of individuals.

11   There have been numerous government attempts at remedying the list of problems I mentioned earlier. Here and there a program has worked; many more have been failures. Clearly, we should find the ones that do work and have more of them. But my deepest feeling is that, in a society of increasingly limited resources, there will never be enough programs to meet the need. We black Americans will never be saved or even assisted terribly much by others, never be repaid for our suffering, and never find that symmetrical, historical justice that we cannot help but long for.

12   As Jean-Paul Sartre once said, we are the true "existential people." We have always had to create ourselves out of whole cloth and find our own means for survival. I believe that black leadership must recognize the importance of this individual initiative. They must preach it, tell it, sell it, and demand it. Our leadership has looked at government and white society very critically. Now they must help us look at ourselves. We need our real problems named and explained, otherwise we have no chance to overcome them. The impulse of our leaders is to be "political," to keep the society at large on edge, to keep them feeling as though they have not done enough for blacks. And, clearly, they have not. But the price these leaders pay for this form of "politics" is to keep blacks focused on an illusion of deliverance by others, and no illusion weakens us more. Our leaders must take a risk. They must tell us the truth, tell us of the freedom and opportunity they have discovered in their own lives. They must tell us what they tell their own children when they go home at night: to study hard, to pursue their dreams with discipline and effort, to be responsible for themselves, to have concern for others, to cherish their race and at the same time build their own lives as Americans. When our leaders put a spotlight on our victimization and seize upon our suffering to gain us ineffectual concessions, they inadvertently turn themselves into enemies of the truth, not to mention enemies of their own people.

13 I believe that black Americans are freer today than ever before. This is not a hope; this is a reality. Racial hatred has not yet left the American landscape. Who knows how or when this will occur. And yet the American black, supported by a massive body of law and, for the most part, the goodwill of his fellow citizens, is basically as free as he or she wants to be. For every white I have met who is a racist, I have met twenty more who have seen me as an individual. This, I am not ashamed to say, has been my experience. I believe it is time for blacks to begin the shift from a wartime to a peacetime identity, from fighting for opportunity to seizing it. The immutable fact of late-twentieth-century American life is that it is there for blacks to seize. Martin Luther King did not live to experience this. But then, of course, on the night before he died, he seemed to know that he would not. From the mountaintop he had looked over and seen the promised land, but he said, "I may not get there with you." I won't say we are snuggled deep in the promised valley he saw beyond the mountain; everyday things remind me that we are not. But I also know we have it better than our greatest leader. We are on the other side of his mountaintop, on the downward slope toward the valley he saw. This is something we ought to know. But what we must know even more clearly is that nothing on this earth can be promised except a chance. The promised land guarantees nothing. It is only an opportunity, not a deliverance.

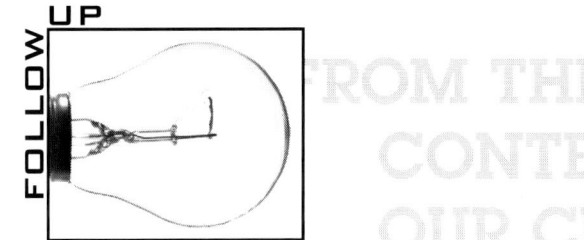

FOLLOW UP FROM THE CONTENT OF OUR CHARACTER

Exploring Language

collectivism: the theory or practice of group ownership and control, especially over production, distribution, and land.
élan: spirit or enthusiasm.
esoteric: limited to or understood by a smll group.
espouse: to support or advocate.
ineffectual: not producing the intended effect.

USAGE Look up *élan* in a thesaurus and discover other lively words that have similar connotations.

Thinking and Talking Points

1. What is Steele's thesis?
2. What is Steele defining?
3. What strategies does Steele use to develop his definition?
4. Steele's book, *The Content of Our Character,* has been both praised and condemned. From reading this excerpt, what do you think makes it so controversial?
5. Look up the word *existential*. What does Steele mean when he uses this term?

Styling

Reread paragraph #1 and study the list Steele writes to underscore the problems facing black America. He uses a complete sentence and a colon followed by a list of problems separated by semicolons. Though semicolons usually separate complete sentences, they can be used to separate items in a series when too many commas might confuse the reader.

> There are many profound problems facing black America today: a swelling black underclass; a black middle class that declined slightly in size during the Eighties; a declining number of black college students; an epidemic of teenage pregnancy, drug use, and

gang violence; continuing chronic unemployment; astoundingly high college and high school dropout rates; an increasing number of single-parent families; a disproportionately high infant mortality rate; and so on.

The phrase *an epidemic of teenage pregnancy, drug use, and gang violence* contains a mini-list requiring commas; if Steele had used commas instead of a semicolons after *a declining number of black college students* and after *gang violence,* the reader might be confused, not knowing which items went with which phrase.

PRACTICE Fill in the blank after the colon with a list of items separated by semicolons, one containing internal commas.

Ryota filled the stereo with his favorite CDs: _____
_____

YOU TRY IT Write three complete sentences followed by colons and lists separated by semicolons, with at least one of the phrases in each sentence containing a mini-list requiring commas.

Teaming Up

1. In your group, make a list of support Steele uses in his argument. Next, make a list of arguments and examples from an opposing view and discuss the results.
2. **A Good Warm-up for Writing Idea #1.** Before class, brainstorm a list of qualities that define you. Type the list, but don't put your name on it. In your group, collect all the responses and shuffle them, redistributing one to each member (if you get your own, shuffle again). Read the lists aloud, trying to guess whose list you have. How accurate were your guesses? Did you learn anything new about your group members?

Writing Ideas

1. Using your list from Teaming Up activity #2, write an essay that defines you, telling what experiences shaped who you are today, and how you arrived at your list.
2. Choose a quality or personality trait and write an extended definition. Some ideas: loneliness, earnestness, depression, serenity, kindness, anger, pity, shame, indignation.

3. Visit your college or local library and use an online database like Infotrac or a newspaper database to research articles on another controversial topic involving an ethnic group, like Native American casinos, whale hunting, affirmative action. Write an essay discussing the controversy. Express and support your point of view.

Essay and Film Connections

Leslie Marmon Silko's "Indian With a Camera" recounts her experience with prejudice against Native Americans. One of the themes in John Sayles's film *Lone Star* is racial identity of a Hispanic community not only in relation to the Caucasian population, but among themselves.

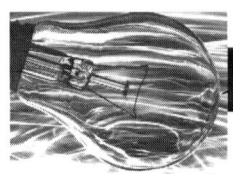

LETTER TO HIS MASTER

Frederick Douglass

Frederick Douglass—an American slave known as Frederick Augustus Washington Bailey—escaped to Massachusetts, becoming a famous writer and lecturer, speaking out against the evils of slavery, and advising Abraham Lincoln. In this eloquent letter, Douglass writes to his former master, demanding to know the fate of his family, still owned by Thomas Auld.

DUSTBIN OF HISTORY AND CULTURE

WILLIAM LLOYD GARRISON: (1805–1879) American abolitionist who founded *The Liberator*, an anti-slavery newspaper.

1   Thomas Auld:

2   Sir—The long and intimate, though by no means friendly relation which unhappily subsisted between you and myself, leads me to hope that you will easily account for the great liberty which I now take in addressing you in this open and public manner. The same fact may possibly remove any disagreeable surprise which you may experience on again finding your name coupled with mine, in any other way than in an advertisement, accurately describing my person, and offering a large sum for my arrest. In thus dragging you again before the public, I am aware that I shall subject myself to no inconsiderable amount of censure. I shall probably be charged with an unwarrantable, if not a wanton and reckless disregard of the rights and proprieties of private life. There are those North as well as South who entertain a much higher respect for rights which are merely conventional, than they do for rights which are personal and essential. Not a few there are in our country, who, while they have no scruples against robbing the laborer of the hard earned results of his patient industry, will be shocked by the extremely indelicate manner of bringing your name before the public....

3   I have selected this day on which to address you, because it is the anniversary of my emancipation; and knowing of no better way I am led to this as the best mode of celebrating that truly important event. Just ten years ago this beautiful September morning, yon bright sun beheld me a slave—a poor, degraded chattel—trembling at the sound of your voice, lamenting that I was a man, and wishing myself a brute.

The hopes which I had treasured up for weeks of a safe and successful escape from your grasp, were powerfully confronted at this last hour by dark clouds of doubt and fear, making my person shake and my bosom to heave with the heavy contest between hope and fear. I have no words to describe to you the deep agony of soul which I experienced on that never to be forgotten morning—(for I left by daylight). I was making a leap in the dark. The probabilities, so far as I could by reason determine them, were stoutly against the undertaking. The preliminaries and precautions I had adopted previously, all worked badly. I was like one going to war without weapons—ten chances of defeat to one of victory. One in whom I had confided, and one who had promised me assistance, appalled by fear at the trial hour, deserted me, thus leaving the responsibility of success or failure solely with myself. You, sir, can never know my feelings. As I look back to them I can scarcely realize that I have passed through a scene so trying. Trying however as they were, and gloomy as was the prospect, thanks be to the Most High, who is ever the God of the oppressed, at the moment which was to determine my whole earthly career. His grace was sufficient, my mind was made up. I embraced the golden opportunity, took the morning tide at the flood, and a free man, young, active and strong, is the result. . . .

4   Since I left you, I have had a rich experience. I have occupied stations which I never dreamed of when a slave. Three out of the ten years since I left you, I spent as a common laborer on the wharves of New Bedford, Massachusetts. It was there I earned my first free dollar. It was mine. I could spend it as I pleased. I could buy hams or herring with it, without asking any odds of any body. That was a precious dollar to me. You remember when I used to make seven or eight, or even nine dollars a week in Baltimore, you would take every cent of it from me every Saturday night, saying that I belonged to you, and my earnings also. I never liked this conduct on your part—to say the best, I thought it a little mean. I would not have served you so. But let that pass. I was a little awkward about counting money in New England fashion when I first landed in New Bedford. I like to have betrayed myself several times. I caught myself saying phip, for fourpence; and at one time a man actually charged me with being a runaway, whereupon I was silly enough to become one by running away from him, for I was greatly afraid he might adopt measures to give me again into slavery, a condition I then dreaded more than death.

5   I soon, however, learned to count money, as well as to make it, and got on swimmingly. I married soon after leaving you: in fact, I was engaged to be married before I left you; and instead of finding my companion a burden; she was truly a helpmeet. She went to live at service and I to work on the wharf, and though we toiled hard the first winter, we never lived more happily. After remaining in New Bedford for three years, I met with Wm. Lloyd Garrison, a person of whom you have *possibly* heard, as he is pretty generally known among slaveholders. He put it into my head that I might make myself serviceable to the cause of the slave by devoting a portion of my time to telling my own sorrows, and those of other slaves which had come under my observation. This was the commencement of a higher state of existence than any to which I had ever aspired. I was thrown into society the most pure, enlightened and benevolent that the country affords. Among these I have never forgotten you, but have invariably made you the topic of conversation—thus giving you all the notoriety I could do. I need not tell you that the opinion formed of you in these circles, is far from being favorable. They have little respect for your honesty, and less for your religion.

6   But I was going on to relate something of my interesting experience. I had not long enjoyed the excellent society to which I have referred, before the light of its excellence exerted a beneficial influence on my mind and heart. Much of my early dislike of white persons was removed, and their manners, habits and customs, so entirely unlike what I had been used to in the kitchen-quarters on the plantations of the South, fairly charmed me, and gave me a strong disrelish for the coarse and degrading customs of my former condition. I therefore made an effort so to improve my mind and deportment as to be somewhat fitted to the station to which I seemed almost providentially called. The transition from degradation to respectability was indeed great, and to get from one to the other without carrying some marks of one's former condition, is truly a difficult matter. I would not have you think that I am now entirely clear of all plantation peculiarities, but my friends here, while they entertain the strongest dislike to them, regard me with that charity to which my past life somewhat entitles me, so that my condition in this respect is exceedingly pleasant. So far as my domestic affairs are concerned, I can boast of as comfortable a dwelling as your own. I have an industrious and neat companion, and four dear children—the oldest a girl of nine years and three fine boys, the oldest eight, the next six, and the youngest four years old. The three oldest are now going regularly to

school—two can read and write, and the other can spell with tolerable correctness words of two syllables. Dear fellows! they are all in comfortable beds, and are sound asleep, perfectly secure under my own roof. There are no slaveholders here to rend my heart by snatching them from my arms, or blast a mother's dearest hopes by tearing them from her bosom. These dear children are ours—not to work up into rice, sugar and tobacco, but to watch over, regard, and protect, and to rear them up in the nurture and admonition of the gospel—to train them up in the paths of wisdom and virtue, and, as far as we can to make them useful to the world and to themselves. Oh! sir, a slaveholder never appears to me so completely an agent of hell, as when I think of and look upon my dear children. It is then that my feelings rise above my control. I meant to have said more with respect to my own prosperity and happiness, but thoughts and feelings which this recital has quickened unfit me to proceed further in that direction. The grim horrors of slavery rise in all their ghastly terror before me, the wails of millions pierce my heart, and chill my blood. I remember the chain, the gag, the bloody whip, the death-like gloom overshadowing the broken spirit of the fettered bondman, the appalling liability of his being torn away from wife and children, and sold like a beast in the market. Say not that this is a picture of fancy. You well know that I wear stripes on my back inflicted by your direction; and that you, while we were brothers in the same church caused this right hand, with which I am now penning this letter, to be closely tied to my left, and my person dragged at the pistol's mouth, fifteen miles, from the Bay side to Easton to be sold like a beast in the market for the alleged crime of intending to escape from your possession. All this and more you remember, and know to be perfectly true, not only of yourself, but of nearly all of the slaveholders around you.

7   At this moment, you are probably the guilty holder of at least three of my own dear sisters, and my only brother in bondage. These you regard as your property. They are recorded on your ledger, or perhaps have been sold to human flesh mongers, with a view to filling your own ever-hungry purse. Sir, I desire to know how and where these dear sisters are. Have you sold them? or are they still in your possession? What has become of them? are they living or dead? And my dear old grandmother, whom you turned out like an old horse, to die in the woods—is she still alive? Write and let me know all about them. If my grandmother be still alive, she is of no service to you, for by this time she must be nearly eighty years old—too old to be cared for by one to whom she has ceased to be of service, send her to me at

Rochester, or bring her to Philadelphia, and it shall be the crowning happiness of my life to take care of her in her old age. Oh! she was to me a mother, and a father, so far as hard toil for my comfort could make her such. Send me my grandmother! that I may watch over and take care of her in her old age. And my sisters, let me know all about them. I would write to them, and learn all I want to know of them, without disturbing you in any way, but that, through your unrighteous conduct, they have been entirely deprived of the power to read and write. You have kept them in utter ignorance, and have therefore robbed them of the sweet enjoyments of writing or receiving letters from absent friends and relatives. Your wickedness and cruelty committed in this respect on your fellow-creatures, are greater than all the stripes you have laid upon my back, or theirs. It is an outrage upon the soul—a war upon the immortal spirit, and one for which you must give account at the bar of our common Father and Creator. . . .

8   I will now bring this letter to a close, you shall hear from me again unless you let me hear from you. I intend to make use of you as a weapon with which to assail the system of slavery—as a means of concentrating public attention on the system, and deepening their horror of trafficking in the souls and bodies of men. I shall make use of you as a means of exposing the character of the American church and clergy—and as a means of bringing this guilty nation with yourself to repentance. In doing this I entertain no malice towards you personally. There is no roof under which you would be more safe than mine, and there is nothing in my house which you might need for your comfort, which I would not readily grant. Indeed, I should esteem it a privilege, to set you an example as to how mankind ought to treat each other.

9   I am your fellow man, but not your slave.

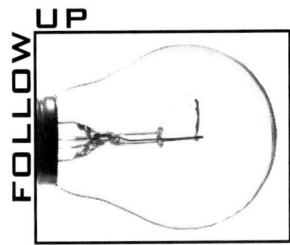

LETTER TO HIS MASTER

Exploring Language

censure: to criticize or reprimand.
chattel: personal possession or property.
deportment: manners, conduct.
disrelish: dislike or distaste.
notoriety: fame, usually with negative implications, like a "notorious criminal."
providentially: luckily or by timely opportunity, sometimes referring to divine interference.
subsist: to exist; to keep alive or provide food for.
unwarrantable: unjustifiable, indefensible.
wanton: cruel or malicious; mischievous.

USAGE Look up the word wanton and study its different meanings. Write two sentences that use different meanings of the word.

Thinking and Talking Points

1. What examples in the essay illustrate the effects of slavery? How do these examples evoke sympathy?
2. What tone does the letter take? Is he respectful to Auld? Does he tell him off?
3. Douglass writes that refusing to allow slaves to read and write is more cruel than "all the stripes you have laid upon my back, or theirs." Why?
4. In the opening, Douglass writes, "I shall probably be charged with an unwarrantable, if not a wanton and reckless disregard of the rights and proprieties of private life." Read the rest of the paragraph. Is he being ironic or mocking? If so, how?
5. How does the letter refute the justification made by slaveholders that slaves were less intelligent and therefore less human than the slaveholders?

Styling

Douglass, like all good writers, uses a variety of sentences styles and lengths. Short sentence: "It was mine." Medium sentence: "Since I left you, I have had a rich experience." Long sentence:

> The same fact may possibly remove any disagreeable surprise which you may experience on again finding your name coupled with mine, in any other way than in an advertisement, accurately describing my person, and offering a large sum for my arrest.

Like many of Douglass's long sentences, this one uses a **loose** structure, but it does so in a unique way: after the first statement, each clause focuses in on a detail in the clause before it. He begins with a complete sentence: The same fact may possibly remove any disagreeable surprise which you may experience on again finding your name coupled with mine.

The next phrase is dependent (in English grammar jargon), a prepositional phrase focusing on *coupled,* giving a closer detail: in any other way than in an advertisement

The next dependent group of words gives a detail about the advertisement: accurately describing my person.

The last dependent group of words gives another detail about the advertisement, linking it to the previous one with a conjunction, and: and offering a large sum for my arrest.

Note: The conjunction *and* is an option. The sentence would be correct without it. Here's a student example based on the Douglass model:

> The lightning flashed incandescently across the storm-troubled sky, illuminating the skeletal limbs of the maple grove that whipped violently back and forth in the fierce wind, casting shadows resembling nightmarish monsters against the sodden ground.

Notice that each dependent grouping provides a detail about the clause before it, getting closer each time, moving from the sky, to the limbs of the trees, and finally to the ground.

PRACTICE Fill in the blanks below with dependent word groups, each time focusing in closer to the object or place. I've completed the first element for you.

> The fog comes in at night like an uninvited guest, *creeping through the quiet streets,* _____, _____.

> A hawk bolted from the mountain, *soaring into the valley below,* _____, _____.

YOU TRY IT Write five sentences in this structure. Use this sentence style in your next writing assignment.

Teaming Up

1. **A Good Warm-up for Writing Idea #2.** Have each member of the group bring in a current newspaper or magazine article about someone in the public eye he or she disagrees with on moral or ethical grounds. Pick out one article you all agree would make a good target, and make a list in the following order:
   a. Explain what the person or group has done that's wrong.
   b. Explain what's wrong with the behavior.
   c. Explain how the behavior hurts others.
   d. Invite the person or group to respond to the allegations.

   Now, draft a letter to this person or group. Have each member of the group take a copy of the letter home to revise and edit. At the next class period, choose the best revision to read to the class.

   For more on this type of argument, see *Adios, Strunk and White* by Gary and Glynis Hoffman.

2. **A Good Warm-up for Writing Idea #3.** Have one person visit the Web site mentioned in Writing Idea #3 and bring in a copy of the Douglass speech. The other members of the group will bring in information on free speech and censorship. Compare the issues to those Douglass brings up. What similarities do you find in the defense of free speech? Which ones do you agree or disagree with? Have the arguments changed since Douglass wrote his speech?

Writing Ideas

1. Imagine what it would be like to be denied the right to read and write. Write an essay as if you're talking to someone who has the power to grant you this right, arguing why you should be allowed to learn.
2. Write an essay to a public figure you think has committed a moral or ethical outrage on society. Follow the format in Teaming Up activity #1.
3. Research and read a speech by Douglass on free speech, then compare it to current arguments on the topic. What principles in the Douglass speech apply today? Are there any that don't? Write an essay comparing these issues, giving your opinion on the free speech debate.

Essay Connections

Another Frederick Douglass essay in this book, "Learning to Read and Write," focuses in depth on the denial of this right to slaves. Both of these essays—and his autobiography—are important historical documents, as well as moving accounts of slavery. Shelby Steele's "The Content of Our Character" focuses on current problems in the African-American community. "Indian With a Camera" by Leslie Marmon Silko explores prejudice against Native Americans.

SECTION FOUR

Laughing Out Loud: Essays That Satirize and Amuse

INTRODUCTION

Laugh therapy? Sounds like quack medicine, but many researchers claim that getting sick people to laugh changes body chemistry, releasing endorphins and natural cortisone, helping the sick feel better and heal faster. Most people enjoy a good laugh—whether or not they think it has healing power—though what each thinks is funny can vary widely.

This section offers a variety of humorous and satirical styles to tickle your funny bone. Some have a gentle humor, like Bailey White's "Mortality," where the author compares her aging body to her ancient car that keeps running despite falling apart. P. J. O'Rourke's biting, outrageous essay "How to Drive Fast" satirically chides—in a non-finger-wagging manner— teens tempted to drink and drive. In "Cat Bathing as Martial Art," Bud

Herron, in a bullet-point process analysis teaches the best way to wash a cat. From Mark Twain to David Sedaris, these essays take on serious and not-so-serious subjects, artfully poking fun, generating laughter, provoking thought. Enjoy.

CAT BATHING AS MARTIAL ART

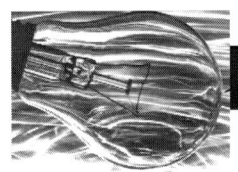

Bud Herron

You can find Bud Herron's work at humor Web sites—where this essay is posted. This humorous process-analysis essay gives pointers on bathing a cat and will amuse anyone who has tried this risky business.

1. Some people say cats never have to be bathed. They say cats lick themselves clean. They say cats have a special enzyme of some sort in their saliva that works like new, improved Wisk—dislodging the dirt where it hides and whisking it away.

2. I've spent most of my life believing this folklore. Like most blind believers, I've been able to discount all the facts to the contrary: the kitty odors that lurk in the corners of the garage and dirt smudges that cling to the throw rug by the fireplace. The time comes, however, when a man must face reality, when he must look squarely in the face of massive public sentiment to the contrary and announce: "This cat smells like a port-a-potty on a hot day in Juarez." When that day arrives at your house, as it has at mine, I have some advice you might consider as you place your feline friend under your arm and head for the bathtub:

3. - Know that although the cat has the advantage of quickness and lack of concern for human life, you have the advantage of strength. Capitalize on that advantage by selecting the battlefield. Don't try to bathe him in an open area where he can force you to chase him. Pick a very small bathroom. If your bathroom is more than four feet square, I recommend that you get in the tub with the cat and close the sliding-glass doors as if you were about to take a shower. (A simple shower curtain will not do. A berserk cat can shred a three-ply rubber curtain quicker than a politician can shift positions.)

4. - Know that a cat has claws and will not hesitate to remove all the skin from your body. Your advantage here is that you are smart and know how to dress to protect yourself. I recommend canvas overalls tucked

"Cat Bathing as Martial Art" by Bud Herron as appeared in *The Saturday Evening Post*, October, 1985. © 1985 SEPS: Licensed by Curtis Publishing, Indianapolis, IN. All rights reserved. www.curtispublishing.com.

into high-top construction boots, a pair of steel-mesh gloves, an army helmet, a hockey face mask, and a long-sleeved flak jacket.

5. • Prepare everything in advance. There is no time to go out for a towel when you have a cat digging a hole in your flak jacket. Draw the water. Make sure the bottle of kitty shampoo is inside the glass enclosure. Make sure the towel can be reached, even if you are lying on your back in the water.

6. • Use the element of surprise. Pick up your cat nonchalantly, as if to simply carry him to his supper dish. (Cats will not usually notice your strange attire. They have little or no interest in fashion as a rule. If he does notice your garb, calmly explain that you are taking part in a product testing experiment for J. C. Penney.)

7. • Once you are inside the bathroom, speed is essential to survival. In a single liquid motion, shut the bathroom door, step into the tub enclosure, slide the glass door shut, dip the cat in the water, and squirt him with shampoo. You have begun one of the wildest 45 seconds of your life.

8. • Cats have no handles. Add the fact that he now has soapy fur, and the problem is radically compounded. Do not expect to hold on to him for more than two or three seconds at a time. When you have him, however, you must remember to give him another squirt of shampoo and rub like crazy. He'll then spring free and fall back into the water, thereby rinsing himself off. (The national record for cats is three latherings, so don't expect too much.)

9. • Next, the cat must be dried. Novice cat bathers always assume this part will be the most difficult, for humans generally are worn out at this point and the cat is just getting really determined. In fact, the drying is simple compared to what you have just been through. That's because by now the cat is semipermanently affixed to your right leg. You simply pop the drain plug with your foot, reach for your towel and wait. (Occasionally, however, the cat will end up clinging to the top of your army helmet. If this happens, the best thing you can do is to shake him loose and to encourage him toward your leg.) After all the water is drained from the tub, it is a simple matter to just reach down and dry the cat.

10. In a few days the cat will relax enough to be removed from your leg. He will usually have nothing to say for about three weeks and

will spend a lot of time sitting with his back to you. He might even become psychoceramic and develop the fixed stare of a plaster figurine. You will be tempted to assume he is angry. This isn't usually the case. As a rule he is simply plotting ways to get through your defenses and injure you for life the next time you decide to give him a bath. But at least now he is clean.

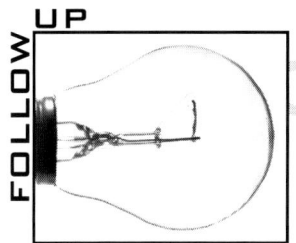

CAT BATHING AS MARTIAL ART

Thinking and Talking Points

1. Herron uses exaggeration, a common technique among humorists. Find examples in the essay where he exaggerates. Which ones do you think work best?
2. Herron uses bullets—points separated by spacing and dots to mark each point—useful in business and Web articles that people scroll through to read. How else does he organize his essay? Could it be written in paragraph format instead of using a bulleted list, or would he need to make changes? If so, what changes?
3. Herron titles the essay "Cat Bathing as Martial Art" but never specifically mentions a martial art. How, then, is cat bathing a martial art? Who is the superior martial artist, Herron or the cat? Why?
4. Examine Herron's use of language, marking or listing lively words and **figurative language**. How does the language enhance the humor?

Teaming Up

1. **A Good Warm-up for Writing Idea #1.** In your group, discuss pets you've owned and the difficulties that arise with pet care. Brainstorm a list of pet-care chores that lend themselves to giving advice, like getting a pill down a cat's throat. Choose one and make a second list consisting of advice—either serious or humorous—on how to complete the chore.
2. **A Good Warm-up for Writing Idea #2.** At home, read Ann Hodgman's "No Wonder They Call Me a Bitch" and compare the humor to Herron's essay. Make a list of similarities and differences in language, tone, and style. Decide which essay you like better and why. In your group, compare your responses.

Writing Ideas

1. Write a how-to essay, advising your reader, step by step, on a process. You can use either the ideas generated in Teaming Up #1 or a different

topic like how to grow orchids, watch football, do a particular skateboarding trick. Think of your hobbies and activities for possible ideas. Know your topic, supplementing research when you aren't sure.

2. Find another humorous essay you like (perhaps one in this section). Write an essay analyzing the humor, focusing on the writer's language, style, exaggeration, or other techniques you think make the essay funny.

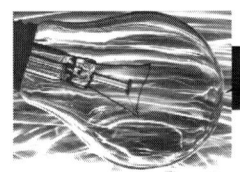

NAME THAT TONE

Louis Menand

Louis Menand—staff writer for the New Yorker, Harvard professor of English and American literature and language, Pulitzer Prize winner for The Metaphysical Club-makes a humorous connection between the Mosquito cell phone ring tone that can only be heard by those under twenty and aging in this essay "Name That Tone," which also appeared in The New Yorker and is part of the 2007 Best American Essays.

DUSTBIN OF HISTORY AND CULTURE

GEORGE BERNARD SHAW **(1856–1950):** Born in Ireland, prominent playwright, literary and music critic, is best known for his numerous plays, among them *Man and Superman, Pygmalion,* and *Candida.*

BOB DOLE: U.S. senator and congressional leader; Republican candidate for president 1996.

GEORGE ELIOT **(1819–1880):** English Victorian novelist (real name Mary Ann Cross) who wrote under the pseudonym George Eliot. Novels include *Middlemarch, Adam Bede,* and *The Mill on the Floss.*

1   There is a new cell-phone ring tone that can't be heard by most people over the age of twenty, according to an NPR report. The tone is derived from something called the Mosquito, a device invented by a Welsh security firm for the noble purpose of driving hooligans, yobs, scamps, ne'er-do-wells, scapegraces, ruffians, tosspots, and bravos away from places where grownups are attempting to ply an honest trade. The device emits a 17 kilohertz buzz, a pitch that is too high for older ears to register but, as we learn from additional reporting by the *New York Times,* is "ear-splitting" for younger people. A person or persons unknown have produced a copy of the Mosquito buzz for use as a cell-phone ring tone, evidently with the idea that it will enable students to receive notification of new text messages while sitting in class, without the knowledge of the teacher.

2   The *Times,* in a welcome but highly uncharacteristic embrace of anarchy, celebrated this development as an ingenious guerrilla tactic in youth's eternal war against adult authority—"a bit of techno-jujitsu,"

"Name That Tone" by Louis Menand. First published in *The New Yorker,* June 26, 2006. Copyright © 2006 by Louis Menand, reprinted with permission of The Wylie Agency LLC.

as the paper put it. But it's not entirely clear which side is the winner here. When you hear the tone, it apparently sets your teeth on edge, which means that, if the entire class suddenly grimaces, it's a good bet that one of the students just got a text message. (Which probably says "sup." Youth, as George Bernard Shaw correctly observed, is wasted on the young.) Anyway, what was wrong with "vibrate only"?

3   The real interest of the story, of course, lies elsewhere. The news is not that students are fooling their teachers, which was never news, even in ancient Greece, or that technology is rapidly unraveling the fabric of trust and respect on which civil society depends, which everyone already knows. It is that one more way for middle-aged people to feel that they're losing it has been discovered. The public concern over natural hearing loss—the *Times* explains that the medical term is "presbycusis"—is part of a trend that started when Bob Dole told the nation that he had trouble getting an erection. Now television commercials inform us that thirty million American men may have trouble getting an erection. Wow. And these are big, friendly, touch-football-playing guys, with George Clooney smiles and luscious, adoring, patient wives. Decay is everywhere discussed, though it is always, weirdly, disguised. Young women with luminous skin explain the importance of fighting premature wrinkling. Thirty is the new forty. We know that this is just anxiety manufactured to sell products, but it does have an impact. People worry about being old before they get old. Americans are living longer but, somehow, aging sooner.

4   People tend to regard the gradual yet irreversible atrophying of their faculties as a bad thing. Is it, though? Sure, it's tied up with stuff that you don't want to think too much about. One day, you learn that you can't hear a sound that is perfectly audible to teenagers and dogs. (Any significance in that symmetry, by the way? Do we feel diminished as a species because dogs can hear a noise that we can't?) Soon after that, you realize that you have forgotten how to calculate the area of a triangle, and how many pints there are in a quart. From there, it's not long until you find that you are unable to stop talking about real estate, which is the first step down an increasingly rocky and overgrown path that leads, almost always—all right, always—to death. What is there to like about any of this?

5   Well, first of all, who *wants* to hear someone else's cell phone? The Mosquito tone is like the squirrel's heartbeat that George Eliot refers to in *Middlemarch:* "If we had a keen vision and feeling of all ordinary human life, it would be like hearing the grass grow and the squirrel's heart beat, and we should die of that roar which lies on the

other side of silence. As it is, the quickest of us walk about well wadded with stupidity." The Mosquito tone is one of those things you're better off not knowing. The world is probably full of such things (though how would you know?). Maybe the area of a triangle isn't that important either. Maybe, in the end, it is all about real estate. The point is that mental and physical development never stops, no matter how old you are, and development is one of the things that make it interesting to be a being. We imagine that we change our opinions or our personalities or our taste in music as we ripen, often feeling that we are betraying our younger selves. Really, though, our bodies just change, and that is what changes our views, our temperament, and our tolerance for Billy Joel. We can't help it. The chemistry has altered.

6   This means that some things that were once present to us become invisible, go off the screen; the compensation is that new things swim into view. Ramps are an example. Try getting a teenager to appreciate a grilled ramp. Try getting a teenager to appreciate another person, for that matter. We may lose hormones, but we gain empathy. The deficits, in other words, are not all at one end of the continuum. Readers who are over twenty may not hear the new ring tone; if they had it on their phones, it might as well be silent. But most readers who are under the age of twenty will not be able to "hear" this Comment. Yes, they will see the words, and they will imagine that they are reading something, and that it makes sense; but they can never truly "get it." The Comment is simply beyond the range of their faculties. For all intents and purposes, if you're under twenty, this page might as well be blank.

FOLLOW UP: NAME THAT TONE

Exploring Language

anarchy: a society without government or law, resulting in chaos and disorder.
atrophy: deterioration, wasting away.
continuum: continuous series or whole; also mathematical term.
guerrilla: irregular warfare comprised of small bands that engage in raids and sabotage.
symmetry: regularity of form, as in both sides of the face are symmetrical (one side matches the other); also applies to mathematical forms.

Thinking and Talking Points

1. Menand writes, "The news is not that students are fooling their teachers, which was never news, even in ancient Greece, or that technology is rapidly unraveling the fabric of trust and respect on which civil society depends, which everyone already knows." Is he jesting or serious? What does he mean by technology unraveling trust and respect?
2. Menand also implies that there is a "war against adult authority." What is the context of this comment? In what way do youth wage war against adult authority? Can you think of examples?
3. Study where he uses the words "grownups" and "noble." What are the implications of these word choices?
4. What is Menand's view on aging? What contrasts does he make to youth?
5. What is the tone of the essay?

Styling

The title of an essay, story, novel, poem, article or other periodical is the first thing a readers sees, so a catchy title is important. Many writers use lines from literature, history, music, or pop culture to find titles. Sometimes, they change a word or two to fit the situation (for a similar exercise on titles, see the Styling with "Roll Over Bach, Too" by Jack

Kroll). In Menand's essay, he plays on the title of an old game show called *Name That Tune,* changing *tune* to *tone.*

PRACTICE Fill in the blanks of the missing pieces of these game show titles with words of your own to create a new title. The rest of the original game show title is in parentheses.

Wheel of _____. (Fortune)
Deal or _____. (No Deal)
The Price is _____. (Right)
Hollywood _____. (Squares)
Beat the _____. (Clock)
The Newlywed _____. (Game)

Note: You're not limited to these choices. Play with them and change some of the other words instead of the ones in parentheses if you like. It's up to you.

Next to each new title, write a possible essay topic that might go with that title.

YOU TRY IT Make a list of television shows by genre. For example, instead of game shows, make lists according to whether they're dramas, sitcoms, or reality shows. Try to have four or five titles per category. Then think of possible essay topics that might go well with those titles or a variation of those titles like in the above practice and write them next to the title. (For example, *Deal or No Deal* might be an essay on computer dating and the types of deal-breakers people list as dating criteria). If you're currently working on an essay, the exercise might help you come up with a catchy title.

Teaming Up

1. The above Styling works well in a group setting. Each member of the group is responsible for a genre of television shows. Then as a team, brainstorm ways the titles might be tweaked to create a play on words. Next to each new title, write a possible essay topic or theme.

2. **A Good Warm-up for Writing Idea #1.** Brainstorm a list of possible differences in thought, belief, or behavior of the young and old. For example, how would grandparents view morality compared to their

teenage or twenty-something grandchildren? Think of at least five categories. Choose one and co-write a paragraph about these differences.

Writing Ideas

1. In Menand's essay, he writes about the viewpoint of aging from the perspective of youth and people who are aging. Think of another contrast in belief and/or behavior between young and old, and write an essay that discusses this difference, outlining both views. You might consider interviewing someone in the opposite age group about your topic.
2. Menand defends aging in his essay, showing the positive aspects. Write an essay defending another aspect of an age group that is usually viewed as negative.
3. Compare the ideas in Menand's essay to Thich Nhat Hanh's "Nourishing Awareness in Each Moment." Do they have a point about the negative or unnecessary use of some technology?

Essay Connections

In addition to Thich Nhat Hanh's piece "Nourishing Awareness in Each Moment," Lawrence Weschler's "Modern Times" offers another view of technology. Bailey White's "Mortality" offers a humorous look at aging, as does Saul Bellow's "Graven Images."

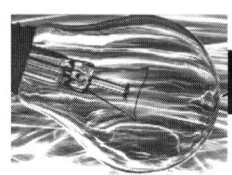

FROM HOW TO DRIVE FAST

P. J. O'Rourke

P. J. O'Rourke is a humorist and former foreign correspondent for Rolling Stone. The following is an excerpt from an essay in his book Republican Party Reptiles. O'Rourke satirizes young people who insist on drinking or taking drugs and then driving a car.

DUSTBIN OF HISTORY AND CULTURE

CHIVAS: A type of whiskey.
SIGMUND FREUD: A 19th-century doctor who founded psychoanalysis and the theory called the Oedipus Complex, which says that children will have an erotic attachment to the parent of the opposite sex.
CHERYL TIEGS: A supermodel in the 1970s and 1980s (O'Rourke's age is showing).
ALBERTO ASCARI: An Italian race-car driver who was killed in the 1950s during a race.
THE ILIAD: Epic poem by Homer written sometime around the 9th century B.C., set in the final year of the Trojan War.
ADIRONDACKS: Mountains in New York State.

See "Writing Idea" #1.

1   When it comes to taking chances, some people like to play poker or shoot dice; other people prefer to parachute jump, go rhino hunting, or climb ice floes, while still others engage in crime or marriage. But I like to get drunk and drive like a fool. Name me, if you can, a better feeling than the one you get when you're half a bottle of Chivas in the bag with a gram of coke up your nose and a teenage lovely pulling off her tube top in the next seat over while you're going a hundred miles an hour down a suburban side street. You'd have to

© iofoto, 2009. Used under license from Shutterstock, Inc.

From "How to Drive Fast on Drugs" from *Republican Party Reptile* by P. J. O'Rourke. Copyright © 1987 by P. J. O'Rourke. Used by permission of Grove/Atlantic, Inc.

SECTION FOUR *Laughing Out Loud: Essays That Satirize and Amuse*

watch the entire Mexican air force crash-land in a liquid petroleum gas storage facility to match this kind of thrill. If you ever have much more fun than that, you'll die of pure sensory overload, I'm here to tell you.

2   But wait. Let's pause and analyze *why* this particular matrix of activities is perceived as so highly enjoyable. I mean, aside from the teenage lovely pulling off her tube top in the next seat over. Ignoring that for a moment, let's look at the psychological factors conducive to placing positive emotional values on the sensory-end product of experientially produced excitation of the central nervous system and smacking into a lamppost. Is that any way to have fun? How would your mother feel if she knew you were doing this? She'd cry. She really would. And that's how you know it's fun. Anything that makes your mother cry is fun. Sigmund Freud wrote all about this. It's a well-known fact.

© MaxFX, 2009. Used under license from Shutterstock, Inc.

3   Of course, it's a shame to waste young lives behaving this way—speeding around all tanked up with your feet hooked in the steering wheel while your date crawls around on the floor mats opening zippers with her teeth and pounding on the

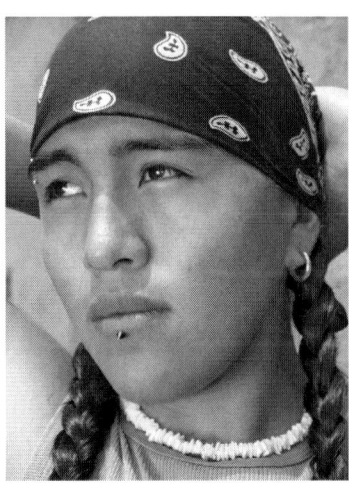
© Mona Makela, 2009. Used under license from Shutterstock, Inc.

accelerator with an empty liquor bottle. But it wouldn't be taking a chance if you weren't risking *something.* And even if it is a shame to waste young lives behaving this way, it is definitely cooler than risking old lives behaving this way. I mean, so what if some fifty-eight-year-old butthead gets a load on and starts playing Death Race 2000 in the rush-hour traffic jam? What kind of chance is he taking? He's just waiting around to see what kind of cancer he gets anyway. But if young, talented *you,* with all of life's possibilities at your fingertips, you and the future Cheryl Tiegs there, so fresh, so beautiful—if the two of *you* stake your handsome heads on a single roll of the dice in life's game of stop-the-semi—now *that's* taking chances! Which is why old people rarely risk their lives. It's not because they're chicken—they just have too much dignity to play for small stakes.

4   Now a lot of people say to me, "Hey, P.J., you like to drive fast. Why not join a responsible organization, such as the Sports Car Club of America, and enjoy participation in sports car racing? That way you could drive as fast as you wish while still engaging in a well-regulated spectator sport that is becoming more popular each year." No thanks. In the first place, if you ask me, those guys are a bunch of tweedy old barf mats who like to talk about things like what necktie they wore to Alberto Ascari's funeral. And in the second place, they won't let me drive drunk. They expect me to go out there and smash into things and roll over on the roof and catch fire and burn to death when I'm sober. They must think I'm crazy. That stuff scares me. I have to get completely shit-faced to even think about driving fast. How can you have a lot of exciting thrills when you're so terrified that you wet yourself all the time? That's not fun. It's just *not fun* to have exciting thrills when you're scared. Take the heroes of the *Iliad*, for instance—they really had some exciting thrills, and were they scared? No. They were drunk. Every chance they could get. And so am I, and I'm not going out there and have a horrible car wreck until somebody brings me a cocktail.

5   Also, it's important to be drunk because being drunk keeps your body all loose, and that way, if you have an accident or anything, you'll sort of roll with the punches and not get banged up so bad. For example, there was this guy I heard about who was really drunk and was driving through the Adirondacks. He got sideswiped by a bus and went head-on into another car, which knocked him off a bridge, and he plummeted 150 feet into a ravine. I mean, it killed him and everything, but if he hadn't been so drunk and loose, his body probably would have been banged up a lot worse—and you can imagine how much more upset his wife would have been when she went down to the morgue to identify him.

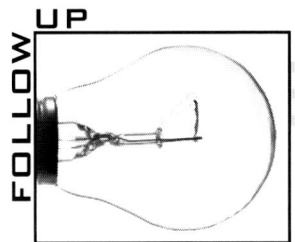

FOLLOW UP FROM HOW TO DRIVE FAST

Exploring Language

matrix: a mold or pattern from which something else originates or develops.
conducive: helping or contributing.
experientially: relating to experience.

USAGE If you look this word up in the dictionary, you'll see a collection of meanings. Try to explain in a sentence or two how the meaning given above applies to O'Rourke's phrase "matrix of activities."

Examine the sentence in which *conducive* appears (paragraph #2). O'Rourke does something English teachers call a "shift in diction," meaning the writer mixes formal words with casual ones. Usually writers avoid this shift. Why does O'Rourke purposely mingle dressed up words like *conducive* with the phrase "smacking into a lamppost"?

Rewrite the sentence where *experientially* appears (paragraph #2) using slang or casual language. Does the sentence lose some of its impact?

Thinking and Talking Points

1. This type of satire is tongue-in-cheek irony, which means the writer says the opposite of what he or she means. O'Rourke *says* he's in favor of drinking and driving, but he *means* just the opposite—drinking or taking drugs and driving are stupid activities that can get you killed. But how does he accomplish his goal? How do we know he's not serious? Look through the essay and find several (four or five) word choices and phrases that clearly tell the reader O'Rourke isn't in favor of drunk driving. Explain why you think these phrases show that O'Rourke isn't serious.

2. Some critics argue that satirical essays—while entertaining—are not "real" argument. Refute these critics by writing a paragraph arguing in favor of "How to Drive Fast" as a more effective argument for its intended audience (teens) than a finger-wagging straight lecture. Be specific. Use examples and quotes from O'Rourke's essay and your own experience to support your stand. Even if you disagree, it's good critical thinking to take an opposing view.

3. Notice that O'Rourke organizes his essay in traditional structure: introduction with a **thesis**, body paragraphs with **transitions**, and a conclusion that slaps reality in the reader's face with the consequence of this type of behavior—death. Identify his thesis and transitions; find other areas where he uses *real* consequences of foolish behavior to keep the reader aware that drinking and driving is stupid.
4. Some readers object to O'Rourke's style of humor. What makes his essay controversial? Does the shock value of the essay work for or against him?
5. What is ironic about the Alberto Ascari example?

Styling

While satire is a style all its own, O'Rourke does use a variety of sentence patterns to add flow to his essay. Here's one example:

> Of course, it's a shame to waste young lives behaving this way—*speeding* around all tanked up *with* your feet hooked in the steering wheel *while* your date crawls around *on* the floor mats opening zippers *with* her teeth *and* pounding *on* the accelerator *with* an empty liquor bottle.

This pattern uses a simple, complete sentence followed by a dash. Next comes a series of incomplete sentences (if they were complete it would be a grammatical problem called a run on sentence). The incomplete sentences explain the behavior mentioned in the simple sentence. The first one begins with an "ing" word, *speeding.* The rest of the incomplete sentences use connecting words, italicized in the example.

PRACTICE Complete the sentence below with at least three incomplete sentences. Start each with one of the connecting words or prepositions italicized above.

Fly fishing is a relaxing way to spend a vacation—_____, _____, _____.

YOU TRY IT Now, create your own sentence. Start with a complete sentence followed by a dash. Next, write at least three incomplete sentences that explain or describe the complete sentence.

The first incomplete sentence does not have to start with *ing*—you can use any of the linking words or prepositions.

CAUTION Be on the watch for **run-on sentences** and **fragments**. A **run-on sentence** consists of two or more sentences run together when instead they should be separated by a period, a semicolon, or a comma with a conjunction. For example, in paragraph #1, if O'Rourke had written "Some people like to play poker or shoot dice other people prefer to parachute jump," he would be guilty of creating a run-on sentence. Instead, he uses a semicolon to separate the statements.

O'Rourke does use several **fragments (incomplete sentences)** in his essay. Near the end of paragraph #4, for example, he writes: "Every chance they could get." While writers often use fragments for a particular effect, I caution beginning writers against using them until they have mastered **complete sentences**.

Teaming Up

1. In groups of three to five members, brainstorm a list of harmful or simply rebellious teen behavior. For the next class meeting, have each person bring in an article about one of these behaviors. Before coming to class, each person should prepare a summary of the article to present to the group. After discussing the articles, highlight passages from each that you all agree would be useful in writing an essay on that type of behavior. Practice incorporating these passages into writing by introducing them with the writer's name and words such as *states, shows, disagrees, agrees, argues, claims, according to*.

    EXAMPLE: Joe Brown states . . .

    Note: For the proper documentation of quotes, see the Basic Documentation section.

2. This activity works best with three people but can be adapted to larger groups. Read Writing Idea #2. Decide on a topic to satirize. Brainstorm a thesis and at least three paragraph ideas for support. Have each member of the group develop one idea into a satirical paragraph. Co-write an introduction and conclusion. Then decide how to organize the body paragraphs. Use transitions between paragraphs.

Writing Ideas

1. **Photo Connection:** Examine the photographs of the pierced and tattooed teens. For an introduction to an essay, put yourself in one of the photographs and write a descriptive paragraph using the senses—

sound, smell, sight, taste, touch. If you've had a body piercing—other than ears—you can use your own experience. If not, imagine what it would feel like or interview someone. Next, think about motivation. Why do people get body piercings? Tattoos? Finally, do some research on teen behavior. Focus on body piercing or tattoos. Write an essay which attempts to explain why some teens get tattoos or body piercings. Use the sentence pattern in the Styling section in your final draft.

2. Find a copy of *The Onion*—a satirical newspaper (available at www.theonion.com)—and read one of the satirical news articles. Find a nonsatirical article on the same topic in a newspaper. Write an essay that analyzes the two pieces, explaining what's being satirized, why, and whether you agree that the topic deserves to be satirized.

3. Write a five-paragraph satirical essay using O'Rourke's strategy. Your target should be a behavior that you think is stupid, one that people usually ignore sensible arguments about: steroid use, breast implants, political issues, drugs (narrow to a specific one like cocaine or amphetamines). Use the techniques explored in Thinking and Talking Points #1. This strategy is key to making the essay work.

Essay and Film Connections

Jonathan Swift's "A Modest Proposal," one of the best satires in the English language, is easy to find on the Web. The film *Election* outrageously satirizes high school elections and other behaviors.

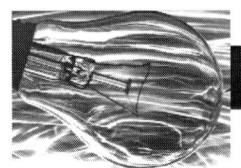

MORTALITY

Bailey White

> In this excerpt from her book *Mama Makes Up Her Mind and Other Dangers of Southern Living*, Bailey White—a first grade teacher, writer, radio commentator—writes about her life in the South, where she lives with her eccentric mother. Here, with gentle humor, she compares her aging car to her new car as well as her aging body.

DUSTBIN OF HISTORY AND CULTURE

GRACIE ALLEN: (1906–1964) American film and TV comedian, married to comedian George Burns.
VIVALDI: (1678–1741) Italian composer and violinist.

1   It really makes you feel your age when you get a letter from your insurance agent telling you that the car you bought, only slightly used, the year you got out of college, is now an antique. "Beginning with your next payment, your insurance premiums will reflect this change in classification," the letter said.

2   I went out and looked at the car. I thought back over the years. I could almost hear my uncle's disapproving voice. "You should never buy a used car," he had told me the day I brought it home. Ten years later I drove that used car to his funeral. I drove my sister, Louise, to the hospital in that car to have her first baby, and I drove to Atlanta in that car when the baby graduated from Georgia Tech with a degree in physics.

3   "When are you going to get a new car?" my friends asked me.

4   "I don't need a new car," I said. "This car runs fine."

5   I changed the oil often, and I kept good tires on it. It always got me where I wanted to go. But the stuffing came

See "Teaming Up" #1.

© Ivan Cholakov, 2009. Used under license from Shutterstock, Inc.

"Mortality" from *Mama Makes Up Her Mind and Other Dangers of Southern Living* by Bailey White. Copyright © 1993 by Bailey White. Reprinted by permission of Da Capo Press, a member of Perseus Books Group.

out of the backseat and the springs poked through, and the dashboard disintegrated. At 300,000 miles the odometer quit turning, but I didn't really care to know how far I had driven.

6   A hole wore in the floor where my heel rested in front of the accelerator, and the insulation all peeled off the fire wall. "Old piece of junk," my friends whispered. The seat-belt catch wore out, and I tied on a huge bronze hook with a fireman's knot.

7   Big flashy cars would zoom past me. People would shake their fists out the windows. "Get that clunker off the road!" they would shout.

8   Then one day on my way to work, the car coughed, sputtered, and stopped. "This is it," I thought, and I gave it a pat. "It's been a good car."

9   I called the mechanic. "Tow it in," I said. "I'll have to decide what to do." After work I went over there. I was feeling very glum. The mechanic laughed at me. "It's not funny," I said. "I've had that car a long time."

10 "You know what's wrong with that car?" he said. "That car was out of gas." So I slopped a gallon of gas in the tank and drove ten more years. The gas gauge never worked again after that day, but I got to where I could tell when the gas was low by the smell. I think it was the smell of the bottom of the tank.

11 There was also a little smell of brake fluid, a little smell of exhaust, a little smell of oil, and after all the years a little smell of me. Car smells. And sounds. The wonderful sound when the engine finally catches on a cold day, and an ominous tick tick in July when the radiator is working too hard. The windshield wipers said "Gracie Allen Gracie Allen Gracie Allen." I didn't like a lot of conversation in the car because I had to keep listening for a little skip that meant I needed to jump out and adjust the carburetor.

See "Teaming Up" #1.

© Michael Shake, 2009. Used under license from Shutterstock, Inc.

12 I kept a screwdriver close to hand—and a pint of brake fluid, and a new roter, just in case. "She's strange," my friends whispered. "And she drives so slow."

13 I don't know how fast I drove. The speedometer had quit working years ago. But when I would look down through the hole in the floor and see the pavement, a gray blur, whizzing by just inches away

from my feet, and feel the tremendous heat of internal combustion pouring back through the fire wall into my lap, and hear each barely contained explosion just as a heart attack victim is able to hear his own heartbeat, it didn't feel like slow to me. A whiff of brake fluid would remind me just what a tiny thing I was relying on to stop myself from hurtling along the surface of the earth at an unnatural speed, and when I finally arrived at my destination, I would slump back, unfasten the seat-belt hook with trembling hands, and stagger out. I would gather up my things and give the car a last look. "Thank you, sir," I would say. "We got here one more time."

14   But after I got that letter, I began thinking about getting a new car. I read the newspaper every night. Finally I found one that sounded good. It was the same make as my car, but almost new. "Call Steve," the ad said.

See "Teaming Up" #1.

15   I went to see the car. It was parked in Steve's driveway. It was a fashionable wheat color. There was carpet on the floor, and the seats were covered with a soft, velvety-feeling stuff. It smelled like acrylic and vinyl and Steve. The instrument panel looked like what you would need to run a jet plane. I turned a knob. Mozart's Concerto for Flute and Harp poured out of four speakers. "But how can you listen to the engine, with music playing?" I asked Steve.

© David Benton, 2009. Used under license from Shutterstock, Inc.

16   I turned the key. The car started instantly. No desperate pleadings, no wild hopes, no exquisitely paired maneuvers with the accelerator and the choke. Just instant ignition. I turned off the radio. I could barely hear the engine running, a low, steady hum. I fastened my seat belt. Nothing but a click.

17   Steve got in the passenger seat, and we went for a test drive. We floated down the road. I couldn't hear a sound, but I decided it must be time to shift gears. I stomped around on the floor and grabbed Steve's knee before I remembered it had automatic transmission. "You mean you just put it in 'Drive' and drive?" I asked.

18   Steve scrunched himself way over against his door and clamped his knees together. He tested his seat belt. "Have you ever driven a car before?" he asked.

19   I bought it for two thousand dollars. I rolled all the windows up by mashing a button beside my elbow, set the air-conditioning on "Recirc," and listened to Vivaldi all the way home.

20   So now I have two cars. I call them my new car and my real car. Most of the time I drive my new car. But on some days I go out to the barn and get in my real car. I shoo the rats out of the backseat and crank it up. Even without daily practice my hands and feet know just what to do. My ears perk up, and I sniff the air. I add a little brake fluid, a little water. I sniff again. It'll need gas next week, and an oil change.

21   I back it out and we roll down the road. People stop and look. They smile. "Neat car!" they say.

22   When I pull into the parking lot, my friends shake their heads and chuckle. They amble into the building. They're already thinking about their day's work. But I take one last look at the car and think what an amazing thing it is, internal combustion. And how wonderful to be still alive!

Thinking and Talking Points

1. Why does White title her essay "Mortality"?
2. Find sensory details in the essay. How do these details enhance the humor?
3. Most people are excited about the prospect of owning a new car. Why is White so reluctant to relinquish her old clunker?
4. How is White's old car a metaphor? What clues are there in the essay to support a metaphorical subtext?
5. Is White simply trying to entertain her reader or is she making a point?

Styling

In Thinking and Talking Points #2, you located sensory details, a strong tool writers use to enhance writing, to make the reader feel, hear, taste, smell, and see the experience.

PRACTICE Sit in your car or another spot and **freewrite** on each of the senses for five minutes.

YOU TRY IT Use the best details from your freewrite above to write a paragraph describing your car or other spot. Now you have a start on Writing Idea #1.

Teaming Up

1. **Photo Connection and a Good Warm-up for Writing Idea #2.** In your group, co-write a paragraph describing and comparing each car and the type of person who would drive each vehicle. Make a list of the stereotypes you created about each person. Then debunk each stereotype (noting how each stereotype might be refuted).
2. Before class, write a paragraph describing an object or place—your car or perhaps your room—and what it reveals about your personality. In class—without yet revealing your writing—team up with

another person and tell each other what object you chose. Now write what you think the other person's choice reveals about his or her personality. Compare. Did your speculations match?

Writing Ideas

1. What you drive—like hairstyle and clothing—can reveal personality. Write an essay describing your car—or dream car—and what it says about your identity.
2. Observe several people and their cars, and write an essay that classifies people and the types of cars they drive, illustrating how what we drive can reveal something about our personalities. Admit that you are generalizing and there are always exceptions to your classification; otherwise, you might get accused of committing a logic error.
3. Write an essay that discusses what the automobile says about American culture. If you like, you can restrict your discussion to the culture of a particular region like New York or California.

Essay Connections

Diane Ackerman's "Hair" is about other revealing aspects of culture: hairstyle and identity. Joseph Epstein explores America's obsession with celebrities in "The Culture of Celebrity."

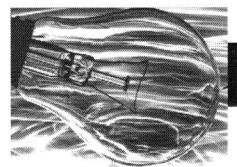

TURBULENCE

David Sedaris

> Essayist and funny man David Sedaris has several collections to his credit: Me Talk Pretty One Day, Naked, Holidays on Ice, and Dress Your Family in Corduroy and Denim (a grammy winner for best spoken-word album). He's also a frequent contributor to The New Yorker magazine, where "Turbulence" appeared.

1   On the flight to Raleigh, I sneezed, and the cough drop I'd been sucking on shot from my mouth, ricocheted off my folded tray table, and landed, as I remember it, in the lap of the woman beside me, who was asleep and had her arms folded across her chest. I'm surprised that the force didn't wake her—that's how hard it hit—but all she did was flutter her eyelids and let out a tiny sigh, the kind you might hear from a baby.

2   Under normal circumstances, I'd have had three choices, the first being to do nothing. The woman would wake up in her own time, and notice what looked like a shiny new button sewn to the crotch of her jeans. This was a small plane, with one seat per row on Aisle A, and two seats per row on Aisle B. We were on B, so should she go searching for answers I would be the first person on her list. "Is this yours?" she'd ask, and I'd look dumbly into her lap.
   "Is what mine?"

3   Option No. 2 was to reach over and pluck it from her pants, and No. 3 was to wake her up and turn the tables, saying, "I'm sorry, but I think you have something that belongs to me." Then she'd hand the lozenge back and maybe even apologize, confused into thinking that she'd somehow stolen it.

4   These circumstances, however, were not normal, as before she'd fallen asleep the woman and I had had a fight. I'd known her for only an hour, yet I felt her hatred just as strongly as I felt the stream of cold air blowing into my face—this after she'd repositioned the nozzle above her head, a final fuck-you before settling down for her nap.

5   The odd thing was that she hadn't looked like trouble. I'd stood behind her while boarding and she was just this woman—forty at most—wearing a T-shirt and cutoff jeans. Her hair was brown, and

"Turbulence" by Sedaris: From *When You are Engulfed in Flames* by David Sedaris. Copyright © 2008 by David Sedaris. By permission of Little, Brown & Company.

fell to her shoulders, and as we waited she gathered it into a ponytail and fastened it with an elastic band. There was a man beside her, who was around the same age and was also wearing shorts, though his were hemmed. He was skimming through a golf magazine, and I guessed correctly that the two of them were embarking on a vacation. While on the gangway, the woman mentioned a rental car, and wondered if the beach cottage was far from a grocery store. She was clearly looking forward to her trip, and I found myself hoping that, whichever beach they were going to, the grocery store wouldn't be too far away. It was just one of those things that go through your mind. Best of luck, I thought.

6   Once on board, I realized that the woman and I would be sitting next to one another, which was fine. I took my place on the aisle, and within a minute she excused herself and walked a few rows up to talk to the man with the golf magazine. He was at the front of the cabin, in a single bulkhead seat, and I recall feeling sorry for him, because I hate the bulkhead. Tall people covet it, but I prefer as little leg room as possible. When I'm on a plane or in a movie theatre, I like to slouch down as low as I can, and rest my knees on the seat back in front of me. In the bulkhead, there is no seat in front of you, just a wall a good three feet away, and I never know what to do with my legs. Another drawback is that you have to stow all of your belongings in the overhead compartment, and these are usually full by the time I board. All in all, I'd rather hang from one of the wheels than have to sit up front.

7   When they announced our departure, the woman returned to her seat, and hovered a half foot off the cushion, so she could continue her conversation with the man she'd been talking to earlier. I wasn't paying attention to what they were saying, but I believe I heard him refer to her as Becky, a wholesome name that matched her contagious, almost childlike enthusiasm.

8   The plane took off and everything was as it should be until the woman touched my arm, and pointed to the man she'd been talking to earlier. "Hey," she said, "see that guy up there?" Then she called out his name—Eric, I think—and the man turned and waved. "That's my husband, see, and I'm wondering if you could maybe swap seats so that me and him could sit together."

9   "Well, actually—" I said, and before I could finish her face hardened, and she interrupted me, saying, "What? You have a problem with that?"

10   "Well," I said, "ordinarily I'd be happy to move, but he's in the bulkhead, and I just hate that seat."

11 "He's in the what?"

12 "The bulkhead," I explained. "That's what you call that front row."

13 "Listen," she said, "I'm not asking you to switch because it's a bad seat. I'm asking you to switch because we're married." She pointed to her wedding ring, and when I leaned in closer to get a better look at it she drew back her hand, saying, "Oh, never mind. Just forget it."

14 It was as if she had slammed a door in my face, and quite unfairly, it seemed to me. I should have left well enough alone, but instead I tried to reason with her. "It's only a ninety-minute flight," I said, suggesting that in the great scheme of things it wasn't that long to be separated from your husband. "I mean, what, is he going to prison the moment we land in Raleigh?"

15 "No, he's not going to prison," she said, and on the last word she lifted her voice, mocking me.

16 "Look," I told her, "if he was a child I'd do it." And she cut me off saying, "Whatever." Then she rolled her eyes and glared out the window.

17 The woman had decided that I was a hard-ass, one of those guys who refuse under any circumstances to do anyone a favor. But it's not true. I just prefer that the favor be my idea, that it leaves me feeling kind rather than bullied and uncomfortable. So, no. Let her sulk, I decided.

18 Eric had stopped waving, and signalled for me to get Becky's attention. "My wife," he mouthed. "Get my wife."

19 There was no way out, and so I tapped the woman on the shoulder.

20 "Don't touch me," she said, as if I had thrown a punch.

21 "Your husband wants you."

22 "Well, that doesn't give you the right to touch me." Becky unbuckled her seat belt, raised herself off the cushion, and spoke to Eric in a loud stage whisper: "I asked him to swap seats, but he won't do it."

23 He cocked his head, sign language for "How come?," and she said, much louder than she needed to, " 'Cause he's an asshole, that's why."

24 An elderly woman across the aisle turned to look at me, and I pulled a Times crossword puzzle from the bag beneath my seat. That always makes you look reasonable, especially on a Saturday, when the words are long and the clues are exceptionally tough. The problem is that you have to concentrate, and all I could think of was this woman.

25 Seventeen across. A fifteen-letter word for enlightenment. "I am not an asshole," I wrote, and it fit.

26 Five down. Six-letter Indian tribe. "You are."

27   Look at the smart man, breezing through the puzzle, I imagined everyone thinking. He must be a genius. That's why he wouldn't swap seats for that poor married woman. He knows something we don't.

28   It's pathetic how much significance I attach to the Times puzzle, which is easy on Monday and gets progressively harder as the week advances. I'll spend fourteen hours finishing the Friday, and then I'll wave it in someone's face and demand that they acknowledge my superior intelligence. I think it means that I'm smarter than the next guy, but all it really means is that I don't have a life.

29   As I turned to my puzzle, Becky reached for a paperback novel, the kind with an embossed cover. I strained to see what the title was, and she jerked it closer to the window. Strange how that happens, how you can feel someone's eyes on your book or magazine as surely as you can feel a touch. It only works for the written word, though. I stared at her feet for a good five minutes, and she never jerked those away. After our fight, she'd removed her sneakers, and I saw that her toenails were painted white, and that each one was perfectly sculpted.

30   Eighteen across: "Not impressed."

31   Eleven down: "Whore."

32   I wasn't even looking at the clues anymore.

33   When the drink cart came, we fought through the flight attendant.

34   "What can I offer you folks?" she asked, and Becky threw down her book saying, "We're not together." It killed her that we might be mistaken for a couple, or even friends. "I'm travelling with my husband," she continued. "He's sitting up there. In the bulkhead."

35   You learned that word from me, I thought.

36   "Well, can I offer—"

37   "I'll have a Coke," Becky said. "Not much ice."

38   I was thirsty, too, but more than a drink I wanted the flight attendant to like me. And who would you prefer, the finicky baby who cuts you off and gets all specific about her ice cubes, or the thoughtful, nondemanding gentleman who smiles up from his difficult Saturday puzzle saying, "Nothing for me, thank you"?

39   Were the plane to lose altitude and the only way to stay aloft was to push one person out the emergency exit, I now felt certain that the flight attendant would select Becky rather than me. I pictured her clinging to the door frame, her hair blown so hard it was starting to fall out. "But my husband—" she'd cry. Then I would step forward saying, "Hey, I've been to Raleigh before. Take me instead." Becky would see that I am not the asshole she mistook me for, and in that instant she would lose her grip, and be sucked into space.

40   Two down: "Take that!"

41   Its always so satisfying when you can twist someone's hatred into guilt—make them realize that they were wrong, too quick to judge, too unwilling to look beyond their own petty concerns. The problem is that it works both ways. I'd taken this woman as the type who arrives late at a movie, then asks me to move behind the tallest person in the theatre so that she and her husband can sit together. Everyone has to suffer just because she's sleeping with someone. But what if I was wrong? I pictured her in a dimly lit room, trembling before a portfolio of glowing X-rays. "I give you two weeks at the most," the doctor says. "Why don't you get your toenails done, buy yourself a nice pair of cutoffs, and spend some quality time with your husband. I hear the beaches of North Carolina are pretty nice this time of year."

42   I looked at her then, and thought, No. If she'd had so much as a stomach ache, she would have mentioned it. Or would she? I kept telling myself that I was within my rights, but I knew it wasn't working when I turned back to my puzzle and started listing the various reasons I was not an asshole

43   Forty across: "I give money to p—"

44   Forty-six down: "—ublic radio."

45   While groping for reason No. 2, I noticed that Becky was not making a list of her own. She was the one who had called me a name, who had gone out of her way to stir up trouble, but it didn't seem to bother her in the least. After finishing her Coke, she folded up the tray table, summoned the flight attendant to take her empty can, and settled back for a nap. It was shortly afterward that I put the throat lozenge in my mouth, and shortly after that that I sneezed, and it shot like a bullet onto the crotch of her shorts.

46   Nine across: "Fuck!"

47   Thirteen down: "Now what?"

48   It was then that another option occurred to me. You know, I thought. Maybe I will swap places with her husband. But I'd waited too long, and now he was asleep as well. My only way out was to nudge this woman awake, and make the same offer I sometimes make to Hugh. We'll be arguing, and I'll stop in mid-sentence and ask if we can just start over. "I'll go outside and when I come back in we'll just pretend this never happened, O.K.?"

49   If the fight is huge, he'll wait until I'm in the hall, then bolt the door behind me, but if it's minor he'll go along, and I'll reenter the apartment saying, "What are you doing home?" Or "Gee, it smells good

in here. What's cooking?"—an easy question, as he's always got something on the stove.

50 For a while, it feels goofy, but eventually the self-consciousness wears off, and we ease into the roles of two decent people, trapped in a rather dull play. "Is there anything I can do to help?"

51 "You can set the table if you want."

52 "All-righty then."

53 I don't know how many times I've set the table in the middle of the afternoon, long before we sit down to eat. But the play would be all the duller without action, and I don't want to do anything really hard, like paint a room. I'm just so grateful that he goes along with it. Other people's lives can be full of screaming and flying plates, but I prefer that my own remains as civil as possible, even if it means faking it every once in a while.

54 I'd gladly have started over with Becky, but something told me she wouldn't go for it. Even asleep, she broadcast her hostility, each gentle snore sounding like an accusation. Ass-hole. Ass-ho-ole. The landing announcement failed to wake her, and when the flight attendant asked her to fasten her seat belt she did it in a drowse, without looking. The lozenge disappeared beneath the buckle, and this bought me an extra ten minutes, time spent gathering my things, so that I could make for the door the moment we arrived at our gate. I just didn't count on the man in front of me being a little bit quicker, and holding me up as he wrestled his duffelbag from the overhead bin. Had it not been for him, I might have been gone by the time Becky unfastened her seat belt, but as it was I was only four rows away, standing, as it turned out, right beside the bulkhead.

55 The name she called me was nothing I hadn't heard before, and nothing that I won't hear again, probably. Eight letters, and the clue might read, "Above the shoulders, he's nothing but crap." Of course, they don't put words like that in the Times crossword puzzle. If they did, anyone could finish it.

FOLLOW UP: TURBULENCE

Thinking and Talking Points

1. Analyze the behavior of both people. Should he have moved his seat? Why or why not? If the woman were to tell the story, how would she tell it? Outline both points of view.
2. Though not everyone has the same sense of humor, the essay has intended humor. Whether or not you think the essay is funny, discuss strategies Sedaris uses to convey humor.
3. What is the main point of the story?
4. Much of the story is told using dialogue. Rewrite a section of the dialogue into prose. What does the story lose by this change?
5. What is the purpose of the example of how he resolves conflicts with Hugh?

Styling

You might come across a writing situation where dialogue is appropriate or necessary to get across your point, tone, or characterization. Dialogue can liven up a section of otherwise dull prose.

Notice that in Sedaris's essay, whenever the speaker changes, a new paragraph begins (the proper format for dialogue). Punctuation goes inside the quotation marks:

> "Well," I said, "ordinarily I'd be happy to move, but he's in the bulkhead, and I just hate the bulkhead."
> "He's in the what?"
> "The bulkhead," I explained. "That's what you call that front row."

Also note that when an interruption like "I said" or "said Rob" occurs in the middle of the sentence being quoted, a comma goes after it, and you would not capitalize "ordinarily" because it's part of the sentence containing the word "well."

PRACTICE Put the following exchange between Alice and the Caterpillar —from *Alice's Adventures in Wonderland* by Lewis Carroll—in dialogue form, using correct punctuation, quotation marks, and a new line when the speaker changes.

What do you mean by that? said the Caterpillar, sternly. Explain yourself! I can't explain myself, I'm afraid Sir, said Alice because I'm not myself, you see. I don't see said the Caterpillar. I'm afraid I can't put it more clearly Alice replied, very politely for I can't understand it myself, to begin with; and being so many different sizes in a day is very confusing. It isn't said the Caterpillar.

You can see how confusing it is when each speaker is not clarified with punctuation, quotation marks, and a new paragraph.

YOU TRY IT In dialogue form, write down a recent conversation, or rewrite a section of your last essay to include dialogue. You can also write down an exchange from a favorite film.

Teaming Up

1. Discuss the situation in the essay, and how you think the woman, Becky, would tell her side of the story. After brainstorming, rewrite the situation from Becky's point of view. Use proper dialogue form. Be prepared to read your paper to the rest of the class.

2. Individually, make a list of Pet Peeves (minor, annoying things that other people do that bother you). Next share your list. Chances are that at least one item on someone else's list is something that you're guilty of doing. Discuss ways to resolve such conflicts or control the behavior in ways acceptable to all in the group.

Writing Ideas

1. Write a narrative essay about a ridiculous, embarrassing, or otherwise unpleasant encounter you've experienced. Describe the situation and use dialogue. Explain how you resolved—or wish you had resolved—the conflict.

2. Write an essay about everyday annoyances, social niceties that people sometimes ignore, and the conflicts or misunderstandings they can cause. Give advice on how these situations might be peaceably resolved. Consider splitting types of annoyances into classifications (see Writing Strategies for Classification in Section Five), perhaps from minor offenses to more major ones.

3. Think of something to which you attach a significance (for Sedaris, it's the *New York Times* crossword puzzle); it can be an object, a ritual, anything that has meaning for you in some small way. Avoid

major social rituals like attending church or getting married. Find something that you do on a regular basis that has significance. Write an essay describing the object or ritual, and explain its significance and perhaps analyze whether or not there's anything absurd in your attachment.

Essay Connections

P. J. O'Rourke's "How to Drive Fast" and Mark Twain's "Advice to Youth," both have themes of bad behavior.

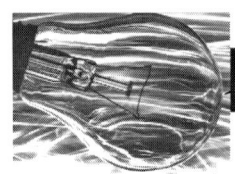

ADVICE TO YOUTH

Mark Twain

Mark Twain (1835–1910), real name Samuel Longhorn Clemens, American writer and humorist, is best known for The Adventures of Huckleberry Finn and Tom Sawyer, but he wrote many other novels, short stories, and essays. In "Advice to Youth," an address to students, he satirizes the arrogance of youth who lie, manipulate parents, and think they're superior.

DUSTBIN OF HISTORY AND CULTURE

GATLING GUN: A machine gun invented by Richard J. Gatling.
INNOCENTS ABROAD: A book by Mark Twain (see Teaming Up #2).
ROBERTSON: Frederick Robertson (1816–1853), English Anglican clergyman (see Teaming Up #2).
SAINT'S REST: A work written by English Puritan clergyman Richard Baxter (1615–1691) (see Teaming Up #2).

1   Being told I would be expected to talk here, I inquired what sort of a talk I ought to make. They said it should be something suitable to youth—something didactic, instructive, or something in the nature of good advice. Very well. I have a few things in my mind which I have often longed to say for the instruction of the young: for it is in one's tender early years that such things will best take root and be most enduring and most valuable. First, then, I will say to you, my young friends—and I say it beseechingly, urgingly—

2   Always obey your parents, when they are present. This is the best policy in the long run, because if you don't they will make you. Most parents think they know better than you do, and you can generally make more by humoring that superstition than you can by acting on your own better judgment.

3   Be respectful to your superiors, if you have any, also to strangers, and sometimes to others. If a person offends you, and you are in doubt as to whether it was intentional or not, do not resort to extreme measures; simply watch your chance and hit him with a brick. That will be sufficient. If you shall find that he had not intended any offense, come out frankly and confess yourself in the wrong when you struck him; acknowledge it like a man and say you didn't mean to. Yes, always avoid violence; in this age of charity and kindliness, the time has gone by for such things. Leave dynamite to the low and unrefined.

4   Go to bed early, get up early—this is wise. Some authorities say get up with the sun; some others say get up with one thing, some with another. But a lark is really the best thing to get up with. It gives you a splendid reputation with everybody to know that you get up with the lark; and if you get the right kind of a lark, and work at him right, you can easily train him to get up at half past nine, every time—it is no trick at all.

5   Now as to the matter of lying. You want to be very careful about lying; otherwise you are nearly sure to get caught. Once caught, you can never again be, in the eyes of the good and the pure, what you were before. Many a young person has injured himself permanently through a single clumsy and ill-finished lie, the result of carelessness born of incomplete training. Some authorities hold that the young ought not to lie at all. That, of course, is putting it rather stronger than necessary; still, while I cannot go quite so far as that, I do maintain, and I believe I am right, that the young ought to be temperate in the use of this great art until practice and experience shall give them that confidence, elegance, and precision which alone can make the accomplishment graceful and profitable. Patience, diligence, painstaking attention to detail—these are the requirements; these, in time, will make the student perfect; upon these, and upon these only, may he rely as the sure foundation for future eminence. Think what tedious years of study, thought, practice, experience, went to the equipment of that peerless old master who was able to impose upon the whole world the lofty and sounding maxim that "truth is mighty and will prevail"—the most majestic compound fracture of fact which any of woman born has yet achieved. For the history of our race, and each individual's experience, are sown thick with evidence that a truth is not hard to kill and that a lie told well is immortal. There in Boston is a monument of the man who discovered anesthesia; many people are aware, in these latter days, that that man didn't discover it at all, but stole the discovery from another man. Is this truth mighty, and will it prevail? Ah no, my hearers, the monument is made of hardy material, but the lie it tells will outlast it a million years. An awkward, feeble, leaky lie is a thing which you ought to make it your unceasing study to avoid; such a lie as that has no more real permanence than an average truth. Why, you might as well tell the truth at once and be done with it. A feeble, stupid, preposterous lie will not live two years—except it be a slander upon somebody. It is indestructible, then, of course, but that is no merit of yours. A final word; begin your practice of this gracious

and beautiful art early—begin now. If I had begun earlier, I could have learned how.

6 Never handle firearms carelessly. The sorrow and suffering that have been caused through the innocent but heedless handling of firearms by the young! Only four days ago, right in the next farmhouse to the one where I am spending the summer, a grandmother, old and gray and sweet, one of the loveliest spirits in the land, was sitting at her work, when her young grandson crept in and got down an old, battered, rusty gun which had not been touched for many years and was supposed not to be loaded, and pointed it at her, laughing and threatening to shoot. In her fright she ran screaming and pleading toward the door on the other side of the room; but as she passed him he placed the gun almost against her very breast and pulled the trigger! He had supposed it was not loaded. And he was right—it wasn't. So there wasn't any harm done. It is the only case of that kind I ever heard of. Therefore, just the same, don't you meddle with old unloaded firearms; they are the most deadly and unerring things that have ever been created by man. You don't have to take any pains at all with them; you don't have to have a rest, you don't have to have any sights on the gun, you don't have to take aim, even. No, you just pick out a relative and bang away, and you are sure to get him. A youth who can't hit a cathedral at thirty yards with a Gatling gun in three-quarters of an hour, can take up an old empty musket and bag his grandmother every time, at a hundred. Think what Waterloo would have been if one of the armies had been boys armed with old muskets supposed not to be loaded, and the other army had been composed of their female relations. The very thought of it makes one shudder.

7 There are many sorts of books; but good ones are the sort for the young to read. Remember that. They are a great, an inestimable, an unspeakable means of improvement. Therefore be careful in your selection, my young friends; be very careful; confine yourselves exclusively to Robertson's Sermons, Baxter's *Saint's Rest, The Innocents Abroad,* and works of that kind.

8 But I have said enough. I hope you will treasure up the instructions which I have given you, and make them a guide to your feet and a light to your understanding. Build your character thoughtfully and painstaking upon these precepts, and by and by, when you have got it built, you will be surprised and gratified to see how nicely and sharply it resembles everybody else's.

ADVICE TO YOUTH

Exploring Language

didactic: intended to teach, but often refers to teaching in a preachy, moralistic manner.
eminence: fame or prominence.
temperate: mild, moderate.

USAGE Locate the sentences where Twain uses these Exploring Language words in paragraphs #1 and #5, and study their usage. Here's a challenge: use all three of these words in one sentence.

Thinking and Talking Points

1. In this type of satirical humor, writers say one thing but mean the opposite. Find examples in the essay that illustrate that Twain isn't advocating lying, feeling superior, or shooting one's grandmother. How effective is this type of humor?
2. Why do you think Twain gives satirical advice to students in his address rather than instructive advice as he claims?
3. Why does Twain write that slander is indestructible? Do you agree? Is this type of lie worse than other lies Twain mentions?
4. What is Twain's view of youth? To what extent do you agree with his view? Is his "advice" relevant today?
5. What point does he make in the last line of the essay?

Styling

Though satire has a unique style, good humorists also use strong writing techniques such as sentence variety. Notice that Twain uses some very long sentences, some very short, others medium. Sentence variety keeps the reader alert, like a song with varying beats and tones. Because you know how to write short and medium sentences, practice modeling one of Twain's longer sentences:

> Only four days ago, right in the next farmhouse to the one where I am spending the summer, a grandmother, old and gray and sweet,

one of the loveliest spirits in the land, was sitting at her work, when her young grandson crept in and got down an old, battered, rusty gun which had not been touched for many years and was supposed not to be loaded, and pointed it at her, laughing and threatening to shoot.

Don't let long sentences intimidate you; they're just short sentences dressed up. If you analyze Twain's sentence, you'll find the short sentence:

Only four days ago a grandmother was sitting at her work.

The rest of the sentence consists of word groups that dress up this simple sentence, describing and giving more information. Twain could have split some of this information into separate sentences, but he knew a well-written long sentence gives what English teachers refer to as "flow" to an essay. Let's examine the rest of the word groups to determine their purpose. The first one is an interrupter placed between "ago" and "a grandmother," giving extra information about Twain's whereabouts: right in the next farmhouse to the one where I am spending the summer.

Notice that the word group is **dependent**—it can't stand alone as its own sentence. The next two dependent word groups come after "grandmother," describing her:

old and gray and sweet

one of the loveliest spirits in the land

The next series of dependent word groups provides action—read them again (in the complete sentence above), writing them out separately on a sheet of paper, noticing that they, too, are dependent.

PRACTICE Fill in the blank in the simple sentence below, adding a dependent clause that describes the teller:

Last week a bank teller, _____, sat innocently at her window.

Next, replace the period after window with a comma, and add a dependent clause describing what the teller is doing:

Last week a bank teller, _____, sat innocently at her window, _____,

Now, give a series of action clauses:

Last week a bank teller, _____, sat innocently at her window, _____, when _____, _____, and _____, and _____.

YOU TRY IT   Write three more sentences based on the above model. Use this structure in your next writing assignment.

   Look Out. Don't get discouraged if you commit comma splices at first. Writing correct long sentences sometimes takes several practice tries.

Teaming Up

1. In groups of three or four members, decide on a topic that might lend itself to satirical advice, like cheating. Brainstorm a list of satirical reasons advocating the topic. Choose one of the reasons to develop into a paragraph, and then co-write the paragraph.

2. Have each group member do a little research on the works Twain recommends students read: *The Innocents Abroad,* Frederick Robertson's Sermons, and Richard Baxter's *Saint's Rest* (the latter two available on the Web). You should be able to find enough information in a good encyclopedia to give you clues. In your group, discuss the findings and why Twain suggests young people should read works like these exclusively.

Writing Ideas

1. Write an essay about an experience you had with lying or slander, either by you or aimed at you, explaining the situation and the damage caused.
2. Write an essay that gives advice, either serious or satirical. You can give moral or ethical advice, as Twain does, or write a "how to" piece, a type of essay English teachers call Process Analysis: how to develop a roll of film, how to buy a car, how to inline skate; the possibilities are endless.
3. Visit a library that has an online periodicals database and research political campaign slander. Write an essay arguing for or against this type of campaign strategy, not only whether it works, but its moral and ethical implications. Use your research to provide examples in your essay. For more on writing research papers, see the Research section in this book.

Essay and Film Connections

P. J. O'Rourke's "Driving Fast" and Jonathan Swift's "A Modest Proposal" (not in this book) are essays that satirize behavior. "Turbulence" by David

Sedaris is a humorous account of behavior he has encountered. The Swift piece is easy to find on the Web. Just use a good search engine—like google.com—and type in Swift Modest Proposal. The film *Election* is a good satire.

SECTION FIVE

Writing Strategies

WRITING BASIC COLLEGE ESSAYS

Getting Started

You stare at a blank sheet of paper or computer screen. Nothing. "Writer's block," you say, and head for the TV and the next episode of *American Idol*. Unless you're writing an essay about reality television programs, resist the temptation.

I don't believe in writer's block and neither should you. If I did, you wouldn't be reading this book. As appealing as that idea might sound to you right now, look at it this way: you'd just be reading somebody's else's book, so dive in, and maybe I can give you some swimming lessons.

Most writer's have trouble getting started, but if you want to pass your English class—or any other college course that requires writing— you need determination and a plan. Most writers have a **prewriting** process, though each writer might approach that process differently. The traditional brainstorming methods—clustering, listing, freewriting—you may have covered in high school or another college English course, but in case you missed class that day, or it's been a while and you've forgotten, I'll go over them at the end of this section.

The traditional brainstorming didn't work for me when I was in college, and still doesn't, but I do have a process: I run. As I runner, I find it's lonely and painful out on the track, so I need to keep my mind off the huffing and puffing, muscle aches and stomach cramps. I plan my writing in my head while I'm running, keeping a pencil and note pad in the car to jot down ideas as soon as I'm finished with my workout.

But that isn't my only prewriting technique, so for you couch potatoes, here's another way. Often, ideas occur to me at odd moments—when I'm reading, watching television, talking on the phone, riding in the car, cooking dinner—so I keep sticky notes handy to keep track of flashes of brilliance that can turn into junk or jewels, discarded or used accordingly. Although I wind up with sticky notes pasted all over my office, car, kitchen, books, day planner, sofa, or wherever I happen to he at the moment, it's worth it when one of those ideas works. My daughter calls her brainstorming "shower thinking" because she gets her best ideas while taking a shower (I tell her that's because she stays in there so long she's bound to think of something). Ernest Hemingway wrote in *A Moveable Feast* about the writing process, "But sometimes when I was starting a new story and I could not get it going, I would sit in front of the fire and squeeze the peel of the little oranges into the edge of the flame and watch the sputter of blue that they made. I would stand and look out over the roofs of Paris and think, 'Do not worry. You have always written before and you will write now. All you have to do is write one true sentence.'" Good advice. If you write one sentence, another will follow, and soon, you'll be writing.

Whether you're a Hemingway, an English teacher, or a college student, the point is to keep your topic in mind and be prepared to write down ideas, even the ones you think you might not use. Students often say to me, "Gee, I had a really good idea for that paragraph, but I forgot it." So buy a notebook or sticky pad and keep a pencil handy. And write.

Once you have some ideas on your topic, you need to find information: visit the library, interview an expert, talk with friends, brainstorm ideas. Gather more information than you think you'll need. You can always discard some of it later. If you use information out of books, from an interview with an expert, or off the Internet or any other source, document correctly or you risk being accused of **plagiarism**. The Research section at the end of the book covers the basics of documentation.

Organizing and Writing

You have great ideas and lots of information. Now what? A lot depends on the type of essay, and strategies for writing particular types of papers are in this section. Basically, though, essays consist of an introduction with a thesis, body paragraphs, and a conclusion. Sometimes it helps to have a thesis in mind before you begin to write, but be open to changing your thesis because you might change your mind as you develop your thoughts.

THESIS STATEMENTS A thesis statement is your main point, often expressed as an opinion. Though not all papers require a thesis, most college writing does. There are a few rules to keep in mind when writing an argument-type thesis:

1. A thesis cannot be a fact. It should express a point of view or opinion.
2. A thesis should not be too broad: For example, "There are many issues in American politics," cannot be a thesis because there is too much to cover. Narrow it down to one issue. Also, this statement qualifies as a fact (see #1).
3. A thesis should not announce its topic. Avoid phrases like "I will discuss" or "this essay will show." That language does not express a point of view. If you wrote, "This essay will analyze the controversy surrounding television's coverage of presidential campaigns," you would not have an appropriate thesis. You're not expressing an opinion.

To build a good thesis, first start with a broad topic:

American politics

Next, narrow that topic by carving out a special area, in this example, politics:

Television's coverage of presidential campaigns

Take a stand on the topic and give your reason or reasons for your opinion:

Although many might argue that limiting television coverage of presidential campaigns violates the idea of free press and free speech, the media's bias for or against a candidate misleads and unfairly influences the public's view, giving the press too much power over the outcome of elections.

Now you have a thesis that is not too broad, expresses your opinion, and does not announce the topic. Keep in mind that a thesis might change as you explore the topic, so be flexible. (For more on thesis statements see the different writing strategies in this section.)

With a working thesis crafted, you're ready to organize each point you want to make to support your thesis.

Let's say that your thesis is "Children spend too much time in structured social activities such as soccer, ballet, and Little League; although there are a lot of benefits to these activities, sometimes children need to be left alone as a group to learn how to problem solve, make their own rules, and learn independence." You might organize the essay like this: paragraph one, introduction with thesis; paragraph two, problem solving; paragraph three, making their own rules; paragraph four, learning independence; paragraph five, conclusion. Notice how the topics are discussed in the order they appear in the thesis? Following this strategy will keep your paper organized.

Keep in mind that this structure is basic; as you develop as a writer, you will want to develop more complex ways of organizing your essay.

Now you have ideas, a thesis, and an organizational plan, so write the draft. Don't panic. Jump in. The water's fine.

Revising and Editing

It's midnight the night before the paper is due. You've written a draft, so you're in good shape, right? Wrong. Most students think that having a draft means they can just hit spell check on the computer and then print. I admit that occasionally a student can pull this tactic off, but for the rest of us, we've only just begun. Writing means rewriting, rewriting, and more rewriting.

First, revise your paper. Revising means big changes, like adding or deleting information, reorganizing the essay, rewriting sentences, checking that the ideas are fully developed. Here's a list of questions to ask yourself about each developmental paragraph of your essay:

1. Can I add another example?
2. Can I add more information?
3. Can I describe something and make it more vivid for the reader?
4. Can I add a statistic or quote as evidence to strengthen my claim?
5. Can I explain a quote so the reader is clear on why I used it?
6. Have I related all of the material to my thesis statement or topic sentence?
7. Are there terms my reader may not understand (for example, surfing jargon) that I need to define?

All of these questions may not apply to every paper, but most of them will. You can always add an example or more information or description, and you should check to make sure that all of your material relates to the thesis or topic sentence.

TRANSITIONS An organized, well-written essay needs transitions between paragraphs and between ideas within paragraphs. There are many ways to smooth out an essay with transition, depending on what you are writing (for transitions with narratives, see Strategies for Writing from Memory). In general, you want to be certain that the concluding line of one paragraph has some link to the beginning line—topic sentence—of the next paragraph. That link can take on the different form of the same word—for example, you might end one paragraph with a sentence containing the word death, and begin the next sentence with deathly or die. You can also use words that mean the opposite: death and life. Using a word with a similar meaning or idea (synonym) works, too: troubled and depressed. For more on transitions, see the Styling section in "About Men" by Gretel Ehrlich.

Don't assume you're done after revising your draft once. I tell students to write their first draft at least one week in advance, put it away for two days, revise again, put it away a second time, go back and revise a third time, and then they can begin editing.

Now you can spell check. But don't stop there. Check for other errors like **run-on sentences** and **fragments** or other grammatical errors. Remember that your computer's spell-check program won't catch misused words. If you write *desert* when you should have written *dessert*, spell check is useless.

You're not done yet. Now that you've cleaned house, decorate with style techniques in this book to give your essay some spark.

Titles, Introductions, Conclusions

TITLES You're browsing through your favorite magazine, trying to decide which articles appeal to you: "Hairstyles of the Stars" or "Tiger Woods Wins Again." If you don't care about hairstyles or golf, you're probably going to move on. Titles are the first thing readers see, so you need a lively one to hook and reel them in, and just because your teacher has to read your paper, whether it has a strong title or not, doesn't mean you should neglect it.

Don't bore the reader with one of those my-summer-vacation titles: "Essay #1" or "Comparison Essay" or "Animal Rights." Those titles don't exactly thrill anyone into wanting to read more. If your title is "Animal Rights" you've probably already lost your reader; very few people want to read yet another essay on that topic. But if your title is something like "Save the Whales, Screw the Shrimp" (an animal rights essay by Joy Williams), or "Am I Blue?" (by Alice Walker, about animal rights and a horse named Blue), the reader might be intrigued enough to at least read the introduction.

So where do writers get these great titles? Sometimes titles word-play on great literature, history, or song. For example, P. J. O'Rourke's essay about the "bad logic" of charitable concerts like Band Aid and Live Aid is cleverly titled "Fiddling While Africa Starves," a play on the line about Emperor Nero, who is said to have fiddled while Rome burned. The novel *Of Mice and Men* by John Steinbeck borrows from an 18th-century poem by Robert Burns (of "Auld Lang Syne" fame, which we sing on New Year's Eve) titled "To a Mouse": "The best-laid schemes o' mice an' men / Gang aft a-gley" (go often awry).

You don't have to know history or great literature to come up with a sharp title. You can borrow from music, TV shows, slogans. Remember how those *Got Milk?* ads took off? Got _____? People fill in the blank with just about everything. Jack Kroll's essay on the Beatles plays on one of their tunes, "Roll Over Beethoven," by changing it to "Roll Over Bach, Too." Kroll's essay "Monster Mash," about horror films, borrows from another old song. One student, Juan Diaz, titled his paper "Milk Not Included," a play on the "Batteries Not Included" slogan seen on most electronic toys. His paper was on cereal icons like Tony the Tiger. Think about your titles. Make them meaningful.

INTRODUCTIONS You're still browsing through that magazine, and a title ignites some interest, so you read on, only to find that after the introduction, you're bored senseless and can't read another word. You want to welcome your readers in, not send them into comas. Once you have that snazzy title, you're obligated not to disappoint your reader with a novocaine introduction. English books abound in suggestions for writing introductions: tell a little story, describe a scene, ask questions, use a startling quote, remark, or statistic. All of these tips work, but there's another way: read introductions to essays that you admire, that catch your interest from the first line, and study what the writer does to hook you. Then model that style.

In "Musical Awakenings," Clayton Collins opens his essay with short, catchy phrases: "Oliver Sacks danced to the Dead. For three solid hours. At sixty. And with 'two broken knees.'" Each phrase introduces a more remarkable point than the one before it. The fact that Oliver Sacks danced to the Dead doesn't seem that incredible, but by the time I get to that last phrase about the two broken knees, I'm hooked. I have to read on. David Huddle's "Museum Piece" creates an immediate intimacy by addressing the reader as *you:* "Jan Vermeer's 'The Girl with the Red Hat' always appealed to you because of that hat." You feel as if you're in the museum viewing the paintings with Huddle, mesmerized by the first line. Ann Hodgman in "No Wonder They Call Me a Bitch" opens her essay with a series of questions: "Is a Gaines burger really like a hamburger? Can you fry it? Does dog food 'cheese' taste like real cheese? Does Gravy Train actually make gravy in the dog's bowl, or is that brown liquid just dissolved crumbs? And exactly what *are* by-products?" Brenda Peterson in "Growing Up Game" starts her essay off with a personal story that contains a startling remark: " When I went off to college, my father gave me, as part of my tuition, fifty pounds of moose meat." Moose meat? Who gives their child moose meat? I don't know about you, but I have to read on to find out the answer.

When you're stuck on writing an introduction, just flip through this book and read several introductions to the professional essays until one intrigues you. Study it and try to imitate it. Give it a try. It might work.

CONCLUSIONS   You're at the end of your paper. You're tired. Brain dead. Nerves jitter from excess coffee. You still have to write a conclusion. "Easy. I'll just restate the ideas in my paper," you say to yourself. I know this worn out tactic for conclusions tempts you, but stand strong. Don't disappoint your readers now. They deserve better.

Tactics for writing a conclusion aren't that different from the tactics for writing an introduction. You can describe a closing scene, finish with an appropriate story, end with a question to leave the reader thinking, polish off with a fabulous quote. Again, you can model good writers. Collins ends "Musical Awakenings" with a one-line conclusion: "That would have Sacks dancing in the aisles." "That" refers to discussion in the previous paragraph, but by setting off that one line, Collins leaves us with a strong punch that closes up his essay—which begins with Sacks dancing. Nicely done. Huddle ends "Museum Piece" imagining what the girl in the painting is saying to the modern viewer, a creative touch. Peterson ends her piece summing up her mixed feelings about eating wild game, the horror and the awe. In "Joyas Voladoras," Brian Doyle surprises the reader with a list of heartbreaks.

My last word on conclusions repeats the advice for introductions: flip through the essays in this book, read several conclusions, find one you like, and try to imitate it.

Traditional Brainstorming

FREEWRITING Freewriting, a simple but useful technique, can help unstick you. The idea is to write down any weird or not-so-weird idea buzzing about in your head, without any thought to structure, grammar, or spelling. Just write nonstop. Don't even think. Just write, write, write. Though most of what comes out might look like alien messages from deep space, a brilliant idea or two might be lurking, waiting for you to discover and develop it.

CLUSTERING Write your topic in the center of a piece of paper and draw a circle around it. Draw lines out from your topic, like spokes of a wheel, and draw bubbles, like balloons, at the end of each line. Fill in each bubble with one thing that pops into your mind about your topic. Repeat this technique for each bubble.

LISTING If you're the type of person who likes to make daily lists, here's the brainstorming technique for you. Simply write your topic at the top of a sheet of paper and list whatever flashes into your head about that topic. A list might look like this:

Children

no free time to play

too many structured activities

what happened to playing baseball in the park with no adults?

need to learn independence

too much pressure

don't learn decision making

can't solve their own problems

must have some supervision and guidance, of course

Next, choose three or four interesting ideas from the list and write them at the top of a sheet of paper:

independence	*problem solving*	*decisions*
wimps	can't fix things	which college
too afraid	run to mom and dad	which major
live at home	disagreements	which job
can't grow up		

You could keep this up into infinity, but you only need to keep listing until you feel you have some solid ideas to start your essay. What you now have is an idea for a thesis and three developmental paragraphs and ideas for examples to support each idea.

STRATEGIES FOR WRITING FROM MEMORY

Storytelling comes naturally. You tell stories almost every day. "Guess what happened!" you exclaim, and proceed to give the details. Your friends or relatives may be excited or sad for you, depending on the tale you tell, and might ask for more details or—if you blather on too much—cry "Enough already!" When trying to tell your story in writing, however, you have to keep in mind that the reader can't ask questions or tell you, "Get to the point!" It's up to you to hold the reader's attention, make a point, keep to the story, evoke a sense of time and place. If you don't follow these strategies, you're in danger of boring your reader, a sin in the storytelling realm.

Purpose

Why are you writing this story, sharing this memory? You might be tempted to reply, "Because the teacher told me to." As true as that might be, you still need a point to your story. Though your purpose might be implied rather than stated directly, that purpose should be clear. Are you trying to inform, explain, teach, warn? Also, would anyone be interested in what you're writing other than you? If you write about the time you were in a car accident or the horror of finding a significant other cheating on you, some readers might sympathize, but while those stories are meaningful to you, they don't offer much to the reader, even those who might have had the same experience. What kind of point can you offer that won't sound worn out? Don't drink and drive, or watch out for deceptive boyfriends or girlfriends, husbands or wives? You won't be offering your reader anything unique.

Zooming In

Most narratives zoom in on a small time period, and most writing books advise you to stick to a 24-hour time period or less. For beginning writers, that's generally very good advice. If you try to write your life's story in a three-page essay, you won't have much room for detail and description. While experienced writers do sometimes flash forward or backward in time, like Edward Hoagland does in "the Courage of Turtles, many good narratives zoom in tight, like Lawrence Weschler's "Modern Times," which takes place in a few minutes in his office at work. The idea is to focus on a slice of life, to capture a meaningful moment in time. If you go much outside the 24-hour time frame, you could get into trouble with chronological order or confuse your reader by jumping in time without the proper transition.

Transitions

Transitions—words or phrases that help you move smoothly from one idea to another—are crucial in narrative. When writing from memory, you make automatic adjustments in time in your head, but if you leap in time without informing your reader, confusion results. When you move your story in time, let the reader know with phrases like *later that day* or *the following morning.* If you do decide to make big leaps in time, it's crucial to use proper transition. Use time indicators like "When I was five" or "After I entered high school" to help your reader travel in time with you. If you don't, the reader might be confused, thinking a small child is doing something like driving a car.

Evoking Senses

Another crucial element in writing memories is creating a vivid picture through description and sensory detail. You want your reader to hear, smell, taste, feel, see your experience. In "A Voice for the Lonely" Stephen Corey, instead of just telling the reader that it was quiet in the early mornings when he delivered newspapers, writes, "I recall stopping my brisk walk sometimes, especially in winter when every step squeaked and crunched on the snow that nearly always covered the ground, and marveling at how there were no sounds except those of my own making." He uses sound—squeaked and crunched—to show the silence. For more on using strong description and senses, flip through the Styling sections in this book, or look in the index under senses.

Point of View

Usually when you write from memory, you're writing in the first person, *I*. They are, after all, your memories. But sometimes you want to assume another identity, to write as if you are someone else. Some of the narrative assignments in this book ask you to pretend to be a figure from history or to study a photograph and assume the identity of someone in the picture. You're still using the first person, but you're stepping outside yourself, sliding into another's role, imagining a step back into another's time or culture. This style of storytelling can help you avoid mundane my-summer-vacation essays and spark more imaginative writing.

WRITING STRATEGIES FOR EXPLAINING AND EXPLORING IDEAS

For many essays where you attempt to explain a concept or explore an idea, you can use the basic structure discussed in the section on Writing Basic College Essays. Sometimes, though, you may be attempting to compare, show a cause-effect relationship, define a term, or explain a process, so I've outlined those strategies below, along with some writing tips. Keep in mind that most good essays rely on a clear purpose, organized paragraphs with strong examples, vivid description, sentence variety, and specific details. It's wise to have a snappy title and a hook introduction.

Good essays often blend modes: a comparison essay might begin with a personal narrative, a cause-effect essay might contain a definition paragraph, and a process essay might rely heavily on description. You can combine any of these strategies. Most writers do.

Comparison and Contrast

In a comparison or contrast essay, you're attempting to hold one thing up to another to make a point. In Pauline Kael's review of *The Little Mermaid*, she contrasts Disney's film version to the original story by Hans Christian Andersen to illustrate the inferiority of the Disney cartoon. Comparison shows similarities to make a point, while contrast focuses on differences. For beginning writers, it's sometimes easier to make a point if you're writing about differences, so the example illustrates a contrast.

Usually, you choose between two methods of organization for writing a comparison or contrast paper: one side at a time or point by point. In the one-side-at-a-time method—sometimes called the block method—you spend the first half of the essay discussing one topic and the second half comparing or contrasting the other topic. Let's say you're writing a paper like Kael's "The Little Mermaid," contrasting Disney's *Cinderella* film with the old folktale from Grimms'. You might organize it like this:

Paragraph 1:   I. Introduction and Thesis
Paragraph 2:   II. Disney Film
                a. Weak charcterization
                b. Beauty Wins as a primary lesson
                c. Spiritual element reduced to ninny fairy godmother
Paragraph 3:   III. Grimms' Story
                a. Strong characterization
                b. Beauty comes from within

                        c. Spiritual element in form of dead mother's
                           spirit
Paragraph 4:   IV. Conclusion

Notice that the same points are covered for both versions. If you were to write in the second method, point by point, you would organize the essay this way:

Paragraph 1:   I. Introduction and Thesis
Paragraph 2:   II. Characterization
                        a. Disney: weak
                        b. Grimm: strong
Paragraph 3:   III. Beauty
                        a. Disney: beauty wins is primary lesson
                        b. Grimm: beauty comes from within
Paragraph 4:   IV. Spiritual Element
                        a. Disney spiritual element reduced to ninny fairy godmother
                        b. Grimm spiritual element in form of dead mother's spirit.
Paragraph 5:   V. Conclusion

Paragraphs don't always lay out so neatly into this formula. If your paragraphs get too long, you might need to break them up. For example, in the point-by-point method, you might want to break Characterization into two paragraphs: one for Disney and one for Grimm. Use your judgment.

When comparing or contrasting, it's important to let the reader know which subject you're discussing by using transitions. Here's a list of transitions commonly used in comparison and contrast essays: *on the other hand, by contrast, similarly, by comparison.*

CAUTION   Don't just show how two things are alike or different. There's no point to your essay if you fail to have an opinion. Why are you comparing? To show one's superiority over the other? To warn the reader? To promote understanding of an idea? You must have a **thesis statement**.

Cause and Effect

Why do some young girls mutilate themselves? Why did the Anasazi Indians live in the remote cliffs and resort to cannibalism? What's causing the failure of our educational system? What caused the Los Angeles riots? Does excess television cause obesity in children? Cause and effect essays attempt to explain why something happens—causes—and the results of incidents—effects.

Usually results have many causes, so you want to examine your topic closely for hidden reasons. After the Los Angeles riots, many people blamed the failure of our court system to convict the police officers involved in the Rodney King beating, and while that event certainly triggered the riots, the causes are much more complex, rooted in many years of police brutality and poverty, among other things. If you're going to blame television for obesity in children, you'd better examine the children's eating habits and social lives. It could be that children who watch television and eat excessively do so because of another problem like being picked on in school or trying to escape painful family problems or abuse. It's rare that you can say "this caused that."

There's no one organizational strategy for writing cause and effect essays, but generally you want to explain the problem and then examine the causes. For example, the causes of self-mutilation are complex: pressures of adolescence, self-blame, shame, anger, feelings of abandonment. To neglect one of these causes of this serious problem would result in simplistic thinking.

However you decide to organize your essay—comparison or contrast, argument, narrative, emphatic or chronological order, or some other strategy or combination of strategies—keep the principles of good writing in mind (see the Writing Basic College Essays section).

Explaining a Process

How do you watch a hummingbird? What's involved in developing a roll of film? How did you get those tomatoes to grow so big? Can you show me how to tile my kitchen floor? How do I download information from the Internet? We ask questions like this every day, and hopefully, some kind soul will explain. That explanation is called process analysis, or the how-to essay.

Explaining or analyzing a process in writing isn't that different from showing it to a friend, though when you're writing, your friend isn't there to ask for clarification, so you need to be sure you explain each step thoroughly and don't leave out any steps. Also remember to explain the steps in order. If you're writing out your favorite chocolate chip cookie recipe for a friend, and you list ingredients and baking instructions, your friend will probably read the recipe as he or she cooks, following your directions, happily putting the cookies in the oven, only to realize that you wrote at the bottom of the page, "Oh, yeah, and add one teaspoon of salt." Your friendship might suffer a bit.

You also need a purpose for writing the essay, indicating your attitude about the topic. If you're attempting to teach your reader how to grow orchids, your purpose might be to show that though these flowers have a reputation for being difficult, growing them is easy with a few simple tricks. Without a purpose, your process essay will resemble a grocery list.

Having a clear purpose and step by step instructions won't help your reader if you haven't considered your audience's level of expertise. If you're writing a how-to-grow-orchids essay, can you assume your reader has some gardening experience? Better not, unless you're writing for your garden club newsletter, where you wouldn't need to explain basic gardening terms. For a general audience like your English class, you'd have to be more specific. Don't leave your audience mystified; explain the process clearly and carefully.

Some of the Writing Ideas in this book ask you to explain a process, like one that accompanies Diane Ackerman's "Mute Dancers: How to Watch a Hummingbird," where the idea is to write an essay explaining how to watch another animal. How-to essays can be fun to write. Helping someone learn how to do something—whether it's fixing a car or a glass of lemonade—is rewarding and gives you a chance to show off your expertise.

WRITING STRATEGIES FOR DEFINING TERMS

Words can be slippery. They change meaning, wear disguises, take on new personas depending on who's using them. Charity wears many masks, kindness one day, an insult to pride the next, sometimes a veil for greed. What determines greed for one person constitutes ambition for another. Words are master chameleons.

Purpose

When writing a definition essay, your job is to rip off the masks, expose secrets; don't be content with worn out definitions. If you write what everyone already knows about the word, why bother? For a more interesting paper, look at the side of the word nobody talks about. Let's say you're writing a paper defining the word *lonely*. If you fall into the pity-all-the-lonely-people trap, you won't offer your reader anything new; if, on the other hand, you take the road less traveled, as one student did, and write, "Loneliness doesn't deserve pity or guilt. It deserves to be crushed in the street, crumpled under tires like dead leaves, crunched like a paper bag. Maybe then, like the Phoenix that goes up in flames and rises from its own ashes, the lonely will create their own lives, stop hermiting themselves, learn to paint or take a dance class, volunteer for meals-on-wheels, join a singles club, and quit tormenting the rest of us with their sorrowful lives." This thesis shocks the reader out of complacency.

Language Resources

Finding a new angle for a thesis can be a difficult task, but looking up the word in various language resources might help you find an edge. Many language resources are available online and in the library or a bookstore. While a standard dictionary might be helpful, other, more exciting sources abound: dictionaries of quotations, dictionaries of slang, a thesaurus, *The Oxford English Dictionary*. If you do decide to use a standard dictionary like *Webster's*, avoid boring phrases like "According to *Webster's* . . ." These phrases numb the mind, and your reader will be reluctant to read further. For the paper on loneliness, the student first used a dictionary of quotations to discover what others have said about the term, finding a quote by Paul Elmer More stating that people "hold themselves aloof in chosen loneliness of passion," giving her the idea to focus on loneliness as self-pitying, self-inflicted isolation. She uses this quote in her essay as part of her conclusion.

Next, she visited a thesaurus, finding a bonanza of words to string together, creating an engaging inventory to underscore her point: "Loneliness is self-abandonment, icy isolation, me and my shadow, me-myself-and-I narcissism; single, solo, solitary, stag, I-travel-light baby; unescorted, unaccompanied, unaided, unassisted, pride run rampant." Notice the thoughtful word arrangement. Rather than repeating a list from the thesaurus, she braids them—except for the first string—with **alliteration**, chaining together words beginning with *s*, following with a string of *u* words, using a semicolon to separate the strings. Both strands end with a punch, a more-than-one-word phrase breaking the monotony of a single-word list, emphasizing her notion that most people choose their loneliness. The first strand—notice the complete sentence—contains some alliteration (*m*), but mostly establishes the cold, selfish aspect of the term.

To further defend her definition, the student investigated *The Oxford English Dictionary* (or OED), a several volume set chronicling the history of the English language. She discovered that the word *lonely* derives from *alone,* which stems from Middle English, a combination of *all* plus *one,* or all one. From there she reasoned that *all one* has a selfish, me-me-me implication, further validating her view.

Examples

After you have your purpose for defining the word, you need to provide numerous examples. In the essay on loneliness, the student gives specific examples of sorrowful lives: the lonely business man, married to his job; the housewife stuck in an unhappy marriage; the whore on Harbor Boulevard. The student discusses each example, showing how most lonely people bring about their own loneliness, admitting that some loneliness results from mental illness, "but most lonely people wear their isolation like a crown of thorns." She also harvests examples from pop culture, using the Beatles' album *Sergeant Pepper's Lonely Heart's Club Band,* citing song lyrics that express America's frenzy of pity for the lonely. Without specific, thoroughly discussed examples, the reader wouldn't be convinced of such an unconventional point of view.

Debunking Misconceptions and Preconceived Ideas

Don't just rely on the obvious when writing a definition; be original. For example, you can argue from negation, or what a word is not. In his essay "Charm," from *I Can't Stay Long,* Laurie Lee writes, "Certainly, charm is not a question of learning palpable tricks, like wrinkling your nose, or having a laugh in your voice, or gaily tossing your hair out of your dancing eyes and twisting your mouth into succulent love-knots." He busts the standard view of charm, following with specifics defining charm: "Charm can't withhold, but spends itself willingly on young and old alike, on the poor, the ugly, the dim, the boring, on the last fat man in the corner."

Learning to write strong extended definitions is an important writing and thinking skill. Whether you're writing an essay defining Romanticism for art history, existentialism for philosophy, or Puritanism for religious studies, learning to capture elusive words and make them concrete challenges your mind, your assumptions, broadening your view of the world.

WRITING STRATEGIES FOR ARGUING

Standing up to the high school bully. Wondering whether technology keeps us too much in touch. Deciding if we've lost the war on drugs.

Rethinking the value of television talk shows. Your opinion on these topics—and many others—forms the basis for argument. The trick, though, when writing an argument essay is to support your opinion with solid evidence. Your goal is persuasion—don't just spout your opinion. To convince a reader—especially one who doesn't agree—you need to state your point clearly, back it up with proof, and refute points from the other side.

Stating Your Point

Your point is your **thesis statement**, your opinion on the topic. "Drugs should be legalized because we've already lost the war" states an opinion without using *I*. Generally, in college argument essays, you want to avoid using *I*. First, it's redundant: if you state it, then it is your opinion, no *I* needed. Second, it's considered weak, wishy-washy to write *I think* or *I believe*. It's akin to saying, "It's only my opinion, so don't take me that seriously." Stand up for your convictions with a forceful statement. Notice, too, that the above statement contains *should* and *because*. Those two words signal your opinion—*should*—and your reasons for that opinion—*because*. As you become more practiced at writing thesis statements, you'll want to drop the obvious use of should and because, writing your statement in a more polished manner, as Gore Vidal does in "Drugs": "It is possible to stop most drug addiction in the United States within a very short time. Simply make all drugs available and sell them at cost." Of course, if Vidal doesn't support that statement with solid evidence, we'd simply ignore him.

Supporting Your Point

You support your point in an argument essay the same way you do in any essay (see the section on Writing Basic College Essays), with strong examples, statistics, quotes, details. You want to know your topic, so you may need to do research. Explore both sides of the issue so you can refute the other side.

Refuting the Opposition

When my daughter was a young teen, she wasn't very good at refuting the opposition—her mother. She'd ask to go to a party, and when I'd object based on facts like I didn't know the parents or the crowd of teens, she didn't know how to answer except to say, "But everybody's going," which I pointed out was a generalization because *every* student in the school couldn't possibly be attending the same party. As she got older, she got better at anticipating my questions. When I asked about parental supervision, she'd respond, "Yes, Travis's parents will be there. You know them from band. Here's the phone nmber. You can call and check." She'd have an answer ready for all of my objections. Clever girl. What could I say but go, have fun?

This strategy is basically the same for writing an argument paper. You have to know the other side's objections to your argument and respond in your essay, showing how they might be wrong or misguided. One approach is to bring up their objections, either in the form of a quote or paraphrase, and then respond: "Those who oppose legalizing drugs claim that legalization will lead to more drug addiction. Not so. People who are going to take drugs will do so, legal or not. During Prohibition, when alcohol was illegal, the law didn't stop alcoholism or drinking; it just turned it into a criminal activity." This strategy states the other side's view and then refutes it. The key is to be sure you let your reader know when you are presenting an opposing view. If you forget to use phrases like "Opponents believe," you're in danger of confusing your reader.

Organization

You can use a basic organization for argument essays: introduction with thesis, developmental paragraphs, and a conclusion. The only difference is where to work in refuting the other side. You can use statements from opponents as topic sentences to open each paragraph, refuting and presenting your ideas on that point. In the drug example above, you could further develop the point into a full paragraph, providing statistics on prohibition as well as information on illegal drug use.

Another strategy would be to spend three or four paragraphs discussing your views, and then present the opposition's views in one paragraph and refute them. Either strategy is fine, as long as you address your opponent.

WRITING STRATEGIES FOR CLASSIFICATION

When you go to Disneyland or Disney World, you find your way around by looking at a map divided into different areas, classified according to time or place: Frontierland, Tomorrowland, Fantasyland, Adventureland, Main Street USA, Critter Country, and so on. These classifications orient you to the park and let you know what to expect. Even a first-time visitor will probably figure out that Space Mountain is in Tomorrowland, not

Frontierland. The descriptive names make sense of an otherwise chaotic place. You divide and classify your closet: summer clothes, work attire, winter wardrobe; your pantry: canned goods, spices and baking supplies, breakfast items, boxed foods; your notebook: science, English, math, history, geology. If you walked into your hardware store and the paint was heaped in with the garden tools, the faucets in with the tulip bulbs, you'd walk out.

Writers often classify to make sense of a complex topic, poke fun or satirize, explain a comparison involving more than two subjects. As a student, you might be asked to write a paper for your sociology class discussing parenting styles; periods of art in an art history class; types of earthquakes in a geology class. Classification can be useful for many topics.

In her essay "Friends, Good Friends—and Such Good Friends" (not in this book), Judith Viorst classifies her friends into seven categories: convenience friends, special-interest friends, historical friends, crossroads friends, cross-generational friends, part-of-a-couple friends, men who are friends. Viorst follows good rules of classification to write her essay:

Purpose

1. Make a point. Before you write, ask yourself, "Why am I making this classification?" If you write an essay classifying teenagers according to high school cliques, and you just list the types, you aren't doing your reader a service. Anyone can make a list of types. You need to have a thesis. Are you trying to warn the reader about a certain type of clique? Argue that cliques are detrimental to student learning? Illustrate that strict conformity leads to problems later in life? In Viorst's essay, she doesn't just discuss the types of friends; she makes a point:

   > I once would have said that a friend is a friend all the way, but now I believe that's a narrow point of view. For the friendships I have and the friendships I see are conducted at many levels of intensity, serve many different functions, meet different needs and range from those as all-the-way as the friendship of the soul sisters mentioned above to that of the most nonchalant and casual playmates.

   She then discusses each class of friends, pointing out how the class fits into her definition of friendship. Notice that she busts the standard view of friendship as being the no-matter-what kind.

Ruling Principle

2. Tie each category back to your thesis. For Viorst, it's the level of intimacy that ties the essay together. In English teacher jargon, this would he called the "Ruling Principle of Classification," how you divide the topic. If you're classifying rocks, do you do it by size, color, shape, composition? You need to pick one ruling principle and stick to it. If Viorst suddenly threw in a class of friends and didn't mention the intimacy factor, we would wonder why she added that category. If you classified Adventure films according to character types and then discussed a group by dialogue, you would be straying from the ruling principle, and your essay would not stick together. The ruling principle is the glue of your essay.

3. Use numerous examples. Every essay needs strong examples. In her category on Convenience friends, after defining what she means by convenience, Viorst lists the types of things these women do for each other: "Convenience friends are convenient indeed. They'll lend us their cups and silverware for a party. They'll drive our kids to soccer when we're sick. They'll take us to pick up our car when we need a lift to the garage. They'll even take our cats when we go on vacation." Listing specific good-neighbor chores gives her point weight. She goes on to give examples of what she would and would not discuss with a convenience friend, the intimacy factor, gluing her essay back to its point.

Support

Every essay needs strong specific examples. Use numerous examples so the reader understands the basic characteristics of the categories or types you are writing about, and the differences between them.

4. Avoid simplifying. Acknowledge that the topic may be more complex than your classification covers. Admit that you are generalizing, and mention possible exceptions to your categories. If you're writing a paper on high school cliques, admit that not every student fits neatly into one of these groups. Your conclusion might be a good place to write a disclaimer.

Labels

5. Label your groups. Notice that Viorst has descriptive labels—like Disneyland—that hint at the topic and give it flavor. You can tell by the label what to expect. When brainstorming a list of high

school cliques, my students came up with the following groups: Rah Rahs (jocks and cheerleaders), Bandos (students in the band), Brains (formerly referred to as nerds), Misfits (students who dress and act in opposition to the rest of the crowd), Stoners (speaks for itself), Clubbies (students who always join clubs or run for office).

Organization

6. Organize your paper. There are many ways to organize your material for classification, depending on your topic, but here are two common methods: chronological and emphatic order. If you're classifying historical time periods, you might want to organize chronologically—time order—in the order the events occurred in time. If you're organizing friends, you might want to use emphatic order—least important category or shortest category first, and the most important or longest last.

SUMMARIZING

A summary is a restatement—in your own words—of another writer's work. In college, you might be asked to summarize a chapter in a textbook, summarize an article and then respond in an essay to the writer's ideas, or summarize to demonstrate understanding in a reading class. Why do you need to learn to summarize material? Is it just busy work? Learning to summarize helps you in several ways: you absorb material for tests, improve reading comprehension, and learn to identify key points. You summarize material almost daily. If a friend asks you what the latest movie you've seen is about, you respond with a summary of the film, briefly telling in *your own words* the main plot. You might occasionally quote from a character, but essentially, you retell the story in your own words. To summarize correctly, follow these steps:

1. Read the article through once to get the general idea.
2. Read a second time, highlighting key ideas—or taking notes if you don't want to defile your book.
3. Then—without looking at the text—write one-sentence summaries for each paragraph of the writer's main ideas.
4. Now write a draft of the summary from your sentences, providing examples from each paragraph that support the main ideas.
5. Check your summary against the author's work, making sure your writing is in your own words. If you use any of the author's

original words, put them in quotation marks. It's okay to put quotation marks around parts of a sentence to distinguish the writer's words from your own. For example, if you are summarizing Shelby's Steele's piece from his book *The Content of Our Character*, you might write a sentence like this:

> Although Steele concedes that prejudice against blacks is still a problem in America, overall, he thinks "there is also much opportunity."

Note: See the Paraphrasing section for information on how to paraphrase correctly.

Tips for Writing Summaries

1. A summary should be about one-quarter the length of the article you are summarizing. If your summary is longer than one page, you may have to break it into paragraphs. A good rule is to change paragraphs when you begin to summarize a new idea.
2. Do not give your opinion in a summary. Save your views for critiques.
3. Always give the title of the text you are summarizing as well as the author's name in your introduction. Don't just write the title of the piece at the top of the page. Introduce the writer and the work:

   > In the article "Drugs" by Gore Vidal, the author argues in favor of legalizing all drugs.

   Notice that this opening sentence introduces the title, the author, and the author's thesis.
4. Be sure to paraphrase correctly (see below).

PARAPHRASING

Paraphrasing—simply put—means rewording. When you take an in-class essay examination based on material from a text, you repeat the material on the test in your own words. You're not quoting from the text but writing what you remember. You might use paraphrasing in a research paper to liven up another writer's words by using your own style, replacing a style that might otherwise sound dry.

A direct quote would look like this (the number in parentheses is the page number where the original statement is found):

> Joseph Verrengia reports, "Laboratory tests on some of the artifacts, including a piece of human excrement, have revealed

traces of a human protein that scientists say is the first direct evidence of cannibalism among the Anasazi" (15).

A paraphrase of the above quote might look something like this:

> According to Joseph Verrengia, science has proven—using tests on human waste left at the scene of the crime—that the Anasazi did, indeed, chow down on their brethren, slicing and dicing, roasting and toasting their own kind, a grisly banquet for reasons unknown (15).

Notice that the source is given in both instances. While you don't have to cite every line of your paraphrase when writing a summary—you've already told the reader that you are rewording another writer's work—you do have to give credit to other writers when you use their ideas or words when paraphrasing in an essay. It doesn't matter that you've reworded it. You still must give the source. Otherwise, you're guilty of **plagiarism**.

Be sure to *completely* reword the material or put quotation marks around partially quoted material. If you use any of the writer's original words, you must put quotation marks around them. If in the Verrengia example above you had written "piece of human excrement" instead of "human waste" and didn't put quotation marks around Verrengia's words, you would be guilty of plagiarizing. See #5 under Summarizing.

PLAGIARISM AND GENERAL ADVICE FOR USING SOURCES

> *"This above all: To thine own self be true."*
> —William Shakespeare

Many students come to college with mistaken or vague definitions of **plagiarism**. Most know that it's wrong to download a paper off the Internet or borrow another student's work and present it as their own—a revolting practice—but knowing when to document a source can sometimes be confusing. I like to believe that most students have integrity and wouldn't plagiarize on purpose, but some students pillage sources unintentionally. When I ask students, "When you paraphrase another writer's words or ideas instead of quoting exactly, do you still have to give a parenthetical reference or otherwise indicate where you found the material?" Often they answer no, thinking that as long as it's in their own words, it's all right. *Wrong.* You must give credit to every source. This is tricky business. However, if you remember some general guidelines, you'll be safe.

1. Always give an in-text citation showing where you got material. See the section on Basic Documentation for information on how to correctly cite material within your essay.
2. If information is common knowledge, or something you already know, you do not have to cite a source because *you* are the source. If you're writing a paper on AIDS, it's not necessary to cite a source on the transmission of the virus. For most people, that's common knowledge. If you're a saltwater aquarium hobbyist writing an essay on how to start an aquarium, then you're probably an expert on many aspects of this exotic pastime, so you don't have to cite that information unless it's something you have to look up.
3. Avoid overquoting or overparaphrasing—stringing material together with little of your own writing. Instead, comment on material, giving your own opinion. Ask yourself, "Do I agree with this writer? What do I think? How does the quote or paraphrase support or refute my own opinion? Is the material logical? Helpful to the reader?"
4. Blend quotes smoothly. Don't just leave them dangling. See the Basic Documentation section for how to blend quotes. The Summarizing section, above, also has ideas for blending quotes.
5. Make sure you've interpreted the quote correctly and that it's relevant to your point.
6. Be fair to the writer you are quoting or paraphrasing. To partially quote someone is okay as long as the partial quote doesn't change the meaning and you put quotation marks around the quoted material. Political commercials sometimes partially quote a rival, intentionally misrepresenting his or her ideas. That's shoddy practice.

SECTION SIX

Research

When writing college essays, you will probably be required to do some research and incorporate it into your own writing. If you use researched material, you must document it correctly. Remember that any words or ideas that are not your own must be documented (see Plagiarism). This section teaches you how to find materials, site information within your essay, and assemble Works Cited pages using the MLA (Modern Language Association) style of documentation. Not every school or department uses MLA format, but most English Departments do. Other styles include APA (American Psychological Association) and Chicago Manual of Style. If a teacher requires that you use a style other than the MLA, visit the library or search the reference section of a Web site like Yahoo! or Internet Public Library (see Favorite Search Engines). Another site that can help you with your works cited page is EasyBib.com.

BASIC SOURCES

The library is king of information. Libraries pay for services and databases that you cannot get for free on the Web. Infotrac, for example, contains articles from periodicals like magazines and journals and specific newspaper databases. You can search for hours on the Web and find nothing reliable on a topic and spend ten minutes in your library databases and find a bonanza of materials. And the library has librarians to

337

help you. You won't find that kind of service on the Web (see "The Internet" below).

The library has a book catalogue, usually on computer, where you can instantly find books on your topic. They also have reference materials like dictionaries and encyclopedias specific to a subject; you'll find art dictionaries, symbol dictionaries, reptile dictionaries. They have copy machines, computers, and access to other libraries. Seek and ye shall find.

Don't limit yourself to books or the Web. Use a variety of sources to ensure you've found the best information on your topic. You can interview people, experts in the field. For example, if you're writing an essay on reptiles, you can phone the local zoo and speak to the keeper of the reptile house. If writing about a social or community issue, you can write to or call city officials like parole officers and social workers. You can talk to professors in colleges who are experts in their fields. The list goes on.

Don't forget that grab bag, the television. Proceed with caution, as with the Web. Avoid talk shows—unless you're writing a paper on the intellectual deterioration of America and want to use talk shows for examples. Rely on PBS stations that show quality programs. Stations with a focus on history, animals, and science generally have reliable information, but again, be cautious: these shows might also have a bias.

THE INTERNET

While the Internet is a great tool that helps you look up information quickly, it also contains a lot of false or biased material. Junk clutters the information superhighway. Anyone can put up a Web page, so be certain that you use valid sites. Don't be a lazy researcher. If you rely on Web sites for research, your paper will be considered unscholarly; some professors will dismiss it with a failing grade, no matter how well-written. In general, *only use databases that your school library subscribes to.* College libraries pay a lot of money to provide you with access to academic, valid research. Take advantage of that privilege. With a student identification number, you can still work at home in your pajamas or at the coffee shop. Ask your school's librarian for help if you're not familiar with these services. Keep in mind this simple rule: if it's not paid for by a college library, proceed with caution. Even if it's an online encyclopedia, it can contain wrong information. Legitimate online encyclopedias—like Britannica Online—charge for the service.

Evaluating Internet Sites and Other Sources

There's a T-shirt/bumper sticker slogan that states, "Question Authority, But Raise Your Hand First." Use this as your **mantra** when evaluating sources, whether from a library, periodical database, interview, television program, film, radio, or the Internet. Again, be especially cautious using the Internet. It's not considered academic to rely on the Internet instead of books or periodicals. But if you do use an Internet site, evaluate sources critically and respectfully. Here are a few guidelines:

1. Is the source trustworthy? Can the site be counted on for accurate, up-to-date information? Find out what organization or individual runs the site. Consider asking your school's librarian.
2. Does the site contain a **bias**? Most do, so don't necessarily rule out an Internet source for this reason, but try to determine whether the information is too far out of the mainstream to be credible. A source that claims the Holocaust didn't happen would not be considered dependable. A Web site maintained by a political group—Republican, Democratic, Libertarian—will have a distinct bias.
3. Don't rely on only one source. If you're writing a paper on the medical use of marijuana and only rely on a Web page sponsored by medical marijuana advocates, your essay will not be thoroughly researched. Use a variety of sources on both sides of the issue.
4. Always cite the Internet source correctly. See the Basic Documentation section.
5. Does the source provide new, interesting information you hadn't considered that will add to your essay?
6. What is the writer's style? Is the **tone** too emotional? Does the writer rely on **jargon**? Are the ideas clear?

Favorite Search Engines

While search engines abound, I've listed a few of my favorites below and the reasons I like them. You may have favorites as well. If so, I'd be happy to hear about them. These engines are fast and easy to use.

GOOGLE.COM You may be familiar with this famous engine, one of the fastest, listing sites by popularity. It seems to weed out a lot of the junk that comes up with other search engines.

ABOUT.COM This search engine has many specific categories to choose from. I particularly like the science category, which breaks into the different sciences: computer, engineering life, social, molecular. I clicked on *Life Science,* which gave me another generous list to choose from. I clicked on *Insects/Spiders,* which gave me a list of creatures, each entry containing clearly written, useful information. Click, click, click, and you're there.

IPL.ORG The Internet Public Library, while not strictly a search engine, is such a great research tool that I've included it here. It gives you access to databases, evaluates Internet sites, and has a terrific reference section where you can ask librarians questions. A must see.

YAHOO.COM Another famous engine, but I didn't want to leave it out in case you are new to the Internet and not familiar with it. Though it contains a lot of information on restaurants and other entertainment, it also contains a strong reference section and has some good academic categories to search.

BASIC DOCUMENTATION

I'm keeping to the basics of MLA documentation, covering the most commonly used sources, so if you come across a source documentation problem not discussed here, your library should have a copy of *The MLA Handbook for Writers of Research Papers* or the *MLA Style Manual,* which provide more in-depth documentation information. Some of the search engines previously mentioned contain reference centers that explain MLA documentation and EasyBib.com will create a works cited page for you if you have all of the proper information.

Format

Do not use a title page for your research paper unless specifically requested to by your teacher. Instead, in the upper left corner of the page, put your name, the teacher's name, the class, and the date. In the upper right corner, put your last name and the page number. Put your last name and page number on every page of your document, but the left corner information goes only on the first page. (See the sample at the end of the documentation section.)

Double space your entire document. Do not put extra spaces between paragraphs. Indent the first line of each paragraph.

Use one-inch margins all around your paper, and use a standard type size like 12 point. If you use huge type, it will look like you've run out of things to say and are trying to take up space by using big type.

Parenthetical References

A parenthetical reference is information about a source that you provide in parentheses. When you're writing a paper using information and quotes from books, magazines, journals, newspapers, interviews, the Internet, you must give a parenthetical reference next to the quote or information. Generally, you put the writer's last name and the page number where you got the information.

Do not use a comma to separate the author's name from the page number, nor should you write *p.* for page. Cite your source just like the examples below. If you use the writer's name to introduce the quote, then you only need the page number in parentheses. Keep parenthetical references as brief as possible, saving detailed information for the Works Cited pages. Here's an example of blending a quote with your own writing:

> Fairy tales teach children about the real world. We grow up to find out, "As we had suspected, the fairy tales had been right all along—the world was full of hostile, stupid giants and perilous castles and people who abandoned their children in the nearest forest" (Lurie 18).

Notice that the period goes outside the parentheses. Here's another example, one that uses the writer's name to introduce the quote:

> Fairy tales teach children about the real world. According to Alison Lurie, we grow up to find out, "As we had suspected, the fairy tales had been right all along—the world was full of hostile, stupid giants and perilous castles and people who abandoned their children in the nearest forest" (18).

Because the writer's name introduces the quote, there's no need to repeat it in the parenthetical reference.

If two people wrote the work, put both names in parentheses: (Brown and Smith 44). If a group of people wrote the article or book, then the reference looks like this: (Brown et al. 44). The *et al.* stands for "and others."

If the source doesn't list an author, then you can abbreviate the title instead. A book titled *Medicines of the Rain Forest* with no author would be cited like this: (*Medicines* 32).

When using a quote of more than three typed lines, you must set the quote off by indenting *two* tab spaces, eliminating the quotation marks, and putting the period before the parenthetical reference, like this:

> Fairy tales teach children about the real world, how to cope with problems, be kind, and have hope. We grow up to find out:
>
> > As we had suspected, the fairy tales had been right all along—the world was full of hostile, stupid giants and perilous castles and people who abandoned their children in the nearest forest. To succeed in this world you needed some special skill or patronage, plus remarkable luck; and it didn't hurt to be very good-looking.
>
> (Lurie 18)

Warning: Keep long quotations to a minimum or it looks like you're not doing your own thinking and writing, stringing together others' ideas instead.

When citing online sources within your paper, treat them the same way if they have page numbers. If not, then you can mention the writer, director, Web page creator, or so forth in your writing and not give a parenthetical reference. The rest of the information will appear in your Works Cited pages. *Never* use a web address in a parenthetical reference. It clutters the paper. You want to keep the essay clean, only giving brief information so that the reader can identify it on the Works Cited page (where the web address properly belongs). Usually, an abbreviated title of the web page will suffice for text referencing.

For now, this should be enough for you to correctly cite various works within your essay. Next comes the Works Cited section.

Works Sited

Your Works Cited section at the end of your paper is where you list, in alphabetical order by author, information about the sources you used so that the reader can easily find them. It starts on a separate sheet of paper but is numbered in sequence with your essay. I've broken down how to cite common sources like books, magazine articles, newspaper articles, journal articles, electronic sources, the Internet, and I've provided a sample Works Cited page to show you how it all fits together.

BOOKS To cite a book, you'll generally need the following information: author, title, city, publisher, and the year the book was published. You'll find most of this information in the front of the book. Look for a statement like this: Copyright 2009 by Kendall Hunt. Somewhere on the same page, usually near the bottom, you'll find the publisher's city listed, sometimes several. If more than one city is listed, use the first one.

Underline or italicize book titles—either method is correct, but be consistent. A book entry on a Works Cited page will look like this:

Bettelheim, Bruno. <u>The Uses of Enchantment</u>. New York:

Random House, 1975.

If Bettelheim had written the book with someone else, say Jane Brown, the entry would look like this:

Bettelheim, Bruno, and Jane Brown. <u>The Uses of Enchantment</u>.

New York: Random House, 1975.

Notice that when the entry takes up more than one line, subsequent lines are indented one tab space.

If there are more than two authors, the entry would read: Bettelheim, Bruno, Jane Brown, and Joe Smith. More than three, resort to "et al.": Bettelheim, Bruno, et al.

MAGAZINE ARTICLES For magazines, you will need the author, title of the article, title of the magazine, the day and month, the year, and the page numbers the article runs through, like this:

Swartz, Mimi. "You Dumb Babies!" <u>New Yorker</u> 30 Nov. 1998:

60–67.

Notice that the day goes before the month, and a colon after the year. The article title is in quotation marks and the magazine title underlined (or you can italicize the magazine title). Multiple authors would be done the same as for books. Notice the pages the article runs through are after the year with no *p.* or *page*.

NEWSPAPER ARTICLES   Again start with the author's last name, the title of the article in quotation marks, followed by the newspaper title in italics or underlined. Because newspapers have sections, you need to give the section and page. If the newspaper has an early and late edition, you need to specify which one the article came from. An entry with only one edition would look like this:

> Dillow, Gordon. "'Our Kids' Really Can't Be Saved." <u>Orange County Register</u> 20 Feb. 2000, L3.

Here's an example of an entry specifying an edition:

> Brown, Sylvia. "Budget Crimes." <u>Los Angeles Times</u> 20 March 1997, late ed.: D1 +.

The + sign indicates the article is on more than one page; the *1* is the page number; the *D* is the section.

SCHOLARLY JOURNALS   What's the difference between a magazine and a journal? Magazines are aimed at the average reader and usually come out weekly or monthly. Journals—although some are published monthly—usually come out quarterly, biannually, or annually and tend to be specific to a field of study, like the *Shakespeare Quarterly*. If you're not sure if it's a magazine or journal, check the front and inside cover; you should be able to find the term *journal*.

Treat a journal article like a magazine article, with a couple of exceptions: you will need the volume number and possibly issue number, determined by whether or not the journal has continuous pagination. If you pick up, for example, issue 3 of a journal and it begins on page 232 instead of page 1, then the journal is paginated continuously and you do not need to bother with the issue number. Usually this type of pagination covers a year and starts over with page 1 in the new volume in the next year. If each issue starts with page 1, then you need the issue number. You will usually find volume and issue numbers on the front of the journal.

Another quirk about citing journals: put parentheses around the year, followed by a colon and the page numbers. Here is an example of an entry without an issue number:

> Yolen, Jane. "American's Cinderella." <u>Children's Literature in Education</u> 8 (1977): 21–29.

The *8* stands for the volume number. Put quotation marks around the article title and underline or italicize the journal title. Here's an example of an entry with an issue number:

> Hearn, Michael Patrick. "Happily, Ever After: The Resilience of the Fairy Tale." <u>Tall: Teaching and Learning Literature with Children and Young Adults</u> 8.1 (1998): 85–98.

The *8* stand for the volume number and the *1* for the issue number. Notice a period separates the volume and issue.

INTERVIEWS Always begin an interview citation with the name of the person interviewed. If you're interviewing an individual in person, cite the interview like this:

> Roberts, Julia. Personal Interview. 27 July 1999.

If you interviewed the person over the phone, Phone Interview would replace Personal Interview.

If you're citing an interview published in a magazine or newspaper, it would look like this:

> Roberts, Julia. Interview. <u>New York Times</u> 18 Jan. 1999, late ed.: D22.

Cite a television or radio interview similar to the above, but give the interviewer's name when available and the title of the program, underlined or in italics:

> Roberts, Julia. Interview with Barbara Walters. <u>Sixty Minutes</u>. NBC. New York. 18 Jan. 1999.

FILMS Generally, cite a film by giving the title first, followed by the director, major actors, studio, and year of release:

> <u>Lone Star</u>. Dir. John Sayles. Perf. Kris Kristofferson, Matthew McConaughey, Chris Cooper, and Elizabeth Pena. Columbia Tristar, 1996.

Perf. is an abbreviation for Performers.

TELEVISION SHOWS Usually for a television program, you will need the title of the episode (if there is one) in quotation marks, the title of the show (underlined or in italics), name of the network, call letters and city of the local station—if any—and the date the show aired:

> <u>Pythons: A Predator's Perspective</u>. DSC. 15 July 2008.

ELECTRONIC SOURCES AND THE INTERNET Generally, electronic sources and Internet sites are treated like their paper counterparts: a magazine article from an online database would be treated like a magazine article, a newspaper source like a newspaper article, and so forth, though you do need to give the online source and the date of access as well. If you're citing a Web site, then you'll also need the complete Web address. Here's an example of an article from an online database you might find in your library. If the computer service—in this example Gale Group—is available, then cite it:

> Miller, Peter B. "Delacroix: Leading Light of the Romantic Movement." <u>USA Today</u> 15 Nov. 1998. <u>Infotrac</u>. Online. Gale Group. 29 Feb. 2000.

Follow the same guidelines for web addresses, but include the entire Web address after the date of access. A complete Web address might look like this:

> <http://www.gc.maricopa.edu/English/topicarg.html>.

If there is no author for a Web page, cite the title first (see *The Cinderella Project* example in the sample Works Cited page).

Works Cited Sample

Study the following Works Cited sample. Notice the title. It's no longer called a bibliography because that term refers to books and you use a variety of sources. Follow these guidelines:

1. Do not number the entries.
2. Double space the entire section. Resist the temptation to put extra spaces between each entry or between the title of the section and the first entry.

3. Place article titles in quotation marks and italicize or underline book, magazine, and periodical titles.
4. When the entry runs more than one line, indent one tab space for following lines.
5. Put your last name and page number in the upper right corner of the page.
6. Alphabetize by author's last name. If no author is listed for a work, alphabetize the work by title.
7. Place a period at the end of each entry.
8. Use the punctuation shown in the sample entries.

Works Cited

Bettelheim, Bruno. The Uses of Enchantment. New York: Random House, 1975.

The Cinderella Project. Ed. Michale N. Saida. Dec. 1997. Children's Literature Research Collection, U of Southern Mississippi. 15 July 2009 <http://wwwdept.usm.edu//~engdept/cinderella/cindrella.html>.

Mulhearn, Chieko Irie. "Japanese Cinderella as a Pubertal Girl's Fantasy." Southern Folklore Quarterly 44 (1980): 203–14.

Ulanov, Ann, and Barry Ulanov. Cinderella and Her Sisters. Philadelphia: Westminster, 1983.

Warner, Marina. From the Beast to the Blonde. New York: Farrar, Straus and Giroux, 1994.

Yolen, Jane. "America's Cinderella." Children's Literature in Education 8 (1977): 21–29

Zipes, Jack. Don't Bet on the Prince. New York: Routledge, 1989.

Sample First Page

Smith 1

Jane Smith

Professor Diaz

English 100

6 Sept. 2009

Title

Begin typing the first line here. Don't forget to indent. Notice there are no extra spaces between the title and the first line or between the class information and the title. Resist the temptation to include extra spaces.

Also, notice that there are no extra spaces between paragraphs. Just indent one tab space, double space your entire document, and use one-inch margins all around.

Glossary

adjective a word that describes or modifies a noun: "Children's dirty faces peered in the candy shop window." The word *dirty* describes *faces*.

adverb a word that describes or modifies a verb, an adjective, or another adverb: "The girl longingly peered through the shutters." The word *longingly* describes how the girl peered.

alliteration using words close together that begin with the same letter or sound: *feasting* and *flying* both begin with *f*.

allusion an indirect or implied reference; don't confuse with *illusion*, meaning deceptive appearance or delusion.

annotating adding notes or explanation; critical commentary.

appositive a word or phrase that renames, describes, or gives more information about a noun (subject) and helps eliminate clunky clauses using *who* and *which*. The orchids, *cymbidiums,* grew splendidly in the greenhouse." *Cymbidiums* renames *orchids* and is much cleaner than writing *which are cymbidiums*.

bias a tendency or preference; sometimes prejudice.

chronological order organization by time order, or order in which events happened.

classification organizing an essay by grouping ideas or objects according to type or characteristic; an essay classifying high school students might be organized according to the group they associate with: jocks, cheerleaders, band members, nerds, brains, etc.

cliché worn-out phrases such as *drinks like a fish, light as a feather,* or *not playing with a full deck.* General rule: if you've heard it before, don't use it in your writing.

complete sentence a statement that can stand on its own; it expresses a complete thought. See **fragment**.

conjunction a connecting word: *for, and, nor, but, or, yet, so.* In an informal essay, you can begin a sentence or paragraph with a conjunction, but do so sparingly.

connotation a suggestion or implication: "Her words had sinister connotations."

comma splice a writing error in which you join two sentences with a comma. Comma splices can be fixed with a semicolon, a comma with a conjunction, or a period and a capital.

> *Incorrect:* That cat is a Persian, her name is Cleopatra.
> *Correct:* That cat is a Persian; her name is Cleopatra.
> *Correct:* That cat is a Persian, and her name is Cleopatra.
> *Correct:* That cat is a Persian. Her name is Cleopatra.

Sometimes a comma splice can be fixed by making one of the clauses dependent.

> *Incorrect:* I waited in line for tickets to the Dave Matthews Band concert, a storm broke out and it began to rain.
> *Correct:* As I waited in line for tickets to the Dave Matthews Band concert, a storm broke out and it began to rain.

The word *as* makes the first clause dependent.

criticism in the context of this book, criticism refers to essays or articles by professionals commenting on or critiquing the work of others, whether it's film, art, or literature.

dependent clause a clause that cannot stand on its own as a sentence; it is depending on another complete sentence. See **independent clause**.

> *Dependent clause:* When she ice skates
> *Dependent clause introducing an independent clause:* When she ice skates, the crowd roars with applause.

definition In the context of this book, definition refers to a type of essay called extended definition where the entire essay focuses on defining one word in depth. See "Writing Strategies for Defining."

emphatic order organization according to which points are the most important or most developed, saving the strongest or most in-depth discussion for the end of the essay right before the conclusion.

figurative language metaphor, simile, personification, analogy.

first person the *I* point of view.

fragment, sentence fragment the word *fragment* means a piece, so a sentence fragment is a piece of a sentence—it's missing something, either a subject or verb, or it has both of these but doesn't express a complete thought.

freewrite a warm-up or prewriting exercise where you write on your topic without stopping to think, disregarding organization, grammar, spelling, or punctuation.

hyphen a punctuation symbol that joins words together to make one, like *deep-rooted*. Don't confuse hyphens with dashes: a hyphen is shorter than a dash, so when you're typing dashes, use two hyphens.

incomplete sentence see **fragment**.

independent clause a group of words that could stand on its own as a complete sentence; it forms a complete thought. See **dependent clause**.

interrupter a word or phrase that interrupts a sentence, requiring commas, dashes, or parentheses: "I told you, Binh, that the essay was due today." *Binh* interrupts the sentence "I told you that the essay was due today."

interrupting clause a group of words that interrupts a sentence, requiring commas, dashes, or parentheses: "Crystal's hair, cut Winona Ryder style, glistened with auburn highlights." The clause *cut Winona Ryder style* interrupts the sentence "Crystal's hair glistened with auburn highlights." If you want the clause to get more attention, use dashes; if you want it to be less noticeable, use parentheses.

introductory clause a dependent clause that introduces the main sentence: "When I work in my garden, I feel serene." The main sentence is "I feel serene"; *when I work in my garden* introduces the sentence. Use a comma after introductory clauses or phrases.

jargon   language used by a particular group, often not understood by the general population: computer jargon, English teacher jargon (some of the terms in this glossary are English teacher jargon).

loose sentence   a sentence structure that begins with a complete sentence followed by a series of clauses or phrases that add description or information. See **periodic sentence**.

mantra   a word or sound you repeat to help you concentrate during meditation.

metaphor   a direct comparison between two objects not using *like* or *as*. "She is a poem." See **simile**.

narrative   an essay or work of fiction told in story form.

noun   a person, place, or thing.

opposition   in an argument essay, the opposition is the other side; the opposite view.

periodic sentence   a sentence that begins with a series of dependent clauses or phrases describing or giving more information about the main sentence, which comes at the end. See **loose sentence**.

personification   giving human qualities to inanimate objects: "The chair *sulked* in the corner."

point of view   (see First, second, third person).

plagiarism   presenting someone else's words or ideas as your own—a serious academic offense. Always give credit to the proper source.

preposition   a word that links words or phrases by showing relationship, direction, or position: *of, from, by, after, through, in,* etc.

prewriting   the process of figuring out what you want to write about and which direction your writing will take. See the Getting Started and Traditional Brainstorming sections of this book.

rationale   an explanation or reason.

refute   to deny or prove wrong. In an argument essay, you should refute your opposition by presenting the other side's views and discussing how their thinking is illogical or misguided.

run-on sentence, fused sentence   two complete sentences that are run together but should be separated with a period, semicolon, or comma with a conjunction: "That cat is a Persian her name is

Cleopatra." Don't try to fix a run-on with a mere comma. That's like yielding at a stop sign and creates another error called a **comma splice**. Fix a run-on the same way you would a comma splice.

second person   you (a more intimate way to address the reader). *Caution:* Don't use "you" in the general sense, meaning "anyone."

sentence variety   using many different sentence styles in your essay rather than repeating the same structure.

semicolon   a mark of punctuation (;) used to join two complete sentences when the thoughts are closely related. Do not use a semicolon with conjunctions; it replaces them.

simile   a comparison that uses *like* or *as*. "She moves like a poem." See **metaphor**.

specific details, specific examples   details or examples that are not vague words or phrases. Instead of *flower;* write *daisy; beer* becomes *Budweiser; oak* replaces *tree.*

thesis statement   the controlling idea or argument of an essay. A thesis should be specific, contain an opinion rather than fact, and not just announce your topic.

third person   someone else, not *I* (first person) or *you* (second person): *students* are; *she* writes; *researchers* believe.

tone   your writer's voice; the emotional or intellectual attitude, style, or manner of expression in your writing: sarcastic, ironic, comic, nostalgic are examples of tone.

transitions   words or phrases that help move sentences or paragraphs smoothly from one idea to the next. Some common transitions are **conjunctions** (ignore the idea that you can't begin a sentence or paragraph with a conjunction, but do so sparingly); conjunctive adverbs like *however, moreover, nevertheless, therefore;* phrases like *in addition, on the other hand;* single words like *thus, also, first, second, third, finally.* A more sophisticated trick for transitions is to pick up a word or idea at the end of one paragraph and use it in the beginning of the next one. See the Writing Strategies section for more on transitions.

verb   a word that expresses action (*jumped, went, made, drank, ran*) or state of being (*is, are, was, were, be, being, been, am*).

Index

A

About.com, 340
About Men, 73, 121, 209, 219, 228–231, 317
   essay/film connections, 235
   group exercises, 234
   language exploration, 233
   styling, 233–234
   thinking/talking points, 233
Ackerman, Diane, 43, 48, 74–77, 122–126, 129, 143, 187, 296, 326
Adjectives, 217–218
Adverbs, 349
Advice to Youth, 305, 306–308
   essay/film connections, 311–312
   group exercises, 311
   language exploration, 309
   styling, 309–311
   thinking/talking points, 309
   writing ideas, 311
African American culture
   The Content of Our Character, 251–256
   Letter to His Master, 260–264
   See also Fiddling While Africa Starves

Alcohol use. See How to Drive Fast
Allegory, 98
Alliteration, 98, 207–208, 327
Allusion, 349
Ambiguity
   Burl's, 17–26
   See also Morality; Realization
American Children, 61, 137, 144–146
   essay/film connections, 149
   group exercises, 148–149
   language exploration, 147
   styling, 148
   thinking/talking points, 147
   writing ideas, 149
Amusement. See Satirical essays
Analysis. See Argument essays; Explanatory/exploratory essays; Process analysis essays
Andersen, Hans Christian, 191, 195, 250, 323
Annotating, 250
Anthropomorphizing, 40, 42
Appositive, 14–15
Argument essays, 189–190
   About Men, 228–231
   The Content of Our Character, 251–256

356 *Index*

Argument essays *(continued)*
  The Culture of Celebrity, 210–216
  Drugs, 196–198
  Fiddling While Africa Starves, 220–223
  Folktale Liberation, 236–246
  Letter to His Master, 260–264
  The Little Mermaid, 191–192
  Naps, 202–206
  opposition viewpoint, 225
  persuasion and, 189
  refutation, 225, 248
  thesis statements and, 315–316
  writing strategies for, 328–330
  See also Writing strategies
Art appreciation
  American Children, 144–146
  Museum Piece, 57–58
  See also Films; Music effects
Artemisia, 61, 149
Assonance, 98

B

Barthes, Roland, 68–70, 121, 195, 209, 219, 235
Baxter, Richard, 311
Bearskin, 195
Beatles music, 9, 83–85, 328
Beauty and the Beast, 250
Bellow, Saul, 30, 137, 166, 167–172, 219, 283
Berne, Eric, 242
Bettelheim, Bruno, 241, 248
Bias, 71, 338, 339
Biology
  Disposable Rocket, 159–162
  How to Drive Fast, 284–286
  Mortality, 291–294
  Name That Tone, 277–279
  See also Natural history
The Black Widow, 50, 82, 143, 176–182
  essay/film connections, 187
  group exercises, 186
  language exploration, 183
  styling, 184–186
  thinking/talking points, 184
  writing ideas, 186–187
Book citations, 343

Boorstin, Daniel, 212
Borges, Jorge Luis, 245
A Box Filled With Magic, 100–104, 113
  essay/film connections, 107
  group exercises, 106–107
  language exploration, 105
  styling, 106
  thinking/talking points, 105–106
  writing ideas, 107
Brainstorming methods, 313, 314
  clustering, 320
  freewriting, 320
  listing, 66, 320–321
  See also Writing strategies
Brand, Stewart, 11
Braudy, Leo, 214
Bristlelip, 195
Bullet points, 275
Bully Pulpit, 218
Burl's, 17–26, 50, 175
  group exercises, 29
  language exploration, 27
  styling, 28–29
  thinking/talking points, 27–28
  writing ideas, 29–30
Burns, Robert, 318

C

Calvino, Italo, 245
Cape Fear, 113
Cat Bathing as Martial Art, 269, 271–273
  group exercises, 275
  thinking/talking points, 275
  writing ideas, 275–276
Cause/effect essays, 324–325
Celebrity. *See* The Culture of Celebrity; Media effects; Popular culture
Central Station, 50
Chen, Ken, 73, 114–118, 235
Children in the Woods, 44–46
  essay/film connections, 50
  group exercises, 49
  language exploration, 47
  styling, 48–49
  thinking/talking points, 47–48
  writing ideas, 49–50

Chronological order, 322
Circumstance. *See* Fate
City Out of Breath, 73, 114–118, 235
  essay connections, 121
  group exercises, 120
  language exploration, 119
  styling, 120
  thinking/talking points, 119
  writing ideas, 121
Classification, 330–333
Clichés, 41, 235
Clustering technique, 320
Collins, Clayton S., 9, 89, 150–153, 318, 319
Colons, 120, 148, 199–200, 257–258
Commas, 14, 48–49, 59, 60, 80, 119, 120, 128, 258
Comma splices, 311, 353
Compare/contrast essays, 143, 323–324
Comparisons, 141, 142, 143
Complete sentences, 59, 80, 148, 200, 257, 288, 289
Conclusions, 141, 319
Conjunctions, 14, 128, 266, 289, 353
Connecting words, 288
Connotations, 47
The Content of Our Character, 251–256, 268, 334
  essay/film connections, 259
  group exercises, 258
  language exploration, 257
  styling, 257–258
  thinking/talking points, 257
  writing ideas, 258–259
Controversy. *See* Argument essays
Conversation. *See* Dialogue
Cooper, Bernard, 17–26, 50, 175
Corey, Stephen, 3–6, 50, 89, 158
Corice, Gordon, 82, 176–182
The Courage of Turtles, 31–37, 50, 82, 143, 187, 321
  essay/film connections, 43
  group exercises, 42
  language exploration, 39–40
  practice exercise, 41
  styling, 40–41
  thinking/talking points, 40
  writing ideas, 42–43

Cowboys. *See* About Men
Criticism, 60–61
Cruikshank, George, 239
The Crying Game, 30, 175
Culture. *See* Fables; Folktale Liberation; Morality; Popular culture
The Culture of Celebrity, 56, 67, 73, 121, 189, 195, 209, 210–216, 296
  essay/film connections, 219
  group exercises, 218
  language exploration, 217
  styling, 217–218
  thinking/talking points, 217
  writing ideas, 219

D

Dahl, Roald, 192
Dashes, 14, 40, 48, 59–60, 119, 135, 174, 184–185, 218, 288
Davenport Films, 195, 250
Debate. *See* Argument essays
The Deer Hunter, 166
Definition essays, 326–328
Dependent clauses, 266, 310
Description, 40, 225–226, 332–333
Desert Bloom, 175
Desert Storm, 10–12
Details. *See* Description; Specific details/examples
Dialogue, 303–304
Dickinson, Amy, 218
Disposable Rocket, 159–162
  essay/film connections, 166
  group exercises, 165
  language exploration, 163
  styling, 164–165
  thinking/talking points, 163–164
  writing ideas, 165–166
Documents. *See* Research strategies
Douglass, Frederick, 260–264, 268
Doyle, Brian, 43, 50, 82, 138–140, 187, 319
Drugs, 190, 196–198, 329
  essay/film connections, 201
  group exercises, 200
  language exploration, 199
  styling, 199–200

Drugs *(continued)*
  thinking/talking points, 199
  writing ideas, 201
  See also How to Drive Fast
Drunk driving. *See* How to Drive Fast

E
Editing process, 316–317
Ehrlich, Gretel, 73, 121, 209, 219, 228–231, 317
Election, 290, 312
Eliot, George, 278–279
Eliot, T. S., 87, 89–90
Ellison, Ralph, 254
Emotions, 157, 158
Emphatic order, 185, 186
Epstein, Joseph, 56, 67, 73, 121, 189, 195, 209, 210–216, 296
Essays from memory, 1–2
  Burl's, 17–26
  Children in the Woods, 44–46
  The Courage of Turtles, 13–17
  Modern Times, 10–12
  A Voice For The Lonely, 3–6
  writing strategies for, 321–322
  See also Writing strategies
Exaggeration, 98
Examples. *See* Specific details/examples
Explanatory/exploratory essays, 51–52
  American Children, 144–146
  The Black Widow, 176–182
  A Box Filled With Magic, 100–104
  City Out of Breath, 114–118
  Disposable Rocket, 159–162
  Graven Images, 167–172
  Hair, 122–126
  The Indian with a Camera, 130–133
  Joyas Voladoras, 138–140
  Monster Mash, 108–110
  Museum Piece, 57–58
  Musical Awakenings, 150–153
  Mute Dancers, 74–77
  Nourishing Awareness in Each Moment, 62–64
  On the Uncertainty of the Future, 53

  Prince, 91–95
  Roll Over Bach, Too!, 83–85
  Toys, 68–70
  writing strategies for, 323–326
  See also Argument essays; Research strategies; Writing strategies

F
Fables, 43
  About Men, 228–231
  animal myths, 186, 187
  The Black Widow, 176–182
  The Courage of Turtles, 31–37
  Folktale Liberation, 236–245
  The Little Mermaid, 191–192
  Mute Dancers, 74–77
  structuralism and, 243
Fate
  A Voice For The Lonely, 3–6
  See also Fables; Uncertainty
Fiddling While Africa Starves, 99, 189, 219, 220–223, 318
  essay/film connections, 227
  group exercises, 226
  language exploration, 225
  styling, 225–226
  thinking/talking points, 225
  writing ideas, 226
Figurative language, 28, 41, 52, 79, 156, 186, 275
Film citations, 345
Films
  A Box Filled With Magic, 100–104
  The Little Mermaid, 191–192
  Monster Mash, 108–110
  See also Art appreciation; Music effects
First person, 322
Fitzgerald, F. Scott, 194
Flow in an essay, 288, 310
Folktale Liberation, 236–246
  essay/film connections, 250
  group exercises, 249–250
  language exploration, 247
  styling, 248–249
  thinking/talking points, 248
  writing ideas, 250
Fragments, 59, 289, 317

Freewrite, 8, 60, 295, 313, 320
Friendship, 3–6
Fused sentences. *See* Run-on sentences

G

Gates, Henry Louis Jr., 129
Gimme Shelter, 99
Goldsmith, Oliver, 213
Google.com, 312, 339
Graven Images, 30, 137, 166, 167–172, 219, 283
   essay/film connections, 175
   group exercises, 174–175
   language exploration, 173
   styling, 174
   thinking/talking points, 173
   writing ideas, 175
Graves, Robert, 239
Grice, Gordon, 43, 50, 143, 176–182
Grimm brothers, 195, 238, 239, 241, 243, 250, 323
Grizzly Man, 43, 82, 187

H

Hair, 122–126, 296
   essay/film connections, 129
   group exercises, 128–129
   language exploration, 127
   styling, 127–128
   thinking/talking points, 127
   writing ideas, 129
Hair (musical), 129
Hanh, Thich Nhat, 56, 62–64, 283
Hemingway, Ernest, 314
Herron, Bud, 270, 271–273
Hitchcock, Alfred, 113
Hoagland, Edward, 31–37, 50, 82, 143, 187, 230, 321
Hodgman, Ann, 88, 275, 319
Hoffman, Gary, 81, 267
Hoffman, Glynis, 81, 267
Holland, Barbara, 121, 189, 201, 202–206, 219
Hollister, George, 81
Homosexuality
   Burl's, 17–26
   See also Identity

Horror movies. *See* Monster Mash
How to Drive Fast, 201, 269, 284–286, 305, 311
   essay/film connections, 290
   group exercises, 289
   language exploration, 287
   thinking/talking points, 287–288
   writing ideas, 289–290
Huddle, David, 57–58, 137, 149, 319
Humor. *See* Satirical essays
Hyphens, 217–218

I

Icons, 219, 234, 235
Identity
   Burl's, 17–26
   The Content of Our Character, 251–256
   Disposable Rocket, 159–162
   Graven Images, 167–172
   Hair, 122–126
Imagery, 105, 107
In the Company of Men, 166
Incomplete sentences, 200, 288, 289
   See also Fragments
Independent clauses, 127–128
The Indian with a Camera, 121, 130–133, 219, 259, 268
   essay/film connections, 137
   group exercises, 136
   language exploration, 135
   styling, 135–136
   thinking/talking points, 135
   writing ideas, 136–137
Information sources. *See* Internet resources; Research strategies
Infotrac, 30, 129, 259, 337
The Innocents, 113
Internet resources
   annotated fairy tales, 250
   artwork, 60, 165
   criticism and, 61
   information, evaluation of, 338, 339
   Infotrac, 30, 129, 259
   language resources, 327
   online databases, 9, 129, 175, 250, 259, 311
   online source formatting, 342

Internet resources *(continued)*
  research materials, 338–340
  search engines, 312, 339–340
  urban legends, 186, 187
Interrupters, 14, 59, 174, 184–185, 186, 310
Interview citations, 345
Introductions, 318–319
Introductory clause, 128
IPL.org, 340
Irony. *See* Satirical essays

J

James, Henry, 113
Jargon, 339
Joyas Voladoras, 50, 82, 138–140, 187, 319
  essay/film connections, 143
  group exercises, 142
  language exploration, 141
  styling, 141–142
  thinking/talking points, 141
  writing ideas, 143

K

Kael, Pauline, 107, 113, 191–192, 250, 323
Kenko, Yoshida, 53, 67
Key words, 14
Kincaid, Jamaica, 200
Klosterman, Chuck, 9, 89, 91–96
Kroeber, Alfred, 214
Kroll, Jack, 9, 83–85, 99, 107, 108–110, 282, 318

L

Lang, Andrew, 240
Lavers, Annette, 68
Legends. *See* Fables
Letter to His Master, 260–264
  essay connections, 268
  group exercises, 267
  language exploration, 265
  thinking/talking points, 265
  writing ideas, 267
Library resources, 60, 99, 129, 175, 250, 259, 311, 337–338

Listing sentence structure, 135–136, 164–165, 185, 257–258
Listing technique, 66, 106, 120, 156, 320–321
The Little Mermaid, 107, 113, 191–192, 250, 323
  essay/film connections, 195
  group exercises, 194–195
  language exploration, 193
  styling, 193–194
  thinking/talking points, 193
  writing ideas, 195
Lone Star, 259
Loose sentence structure, 14, 266
Lopez, Barry, 44–46
Lurie, Alison, 236–246

M

Magazine article citations, 343
Mantra, 339
March of the Penguins, 43, 187
Marlboro man. *See* About Men
Masson, Jeffrey, 82
Media effects
  About Men, 228–231
  The Culture of Celebrity, 210–216
  Fiddling While Africa Starves, 220–223
  Graven Images, 167–172
  The Indian with a Camera, 130–133
  The Little Mermaid, 191–192
  Nourishing Awareness in Each Moment, 62–64
  See also Films; Music effects; News media
Memories. *See* Essays from memory; Writing strategies
Menand, Louis, 67, 277–279
Metaphor, 28, 29, 40, 48, 52, 65, 79, 98, 113, 156–157, 184
Mitchell, Lucy Sprague, 237, 238, 248
Mob mentality, 220–223
Modern Times, 10–12, 227, 283, 321
  group exercises, 15
  language exploration, 13
  styling, 14–15
  thinking/talking points, 13–14
  writing ideas, 15–16

Monster Mash, 99, 107, 108–110, 318
   essay/film connections, 113
   group exercise, 112
   language exploration, 111
   styling, 112
   thinking/talking points, 111
   writing ideas, 112–113
Morality
   Advice to Youth, 306–308
   The Content of Our Character, 251–256
   Drugs, 196–198
   Fiddling While Africa Starves, 220–223
   Folktale Liberation, 236–246
   Letter to His Master, 260–264
   Naps, 202–206
   See also Popular culture
More, Paul Elmer, 327
Mortality, 269, 283, 291–294
   essay connections, 296
   group exercises, 295–296
   styling, 295
   thinking/talking points, 295
   writing ideas, 296
Movies. *See* Films
Muir, Frank, 214
Museum Piece, 57–58, 137, 149, 319
   essay/film connections, 61
   group exercises, 60–61
   styling, 59–60
   thinking/talking points, 59
   writing ideas, 61
Music effects
   Fiddling While Africa Starves, 220–223
   Musical Awakenings, 150–153
   Prince, 91–95
   Roll Over Bach, Too!, 83–85
   A Voice For The Lonely, 3–6
   See also Art appreciation; Films
Musical Awakenings, 9, 89, 150–153, 318, 319
   essay/film connections, 158
   group exercises, 157–158
   language exploration, 155
   styling, 156–157
   thinking/talking points, 155–156
   writing ideas, 158
Mute Dancers, 48, 74–77, 143, 187, 326
   essay/film connections, 82
   group exercises, 81
   language exploration, 79
   styling, 80
   thinking/talking points, 79–80
   writing ideas, 81–82
Mythology. *See* Fables

N

Name That Tone, 67, 277–279
   essay connections, 283
   group exercises, 282–283
   language exploration, 281
   styling, 281–282
   thinking/talking points, 281
   writing ideas, 283
Naps, 121, 189, 201, 202–206, 219
   essay connections, 209
   group exercises, 208
   language exploration, 207
   styling, 207–208
   thinking/talking points, 207
   writing ideas, 208–209
Narratives, 317
Native American culture, 130–133
Natural history
   The Black Widow, 176–182
   Children in the Woods, 44–46
   The Courage of Turtles, 31–37
   Hair, 122–126
   Joyas Voladoras, 138–140
   Mute Dancers, 74–77
News media
   Modern Times, 10–12
   newspaper article citations, 344
   See also Media effects
Newspaper article citations, 344
Nouns, 14, 48, 217–218
Nourishing Awareness in Each Moment, 56, 62–64, 283
   essay connections, 67
   group exercises, 66–67
   language exploration, 65
   styling, 65–66
   thinking/talking points, 65
   writing ideas, 67

O

Once, 89
On the Uncertainty of the Future, 53, 67
  essay connections, 56
  group exercises, 55
  thinking/talking points, 55
  writing ideas, 55–56
Opposition viewpoint, 225, 329
Orbison, Roy, 4–5, 89, 112
Organization, 30, 233, 314–319, 330, 333
O'Rourke, P. J., 99, 189, 201, 219, 220–223, 269, 284–286, 305, 311, 318
Orwell, George, 214

P

Pan's Labyrinth, 195
Paraphrasing, 334–335
Parentheses, 60
Parenthetical references, 341–342
Period, 128
Periodic sentence structure, 14, 80
Perrault, Charles, 238, 239, 241
Persian Gulf War, 10–12
Personification, 27, 52, 98, 121, 157
Persuasion. *See* Argument essays
Peterson, Brenda, 319
Plagiarism, 314, 335–336, 337
Point of view, 55, 61, 322
  first person, 322
  opposition viewpoint, 225, 329
  second person, 353
  third person, 353
  See also Argument essays
Popular culture
  About Men, 228–231
  Advice to Youth, 306–308
  City Out of Breath, 114–118
  The Content of Our Character, 251–256
  The Culture of Celebrity, 210–216
  Drugs, 196–198
  Fiddling While Africa Starves, 220–223
  Folktale Liberation, 236–246
  Hair, 122–126
  How to Drive Fast, 284–286
  icons, 234, 235
  The Little Mermaid, 191–192
  Mortality, 291–294
  Name That Tone, 277–279
  Naps, 202–206
  Toys, 68–70
Prejudice. *See* The Content of Our Character; Fiddling While Africa Starves; The Indian with a Camera; Letter to His Master
Prepositions, 266, 288
Prewriting process, 313–314
Prince, 9, 89, 91–95
  essay/film connections, 99
  group exercises, 98
  language exploration, 97
  styling, 98
  thinking/talking points, 97–98
  writing ideas, 99
Process analysis essays, 325–326
Proust, Marcel, 215
Psycho, 113
Publicity. *See* The Culture of Celebrity; Media effects
Punctuation, 40, 52, 120, 184, 233, 303

Q

Questions, 65–66

R

Racial prejudice. *See* The Content of Our Character; Fiddling While Africa Starves; The Indian with a Camera; Letter to His Master
Rationale, 352
Reality
  Burl's, 17–26
  City Out of Breath, 114–118
  The Content of Our Character, 251–256
  Disposable Rocket, 159–162
  Graven Images, 167–172
  How to Drive Fast, 284–286
  Toys, 68–70
  See also Media effects; Popular culture

Realization
  Burl's, 17–26
  Joyas Voladoras, 138–140
  Musical Awakenings, 150–153
  Nourishing Awareness in Each Moment, 62–64
The Red Violin, 158
Refuting the opposition, 225, 248, 329–330
Religious imagery, 105
Repetition technique, 97, 98, 148, 207–208
Research strategies, 337
  basic information sources, 337–338
  book citations, 343
  documentation basics, 340–348
  film citations, 345
  first page format, 340, 348
  formatting, 340–341, 348
  information, evaluation of, 338, 339
  Internet resources, 337, 338–340
  interview citations, 345
  library resources, 337–338
  magazine article citations, 343
  newspaper article citations, 344
  online source formatting, 342
  parenthetical references, 341–342
  plagiarism and, 337
  scholarly journal citations, 344–345
  television sources/citations, 338, 346
  works cited sample, 346–347
  works cited section, 342–346
  See also Writing strategies
Revision process, 316–317
Rhetorical modes, 51
Robertson, Frederick, 311
Roll Over Bach, Too!, 9, 83–85, 318
  essay/film connections, 89
  group exercises, 88
  language exploration, 87
  styling, 88
  thinking/talking points, 87–88
  writing ideas, 88–89
Ruiz, Judy, 30
Run-on sentences, 288, 289, 317

S

Sacks, Oliver, 150–153, 155, 156, 318, 319
San Francisco earthquake, 10–11
Sartre, Jean-Paul, 254
Satirical essays, 269–270
  Advice to Youth, 306–308
  Cat Bathing as Martial Art, 271–273
  How to Drive Fast, 284–286
  Mortality, 291–294
  Name That Tone, 277–279
  Turbulence, 297–302
  See also Writing strategies
Scholarly journal citations, 344–345
Scorsese, Martin, 100–104, 113
Search engines, 312, 339–340
Second person, 353
The Secret of Roan Inish, 250
Sedaris, David, 297–302, 312
Segal, Lore, 244
Semi-colon, 40, 120, 128, 248–249, 249, 257, 258, 289
Sendak, Maurice, 192, 244, 245, 249
Sensory information, 7–8, 48, 72, 322
Sentences
  comma splices, 311
  complete sentences, 59, 80, 148, 200, 257, 288, 289
  connecting words, 288
  dependent clauses, 266, 310
  flow in an essay and, 310
  fragments, 59, 289, 317
  incomplete sentences, 200, 288, 289
  independent clauses, 127–128
  interrupters, 14, 59, 174, 184–185, 186, 310
  introductory clauses, 128
  listing sentence structure, 135–136, 164–165, 185, 257–258
  loose sentence structure, 14, 266
  periodic sentences, 80
  run-on/fused sentences, 288, 289, 317
  topic sentence, 194, 317
  variety in, 40, 48, 52, 148, 233, 248–249, 266, 309–310
  See also Writing strategies

Sentence variety, 40, 48, 52, 148, 233, 248–249, 266, 309–310
Sexual ambiguity
  Burl's, 17–26
  See also Identity
Shaw, George Bernard, 278
Shift in diction, 287
Silko, Leslie Marmon, 121, 130–133, 219, 259, 268
Simile, 28, 29, 40, 42, 52, 59, 61, 79, 98, 113, 184
Singer, Isaac B., 245
Slang, 97
Smoke Signals, 137
Sources of information. *See* Internet resources; Research strategies
Specific details/examples, 48, 106, 141–142, 164, 193–194, 328, 332
Spiritual practice
  The Indian with a Camera, 130–133
  Nourishing Awareness in Each Moment, 62–64
Steele, Shelby, 251–256, 268, 334
Steinbeck, John, 318
Stereotypes, 186, 233, 234, 235, 295, 296
  See also The Content of Our Character
Storytelling. *See* Essays from memory; Fables
Summarizing process, 333–334
Supporting the point, 329, 332
Swift, Jonathan, 290, 311
Symbols, 98
  About Men, 228–231
  Fiddling While Africa Starves, 220–223
  Hair, 122–126
  Letter to His Master, 260–264
  See also Fables; Morality
Synonyms, 157

T

Technology
  Modern Times, 10–12
  Mortality, 291–294
  Name That Tone, 277–279
  On the Uncertainty of the Future, 53
  Turbulence, 297–302
  See also Internet resources; Warfare
Television sources/citations, 338, 346
Thank You For Smoking, 219, 235
Thesis statement, 88, 288, 315–316, 324, 329, 332
Third person, 353
Thompson, J. Lee, 113
Titles, 112, 113, 281–282, 317–318, 323
Tolkien, J. R. R., 245
Tone, 136, 207, 339
Topic sentence, 106, 194, 317
Toys, 68–70, 121, 195, 209, 219, 235
  essay connections, 73
  group exercises, 72
  language exploration, 71
  styling, 72
  thinking/talking points, 71
  writing ideas, 73
Traffic, 201
Transitions, 43, 52, 106, 207, 233–234, 288, 317, 322
Trimmer, Sarah, 237, 239
Turbulence, 297–302, 311
  essay connections, 305
  group exercises, 304
  styling, 303–304
  thinking/talking points, 303
  writing ideas, 304–305
Twain, Mark, 305, 306–308

U

Uncertainty
  On the Uncertainty of the Future, 53
  See also Fate
Updike, John, 61, 137, 144–146, 149, 159–162
Urban legends, 186, 187
  See also Fables

V

Verbs, 27, 29, 48, 79, 217–218
Vidal, Gore, 190, 196–198, 329

Visual images
  The Indian with a Camera, 130–133
  See also Art appreciation; Films; Media effects
A Voice for the Lonely, 3–6, 50, 89, 158
  essay/film connections, 9
  group exercises, 8
  language exploration, 7
  styling, 7–8
  thinking/talking points, 7
  writing ideas, 8–9

W

Wadleigh, Michael, 99
Walker, Alice, 318
Warfare
  The Content of Our Character, 251–256
  drug war, 201
  Modern Times, 10–12
Warhol, Andy, 212
Weschler, Lawrence, 10–12, 227, 283, 321
White, Bailey, 269, 283, 291–294
Willa: An American Snow Write, 195
Williams, Joy, 318
Winged Migration, 43, 82, 187
Women's liberation, 238–239, 248
Woodstock, 99
Works cited section, 342–347
Writing strategies
  argument essays, 328–330
  brainstorming methods, 313, 314, 320–321
  cause/effect essays, 324–325
  classification, 330–333
  clustering technique, 320
  college essays, 313–321, 323
  compare/contrast essays, 323–324
  conclusions, 319
  definition essays, 326–328
  descriptive labeling, 332–333
  explanation/exploration writing, 323–326
  extended definitions, 328
  freewriting technique, 320
  introductions, 318–319
  language resources, 327–328
  listing technique, 320–321
  organization and, 30, 314–319, 330, 333
  paraphrasing, 334–335
  plagiarism, 314, 335–336
  point of view, 322
  prewriting process, 313–314
  process analysis essays, 325–326
  purpose, determination of, 321, 326–327, 331
  refuting the opposition, 329–330
  revising/editing processes, 316–317
  ruling principle and, 332
  sensory detail/description, 322
  source crediting, 335–336
  specific examples, 328, 332
  summarizing process, 333–334
  supporting the point, 329, 332
  thesis statements, 315–316, 324, 329, 332
  titles, 317–318, 323
  topic sentence, 317
  transitions, 317, 322
  writing from memory, 321–322
  zooming in, 321–322
  See also Research strategies

Y

Yahoo.com, 340